SAILING, SEAMANSHIP AND YACHT CONSTRUCTION

UFFA FOX WINNING THE FINAL RACE FOR THE INTERNATIONAL CANOE TROPHY, 1933

SAILING, SEAMANSHIP AND YACHT CONSTRUCTION

Uffa Fox

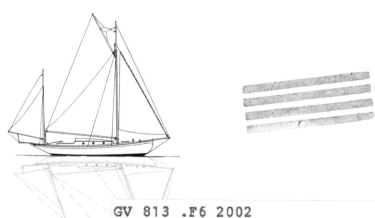

DOVER PUBLICATIONS, INC.
Mineola, New York

Bibliographical Note

This Dover edition, first published in 2002, is an unabridged republication of the third impression of the work originally published in 1936 by Charles Scribner's Sons, New York.

Library of Congress Cataloging-in-Publication Data

Fox, Uffa.
    Sailing, seamanship, and yacht construction / Uffa Fox.
        p. cm.
    Originally published: New York : Scribner's, 1936.
    Includes index.
    ISBN 0-486-42329-8 (pbk.)
    1. Yachting. 2. Yacht building. I. Title.

GV813 .F6 2002

2002071603

Manufactured in the United States of America
Dover Publications, Inc., 31 East 2nd Street, Mineola, N.Y. 11501

DEDICATION

to

NAVAL ARCHITECTS

*Y*ACHTSMEN *looking at vessels developed and designed for their especial benefit, such as are shown in this book, must realise how much they owe to the designers whose lives have been spent in the study of the way of a ship at sea.*

It is only through the kindness of G. L. Watson, Charles Nicholson, William Fife, Alfred Mylne, J. M. Soper, Frederick Shepherd, Morgan Giles, Laurent Giles and Harley Mead of England, and Starling Burgess, Francis Herreshoff, Olin Stephens, Clinton Crane and Cox and Stevens of America that I have been able to illustrate this book with the very best designs, both British and American, of cruising and racing vessels.

INTRODUCTION

SAILING, and so Seamanship, will endure until the end of all things, for sailing is the one thing above all others that offers peace and escape to a man whose brain is weary and tired of the machinery which this age and future ages force and will force upon human beings. A few years ago there was peace and pleasure upon the roads of England; to-day the advent and perfection of the motor-car, besides destroying this peace and quietude, destroys those on the road. But the sea has remained, and will remain to the end, much as it was in the beginning, and I believe the spirit still moves upon the waters, and always will—

> " *Roll on, thou deep and dark-blue Ocean—roll !*
> *Ten thousand fleets sweep over thee in vain ;*
> *Man marks the earth with ruin—his control*
> *Stops with the shore. . . .*"

And so I have written this book in the hope that, even if it is not so enduring as its subject, it will be of value to those whose pleasure it is to go down to the sea in ships.

ACKNOWLEDGMENT

OF the 325 illustrations in this book 152 are photographs by Beken & Son, Edwin Levick, Morris Rosenfeld, W. White, Ivan Kettle, Miss M. Till, and there is no doubt we owe a great deal to these photographers.

For instance, Beken's collection of Yachting subjects numbers over 20,000 indexed negatives from 1880, when photography on the water commenced, to the present day, and I feel very grateful to him and all the photographers above for their help in illustrating this book.

Also to Messrs. Thomas H. Parker Ltd. of Berkeley Square for their help in reproducing de Loutherbourg' picture of " The Glorious First of June ", and to R. F. Patterson for the two pictures he painted of *Dorade* at sea.

A list of the photographs, arranged under the respective photographers' names, will be found at the end of the volume.

CONTENTS

CONTENTS

PART II
RACING

PART I
CRUISING

· I ·

TYPHOON

Length, overall - - - 45 ft. 0 in.		Length, waterline - - 35 ft. 0 in.
Beam - - - - - 12 ft. 0 in.		Draught - - - - 6 ft. 0 in.
Displacement - - - 15¼ tons		Sail area - - - - 950 sq. ft.

Owner and Skipper, WILLIAM W. NUTTING   *Designer*, WILLIAM ATKIN

SEAMEN are made up of deepwater men and coasters, and until I met *Typhoon* and her owner I was a coaster only, not having sailed off soundings ; so *Typhoon* having given me perspective, which, like humour in life, gives a sense of proportion and balance, *Typhoon* shall have the honour of going in to bat first.

Bill Nutting and Billy Atkin were both on the staff of *Motor Boat*, a New York magazine, and if we remember this fact when looking at *Typhoon's* lines they do not appear so unbalanced. The easy hollow bow and the powerful stern are typical of motor boats, which tend to squat by the stern through the propeller kicking away the ground or rather the water from under their quarters. *Typhoon's* lines, every time I look at them, bring to my eyes a picture of two sailing men, lovers of sail, made through force of circumstances prisoners in the offices of a Motor Boat Journal, and while there, being unable to stifle their love of sail any longer, they break out with a sailing boat, which to appear in their paper must bear a strong resemblance to a motor boat. And the fact that when I met her she had already crossed from Nova Scotia to Cowes in 22 days and had sailed the ocean part from Cape Race to the Bishops in 15 days 9 hours, balanced the ends far more in my eyes than I then realised. *Typhoon* arrived in Cowes early in August 1920, and my troop of Cowes Sea Scouts badly wanted me to take them aboard to see her and her crew ; but I could not very well take fifteen or twenty youngsters over a stranger's vessel without some reasonable excuse, and it was not until the end of that month that one came. We heard that *Typhoon* needed two more to make up her crew for the homeward voyage via the trades to New York, so as I wished to be one, and Charles Hookey, one of my boys, who was 6 ft. 2 in. overall, wished to be the other, we took the troop aboard, hoping that the owner would look upon us favourably as candidates for his crew and upon the troop much as he would upon an engine in a steam launch, and not mind.

We found an owner who was kindness itself, and the only excuse we needed was that we were fond of sailing and the sea. Ever since, when feeling shy, I have remembered this and have just dived into rooms full of people, rather like diving into the sea for a swim, knowing that if I had to wade in slowly I should lose my breath and run out frightened, when there would really be no need for the sea and human nature are naturally kind. Both however are alike in the fact, that although naturally kind, liberties must not be taken with either, for then the serene brow becomes ruffled and trouble is found.

And so we visited *Typhoon* in our whaleboat, and I asked Bill Nutting if I could make up his third man, and if he needed another Charles Hookey would be that man. . . . All the troop would have liked to go, but we were the only two that could.

Then next morning I told my family I wished to sail back to America in *Typhoon*, and my father argued with me. *Typhoon*, he said, was an unbalanced boat with her hollow weak bow and her broad stern. I said that she had already crossed the Atlantic, and he was not impressed ; for, he said, if you threw a box overboard in North America it would cross the Atlantic and be unable to help itself coming to England ; and he warmed up to September gales, and the storms of October and November, from which I gathered he was against my starting.

So I went aboard again that evening with the gang, and Nutting said better not come ; he wanted me to, I wanted to, my father did not want me to. So the only thing to do was to toss up. And it came tails, so I passed the penny to the youngest in the troop, and the next two came heads so all was settled. . . . Years afterwards Harry Partridge told me the other two calls came tails too ; hence we learn that the right thing to do is that which you want to do.

It was now late, so as all my gear was aboard the schooner *Black Rose*, in which I had been cruising, we started for Hamble to fetch it, and there being no wind this meant a fourteen mile row in the whaler, and we arrived back aboard *Typhoon* at 3.00 a.m.   Then the skipper fed us with soup, and off we went home to bed at 6.00 a.m. or rather to collect the rest of the gear.

The last day of August found *Typhoon* ready for sea with her owner and Charles in one watch and myself and Jim Dorset in the other, the owner delighting me by giving me charge of that watch.

Those of the troop who could came down in our racing gig to say farewell, and we left Cowes at 1.00 p.m. for New York, under a $7\frac{1}{2}$ horse power one-lung Diesel ; and at 3.00 p.m. we were still without wind, roaring through Hurst with the engine peacefully quiet.   Engines to me seem just like that ; they behave perfectly well until really

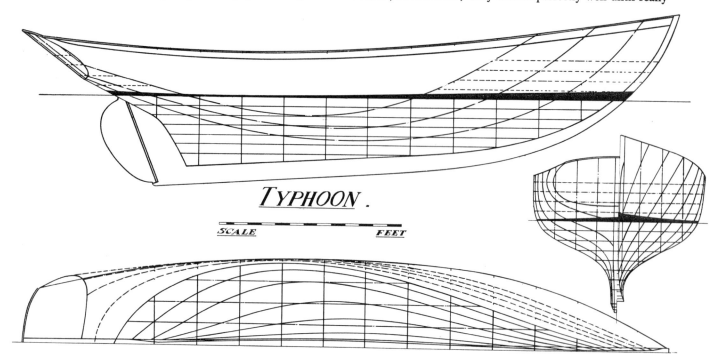

TYPHOON .

SCALE ▭▭▭▭▭▭▭▭▭ FEET

needed and then they drop peacefully to sleep, and here we were with every chance of being swept to the shingles by the fierce ebb without an engine.   Auxiliary power in a sailing vessel does not receive the attention it should have, and the result is that it is often unreliable.   However this case was soon remedied, for it was the stuffing box overheated through being set up too tightly, and easing it off and throwing water over it enabled us to restart the engine and stand over towards the Island shore and safety, with the ebb tide.   On the flood the tide sweeps towards the Island, and vessels should keep near the shingles then.

By 4.00 p.m. we had cleared the Island, and outside the Needles we found a westerly wind making, which by 6.00 was enough to enable us to set sail and steer S.W. by W.; but by dark the wind had fallen away, and we kept the engine going all through the night until 4.00 a.m. the next morning, September 1, when there was enough wind for sailing.   However this faded away for two hours from 8.00 till 10.00 a.m., when it came in again quite strongly, and at 4.00 in the afternoon we had all we could stagger under with full sail.   At 5.00 p.m. we put two reefs in the mainsail, and three hours later we stowed it entirely, as by now it was really blowing hard.   Myself, Jim and Charles were all seasick, so as the skipper was on watch we stretched out in bunks feeling rather small.

At 4.00 a.m. I turned out and discovered everyone turned in, and *Typhoon* steering herself under her headsail only, while away on the port bow was the glow from two lighthouses, which later we found were on a small island to the east of Ile de Batz (the Sept Iles).   And so sitting steering *Typhoon*, with the French coast in sight, there was time to think quietly over everything.   Here we were, four of us crossing the Atlantic, three of us very young and seasick, and a kind-hearted skipper who, rather than disturb our slumbers, had taken the mizen off *Typhoon*, hung a riding light in the rigging, and turned in with us when he felt tired (so the log read between the lines) with the English Channel full of shipping.

It took but a few seconds to realise that when it came to weather our vessel could stand far more than we could, that we three youngsters were the weak links in the chain, and that our too indulgent skipper would let us sleep when we were under the weather, all of which was very humiliating.   So three hours later, while the owner cooked the breakfast, I explained my thoughts and feelings, and he agreed that it was far better for his crew to feel dreadfully seasick than humiliated. . . . And that never more, if it were humanly possible, would *Typhoon* be left alone with the night.

At 10.30 a.m. we reset the mizen and steered S.W. along the French coast, which gradually gained on us, as with the wind ahead we could not weather the point ahead, Ile de Batz. After trying to fight our way to windward in vain for three hours against a strong wind and steep sea, we decided to go in, and away we went between two lighthouses on rocks and ran aground on some mud—it seemed to be the only piece of mud amongst masses of rocks.

The log read 172 from the Needles, and we thought and hoped that the town we saw across the masses of rocks was Roscoff, for having only a small scale chart we were not sure of our position ; and as long as no harm comes of it (as it easily can) there is more fun in cruising on a strange coast with a very small scale chart, as then one feels something of the doubts and fears that beset the earliest explorers.

The young flood was making, and there would be no difficulty in kedging off ; so the dinghy was launched and I was detailed off to buy food. Not speaking French I took a paper plate and a pencil to draw sketches of the food we wished to have, and as drawing is the oldest and most natural form of language I returned triumphant, if stony broke.

The town was Roscoff, and there was a fine little harbour in front which dried out at low water. So we cooked and enjoyed an excellent dinner, and afterwards sailed into the harbour in the twilight and moored alongside the stone quay. We walked through the unlighted streets and then to bed with the feeling that we had an interesting town to wander over the next day. And so ended the night of September 2, 1920.

We spent four days alongside the stone quay. We had our halyards ashore to a ring bolt to prevent *Typhoon* falling outward, but they were never used, it being a far better plan to shift the anchors across the deck and place them amidships on the side nearest the wall, thus giving *Typhoon* an inward list. If we had depended upon the halyards they would have needed tending with the rise and fall of the tide.

These four days were pleasantly spent, visiting the town and its church, and all the while a strong westerly wind made the beat to Ushant uninviting. But at noon on September 6 we put to sea with full jib and mizen, but a two-reefed mainsail, as although the wind was easing there still seemed plenty. Having studied the approaches to Roscoff at low water we sailed out without hitting any of the many rocks.

The wind held strong and ahead till midnight and we tacked along the rocky coast towards Ushant, quite happily catching mackerel, which made our fish course for dinner that night, but after midnight the wind started to fade away and by 2.00 a.m. we were slatting about in a glassy swell with the sails sheeted flat to try and prevent their slamming too hard.

Hell is supposed to be paved with good intentions, but according to Bill Nutting it is paved with glassy ground swells, and this being a new idea of hell's pavement to me, I was first of all tickled and afterwards much taken with the picture, for surely there can be nothing more damnable than slatting about in a heavy swell, which throws the boat about in all directions without rhyme or reason.

We were becalmed for 36 hours, and then a faint breeze came out of the north-east and by 2.00 p.m., Wednesday, September 8, we were sailing with a fair wind at 2 to 3 knots. As it was foggy we decided to go outside Ushant, for although the fog was very patchy it might not be clear when we wanted it to be, and with strong tides the passage inside the island is difficult in fog.

At 6.45 we saw a wondrous sight, several rocky islands appeared as though in the sky, and then with startling suddenness two bright flashes appeared in the sky immediately overhead, for we had nearly run into the bottom of Ushant Light in the fog. So we cleared Ushant for the run across the Bay with no need for cross bearings at all, a good departure, if a startling one ; and ever since, when thinking of Ushant or hearing it spoken of, the picture of those two bright flashes in the sky above comes to my mind's eye very vividly.

With the wind astern we lashed the mizen to its weather shrouds and ran wing and wing for the corner of Spain, 300 miles across the Bay, which was very delightful. A small boat hammering her way against a strong wind is wet and uncomfortable, but when chasing away before it she is a different vessel, sailing upright and dry and lessening the force of wind and sea by giving way to them, whereas close hauled she increases the power of wind and sea, to the discomfort of those aboard. September weather with its easterly winds made the Bay of Biscay a pleasant place.

One night the wind was very strong though fair, and to ease up *Typhoon* we stowed her mizen after putting two reefs in the mainsail, and even with her jib and a double reefed mainsail she was driving along as fast as she could go, and seas were sweeping over her continually, the largest in my watch coming clean over the mizen boom, which was stowed in the crutch. These were not the steep unstable waves of the North Sea, but huge Atlantic seas that gave a small boat every chance to rise to them because of their size. But that hard easterly wind only lasted the one night, and by 10.00 a.m. next morning we shook out the reefs in the mainsail and set the mizen, as the wind was taking off, and by 4.00 in the afternoon we were becalmed only 10 miles off the coast of Spain. We had been steering for Cape Ortegall, but through haze this was invisible. All through the night we were becalmed and fog persisted in hiding the land, and it was not until next morning that the breeze came fitfully and settled down to a light wind from the west, enabling us to steer south close hauled on the starboard tack.

At 9.10 a.m. as I had the deck and was steering, there suddenly appeared the lacework of breakers at the base of rocky cliffs, so I yelled delightedly "Land on the starboard bow," and as we were less than 400 yards off we stood on to about 300 yards off, and came about. As we only had small scale charts we could not see anything to tell us our position, and so the morning was spent very pleasantly tacking along westward close to the mountains, with the heavy swell breaking on rocks or yellow beaches at their base, and a fog that hid the tops of the mountains and only revealed half their beauty—a fine game and very fascinating trying to decide where we were after several days out of sight of land. Round a headland 1,000 feet high at least and still onward we tacked, and then round a cape with a lighthouse. We decided it was Cape Prior as the lighthouse was about 300 feet in the air. All day we

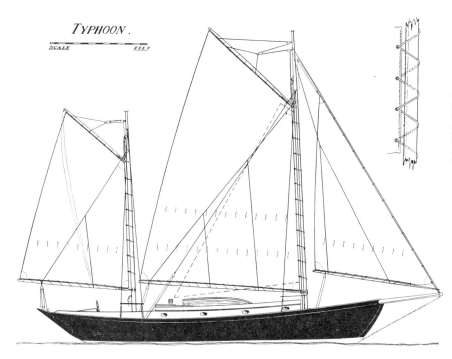

TYPHOON.

SCALE   FEET

← INSET SHOWS TRYSAIL LACING, WHICH MUST AL- WAYS BE DOUBLED BACK OR IT JAMBS ON MAST WHEN HOISTING OR LOWERING.

had seen little fishing boats popping, it seemed, out of the very face of the cliffs, but on going closer there appeared a little bay, and at 5.00 p.m. as the night was coming on and the weather was thick, we sailed into a tiny bight and anchored for the night. It was a delightful anchorage; the Spanish fishermen boarded us with presents of their red vino, lobsters, and some snake-like shellfish, which grow on rocks and on ships' bottoms, these last dreadful looking things to eat, but they shouted instructions as to how we should cook them, which we never understood, and after many mistakes and corrections we managed it in the end. They were very rubbery to chew, though tasting good.

Then we gave them whisky, and not being used to such powerful stuff they dropped off to sleep, and we only put them into their own boats at midnight by main strength. Those fishermen had had what I've since heard described as a good party. They slept all night in the open, for their boats were rather like our sea scouts' whaler, open and double ended with a large dipping lug; and there is no doubt that sleep and fresh air was what they needed.

Next morning at 8.30 a.m. we set sail and continued our beat to windward to Ferrol, whither we were bound, and although we gathered both from the fishermen and the direction of the coast line that we had not yet passed it, we could not tell how far away it was.

By noon we were becalmed close under the high steep cliffs, with the Atlantic swell roaring and breaking 60 feet in the air at their base; and it was not till 3.00 p.m. that a steady westerly wind set in, and soon we rounded a rocky point with a lighthouse, and there stretched before us invitingly a deep channel or fiord with mountains enveloped in the fog on either side, and we sailed in with an ever freshening wind astern, which, clearing the fog away, unveiled the land of Spain. There is no doubt that the Lord is a great scene-shifter; never in my life before or since have I seen such a dramatic unveiling of so beautiful a panorama. It was not done suddenly or hurriedly, but with majestic stateliness, and the eye had just time to take in and explain one scene when another appeared.

And so we entered Ferrol at ever increasing speed until we dropped anchor under the walls of the dockyard that built and fitted out the Invincible Armada; for it was from here that it sailed, and Ferrol is still the Naval Port of Spain. Our log read 455 miles from Roscoff, which showed that in spite of September being the month for easterly winds, we had had to beat against westerly winds for a considerable part of the passage.

Almost before our anchor had reached the bottom the British Vice-Consul's son was aboard. He was very keen on sailing, and he and his father looked after us well and made our short stay very interesting. The Vice-Consul, being a musician, had collected the music of the hills of Spain, and he played it on his piano with great feeling; shutting my eyes, I could hardly believe that I was not in the Highlands of Scotland. There was the same energy and abandon in the music that made the feet itch to be on the move, and the same strange wild beauty. I imagine it to be the effect of the hills upon generations of people, and it is strange how, though thousands of miles apart, you find the same things the world over. On Chesil Beach the fishermen have single thole-pins fixed on the gunwales of their boats and a half-round piece of wood fixed to the loom of the oar drops over the pin, so that they do not have to unship their oars when hauling in lines or going on the beach. This device disappears by the time one is across the weather side of West Bay, but here in Spain is found exactly the same thole-pin and oar.

We chose to dine that night at a very old sailors' restaurant in a room full of Spanish fishermen, who smoked and sang to the guitar. Our choice was sound, for it is generally more fun to be with men who work hard, as when they play they play hard, because their play has been well earned and they enjoy it the more keenly. We thoroughly enjoyed being with them, for we, at our play with the sea, had worked hard too. Then late that evening we wandered round the town, which in the cool of the night was energetic, and for the first time I saw and heard a young Spaniard make love to his sweetheart on her balcony. Instead of being as I'd pictured it, a romantic and pleasing scene, it was a very uncomfortable one, for although he and she did not seem to mind our walking along past them, for they kept going, and although we understood nothing of what was said, we felt that we were listening to words meant for his lady love only. And I wonder when the people who make moving pictures will understand that so many of us avoid them because they show love scenes at which the spectator is only about two feet off, and, knowing that the love birds would dislike us watching, we stay away.

Next day Mr. Martin, the Vice-Consul, invited us to the launching of a trawler and having seen quite a number of launches I was not really interested until we arrived, and there I saw staged the most daring launch imaginable. Instead of the usual twin ways for bilge blocks, there was nothing; the trawler had a single centre way down which she was to slide into the water. The way was steep and deep water close in, but the idea that she would be afloat before she had time to topple over sideways was startling to me, brought up to dry docks and safe ways, on which a ship could spend months half or quarter floated if she wished. As the time for launching drew near I found myself getting very excited and agitated, wanting to clear the people back; but restraining myself I walked about with my hands in my pockets hoping no one would see how nervous I felt. Then the priest did his job and the bottle was smashed, and down she slid on her centre way with a man on either side running along holding up the bilge, and as swift as light she was in the water. We all agreed that the only adequate comparison was that of a seal sliding and diving into the sea. For it was a very graceful and swift launch. But very daring. Then we saw the *Grangetown* discharging coal she had brought for the Spanish Navy. Men shovelled coal into baskets, which women carried on their heads walking in an endless chain, and the job itself seemed endless. When they saw me they rather fancied my white flannel shorts, and being bashful I ran away, which highly amused them.

We left Ferrol at 2.00 p.m. on Sunday, September 19, after a stay of five days, and with a smart breeze took two hours to beat down the fiord or loch to the entrance of Coruna Bay. There the wind fell away, and it was not until after dark that we anchored in the harbour, being almost run down just before 8.00 p.m. by a large steamer leaving the port. We had no side lights up. In watching the changing lights and colours as the day gave way to night we had not realised how completely the darkness had fallen. Outside, the breaking spray rose eighty feet into the air as the Atlantic seas hurled themselves against the rockbound coast of Spain. Somehow we did not wish to go ashore that night, and felt quite contented aboard cooking and eating our dinner, while we watched the lights of the town, wondering what it held for us on the morrow. Drake had burnt Corunna, Sir John Moore was buried there, there the Armada had sheltered, and it was rather enjoyable thinking these things over before going ashore; and so we turned in. The next day we visited a bull ring; there had been a fight the day we had arrived, and instead of seeing bulls killed we saw the sword that had killed them still uncleaned and black with blood. We saw the butcher's shop where the bulls are prepared for the market after they have been killed, and it seems only a matter of time before the spectators will be eating sandwiches of the bull killed in the fight ten minutes earlier. Simply a matter of speeding up the cooking. About 4.00 in the afternoon we set sail for the Azores, and at 6.00 p.m. after tacking out we weathered Point Hercules, steered west to clear Sisargas Island visible 20 miles away, and at 11.00 p.m. were abreast the light on the island, with the Hercules light dropping below the horizon aft, and Villano rising above it farther down the coast. But our course to the Azores now took us away from Spain into the open Atlantic.

We were only doing 3 knots, the night was peaceful, and, as I had the deck to myself there was nothing to stop my thoughts wandering. Our voyage was not unlike a man's voyage through life; with increasing years he goes from the joys of his childhood and boyhood to those of his youth and manhood, each year seeing new joys found and old ones outgrown, and with the new joys, to balance them, greater cares. The blot made on a clean clean page of writing that brought a tear of self pity to the boy would mean nothing to the grown man, able to erase it skilfully with rubber and knife. I felt that, being twenty-three I was as *Typhoon* off the Sirgasas Light; for she was dropping Hercules astern, and although raising and for a time guided by Villano Light, she was headed out into the open Atlantic, the parting of the ways; and I was just emerging from my youth into the joys and cares of man's estate. Soon I should no longer play football, or take part in cross country running, and boxing would become too strenuous, so I must now consider sports that I could continue with a fair chance of success until I had reached the age of three score and ten, and I decided to try and plan my life so that I worked very hard through the winters and then left the summers for sailing and cricket, two things I could play at until the end. And so my watch alone on deck passed all too quickly.

I have often been asked what we did to while away the night watches, and have recalled my thoughts through that watch to try and explain why it is that long voyages in a small sailing vessel are so fascinating once she gets off soundings. There is beauty in the sky at night and in the day, for the Lord is the greatest artist and shifts His scenes with great effect, and when He is not in the mood to show the beauty of the heavens, the man on deck has time to reflect and think. And although this was my first Atlantic crossing in a small sailing vessel, I have since crossed it in two others, and always reached the journey's end with a feeling of regret. For although the might of a heavy gale is frightening, the peace and charm of the ocean is beyond understanding, when it is in its quieter moods.

Next morning, Tuesday, September 21, the mountainous coast of Spain was still in sight over our port quarter, and the wind increasing with the day increased our speed. The wind was E.N.E. and so fair, as it should be in September; but the sea was increasing also, and Charles and I were seasick. Unfortunately for me, after a spell on the nice steady shore I am always sick for a day or so when I start to sail the heaving seas until broken in again. About 5.00 in the afternoon a heavy squall hit us and Jim and myself took in the mainsail in about two seconds, and reset it after the squall had passed. With these heavy squalls about we divided into two watches, so that one man was always ready to stow the mainsail. Squalls give warning, for a heavy black cloud can generally be seen even at night unless the light of the cabin or binnacle deadens the helmsman's eyes; and *Typhoon's* small mainsail and short main boom made stowing or reefing no more than a single-handed job, which was a great comfort. So for twenty-four hours we looked out for the heavy squalls and stowed the mainsail for each, resetting it directly after. It was blowing quite hard between whiles, for as we left Spain the seas were going over the steamers we saw; they, of course, were headed into the sea, while we were chasing away with a fair wind, but we could well have had a reef in the mainsail.

The wind eased off by September 23, and we set the spinnaker and took in the mizen, and still continued on our way happily and peacefully with moonlight nights full of beauty. On the night of the 23rd the skipper cooked the dinner, and very good it was; but at 1.00 a.m. Jim woke me by hitting me on the nose with a shoe remarkably well thrown for one doubled up with indigestion.

So, after getting the castor oil and the instruction book out of the medicine chest, I went to the wheel while the skipper took Jim in hand, and the improvement made by Jim as the skipper advanced with the castor oil had to be seen to be believed; it brightened up the night for quite half an hour afterwards.

It was my watch then till 5.00 a.m., when a really good sunrise was developing; and as artists are unable to paint the sunrises and sunsets seen from small sailing boats in the ocean, a word picture can hardly be expected to either, so I will only copy out the few words set down in my diary at the time, hoping that, however inadequate, they will recall beautiful dawns to those who have seen them.

" 5.00 a.m. Sun still down under cold blue bank of clouds, then orange streaks that turned into vivid red later, extending from east to north. Red sky in the morning may be the sailors' warning but I enjoy beauty while I may. Dawn and Sunset are the most beautiful parts of the day. Rout out Charles whose glum face spoils the picture, I point out the dawn but he can see no beauty in it. Simply asked me to get him a biscuit. ' Breathes there a man with soul so dead.' Expect it is all because he is not yet awake, so turn in on deck as one hour of sleep there is worth two in the cabin."

We had a peaceful day, as the wind was taking off all the while, and that night, not wishing to be disturbed by Jim's indigestion, I cooked the dinner, boiled potatoes, fried corned beef, spinach, onions; and a peaceful night followed, the skipper entering the fact that it was a good dinner in the log.

The next day we were becalmed, and at 10.45 a.m. Charles, who was washing up the breakfast things, gave an excited yell that startled us below, for Charles is not easily excitable, and expecting to see a tidal wave, a waterspout or a sea serpent climbing in over the bow we rushed on deck, to see none of these things, but a little land bird, like a waterwagtail, but yellow and not in the least afraid of man for he was trotting about within a few inches of Charles. The bird was thirsty, as he tried to drink water on the bobstay but was unable to for the plunging of the bow, so we gave him some water and crumbs, and then, quite at home, he inspected the ship and went below, flying and walking all over the boat, having a bath in a teacup, and generally settling down. At 6.30 Charles was sleeping (sunset) and the bird turned in beside him, tucking his head under his wing within two and a half inches of Charles's nose; an impressive and inspiring sight.

We made a nest for him in an empty oatmeal box and he turned in there later. When daylight came next morning, Sunday, September 26, we found our little bird dead and were all very upset; at first we thought we would bury him, and then thinking he'd be happier in the sunshine floating on top of the water, I sealed him up

TYPHOON WITH JIB, MIZEN AND 'DOLLY VARDEN'S' TRYSAIL SET, SAILING TOWARDS HELL GATE

in a jam bottle, and with a card inside telling of his faith in human nature, we set him free to wander over the waves. Strange how we had taken to that little bird, blown four hundred miles off the land and how sad we were at losing him. When men are alone with Nature in mid ocean, their thoughts grow simple and kind.

Yesterday we had seen large schools of porpoises, one with at least two hundred in it, and to see them jumping clear of the water in batches of fifty or so on their way due south was to realise how many fish there were in the sea, and how perfect they were, for these porpoises, about six feet long, were travelling at 30 knots or more, which is an astonishing speed for their length. By noon we were becalmed, and about a quarter of a mile away lay a floating object. Full of curiosity I swam towards it. When almost to it I saw a ripple, and although of all the fish we had seen that day we had not sighted a shark, I immediately thought of sharks and started to swim back to *Typhoon*, which now looked miles away. The skipper yelled to know why I had turned without seeing what I set out for, and though feeling very frightened I made once more for the object. It turned out to be a barrel covered with weed a foot long, and without a second glance I turned tail for *Typhoon* and swam as fast as I was able, feeling an imaginary shark at my feet all the while. We had shot at them with an express rifle quite a lot, for we towed our dish cloths astern on a string to wash them and the sharks used to snap at them; if we were going any speed they missed, for a shark's mouth is on its under side, and to bite things floating on the surface it has to roll over on its back, and generally loses speed in so doing.

The next day, Monday, September 27, we were still becalmed, and spent the day swimming, painting and varnishing *Typhoon*, and replacing worn gear. It was very peaceful with *Typhoon* just fanning herself along, when at

2.00 p.m. we sighted three masts ahead, and altered course towards them. Three and a half hours later we spoke the *Marjorie McGlashen* of St. John with a load of salt fish bound to Malaga.

She had had no wind for six days. We passed each other bound in opposite directions, and as we were then doing 2 knots we soon separated, and at sunset, 6.00 p.m., she was some way off. The sun set right ahead, and as it went down the moon came up dead astern, rather wonderful the big red ball of fire going down ahead and the full yellow moon rising astern, both in sight for some time. A fine picture for a circular room in a lighthouse, the sun setting one side and the moon rising on the other, with the red light from the one toning into the yellow of the other ; perhaps the only way a picture could be painted correctly to show both the sun and full moon at once. Next morning the moon dropped into the sea ahead while the sun rose astern. *Typhoon* had sailed herself all through the night, but at 4.00 a.m., the wind increasing rapidly, she had to be steered, and at 6.00 a.m. we had to double reef the mainsail, and three hours later had to take it in entirely, for by now it was blowing hard. With the south-west wind ahead we could steer W.N.W., and *Typhoon* was very uncomfortable. Driving into a heavy steep sea she smothered herself, and cooking was impossible. Just before dark we stowed the jib and mizen, and hove her to under Dolly Varden's trysail, which Tom Ratsey had given to *Typhoon* just before she left Cowes. We three youngsters were seasick, and as the trysail was easily handled by one and sails were my job, I set it in the intervals between my violent eructations, and am afraid that I messed the sail at times, but the seas soon washed it white again. *Typhoon* rode from four to eight points off the wind, from close-hauled to wind abeam, and was quite quiet throughout the night, taking really heavy seas aboard about once every half hour, till 8.00 a.m. when a tremendous rain squall knocked the heart out of the wind, and it rapidly fell away. Then suddenly it flew into the north and blew as hard as ever again, but this wind was abaft the beam, so we took in the trysail, and setting the jib and mizen, started on our way once more. In a very short time the seas grew to an alarming height and *Typhoon* was continually swept. The skipper taking the noon sight was almost swept away. Salt water did not seem to hurt the sextant, and by now it was used to shower baths of great force.

Our position was still 300 miles from San Miguel, as we had on this part of our cruise either too much or too little wind. On one day without wind we did $2\frac{1}{2}$ miles and on the previous day with a gale $21\frac{3}{4}$ miles.

In the afternoon the wind eased, and we set the double reefed mainsail. While the skipper cooked the evening meal with a blow lamp it eased off still more, and I shook out the reefs, leaving the wheel for short intervals to do so. By 10.00 p.m. the night was perfect, with the moon just past full sailing through a fairly clear sky.

Thursday, September 30, came in with a clear crisp breeze and bright sunshine, and breakfast was a joyful meal, but then the wind fell away to nothing and *Typhoon* flopped and fell helplessly about in the old sea during my watch, and it was very depressing. However, the wind came again from the north-west after two hours and we eased the sheets, which had been pinned in to save slatting, and once more sailed. By now the seas had smoothed out into long hills and valleys with almost a quarter of a mile between the crests.

Just before dark we put a single reef in the mainsail as the weather looked dirty, and in the course of the night we had often to lower the mainsail for heavy squalls, resetting it again when they were over.

At 9.45 a.m., Friday, we shook the reef out and enjoyed good sailing weather, sunshine and a nice breeze, our sights putting us 150 miles to the east of San Miguel, the largest island of the Azores, which was under half an inch long on our chart.

Another day of perfect sailing weather, and suddenly Charles at the wheel yelled " Land Ho," and there on the starboard bow was the faint outline of the volcanic peaks of San Miguel ; for we were on the latitude where the earth's crust is thin, and volcanoes are frequent right round this belt of the earth. We had been two hours under twelve days sailing our 850 miles to make this landfall, three days longer than we should have been and food was getting low, paraffin oil had run out, the wind was dead ahead and freshening, so that we had a hard beat to windward in store.

As the sun set at 6.00 p.m. Charles sighted land on the port bow, which we believed to be Santa Maria. By 9.00 p.m. we were, we thought, close to the Formigas rock, and accordingly sailed *Typhoon* so close to the wind that she only moved through the water at about 2 knots, while we waited for the moon to rise and lighten our darkness. The skipper and Jim kept this watch, for though we only had one in a watch at sea we had two in soundings.

At midnight Charles and I took over and no lights showed from the two islands we had sighted ; but as soon as the moon broke through the clouds San Miguel was visible only about 10 miles away.

By 12.30 the wind and sea had increased so much that we had to put two reefs in the mainsail, and perhaps a description of the method used to reef this 480 sq. ft. sail in a heavy wind and sea will be interesting and instructive. It must be remembered that at frequent intervals throughout the job *Typhoon* was being swept from end to end with seas running three and four feet over her decks, and those below were being thrown up on to the deck above, or rather left up there as their bunks dropped away from under them.

The main sheet was eased, so that although there was enough wind in the sail to keep the boom from being thrown about violently there was not enough weight in it to cause hauling down the reef earings and points to be hard work. The tack was hauled down and made fast, then the outer earing hauled down and the main part of the job was complete. In hauling down the tack I had to slacken off the throat halyard—the peak did not need touching—and so with the two earings lashed down the reef points could be tied ; in the dark care had to be taken to tie the right ones and to tie them with the same strain on each. Here the advantage of having some weight of wind in the sail showed itself, for it was in the position it would be when sailing. Had the mainsail been loose-footed the tying of the reef points would have been easier. The whole reef only took about ten minutes, and there is no doubt that the reefing of a ketch's mainsail is a simpler and easier job than the reefing of a schooner's. The sail is in the middle of the boat where the motion is least, and even with the sheet eased slightly the end of the boom is still inside the rail owing to the beam of the ship at this point, whereas a schooner's mainsail generally extends over the stern of the ship, and there is the wheel, helmsman and cockpit to fall over and into. So although past experience had left me satisfied that the schooner's was the best cruising rig, now, after reefing *Typhoon*, the ketch rig seemed to me the easiest and most desirable. Such is the influence of a contented mind.

In three-quarters of an hour the wind and sea had increased still further, so that the mainsail had to be stowed entirely ; with only her jib and mizen *Typhoon* was over canvassed, and hit the seas, which were very very steep, so hard that the skipper and Jim were unable to sleep at all below.

Sunday, October 3. At 6.00 a.m. the skipper and Jim took over, and by this time we were within 5 miles of the island and should have been in smoother water, but the seas were steep and confused and reminded me of Portland Race with a spring ebb tide against a S.W. gale, but on a larger scale. The seas were irregular and so steep that we hardly made any way against them, although with our jib and mizen we had all the sail set *Typhoon* could carry, and we were continually swept with seas.

It was now daylight, and the sight of the green fields and white houses and the strong smoky smell of the land made us long to be ashore. As there would be no sleep below Charles and myself did not think of turning in, but thought that four on deck could tack *Typhoon* and set the mainsail whenever the wind eased for a while.

But though from 6.00 till noon, six hours, we fought in full daylight to get *Typhoon* just those five miles to the land we could not do it. We tried to tack her under jib and mizen only, and as often as we tried we were frustrated by the seas, for the moment the drive was taken out of the sails *Typhoon* lost what little way she had. We set the double reefed mainsail, and she lay down till the water ran in the companion way. Then at noon in a last effort to get her on the other tack we gybed her, and the seizing on the mizen shrouds gave way, and though we were at last on the other tack we had broken our mizen. So we stowed the mizen and jib and hove to once more under Dolly Varden's trysail, finally settling down below at 2.00 p.m. Eight hours we had been trying to tack that last five miles, without food and wet through the whole time ; in fact Charles and I had been wet through for fourteen hours, as we had just completed our six hour watch when this struggle began.

And so I sat thinking over a vessel with a ketch rig again, and listening to the arguments for it, the greatest of all being that in bad weather she will handle and balance under jib and mizen. And so she will, but when the weather is damned bad she will do nothing under them, neither will she under mainsail alone, and she will not stand mainsail and jib even if the mainsail is well reefed, for all the drive is too far forward. This was of course an unusually hard wind, for it was October and the equinoctial gales were about ; when we finally reached port we found eight large steamers sheltering there, some with boilers shaken loose, and all eight with one trouble or another.

We lay hove to from 2.00 p.m. Sunday, till 8.00 a.m. Wednesday, when the wind having eased we set the double reefed mainsail, and soon after we shook out the reefs and at 10.00 a.m. set the jib and steered S.W., hoping to sight San Miguel by dark.

At 4.15 p.m. Charles, who seemed to be great at landfalls, sighted an island on the port bow, which we took to be Santa Maria, and fifteen minutes later he apparently discovered more land in a mass of cloud on the starboard bow, but we were not sure that this was land at all. Then with sunset came a calm, which lasted all night ; and was succeeded at daybreak by baffling light airs from all points of the compass ; later wind came out of the north about noon strong enough to give us steerage way, then backed to north-west and we slowly made our way towards Santa Maria. By sundown we were only four miles off, and gradually drew inshore through the deepening gloom. We had no chart and were not really certain of the island's identity ; even if it were Santa Maria our chart was no guide ; no lights appeared ashore to help us except one swinging lantern moving over the face of the mountain, probably carried by a farmer to light him on his way. The roar of the surf and the cries of thousands of birds made the night eerie, and we dared not approach any closer, so we stood off-shore again, making short tacks along the coast in search of a cove, or at least what appeared by the chart to be one. Just before pitch darkness set in, finding a low place in the hills above, we thought it must be our cove, so after standing in to four fathoms we let go the anchor, seventeen days from Spain. We were completely out of food, so that we could not help turning in on empty stomachs, wondering what we should find when daylight came.

Friday, October 8. On waking, we found that the houses we had seen the night before and thought empty as no lights showed, were occupied, with terraced gardens behind them, and that the town was alive. So we rowed ashore, directed by yells as to the way in through the rocks and surf, and soon our dinghy was hauled high and dry by the inhabitants, all wondering what sort of vessel it was that had anchored off their town in the night. The island was Santa Maria, and the town San Laurenco; walking up its steep main street we all discovered that we were not very stable on our legs, and that they did not seem very strong, in fact we felt like invalids out of bed for the first time. The people were kindness itself, and made us eat and drink before we were allowed to speak. Without knowing how to thank them we fell to, and after we had fed were shown the wonders of the island. The terraced gardens grew grapes for wine, almost every house having its own wine press; one had a still in which the

THE *Independent Bridge* LIFTS OUT
OUR MIZEN MAST

owner made a powerful brandy. The red and white church was two hundred years old, fires were lit with flint and steel and the pith of a plant for tinder, bread was baked, as it still is in parts of Norfolk and Suffolk, in stone ovens, a fire being first lit in the oven and then raked out, and the bread put in and cooked by the heat held in the stones for several hours. There was so much to see that our brains could not grasp it all, and at 3.00 p.m., after provisioning, we left. The townspeople would not accept payment for anything and came down in a body to bid us farewell. Soon we were away with a double reefed mainsail, for the S.W. wind had set in strong again, but with the darkness it fell away to a calm, and we spent the night rolling helplessly. Throughout the morning we were becalmed, with occasional catspaws from different directions, holding just long enough to move *Typhoon*, and then dying away again.

But in the afternoon a breeze came, and we sailed towards Ponta Delgada, which with all the island of San Miguel had been in sight since daybreak. By sunset we were only three miles from the breakwater, and feeling our way in with the lead we anchored in the harbour just off what we took to be the public landing, and turned in for the night.

We spent ten days at Ponta Delgada as there seemed so much to do, and so many people to visit and dine with that the work proceeded pleasantly if slowly. Our anchorage was just off the inner harbour, where we found a three-masted double-ended lateen-rigged trader which had sailed in just before dark ahead of us. Long parallel lines—she was sixty feet overall and had a crew of twelve—made her fast and easily driven. When we had looked over this interesting vessel her crew came aboard *Typhoon* and showed an equal interest in her. We had already passed the Customs and the Doctor was quite satisfied with our papers. So far there had been no trouble at all with harbour authorities, who all seemed to do their utmost to help us. A walk over the town soon tired us out, and we wondered if the climate of the Azores was the cause or if it was due to the fact that we had not used our legs much for some weeks, or if it was the complicated money system that really laid us low; for there were two sorts of money on the island, the mainland Portuguese milrei being worth five of the island's milreis, so there was weak and strong money and we never knew which was which.

We had anchored to a 60 lb. kedge; this was unfortunate, for the warp chafed through on the hard rocks below, and *Typhoon* blew ashore. Her deep heel aft striking first, she swung round stern to the wind and waves, so we ran out the main anchor from aft in the dinghy and hove her off as she lay, and she hung that way so nicely that we left her so. That night it blew a gale, and though we were inside the end of the breakwater her stern pounded on the short steep seas in a frightening manner. With no mizen we did not dare sail off, and the engine refused duty, so we spent a night moored stern to the waves with the rocks close aboard to leeward. In the morning we swung her round on her anchor, and tried to sail her off. We set the mainsail, and then hauling in hand over hand on the anchor ran her over it with quite a bit of way on, broke it out cleanly, and setting the jib stood farther into the harbour on the port tack. But we could not weather the rocks to leeward, so we stayed her and then stood out of the harbour on the starboard tack. We tried to tack her again before clearing the harbour, but she would not stay, and after several attempts we anchored, not having gained an inch to weather. Then a tug came along, and we gratefully gave him a rope, with which he towed us into the harbour. We might easily have gone out to sea again and spent days getting back. The skipper and I had an argument that night about double enders. I had taken an unfair advantage the night before, for with *Typhoon* hammering her stern hard into every sea he had had to admit our position then was a case where a pointed stern boat would have been happier.

We moored up alongside the *Independent Bridge*, and she lifted out our mizen mast, off the heel of which her carpenter cut two feet. It was then restepped. It only remained to shorten the shrouds, and as these were double with their eyes on the deck it meant shortening one eye only and shifting the seizing at the hounds. . . . The carpenter also made two new cheeks for the hounds, and these he morticed deeper into the mast, and clenched on with a copper bolt through the two, which made a much stronger job than the screws had before.

Having repaired the mast we had to put our supplies aboard for the passage to New York. Food was scarce on the island and none could by law be taken away, so we had to resort to smuggling.

This was a humorous job. The four of us loaded our pockets with eggs, and then proceeded down the crowded streets. We had gone carefully and with infinite skill for about one hundred yards, when the skipper said " damn " under his breath, and walked even more uncomfortably than before. This amused us so much that we all began laughing, only to turn silent one by one as we each broke an egg or so, when it was the skipper's turn to laugh. And so we made our way to the quay laughing at each other's discomfort. The crowds we passed through wondered at the cause of our mirth. When we finally arrived at the boat we had difficulty in climbing aboard not only because of the eggs, but because we were weak through laughing so much. After this only one went for eggs at a time.

We bought 100 lbs. of beef and a bag of flour off the *West View*, a steamer in for repairs, and had to smuggle this aboard under cover of the dark nights, for there were soldiers on every ship as well as along the quays to watch out for such things as food passing between different vessels. What with one thing and another it took time to provision *Typhoon*, but at last we were ready, and then Manson Dillaway, a lawyer from Boston, said he would like to join us for the passage home, which brought our numbers up to five. So we sailed away from Ponta Delgada, where everyone had shown us the utmost kindness, and all the large steamers blew their whistles as we cleared the harbour, a tiny ketch no larger than their lifeboats. Their parting whistles moved us all deeply, so that we could none of us look at each other or speak. " Parting is such sweet sorrow."

The skipper said he would like the first watch, and as we knew how he was feeling we all turned in and left him alone with his thoughts and *Typhoon*, guessing rightly that he would take a much longer watch than he should, for by now we had begun to realise each other's thoughts and moods, and so knew that the skipper would enjoy the night.

This was the night of October 19, 1920. With the wind westerly *Typhoon* sailed close hauled down towards the North East Trades on a course S.S.W. ½ W. By midnight the wind had increased and was still increasing until 1.00 a.m., when we took the mainsail off her, and she sailed on under jib and mizen for twelve hours and then at 1.00 p.m. we set the mainsail once more.

Next day October 21 the wind backed into the south-west and we put about and lay west on the port tack. At 7.30 p.m. that night the wind fell away to a calm, and we flattened in the sails to prevent slatting, but the next morning brought a strong breeze from west-south-west, and we steered N.W. by W. until 3.50 in the afternoon, when the wind backing into the south enabled us to steer W.S.W. But soon the breeze died away and at 6.30 p.m. the engine was started. The clutch, however, would not grip, so the engine was stopped till daylight; " Allah be praised," for with that running below sleep was difficult and uncomfortable. An engine on a sailing vessel should be put in a watertight, fireproof and smellproof room of its own.

Saturday, October 23 (next morning), we started the engine at 10.00 a.m. and away we went at 4¾ knots until three in the afternoon, when the stuffing-box was so hot the engine had to be stopped, and restarted after a two hour rest, when it ran for 13 hours until we stopped it, for a breeze was making. We set sail and steered west with a south-west wind at 6.00 a.m.

As the day grew the wind increased. Towards nightfall we put two reefs in the mainsail, and by midnight it was blowing so hard that we took it in altogether. It was a dirty night, *Typhoon* being continually swept by seas, and those below had no rest, for the motion threw them up on to the deck beams. A heavy rain squall knocked down the seas and also eased the wind slightly in the early morning, and at 9.00 a.m. the mainsail was set, but the wind flew into the north and blew so hard that we stowed it again in a hurry. Then at 4.30 in the afternoon we set Dolly Varden's trysail, which with the jib and mizen gave us 6½ knots, a speed quite fast enough for the sea then running.

We carried along under this rig for 24 hours and then in the afternoon of October 26 we set the mainsail, for the wind was north-east and steady, and we hoped we were in the Trades. The mainsail increased our speed, so that we were now doing 7.4 knots right on our course. And from now on life aboard became very pleasant. The Trades sound nice and settled, but they are full of squalls and blow quite fresh ; being fair for our passage, however, little water found its way below, though the lee scuppers were generally full.

And so we settled down to a pleasant life, steering, cooking and eating meals and smartening up *Typhoon*. Everything was peaceful till sunset on November 2, when we stood by for something to happen, for the sunset had a wicked look. At 6.45 p.m. a squall hit us, full of heavy rain, which practically knocked *Typhoon* on her beam ends, although the mainsail was half down. During the few minutes the squall lasted we stowed both mainsail and mizen.   After it was over we reset the mizen, but did not hoist the mainsail till noon next day, for the squalls followed each other in rapid succession.   Then on November 4 the wind came ahead and blew very hard, so that the skipper and I reefed the mainsail, then the mizen and then the jib.   The water in this latitude was quite warm, so we did all reefing and wet work without any clothes on at all, so that they were dry or fairly so to put on afterwards.   Although reefing her was a single-handed job it was much easier with two and more fun, as there was someone to laugh with.

The wind veered from west to north-west, so we tacked late in the afternoon, and steered West ½ South. Then at 7.00 p.m. the wind fell away, so that at 9.00 p.m. the engine was started, and ran all through the night.

Noon November 5 (next day) the engine gave up the ghost, and expecting it to take some time to start, we all dived overboard and it started immediately.   Charles, the skipper and myself managed to scramble aboard before

WITH FULL JIB AND MIZEN, AT SIX KNOTS, WE PASSED A THREE-MASTED SCHOONER HOVE TO

Typhoon gathered way, but we had to swing her round in a circle to pick up Dillaway who looked like being left behind.   After another two hours under power the circulating water stopped, and so as a breeze was making from the west we stopped it and set sail steering N. by West.   Our position now was Lat. 33.23.16, Long. 53.06 so we were getting towards New York.

For three days we had head winds and heavy squalls, and light winds between the squalls, so our progress was not fast.   Then came another three days of calms, squalls, head winds and engine starting and stopping, so that the afternoon sights of Wednesday, November 10, put us about 800 miles from New York in Lat. 33.48.02 and Long. 60.05.15.

Although this part of the voyage does not seem long, it is a part where heavy gales are to be expected in November.   Everything, however, was fairly quiet till the night of November 12, when at 9.30 p.m. the wind piped up so strong that we had to stow the double-reefed mainsail entirely, and all through the night *Typhoon* drove close hauled into a heavy head sea.

Our good weather was over ; we were out of most of our best food and had been making all sorts of unleavened bread and weird cakes with the flour we still had, but now we could no longer use the coal stove, which warmed and dried and kept *Typhoon* sweet below, and instead had to cook by the primus in gimbals, with the cook lashed on to his job, so violent was the motion.

On November 13 we were struck by a very fierce squall, and for over two hours *Typhoon* with only her jib had all the sail she could stagger under.   It blew with great force from the west, then south-west, then north, and finally settled into a hard north-east wind, when we set the mizen again.   The seas grew rapidly, and to make matters worse were very confused, for the shifting winds had blown hard enough to cause cross seas, but *Typhoon* doing her six knots under jib and mizen made the best she could of it, and we were fairly comfortable if wet.

In the middle of the afternoon we sighted masts ahead, and soon saw there were three, which we took to be those of a three-masted schooner coming our way under shortened sail, but we could not understand why she was so long drawing near.   Then we lifted her hull above water, and at first she seemed to have no sail set at all, but later on we saw that she was hove to under her two inner staysails and her well-reefed mainsail, and although she was so snugged down she was first lifting her bow out of water so that we could see clear under her forefoot a third of her length ; then pitching down as though bound for the bottom.   It needed all hands to take two photographs of her. Charles steered while Jim, Dillaway and myself contrived to hold the skipper on as well as protect the camera from the spray and seas that were flying over us. Three men in oilskins on her quarter-deck were so surprised to see such a small boat sailing while they had had to heave to that they did not return our cheerful wave. Or possibly they thought us such damned fools to be under way in such a seaway that we were beneath their notice, for there was no doubt that seamanship and common sense pointed to heaving to, but our food was almost exhausted and we could not afford the delay.

Towards sunset the glass started to rise and we decided to carry on through the night under jib and mizen ; and by 9.00 a.m. next morning (Sunday, November 14) the wind had eased enough to set the mainsail reefed, when we increased our speed to 7 knots. Then the wind shifted about before settling down to a light easterly breeze that only gave us 4 knots. We were grateful for this light fair wind and the consequent easing up of the motion ; the breaking seas gradually became less formidable, and though it was now cold we were able to light the stove and dry and warm *Typhoon*.

The wind remained moderate to light throughout Sunday, but on Monday morning it freshened from the E.S.E. In an effort to increase our speed we set the spinnaker, but it carried away, and so we were content with the full mainsail, the mizen having been stowed as the wind was aft, rendering it of little or no value.

The skipper's sights on Monday showed that we had made good three hundred miles in the three days of heavy weather, which he thought was disappointing, but which I thought good, for really we should have hove to and made no progress at all.

Tuesday, November 16, came in with another hard gale from the east, and we lowered the mainsail and set the jib under which *Typhoon* ran for some hours ; but at 10.30 a.m. we were afraid that the jib would not last much longer, so we bent Dolly Varden's trysail and stowed the jib. We put extra lashings on the dinghy, stowed sail and generally prepared *Typhoon* for the severest weather, for we all felt that the gale coming was to be much heavier than anything we had yet encountered. The work was exacting and dangerous, for *Typhoon* was flying through and under seas that were very strong, and generally Charles held me like a vice while I stowed and lashed sails ; and although he several times hurt through his excessive force, the very pain gave me confidence to work quietly on without fear of being washed away.

That afternoon Charles took the wheel over from me at 3.00 p.m. *Typhoon* was careering along far too fast for safety ; on top of the seas she would begin gathering way and then rush down the face of the wave at an alarming speed ; every sea that caught her lifted her stern high just before she began this mad rush, and this was the moment the helmsman had to anticipate, for in it lay the whole secret of taking her through that weather. At such moments, with her high buoyant stern in the air, she had no steerage way, since although she was travelling quite fast the breaking crests of course travelled faster ; the rudder had no grip, yet she must be poised exactly right for each downward swoop before it actually began, or she would broach or gybe. I sat by Charles to explain this nice point, and he steered under my direction for some twenty seas, after which I went below feeling he had mastered the situation. But it was apparently not so, for no sooner had I shut the sliding hatch than we broached, and went over on our beam ends. Half expecting this to happen I was not really surprised, and grasped what was happening in a flash. *Typhoon* went over to 90 degrees, and then righted slowly. There was no time to be frightened before she was up again, so the whole thing seemed funny instead, until I thought of Charles, and was afraid he'd been washed away ; but looking through the port I saw him looking so puzzled and worried, that he looked funny too. And I roared with laughter.

A page or so from my diary written at the time will I believe paint the picture more clearly than words written afterwards.

" Tuesday, November 16.

" 6.00 a.m. Lacing of main gaff carried away. Blowing hard. Charles at wheel calls me.

" 6.10. Wind backs E.N.E. blowing harder. Half lower mainsail and hoist jib. Blowing and raining like old Nick. Jim came up to lend a hand and went below to get dry and warm when we had half lowered mainsail. W.W.N. (skipper) woke as Jim was casually dressing. He heard the wind whistling and the mainsail flapping and got wild (we all do when hungry). He chewed Jim up and then rushed forward to me and banged me on the nose with his elbow. Good job I was there or he might have gone overboard (motion of ship pretty bad) but my nose brought him up. Asked him if he'd hurt his elbow, he said ' a bit ' and thought it was the mast he'd hit till I explained afterwards.

" We doused and secured the mainsail in crutch.

" 10.00 a.m. Been running under jib since 6.10 a.m. W.W.N. at wheel thinks wind too much for jib and that it may carry away. Heavy sea.

" 10.30. Jim, Charles and I got out and half hoisted trysail to blanket jib, which then stowed. Oilskins no good as every now and then I went under. Usually up to my waist as standing on bobstay. Jim asked me once if I'd hurt myself as a sea banged me against the bowsprit. I replied ' No, but I've given myself a hell of a twist,' as

I noticed that my oilskins were on the wrong way round.   And then told Jim and Charles the story of the workman, who was late up and dressing in a rush put his trousers on back to front without knowing it; he dashed off to work and was no sooner on the scaffolding of the house he was helping to build than the scaffolding collapsed. When picked up and asked if he was hurt he said ' No,' but looking down and seeing his trousers back to front added ' But I've given myself a hell of a twist.'   Jim and Charles were holding on to the mast, and I was on the bowsprit, so had to shout the story, don't know if they heard it or not but Jim laughed at the right time, but this may have only been his politeness.   W.W.N. at the wheel getting impatient, so take time hoisting trysail; would like a penny for every time I've answered his anxious enquiry with ' Nothing broken only a wheel come off ', a bad

IN SPITE OF THE GALLEY BEING AFT THE COOK HAD TO BE LASHED TO THE STOVE

habit rubbing people the wrong way.   It is rotten of me for W.W.N. owns the ship, and is responsible for irresponsible kids like Jim and myself.

" Sheet tackle got adrift as we were hoisting trysail so Charles held on to my feet, I leant overboard for it, Charles has altered since the gale off San Miguel and is now the busiest man on the ship.

" After we'd finished putting extra lashing on the dinghy I undressed and standing up in the rain in the cockpit bathed with real soap.   W.W.N. was amused and said ' Well, you intend to go to your maker clean anyway.'

" And I replied, ' Well, if we do weather this lot I'd be angry at wasting this nice rainwater.'   Heaviest wind and sea we have had.   W.W.N. at wheel is having a strenuous time, she is a good little ship, wonderful the way she stands up to this wind and sea.   Sincerely hope the schooner we passed is allright.

" 3.10.   Charles relieved me at wheel.   Seas worse, which seemed impossible five hours ago, everything can be worse, but it is not very comforting, when after losing thirty bob, a friend tells you it is better than losing sixty.

" We got knocked down with our masts in the water.   I'd just taken off my oilies when with a bang we went over to port.   I grabbed the table and Dillaway's bunk, he just managed to stay in it.   Jim dropped from his bunk on to W.W.N., who was lying on the port seat.   Jim had an amazed expression as he cleared the ditty box on the dresser.   I wanted to laugh, hadn't time to get frightened before she came up.   Suddenly thought of Charles and looking through the port was relieved to see him sitting at the wheel with a very worried and puzzled expression on his face.   There was the cockpit full of water, and our empty kegs floating about with the last of our salt beef. Charles looked exactly like Robinson Crusoe on his raft just leaving the wreck.   He looked so funny that I laughed, which made W.W.N. wild as he had just discovered his pyjamas covered with fuel oil. Then we had a heated argument, the skipper and I (raised voices but could not wave our arms as we had to hold on either end of the table) about boats' sterns. I believe in pointed sterns and the skipper in broad sterns.

" She is a wonderful boat but I think she'd be more wonderful if she had a canoe stern, or a stern like a Scotch fishing nabbie."

After we had finished our argument, neither side convincing the other, the skipper took the wheel. By now it was dusk, and to make steering easier we trailed two long lines astern, which steadied her as she was on top of the seas. The difference in steering was so great, that we decided to run on through the night rather than heave

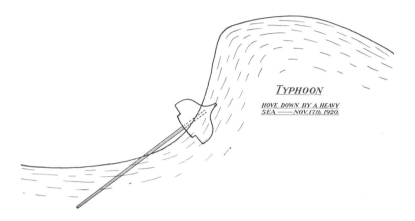

TYPHOON
HOVE DOWN BY A HEAVY SEA —— NOV. 17th. 1920.

to. This was at 4.30 p.m. At 9.30 p.m. the wind fell away quickly, and then we had a salvo of hard squalls from all directions, one close on the heels of the other.

Next morning (Wednesday, November 17) at 3.00 a.m. the skipper and I gybed her by lowering the trysail, and then setting it again on the starboard side. There was a chance of taking out the mast or bursting the sail in gybing with it set. Then we hauled in one of the two lines astern as the wind had eased. The skipper steered till 7.00 a.m., and then Jim took her for two hours, then after my two hours the skipper took her another two. From 7.00 a.m. till 1.00 p.m. the wind had increased, and was still increasing ; the new sea making up over the old was heavier and more confused than the sea we had before encountered, and it was still increasing, while the wind blew harder than ever in a succession of vicious squalls. The tops of the seas were blown off, and the valleys were streaked with spume and spray flying across like snow before a gale. The sting of the spray could be felt under oilskins, and we had already streamed our second rope astern, this time bent on to a heavy iron pail, otherwise no helmsman on earth could have steered *Typhoon* for five minutes. As it was, two hours of it had us all dead beat. With the rising wind and the seas increasing so quickly, not only in size but in steepness and unevenness, the skipper decided to heave to, and we prepared the Voss type sea anchor below, as it was easier to work there than on deck, and then took it to the cockpit to rig, with Charles sitting and lying on it as the wind tried to lift it out of the boat, when it would have blown away to leeward and perhaps turned into a kite. The sea anchor warp was already rove through a fairlead on the bowsprit end to the cockpit, so we had only to drop it over from aft and all would be well.

So we were all ready, Dillaway was to pump bilge water and oil out with the bilge pump, Jim and I were to lower and stow the trysail, then make our way aft and help Charles stream the sea anchor, while the skipper steered. And Jim and I were to put lifelines on, for by now the seas were thundering down on *Typhoon* with alarming frequency and weight. But although Jim and I said " Yes " to the skipper, we foolishly disobeyed orders and did not put them on, feeling that they would hamper our movements. I went first to the mainmast to gather in the trysail halyard and get it all ready to lower before Jim left the cockpit to join me for the actual hauling down of the sail, which we thought would stick in that wind ; for all our halyards and ropes had been swept off their belaying pins and were trailing overboard and astern like the arms and legs of an octopus.

As soon as I had coiled the halyard, I signalled to Jim to come forward. He had just climbed out when one heavy sea came, but he held on to the mizen and I to the mainmast for that one, which was the forerunner of another with tons and tons of water, which broke aboard us from an enormous height. That sea towered above us like a church ; in moments like that size cannot be judged accurately, for the brain is too excited, but to me it looked to have a face that was practically vertical, but with the top overhanging, like an overhanging cliff, and the top seemed to be thirty feet above us, and we had already climbed about fifteen feet from its base. So there *Typhoon* seemed to me to be climbing the face of a plumb cliff, and when she had climbed fifteen feet the other thirty feet crashed down on her. It was pretty grim. Jim, who was half-way between the two masts on his way forward to me, with only the handrail along the deck house to hold on to, had no chance at all and was swept off. I had my legs wrapped round the mainmast and a belaying pin of the spider band in each hand, and held on for a fraction of a second. Then I seemed to be swept miles and miles, and the mainmast came down and hit me, so clutching it grimly, I hung on, and, slowly at first, *Typhoon* righted (for she had been knocked on her beam ends and past). I was lifted out of the water, and found myself clinging to the hounds. Sliding to the deck I gave a heave at the trysail, and it came down as sweetly and as easily as though there had been no wind at all.

I then rushed aft to help with Jim who meantime had caught one of the ropes we had trailed astern, and had been hauled alongside as *Typhoon's* way slackened. Our struggle to hoist him aboard will always live in my memory. It seemed hours before we three could hoist him over the rail, and it was not until the skipper had put a heavy boathook under him and prised down on it, using it as a handspike, which raised Jim to the level of the rail, that we slid him in to safety.

Jim was pushed below, and the sea anchor streamed. But first of all it burst its spreaders, and then the warp carried away, and we fell away again broadside to the seas. Lashing down the trysail heavily, and making things snug on deck, we went below and left *Typhoon* to her own ways ; it was the best thing we could have done, for she seemed quite happy, though about every half hour a heavy sea would thunder down on to her decks and shake her throughout her whole length.

Down below she was in a dreadful state. The inside ballast had burst the floor boards, and, striking the chart case, had slid into the corner of the coach roof ; the ashes from the stove had also found their way on to the roof, which showed how far *Typhoon* had rolled over. The shortness of her masts and the outside ballast on her keel had been just enough to bring her back and no more, for Dillaway below said that when down she lay there some time before slowly rolling her masts out of water. I had assisted in the trials of capsizing a lifeboat, which had to right itself, and do it with outside keel and air boxes, but never for a moment dreamt I should find myself in a vessel hove down as we hove the lifeboat down ; and never will I go to sea with inside ballast again, for that ballast might easily have dropped out through the deck house, and had it done so *Typhoon* would have gone to the bottom and no more would have been heard of her. She must have been within a hair's breadth of it as it was.

We made ourselves as comfortable as we could, spreading towels over the floorboards to keep the broken glass underneath and so out of our bare feet, and then opened the last tin of soup, the last tin of beef, and the last tin of mixed vegetables, which we had put by as an emergency ration ; for we thought how close we had been to missing that last meal altogether, and that we might take it inside us wherever we went. We also opened a bottle of cognac and made a feast of it, after which we sang our best songs, Dillaway and myself being the choir leaders, and then to bed, with the seas crashing down at regular intervals of about half an hour. By this time we had become used to it, and there was no more to do except sleep. We could not sail, the wind and sea were too much, we could not eat as we'd eaten the last of everything, and so to bed. And sleep. " Oh sleep it is a gentle thing beloved from pole to pole."

And we none of us woke till it was broad daylight on Thursday 18 (next day). The wind, though still blowing, had eased, and the seas were not thundering down on to us so heavily or so often. Charles lit the coal stove ; we found some porridge, which had fallen into Dillaway's bunk off the stove, and fried it for breakfast, and with a tiny drop of soup felt braced up and cheerful.

" Joy cometh in the morning," I used to sing without realising how true it was, for how can a boy of twelve know the full meaning of words ? Those who have spent a night of doubts and fears at the bedside of someone dear to them, will understand when they remember the hope the bright gleams of sunshine brought in the morning, how joyful we were and how our joy was further increased by finding the porridge in Dillaway's bunk.

By 2.00 in the afternoon the seas had eased, so that we could work about the deck again. We set the jib and mizen, and by 4.00 p.m., after relacing the head of the mainsail, we were able to set and carry it also. Our position was about 200 miles south-east of New York, with the wind north-west, dead ahead.

A tiny land bird came aboard and rested for an hour or so and then flew away again, and it made us wonder how many small birds able to fly at about 50 miles an hour must be swept off shore and lost by winds above that speed. By 5.30 p.m. the wind had died away completely, but two hours later it filled in again more westerly, allowing us to steer north. All night *Typhoon* steered herself closehauled, so that the man on watch sat in the companionway in the warmth of the coal range with only his head out in the bitter cold of the night.

Friday, November 19, came in colder than ever, with the wind more westerly, so we knew we were clear of the Gulf Stream, and with the continual showers of icy water we had to shorten up the tricks at the wheel, for the lack of food made us unable to withstand the cold. At 8.30 a.m. we were forced to put one reef in the mainsail, and at 1.00 p.m. another, and even then *Typhoon* could only just stagger along with the press of sail she had. A race not against time, but against starvation and hunger urged us on, and had been the cause of our driving on, when we should have hove to during the last two heavy gales. Our afternoon sight put us 150 miles from New York and 115 miles from Montauk Point, so we decided on Montauk and Long Island Sound.

At 3.00 p.m. a steamer steering a north-easterly course passed within a quarter of a mile of us, so being the signalman I semaphored " Please report *Typhoon* from Azores." She repeated the message and reported us, for the Navy stations were on the look-out for us, and they received the message. At 4.45 p.m. we were forced to lower the mainsail entirely, for it was without doubt blowing a gale again and this eased *Typhoon* in her motion. Then we cooked our meal. For some days we had been living on flour and water, which we could eat all day without satisfying our hunger. We had no grease at all, and the way we cooked the little pancakes was to put five little dabs in the pan and turn them over as they began to stick together, the art of the job being to turn them when they began to solidify and before they stuck to the frying pan. Then we ate one each while the next five were in

THE SPANISH STEAMER LOWERS A BAG OF BISCUITS TO THE TYPHOON

the pan, and so our meals lasted hours without satisfying our hunger. This one took three men to cook. The skipper was lashed to the stove, with another lashing to hold him off it, Charles steadied him as well with one hand, and I mixed the batter wedged between the companionway and the oilskin-locker.

After we had taken her mainsail off *Typhoon* steered herself under jib and mizen all through the night; this was a relief to all, as the man on watch, sitting in the cabin with only his head out in the cold, was able to do four hours on, which gave good long spells below for the rest, and we needed sleep to make up for our lack of food. Or at least it seemed so, for we were none of us feeling strong. Saturday, November 20, came in finer, with the wind lessening; at 7.00 a.m. we shook out the reefs in the mainsail, and after repairing the clew set full sail once more. The wind having shifted north let us steer West by North for Montauk Point.

At 11.00 a.m. a ship going east was passing our bow within ¼ mile, and, to make sure that our position and the fact that we were still going strong should be known ashore, I semaphored, " Please report *Typhoon* of New York thirty-one days from the Azores." But she was a Spanish ship and could not read the message; she therefore stopped her engines and hove to while we luffed under her lee. She was the *Guillem Sorolla* of Valencia, and after asking them to report us, the skipper said that our food was low, exchanging cards politely with the captain of the steamer by a boathook, not a footman. Thereupon someone threw over one or two sea biscuits; Charles and Dillaway pounced upon them, broke them in pieces and shared them out so enthusiastically that our plight became apparent. That generous Spanish captain then proceeded to load us with food. He passed us a leg of mutton, a 30 lb. chunk of beef, sugar, ten loaves of bread, rice, a keg of lard, slabs of dried codfish, onions, cabbages, salt pork, apples, pears, tinned fruit, salmon, sardines and two bottles of cognac. The sight of all this food coming aboard was too much for us youngsters, and while the skipper kept up his protests that we had quite enough to go back to Europe with and did not need any more, we kept prancing excitedly about the deck, and our unconcealed joy made the skipper's words unavailing, manna still rained down from heaven. All this time Charles was at our stern and I was at the bow surging our two warps, so that *Typhoon* kept fairly well behaved as she rose and fell in the steamer's lee, for we had just that much control left of our feelings, though Charles's abandon came near imperilling us on more than one occasion.

The captain was quite delighted at having saved us from hunger; when we let go our warps and fell away from the steamer, giving three cheers for her, her captain and crew, and salutes on our foghorn, her powerful steam whistle responded with a succession of deafening blasts.

Then, leaving me to trim *Typhoon* so that she would sail herself, the rest went below. *Typhoon*, knowing that I wished to follow them, sailed herself perfectly at once, and to see that crowd below was a sight worth staying behind for. There was the skipper, who had shown great control on deck, with a great 30 lb. chunk of beef on his lap, fondling, stroking and patting it, as he cut off great chunks, which we fried and ate with the new bread, and for hours we cooked and feasted finishing up with fruit, during all of which time our vessel sailed herself. And then, wondering if it was fair to our " Little Marys " to load them with so much food after they had been empty for so many days, we took five cascaras each and hoped for the best ; the combination seemed to suit our insides, and I suppose that if a man eats even as we did, and needs it, no harm can result. Directly we had finished, the skipper set to work preparing and cooking the dinner of roast beef, with fresh vegetables, and fruit, and the toast in cognac was to the *Guillem Sorolla* and Captain Soler her skipper.

Early next morning Dillaway, who was at the wheel, sighted a flashing light on the port bow ; but instead of the Montauk intervals it showed the triple flash of Shinnecock Light, thirty miles to the west of where we thought we were. With the growing light the skipper recognised the lighthouse as Shinnecock, and, as we had been given our position by the steamer that fed us, we could only conclude that the Labrador current had set us all that way down the coast. With the breeze north-easterly we decided to make a fair wind of it to New York instead of beating back to Montauk and running down the Sound, so we ran alongside the outer edge of Long Island, getting closer and closer in order to gladden our eyes with the unfamiliar sight of land, and at 1.20 we brought Fire Island Light abeam. The skipper steering took her farther and farther inshore while we cooked all sorts of weird dishes, which the skipper helped to eat, for we were a happy ship ; the food and land we had longed for were now ours to enjoy, and we grew careless of the sea, until suddenly the skipper yelled " breakers ahead," and we found that we were over Jones Inlet shoal. Gybing over we went out to sea again, touching only once, but hard enough to frighten us, for there was quite a sea running still.

When we had regained deep water, and were clear of the shoals, we went back on our course again, and this time in gybing the mainsail burst across from leech to luff with a report like a rifle. The mainsail had been through a lot in its passage across the Atlantic and back, and it was a cross cut sail of 10 oz. duck. It was not so much due to wind as to hard wear that the mainsail went, although it was blowing quite hard.

By 10.00 p.m. we cleared Rockaway Point and anchored for the night off the Atlantic Yacht Club in Gravesend Bay, thirty-two days from the Azores. The next day we beat up to Staten Island and moored in between two piers, and then could not get out as a hard wind blew right in on us, and so we spent a night moored at all four corners pitching up and down.

Then with W. P. Stephens, his son Koke, and his confederate Henry Frisch, we started late for tide to beat up the East River, through Hell Gate into Long Island Sound with jib, trysail and mizen. All went well till we were in the lee of the great buildings, and here we were naughty again ; Koke, who had so often sailed this part of the East River, wished us to do so and so, and we left it undone, for Charles and I had never before seen New York, and those lofty buildings whose outlines just showed against the sky looked like fairy palaces, so we did not pay much attention to navigation, and the skipper had so much news to hear from W. P. The natural consequence was that a four knot tide took us into a string of moored barges with a crash which splintered our rail off on the quarter, and started a swearing match between Koke and the skipper of a tug, until he recognised *Typhoon*, and then he towed us into midstream and cast us off with a cheery " Good Luck."

We had missed our tide through Hell Gate, which moreover was not much of a place for us after dark, so we put into the New York Yacht Club's River Station for the night, and next day sailed through Hell Gate and anchored off Whitestone landing, in front of the skipper's house, so ending an eventful Atlantic crossing.

Typhoon had brought us through storm and sunshine ; we had learnt to rely upon her and she never failed us, though we had driven her to the utmost and beyond it on two occasions. We were happy to be in America safe and sound ; and we were sad also, for we should now part, five of us, who had lived as brothers, and perhaps not meet again.

Dillaway left for his home, and so did Jim, Charles and I went to the docks of New York, where we found a job for one as a trimmer on the *Celtic*. So Charles worked his way back to England shovelling coal, and I stayed on till such another job should turn up.

                    *   *   *   *   *   *   *   *   *   *   *   *

The lessons *Typhoon* taught me were many, as she first took me into deep waters.

(1) That a small vessel going to windward could stand far more than her crew, but that chasing away before a gale the crew could drive her beyond her limitations.

(2) That one man could reef or stow a 500 sq. ft. mainsail in all weathers, but not a larger sail.

(3) That as small vessels can and do capsize, inside ballast is a source of danger, and if carried should be fastened down.

ON TRIALS LIFEBOATS ARE HOVE UPSIDE DOWN TO PROVE THEIR SELF-RIGHTING ABILITY

Our National Lifeboat Institution, knowing that boats capsize, have designed self-righting lifeboats which are thoroughly tested for their self-righting powers before being handed over. *Sea Queen* capsized off Japan, *Joan* off Greenland, *Typhoon* between Bermuda and New York, and other cases are known ; these three righted themselves as lifeboats do, and most small vessels would with outside ballast, whereas the tendency of one with inside ballast is to stay there, for this ballast drops on the deck, and holds her down, while of course if it dropped through she would sink.

(4) That an engine in a sailing boat is unnecessary, and if carried should be in a separate compartment that is watertight, fireproof, sound proof, and smell proof. Whenever *Typhoon's* engine ran it turned her from a clean, lovable and happy ship into a dirty, smelly and irritating vessel.

(5) That a ketch will not handle under jib and mizen when there is wind and sea enough for her to shorten down to that, as she will not stay.

(6) That 10 oz. duck is not heavy enough for an ocean cruiser's only suit of sails, and that the cloths should run parallel to the leech, with a leech rope fitted the whole length of the leech. This enables the reef points to be put in seams where they are much stronger.

(7) That the old sailing ship reckoning of 100 miles a day was right for provisioning, but allowances should be made for calms, gales, or spars and sails carrying away, all of which delay a vessel. *Typhoon* sailed roughly 5,000 miles in 50 days.

(8) A crew should be divided much as we were, the owner navigator, Jim engineer, Charles in charge of galley and food, and myself in charge of sails and spars.

(9) That it is asking for trouble to cross the Atlantic during the equinoctial gales in a small vessel.

(10) That although *Typhoon* weathered two gales that distressed large steamers, her broad stern and fine hollow water-lines were not ideal.

(11) That all outside ballast, by giving extra stability and power to carry sail, helps a vessel to tack against a steep heavy sea.

(With all her ballast on her keel, instead of only half, *Typhoon* would probably have come about in that gale off the Azores.)

(12) That the hardest and saddest part of an ocean cruise comes when the crew say " good-bye " at the end.

· 2 ·

DIABLESSE

Length, overall	-	-	-	52 ft. 6 in.	Length, waterline	-	-	46 ft. 0 in.
Beam	-	-	-	15 ft. 6 in.	Draught	-	-	-	7 ft. 3 in.
Displacement	-	-	-	35 tons	Sail area	-	-	-	1,800 sq. ft.

Owner and Skipper, JOHN B. KELLEY

Built from a model in Gloucester (lines taken off by UFFA FOX 1922)

IN the summer of 1921 *Diablesse*, with her owner, his wife and two others, sailed across to Cowes from New York, and when in 1922 the owner offered me the job of forming one of his crew for the voyage back I gladly accepted. We sailed at 4.00 p.m. on June 17 from Cowes, the owner as skipper, his wife as mate, Bobby Somerset navigator, myself in charge of sails, and Bill Waight in charge of food. Everyone had thus a particular function and responsibility, but of course we all helped each other whenever we could, and such an arrangement made a happy ship.

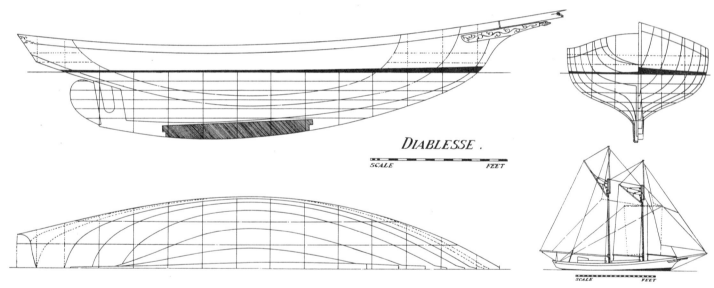

DIABLESSE .

SCALE   FEET

Tern III, with her owner Claud Worth aboard, was under way as we left, to accompany us to the Needles, and as both vessels were very much the same length this part of our cruise turned into a race. Once we had the fisherman's staysail set *Diablesse* drew away from *Tern III*, for with the wind north-westerly it was a reach down the Solent, when our schooner rig was at its best. By 6.45 p.m. we were off Old Harry, and *Tern III* was shaping in for Poole, having lost ground all the while. Had this part of our course been to windward there would in all probability have been a different story to tell, for then *Tern's* cutter rig would have given her the advantage.

And so we started for Madeira happy in the knowledge that at least reaching we were faster than *Tern III*. At 8.30 p.m. we took in the mainsail and set the trysail, for the wind was freshening. It was our first night at sea, and except for the owner and his wife we were strange to *Diablesse*; throughout the first night, therefore, *Diablesse* sailed under jib, staysail, foresail and main trysail. Next morning (June 18) after breakfast we got full sail on her again, and at noon our log read 89 miles, giving an average of 5¼ knots since it had been streamed at 7.00 p.m. near Old Harry.

At 4.00 p.m. on June 19 our position was 10 miles north-east by north off Ushant, thirty-six hours from Cowes; since noon the day before we had averaged just over 7 knots, and the wind having hauled ahead, although making us sheet down hard, enabled us to clear Ushant nicely. So we continued our way to Madeira with one on watch for three hours, giving the rest nine hours off; life on board was easy, for *Diablesse*, being twenty-one years old, had settled down and did not need the constant attention to chafe and small gear that new boats demand. After fourteen days of quiet and peaceful sailing we arrived at Madeira, anchoring in Funchal at 9.00 a.m. on July 1, with the log reading 1,382 miles from Old Harry.

Here we spent four pleasant days. The intake pipe on our engine had broken and let water into *Diablesse*; we loaded her bow down with huge stones off the beach, with the object of lifting her stern high enough to get at the pipe, but it was in vain, and the picture of that heap of stones will always remain in my memory as representing the amount of water a sailing ship could take on her deck without seriously affecting her. We then had recourse to a diver, and it was arranged that I should swim underwater to show him the hole and pipe, as there were two; twice in the course of this operation he almost drowned me, for in the midst of my explanations I would need breath, whereas he, having plenty pumped down to him, did not realise this and held on to me.

BOBBY SOMERSET, NAVIGATOR

RUNNING SOUTH TO THE TRADES

At 7.00 p.m. on July 6 we sailed, with several friends on board. Coehela, who had been most kind to us, steered *Diablesse* out into the night. The full moon made a silvery pathway across the ocean; the reef points pattering on the sail, as *Diablesse*, with her sheets off, rolled quietly along, made a sound like gentle rain, which is one of the pleasantest sounds, for it conjures up a picture of fine weather and a fore-and-aft vessel gently flapping her sails as she lifts her way over the easy seas. Our Funchal friends came further than they intended, for on such a night they could not bring themselves to go back aboard their steam tug; but finally they left us, and we sailed on in the moonlight.

We headed south into the Trades, where *Diablesse* rolled her way along steadily and easily under squaresail and mainsail, with jib set also in case we needed it in a hurry. And in those weeks of pleasant weather *Diablesse* endeared herself to us, for she moved with the graceful ease of a porpoise, lifting to the seas without any effort, so that life aboard was perfection.

We were a little kingdom of our own. The skipper, aged thirty-four, was the father of the family; Bobby and I the elder twins, twenty-four each; and Bill and Miss Ann (as we called the skipper's wife) the younger twins, both being only twenty-one. Day after day passed peacefully by; Bobby reading for an hour every evening out loud to us all in the cockpit, Miss Ann mixing Mint Juleps about 2.00 p.m. every afternoon, a Virginian drink, which first of all produces smiles, then a great feeling of energy, then a powerful desire for sleep, while, as my trick at the wheel generally started soon after sundown, I used to sing for half an hour with Bill as a helpmate, and Bobby would lead us in " Green grow the Rashes, O," which always started off with three verses or so for Bobby to tune up in, and away we'd go with a swing. And so time passed, and we bent south until the sun was plumb overhead, reading 90 degrees on the sextant all round the compass at noon; and after that we bent our way north again for Bermuda, all of which time the squaresail lifted *Diablesse* over the seas, while the mainsail prevented her from rolling.

As we worked our way north we had to cross the Sargasso Sea, the dead spot in the North Atlantic, where there are no currents and usually no wind. Here we felt the heat of the sun, for whereas farther south, directly under it, we had had the fresh Trade winds to cool us, here there were no refreshing breezes, and we were glad when after several days we picked up enough wind to take us away from the deathly stillness of the Sargasso.

The weed was not very thick there, but the place was alive with fish, all quite tame and anxious to take a bent pin without any bait on it, but their mouths were generally too tender and we seldom landed any. It was a relief when first of all fitful squalls and then a steady breeze let us continue on our way.

After twenty-eight days we came to Bermuda, and the whaleboat that brought out the pilot was very pleasing to the eye; long and narrow, with her sweet and easy lines, she brought back memories to Bill and myself of Cowes Seascouts, for I was Scoutmaster and Bill Assistant Scoutmaster, and in Valhalla's whaleboat,[1] very like this Bermudian pilot-boat in shape, we had sailed thousands of miles.

The wind being fresh, we beat in through the coral reefs with the foresail and the main topsail stowed, and *Diablesse* tramped along under jib, staysail and mainsail. At 3.30 p.m. on August 4 we anchored in Hamilton Harbour, there to remain for a week. Our stay was not marred by any noise, for the Bermudians in their wisdom do not allow trains, motor cars on any such things to spoil the beauty and peace of their islands; there, alone in the world, is an island upon which quiet can be enjoyed.

On August 10, our sailing day, we watched their 14-footers racing. With a 35 ft. mast and a 16 ft. bowsprit they set 350 feet of sail, and the crew of six was hardly enough to sit out this amount of canvas. It was a most interesting race to watch. The dinghies were moored either side of the committee boat, which, as there was no stream, lay head to wind. At the starting gun the dinghies sprang off on either tack; then when they met after coming about, instead of the port tack boat giving way they both went about, the idea being that as the two had done equally well to meet after sailing a certain time neither should have any right of way. There is much to be said for this rule, for there is no doubt that our port rule gives the starboard tack boat a great advantage, equal to about three boats' lengths in practice, and such rules make racing a game of tactics like chess rather than one of pure sailing skill.

After the race we set sail and left at 5.00 p.m., foolishly starting the engine for the passage through the reefs to please the pilot by making things easier. This set fire to some oakum resting on the exhaust pipe which soon became red hot, and a serious fire started back in the counter. We none of us thought of going back, and when we had cleared the reefs I rowed the pilot ashore in the dinghy, listening to the warnings and bearings he gave me by which to clear the reefs; and as there were sharks about I had no desire to scratch the dinghy on the reefs or capsize in the seas that broke over them, for it was now dark. Having put the pilot ashore I rowed back as fast as I could towards *Diablesse*, who all this time was proceeding to sea, her crew having too much to attend to with the fire, which had increased greatly since my departing, to think that every mile she sailed away from Bermuda was another for me to row, in a sea that was breaking not heavily, but enough for me, whose mind still dwelt on the sharks the pilot had spoken of so eloquently.

So, rowing as hard as I could without shipping too much spray, I chased after *Diablesse*, and for a long time made no impression. It seemed as if I could never catch her unless a calm came, but imperceptibly the distance between us lessened, and at last, in a state of exhaustion, I was alongside, with only the skipper to help hoist the dinghy because of the fire. We could have done with another on the dinghy job, for with the sea running and the dinghy going up and down, hoisting in was difficult for two. All thoughts of a rest after the hard row were quickly dispelled, however, by the hold the fire had; and as the only way to the counter was from below, and no one could breathe there for smoke and fumes, we started bashing in the cockpit floor with the anchor as a battering ram. It was a job that delighted me, for I was angry first of all at *Diablesse* jilling out to sea almost as fast as I could row, and then with myself for being angry when I discovered why, and then because I had felt rather afraid of those sharks; though there is no doubt that rowing a dinghy in a sloppy sea on a dark night rather lends a man's imagination a hand. It will therefore be understood that I put my heart and soul into the bashing in of the cockpit floor; and then Bobby and Bill set to work, the one aiming the stream of water aft on to the flames while the other pumped with the powerful boat pump. Soon the fire was out and we all turned in except the skipper, who took the first trick at the wheel.

We were now at sea with a self bailing cockpit that would bail itself into the ship, and so next day as ship's carpenter I set to work on the broken floor; and after twelve years the repair still holds, as watertight as when it was completed, and the mystic words " Pol Roget Champagne " can still be read faintly under the mahogany paint on the locker.

It may seem strange that none of us thought of turning back when the fire was at its height, for there can be no doubt that fire at sea is dangerous and often fatal; but we all had such confidence in our ship and ourselves that we sailed on, Miss Ann steering and Bobby pausing just long enough to take a departure from St David's Light.

The weather continued moderate, then light until the night of August 18, when it breezed up, and with all four lowers *Diablesse* smoked along, steering herself with her lee deck awash. During this night, which was one of rain, wind, lightning and bad visibility, we were due to sight Montauk Point. Bobby, who had navigated throughout,

[1] See page 122.

picking up Ushant, Madeira and Bermuda with great exactness, was just a shade anxious, for this would be our landfall ; and besides the feelings all navigators have when making their landfall, there was the fact that when we burst the cockpit floor in we had destroyed the compass-correcting magnet, so that as well as the worry of the chronometer rate, there was that of the compass error. The log was carefully read from time to time by an anxious navigator ; in two hours it gave 22 miles, which at that time I quite believed, for during the whole of my watch I stood in the fore shrouds to leeward with the seas breaking aboard and running past waist high, vainly looking for a lighthouse flashing ashore, and would have believed she had done 12 knots quite easily that night. But now,

DIABLESSE

after twelve years, during which time I've never seen 11 knots logged on a boat under 60 feet waterline, I think *Diablesse's* log must have been read early and then late to give 11 ; I should put her maximum speed at 10 knots.

Be that as it may, all through the night *Diablesse* roared along ; no light appeared, but though the visibility was bad the brilliant flashes of lightning would have been enough to show us land ahead before we were in any danger of striking. On we sailed, therefore, and dawn revealed Long Island and Shinnecock two miles away, the latter's light having failed to pierce the driving rain during the night. A course had been laid for Montauk Point, as in the case of *Typhoon*, and here again we were thirty miles out in our reckoning. Bearing in mind that a steamer had given *Typhoon* her position the day before, and that Bobby had proved himself the most exact of navigators, I am convinced that the Labrador current running south inside the Gulf Stream sometimes sets a small boat much farther south than is generally supposed. We sailed on into Long Island Sound, the weather clearing as the day grew older ; but inside we picked up a very heavy squall, such as is often met in the Sound. Black heavy clouds made up, and then came rain and wind so hard that the water was flattened out and the bowsprit could hardly be seen, and *Diablesse*, lying down with her lee deck under to the coach roof, flew along through a hissing sea. Bobby stood by the main and Bill by the foresail halyards, but if we had started anything in that wind the chances were that the sails would go, so the owner in the hatchway said " Hold till I say the word," or rather shouted it, and *Diablesse* staggered through the squall with her four lowers. Afterwards we were told it blew 60 miles an hour. Then it passed and we sailed peacefully into New London, where we anchored for the night, without going ashore or anyone there knowing we had just arrived from Cowes. Next morning, August 20, we started for City Island and sailed the 83 miles from New London in 10 hours, a passage which shows that *Diablesse* bustles along when she has her wind.

So ended a very very pleasant Atlantic crossing. We had fine weather throughout, for *Diablesse's* mainsail was not reefed once, and the only time we had taken it in and set the trysail was the first night out from Cowes, when the skipper, knowing he had a crew aboard who were new to the ship, and considering that we were not racing, rightly thought a peaceful night was the thing. And it was. We had taken 51 sailing days to sail the 5,000 odd miles from Cowes to New York, which gives the same average as *Typhoon's*, and shows that, as a general rule, in provisioning and preparing for a cruise a man should reckon 100 miles to the 24-hour day, allowing of course food for eventualities that might cause exceptional delay, such as gales, calms, and broken spars.

For two months *Diablesse* loafed about Long Island Sound, and then, with a smart breeze at midnight on October 17, she put to sea from City Island, bound to Gloucester.

Only the owner and myself were left of her Atlantic crew, for Bobby and Bill, after staying to see the 6-metre races between the American and British teams, had departed to England, and the owner's wife, Miss Ann, was in Virginia with her parents. By noon next day we were off Block Island. There was now much more weight in the wind, for it was no longer summer, so we handed the squaresail, which eased *Diablesse* considerably, though she was still hard to steer under her four lowers.

At 2.30 p.m. the jib split right across. I took it in and bent the old one on to the hanks without setting it. Then just after dark *Diablesse* gybed, and carried away her main gaff, which meant that the mainsail had to be stowed, for it looked just like the broken wing of a bird. This was a difficult job, for the broken gaff, flogging about, seemed intent on doing damage, but at last both sail and gaff were stowed. Then we took in the staysail and hove to for the night, under foresail only.

Next morning (Thursday), at 6.00 a.m., we put the staysail on her, and setting the main trysail, continued on our way. Later in the day, the wind having eased, we were able to set and carry the squaresail as well. Throughout the night the owner and I had taken watch and watch, for though *Diablesse* was safe enough with her head under her wing, we were close to the shoals to leeward, and there was also the chance of a steamer coming along, whose lookouts, on such a dirty night, might not become aware of our existence until she hit us.

I repaired the gaff by chopping and splitting down some wood into splints, nailing them along the broken spar and binding the whole with wire seizings, which were tightened by wedges driven in afterwards. Although the job was not very neat the gaff was as strong as ever, and the mainsail was rebent to it, but left stowed until the weather should moderate. Towards evening the squaresail had to come in, as the wind was increasing again ; and then, as darkness settled down, we entered the Musketer Channel, and under staysail, foresail and main trysail, *Diablesse*, with seas breaking over her, threaded her way through the channels inside the Nantucket shoals. The night was dark, but fairly clear, and Kelley yelled the different compass courses from the cabin. When he was not engaged in studying the chart, he was in the lee rigging, looking for lights and buoys, while I handled *Diablesse* alone, for even in this weight of wind, she steered easily under her present rig. Thus we passed the Cross Rip Lightship, and went on through to Cape Cod. For me, steering *Diablesse*, the time went very fast ; when we had cleared the worst of the shoals Kelley asked me to guess the time, and I said " 10.00 p.m.," when it was in fact 3.00 a.m. The two of us were so happy with *Diablesse* and this wild night that we almost fought for the wheel ; although I had been steering some ten hours I still wanted to continue, for the roaring wind, the darkness and the flying spray, made the night so exhilarating that we both wanted the excuse of steering to stay up. In the end we both spent the rest of the darkness on deck ; but dawn found us tired, and the wind ahead was driving *Diablesse* off Cape Cod, and the steep breaking seas were coming aboard hard and often. Soon we came upon a big Gloucester schooner hove to, and decided to follow her example. Taking in the trysail and then the staysail, we put the helm a-lee, and starting the fore sheet, turned in ; for it was daylight, and we were headed off shore to safety ; and so we spent the day sleeping contentedly.

At sunset the wind eased, so we made sail, setting the staysail and trysail, and sheeting in the foresail. We tacked, and stood in for Cape Cod, the skipper taking the first half, and I the second half of the night. By dawn (Saturday) the wind had eased still more. The trysail was taken in, and the mainsail set, and then later the main topsail and jib, and *Diablesse* was again under full sail. But the wind fell away rapidly, and it was dark by the time we were within two miles of Cape Cod.

So far only two people have appeared in this part of the story, and those two, the skipper and myself, worked *Diablesse* to Cape Cod without any bother or fuss. But below we had two men who kept their yacht off Larchmont ; soon after we left City Island they had ceased to take interest in sailing *Diablesse*, for although we had had so much wind and work, they had not appeared on deck, and now they found that they had urgent business in New York, and so wished to be put on shore as soon as possible. The dinghy was launched and I rowed them ashore, where we landed safely in spite of the heavy surf over the flat sand. Here, as almost everywhere, the size of the waves varied, and three large waves were followed by about six smaller ones ; by keeping just clear of the line of breakers till the last of the big waves rolled up, and then driving in on top of it, we got safe ashore, the two men jumping out and running the dinghy high and dry before the next large wave came in. Then, when getting off again, I launched on the last of the large waves, and rowing fast, was clear of the line of breakers before another heavy one came roaring in.

I rowed on out to sea, and when two miles off, looked about for *Diablesse*, but could see no sign of her in the darkness, for she had sailed closer in to the shore. But when I flashed an electric torch all round, she saw it, came out towards me, and soon I was on board and the dinghy in on deck. It was only two hours since I had left, but it seemed much longer; it had been a weird experience landing in the surf, as there was a heavy mist, and this, added to the roar of the breakers, somehow made the minutes seem like hours. The lighted cabin and saloon looked cosy indeed, and as we sat down to the evening meal, which the skipper had cooked meanwhile, *Diablesse* seemed very warm and affectionate.

At 9.00 p.m. the skipper ordered me to bed for five hours, while he stood the first watch, and then at 2.00 p.m. I took over and he turned in till 7.00 a.m., so that we both had five hours of solid sleep. There was little to

THE HENRY FORD STARTS TO WINDWARD OF THE BLUENOSE

disturb us except that twice, in the mist which came up with the light wind, we were almost run down by steamers; but they sheered off in time. The next day (Sunday) was a day of light winds and autumn sunshine, with a mist that cut down visibility to 2 miles, and in the warm sun we sailed quietly towards Gloucester, eventually dropping our anchor in the inner harbour alongside the schooners *Hookah* and *Lloyd W. Berry*.

That night we all went ashore to a roaring dinner; there were Smith, the owner of *Hookah*, Herb Stone the editor of *Yachting*, Bill Nutting the editor of *Motor Boat*, Chris Ratsey (from Cowes), Sid Breeze the owner of *Filatonga*, a couple of Ford brothers, who were cruising late, Captain Wallace the square rigged man, who has written so well of his ships, Roger Griswold, the owner of the *Lloyd W. Berry*, Jack Kelley, owner and skipper of *Diablesse*, and myself; with such a wild gang, all bursting with energy and vitality, the dinner could hardly be expected to be anything but a roaring one from the start. But before we fed, we visited Howard Blacburn, who after his fingers had been frozen off, had twice sailed across to Europe, in the *Great Western* and *Great Republic*, single handed, without fingers or thumbs, the most remarkable of all small boat voyages; and, though he could not feed with us, he wished us a merry evening.

We were in Gloucester, a town I had always wished to see, for the Gloucester schooners, which sail out and fish on the Grand Banks of Newfoundland, are the finest sailing vessels in the world. Designed and built for speed, they have to be seaworthy as well, for their work takes them on the banks where the seas break heavily in a gale. As luck would have it, it was the time of the International Fishing Schooner Races, which accounted for the presence of the crowd with whom we dined, and on the morrow the *Henry Ford* of America was to race the Canadian *Bluenose* for the championship of the North Atlantic.

The first race was held in light winds, and the *Henry Ford* won by two minutes. Then came two days of bright sunshine with smart breezes, when the *Bluenose* won by seven minutes on both occasions. We watched the first race from the destroyer *Paulding* and the second two from the *Isherwood*, and from these two vessels we could tell at any moment not only the wind's speed, but, by steaming abeam of them and adjusting our speed to theirs, the speed of the schooners also. The last day's race was the most interesting of the three. On the reach in the first round the *Bluenose* walked along at 13½ knots with the wind then blowing at 25 miles an hour. On the same reach in the second round, although the wind had increased to 35 miles an hour, and she still carried everything, jib topsail, jib, staysail, foresail, fore topsail, fisherman's staysail, mainsail and main topsail, she went no faster.

THE BLUENOSE TOOK IN HER FORE TOPSAIL AND JIB TOPSAIL

Halfway along this second reach the *Henry Ford* carried away her fore topmast, and so lost her jib topsail and fore topsail; but she did not slow up at all through losing these sails, and soon after the *Bluenose* took in her jib topsail and fore topsail, and she too, continued at her maximum speed of 13½ knots.

We laid *Diablesse* up at Gloucester and so ended the cruise. She too taught me many lessons.

That an Atlantic crossing in the summer months, in such a good little ship, and with such a happy and contented crew, is the pleasantest thing that could happen to any mortal.

That the schooner rig is better than the ketch, for though both mainsails are the same size and that of the ketch easier to handle, because it is amidships, the schooner scores in really bad weather, when with main trysail, foresail and staysail set she has her largest sail amidships, and becomes in effect a ketch for the time being. While if the wind and sea increase and she has to heave to, the trysail and staysail are taken in, and the foresheet started, when she will lay quietly until the time comes to make sail again. Added to this is the fact that, because of the position of the masts, they can be stayed together, and so strengthen each other, whereas on a ketch this cannot be.

· 3 ·

L A N D F A L L

Length, overall - - - 71 ft.	Length, water-line - - 60 ft.
Beam - - - - - 18 ft.	Draught - - - 11 ft.
Displacement - - - 59 tons	Sail area - - - 3,000 sq. ft.

Owner and Skipper, PAUL HAMMOND   *Designer*, FRANCIS HERRESHOFF

PAUL HAMMOND'S invitation to form one of *Landfall's* crew for the Transatlantic Race was accepted like a shot, as besides the honour the invitation carried, there was in store the joy of crewing on a vessel whose owner aimed at perfection in every detail from lead keel to truck.

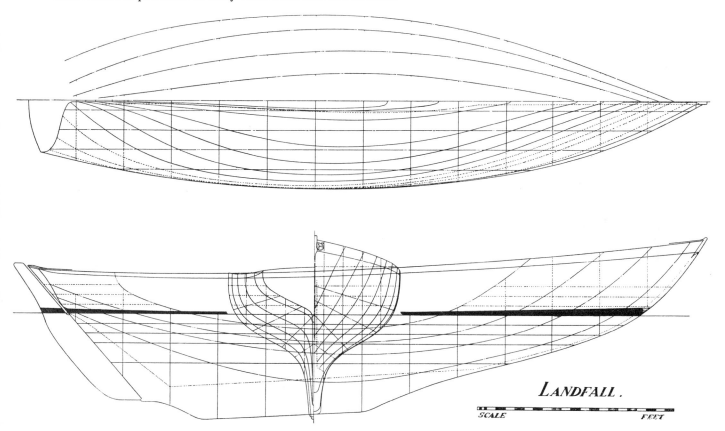

LANDFALL.

SCALE   FEET

To see *Landfall* anchored was to be deceived, for her lack of overhangs, combined with the ketch rig, cheated the eye and brain into thinking her a ponderous old dame without life or energy. But under way she slipped along without effort in light airs, would do $7\frac{3}{4}$ knots within four points of the wind, and crossing the Atlantic on several occasions did $11\frac{1}{4}$ knots (her maximum speed), as she had no overhangs. Beside this ability to ghost along she had the power to carry sail in hard weather, and off the Dutch coast in wind blowing 45 miles an hour stood up to her full sail, close-hauled, without a murmur.

To appreciate her underwater lines at their full value a piece of paper should cover those from the water-line up, when her designer's skill is revealed. The piece was nicked from her keel aft as, having enough lateral resistance without it, this would have added to her wetted surface unnecessarily.

While the faults of a transom stern are not noticeable in smooth water they are in a seaway, where it drags dead water behind it level with the rail each time the bow rises on a sea.

The words

"——that the currents of parted seas,
Closing behind with mighty force,
Might aid and not impede her course"

express every designer's aim, as the way a vessel leaves the water is of greater importance than the way in which she cleaves it.   In a seaway the overhang aft aids, while the transom stern impedes a vessel. *Landfall's* transom stern was forced upon her by the American overall length rule of 71 ft.   Her owner wanting a large vessel for cruising in European waters had her designed 60 ft. on the line, which is the maximum limit for the Royal Ocean Racing Club Rule, and was then forced to chop off her stern to come within the American length limit. . . . English and American yachtsmen always play together and it seems foolish to differ over such a simple rule, lines have a natural ending, and as the present American overall length prevents this, I sincerely hope they will adopt the natural English limit of water-line.

LANDFALL.

SCALE   FEET

Landfall's ketch rig was chosen by her owner because he had not sailed with it before, and apart from wishing to try it, he thought it could be made into a more efficient rig than generally supposed.   The ketch rig with its mainsail amidships is very easy to handle at sea, and to overcome its poor windward qualities a large mainsail was made, which, sheeting to the end of the mizen boom or bumkin, would convert *Landfall* into a cutter on light days. The sail is shown by dotted lines on the sail plan, and although at first allowed it was afterwards disallowed by the rules.

As *Landfall's* sail trimmer, her rig, spars and sails came under my care, for the spars and rigging were well wrapped up in the trimming of sails, it being useless to trim down headsail sheets if their luffs were sagging away to leeward, so the hollow mainmast standing 82 ft. above the deck was seldom out of my thoughts.   Although the mizen only stood 58 ft. above the deck it was more difficult to keep straight, and in its place, than the mainmast, due to *Landfall's* transom stern which only allowed 10 ft. of drift to the mizen backstay.   Most badly-fitting mainsails can be traced to badly-stayed masts, which bend, and so distort the sail.   *Landfall* had such an excellent crew that my duties trimming sails were nil, and this allowed me to spend the time racing across the Atlantic in keeping the masts straight and upstanding.

This job was so difficult that I only gained 12 lbs. crossing, and it brought home to me the fact that the best ocean racer was the best cruiser, as her owner and the designer had in months of forethought prepared her for every emergency.

Landfall carried twenty sails on board, all made of American cotton woven in England, except her four storm-sails, which were of tanned flax (see chapter on sails for further details).

LANDFALL

SCALE.   FEET

BOWSPRIT SHOWS INTERNAL TRACK OUT OF WHICH FORESTAY
SLIDES, SO WHEN JIB NEEDS TAKING IN THE FORESTAY, WITH
THE JIB ON IT IS SLID AFT TO STEMHEAD AND JIB LOWERED IN
THE LEE OF THE STAYSAIL, STRONG PIGTAIL HOOK FOR TACK
OF JIB. STAINLESS STEEL TRACK

RAFEE SQUARESAIL, CAN BE CARRIED WITH THE WIND ABEAM,
GENERALLY TWO SEPARATE SAILS, SPINNAKER BOOM SLID UP
ONE OF THESE INTERNAL TRACKS ON THE FORESIDE OF MAST,
AND ANOTHER BOOM AT BOTTOM OF MAST

Landfall's bowsprit had an internal track for its full length, in which slid a fitting taking the jibstay and tack, so that the lowering of a jib was easily carried out, for with the fitting hauled aft the stemhead the jib could be lowered down the stay in the lee of the staysail, where ten men, if needed, could muzzle it without much risk of falling overboard or of the jib getting under the bow. *Landfall* had a net under her bowsprit to prevent sails getting under the bow in the case of one being lowered down to the bowsprit end, and this was the favourite sleeping-place for her crew, and most afternoons found two of us with mattresses lying out yarning under her bowsprit.

LANDFALL STARTING IN THE TRANSATLANTIC RACE

Her mainmast had one internal track on its foreside, and another on its after-side, the aft side taking up the mainsail slides, on each of which were four small wheels ; and as these worked inside the track there was no fear of them jambing, for from an engineering point of view they were correct, whereas the ordinary male track and female slide is quite wrong and yet is persisted in, and owners getting disgusted with jambing slides wish their vessels were gaff instead of Bermudian rigged.

The track on the foreside took aloft the heel of the square-sail yard, and also allowed the spinnaker boom heel to be adjusted to its best position for any weight of wind. The mizen, too, had a similar internal track and slides, so we had no trouble from slides sticking at all on masts or bowsprit.

There were two spare cots in the fo'c'sle, and in these two we stowed the light weather headsails when not in use, all other sails being stowed in the sail room aft excepting the spare mainsail, which lived on the wardroom floor and made a fine footstool beside the table (for a heavy sail should be stowed amidships, otherwise it alters a vessel's trim) and although here it picked up coffee and jam pots, as her owner remarked they did not affect the shape of the sail.

The mizen staysail was the only sail I did not like to see set, for with its tack at the aft side of the mainmast it had a very strong forward pull against which the mizen backstay with its short drift aft was powerless. A mizen staysail should not, to my idea, come more than halfway between the two masts, and I believe *Landfall's* should have tacked on the fore edge of her deck house. And it will be seen that the mizen mast through being pulled forward let the main topmast forward, spoiling the mainsail's shape and allowing the jibstay to sag to leeward.

Generally across the Atlantic we had the genoa jib set and inside this the balloon staysail. These two sails were cut to fit each other, and although it appeared that they would interfere with each other they actually pulled like a pair of horses as against only one, had one sail been forward of the mast.

In designing a warship I imagine that a designer has to work to instructions from the Lords of the Admiralty, and that they give him a deck plan on which are the guns, torpedo tubes, etc., and the space required to work them, and say, " This is our fighting platform, we want it to travel 40 miles an hour and have quarters for 1,000 men, ammunition, etc., etc." A sailing ship's deck must be regarded as her fighting platform, and arranged so that her crew have every advantage possible in battling with sails. *Landfall's* owner had arranged her decks perfectly for the fray. Wherever a winch was wanted, there it was, or rather a winch was never wanted as it was placed there before the want by the owner's forethought, and so sheeting down, setting up backstays was all made easy, while the halyards, because they were wire, never needed setting up. Rope is nice and kind to handle, but with rope halyards the sails need setting up every watch or more frequently, and as winches take the bite of the wire besides giving enormous power the two combined make an easy cruising vessel. All of *Landfall's* rigging, running and standing, was stainless steel. A complete list of her blocks, with standing and running rigging will be found in the chapters on hollow spars and rigging.

Landfall's accommodation was arranged very well indeed, the fo'c'sle had three cots, and as Joe was the only one forward two were used as sail bins while he used the starboard berth. The anchor winch by Reid was in the fo'c'sle, and as our cable was of stainless steel this wound off the winch on to a drum and stowed easier than chain. The advantage of having the winch below was a clear foredeck from which to set and take in sails, and the weight of the winch was much lower. The advantages of wire are its easy stowage, its lightness and the ease with which it

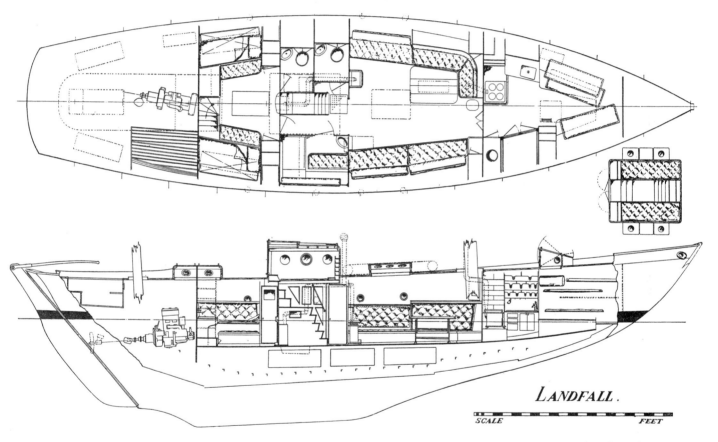

LANDFALL.

SCALE   FEET

comes aboard. In chain 50 per cent. of the load in heaving is in the links over the hawse pipe, while in wire only 10 per cent. The disadvantage of wire is its need for a slightly heavier anchor. The fo'c'sle table covers the winch in time of peace. Directly abaft the fore-hatch was the galley with its combined coal and gas Shipmate range, above which sat a coffee urn, also gas, with two taps in the fo'c'sle and two in the wardroom, one giving coffee and the other boiling water for tea in each place ; and being able to draw off hot coffee day or night made the usual hard luck ocean racing story hard to believe.

" Hard luck " reminds me of the expression " hard up " so often heard these days when it is fashionable to be poor, few realising that the expression is from the helm order, in this case meaning that the helm is " hard up for Poverty Bay."

Directly abaft the fo'c'sle was the large, airy wardroom, with sleeping accommodation for eight, the backs of the bunks swinging up to form the upper berths with adjustable topping lifts from the beams, the lower bunks

NAVIGATOR'S CABIN, TOP INSTRUMENT WIND SPEED, ONE ABREAST BARAGRAPH SPEED THROUGH WATER. ROOT BUNK FOLDED BACK OUT OF WAY—NOTE NOTCHES BELOW CHART TABLE LETTING IT DOWN INTO A SLOPING DESK, WIRELESS AT TOP, SHIELDED READING LAMP OVER CHART TABLE

WARD ROOM. TO LEFT OF MAINMAST, TAP FROM WHICH COFFEE WAS DRAWN. TABLE WEIGHT FOR TABLE PIANO (DULCITONE), SETTEE BACKS SWING UP TO MAKE BUNKS WITH TOPPING LIFTS FROM BEAMS

being adjusted to suit all angles of heel by a fitting inside controlled by the knob seen in the picture of the wardroom The swing table had in place of the usual lead weight a small piano (Dulcitone) the top of which folds to make the music rest. With its gun case, book case, piano, and taps supplying hot coffee or boiling water *Landfall's* wardroom was rather a fine affair for an ocean racer.

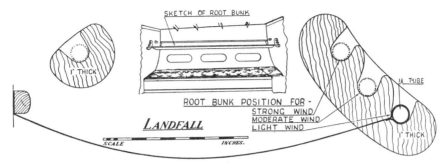

Aft came the navigator's cabin, with a Root folding bunk, instruments that read off the ship's speed and the wind's speed, a wireless set and a chart table that could be lowered in front to form a sloping desk, making it, with its wash-basin, a cell in which a man could be imprisoned months with books and not fret. Abreast this came two wash rooms, the forward leading from the saloon and the after one from the owner's cabin, which came directly abaft the navigator's cabin and wash rooms. Crossing the Atlantic the owner slept in the starboard berth and I in the Root bunk above him, but the little bunk above was so comfortable that several times I'd come below to see the owner's slow smile in my bunk, and I'd stretch out in his.

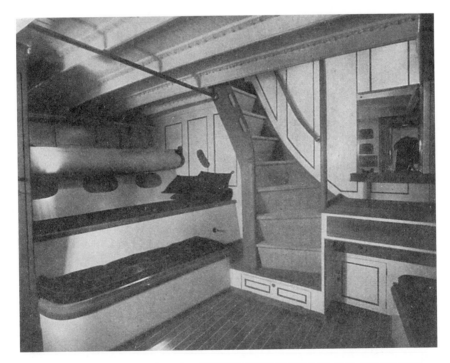

TWISTED STAIRS IN OWNER'S CABIN, OWNER'S BUILT-IN BUNK TO LEFT AND MY ROOT BUNK ABOVE. SHOWS HANDHOLES ON STAIRS TO LEFT AND RAIL TO RIGHT

That Root bunk deserves describing in detail. Easily and cheaply made, it is an adaption of the ordinary pipe cot; a batten fastens the canvas to the ship's side, the canvas bottom, 6 ft. by 2 ft. 3 in., has a pocket sewn in its free edge to take the $1\frac{1}{4}$ in. tube that forms the outer side of the bunk. Two pieces of wood, notched to take the tube, are fastened on the bulkhead at the fore and aft end of the bunk, and the tube is put into the most suitable notch for the weather; when not in use it is folded back into the nearest notch to the ship's side and so stowed neatly. As there is a position to suit any wind, the bunk is very cosy, especially in hard weather when it seems to wrap its arms round the sleeper and say " Off to sleep, my lad, I'll hold you tight till your watch on deck."

The twisted stairs on the bulkhead aft were a delight to use, both going on and coming off watch. We worked the Swedish system of watches and as this gave a long watch of seven hours on deck, it also gave it below, so there

DECKHOUSE

SLIDING HATCH OVER OWNER'S CABIN AND SAIL ROOM

was time in which to get down to some serious sleeping ; 12.00 to 4.00 a.m., 4.00 to 8.00 a.m., 8.00 a.m. to 1.00 p.m., 1.00 to 7.00 p.m., and 7.00 to 12.00 p.m. The finest system that I've met, for with our crew of twelve divided into two watches, the one on deck was strong enough to tackle anything without asking assistance from the watch below.

The chimney of the open hearth fire in the owner's cabin leads through the clothes locker under the stairs from the deck house and combined with the heat from the back of the fireplace quickly dried clothes that needed it. The bulkhead at the after-end of the owner's cabin was fireproof, watertight and sound proof, as it divided the engine room and sail locker from the living quarters, and aft of the engine room came the deep self-bailing cockpit.

FORE DECK SHOWING FORE HATCH WITH SIDEBOARDS WHICH PREVENT WATER GETTING BELOW

On deck, amidships, the deck house has two comfortable full-sized bunks, in which anyone suffering from sea-sickness could soon recover, for it was up in clean, keen salt air, and being amidships, the centre of the seesaw had less motion than any other part of the ship. The rail running round the deck house, besides giving a good hand grip, trapped rain water, which when the valve was opened ran into its tank below for washing. All corners of deck houses and hatches were rounded very carefully and the result was no torn sails, or hard knocks for the crew. Hand grips on the sliding hatches to the owner's cabin and the engine room were of a similar section to the deck house rail, and these extending right across the sliding hatch prevented the water settled on the hatch from dropping below as it usually does. The sideboards on the forehatch preventing water going below, enabled this hatch to be open the whole way across the Atlantic.

Landfall steered very easily and nicely with a tiller until she had reached 9 knots and then, as it was hard work for one to hold her steady in the sea, the steering was done from the tramcar wheel amidships, which could be linked up in a few seconds to the rudder, the helmsman sitting astride the portable saddle seat. All vessels should have two entirely separate steering arrangements when going offshore, for then if an accident happens to one there is the other to use while the damaged one is repaired. Besides this factor of safety *Landfall's* alternate steering positions had the advantage of shifting the helmsman just where he was best ; stowing the mizen he steered amidships out of the way, and stowing the mainsail he could steer with the tiller, leaving a clear deck for those gathering in the sail. And also after say three days of wheel steering the tiller would be used, and gathering round the helmsman for a yarn we all seemed to be on a different ship, that was strangely familiar.

Landfall's name reminds us that the most exciting moments of a ship's life are those during which she first sights land after a long voyage at sea, when full of hope and fear she sails on gamely to the land that might in thick weather cause her death, and the small sigh she gives is hardly heard as she makes still another successful landfall.

LANDFALL.

RUNNING RIGGING LIST

No. Required	Item		Dia. & Construction of Wire	Approx. Strength of Wire	Length of Wire Required with Allowance for Splices	Circumference of Rope	Length of Rope Req. with Allowance for Splices Etc.	Approx. Strength of Rope	
1	Main Halyard	Sheaves at sides of masthead; Cavel at side of mast; 5 1/2" double block shackle to deck pad eye; 9" single block upset front shackle; 5 1/2" double block shackle & becket	3/8" 6x37 Plow Steel	5.3T.	175'	Haly 2 1/2" Jig 1 3/4"	160' 60'	5900# 3150#	
1	Mizen Halyard	Sheaves at sides of masthead; 8" single block upset front shackle; 20'; 110'; Winch at side of mast	5/16" 6x19 Plow Steel	3.9T	118'	2 1/2"	138'	5900#	
1	Jib. Halyard	8" double block front shackle; 8" single block upset fr. shackle; 20'; Winch; 5/16 wire; 152'; 7/16 tack strap; 1'-0"	3/16" & 5/16" 6x19 Plow Steel	7.3T 3.9T	5' 155'	2 1/2"	180'	5900#	
1	Forestay Sail Halyard	8" double block fr. shackle; 8" single block upset fr. shackle; Winch; 20'; 5/16 wire; 128'; 7/16" tack strap; 2'-6"	7/16 & 5/16 6x19 Plow Steel	7.3T 3.9T	6' 130'	2 1/2"	156'	5900#	
1	Mizen Staysail Halyard	Wire strap to go on mizen mast; 8" single block shackle & becket; 8" single block upset side shackle; Double end	3/8" 6x37 Plow Steel	5.3T	8'	2 1/2"	175'	5900#	
1	Spinnaker Halyard	Snap shackle swivel eye; 8" single block fr shackle; Lead block; Winch; Snap shackle swivel eye	5/16" 6x19 Plow Steel	3.9T	75'	2 1/2"	85'	5900#	
1	Balloon Halyard	Shackle; 8" single block fr shackle	5/16" 6x19 Plow Steel	3.9T	75'	2 1/2"	90'	5900#	
1	Main & Mizen Gantline	4 1/2" single block; 116'; 164'; 4 1/2" single block				1 1/2"	280'	2450#	
1	Main Sheet	Double ended; Winch				3	300'	8200#	
1	Mizen Sheet	Shackle				2 1/4"	165'	4900#	
4 1 set to spare	Fore Stay Sail Sheet	Pair of 8" round blocks on shackle; 8" single block screw eye deck plate; Winch				2 1/2"	360'	5900#	
2	Jib Sheet	Shackle; 11'-3/8 wire pennant; 8" single block for rope strap; 8" single block screw eye deck plate; 4 1/2" double block fr shackle; 4 1/2" single block fr. shackle becket; 3/8 wire strap	3/8" 6x37 Plow Steel	5.3T	50'	Sheet 2 1/2 Jib 1 1/2"	150' 90'	5900# 2450#	
2	Main Backstay Runner	7" single block jaw; Hook to chain plate; 1 1/2" manila; 32'-3/8" wire runner; 7" single block fr. shackle to deck eye; 6" single bl shackle becket; Winch; 6" single block fr shackle; 2 manila jib	3/8" 6x37 Plow Steel	5.3T	80'	2" 1 1/2	90' 70'	4000# 2450#	
2	Mizen Backstay Runner	5 1/4" double block jaw; 5 1/4" single block upset side shackle, becket; 5 1/4" single block upset side shackle; Winch				1 3/4"	120'	3150#	
1	Main Topping Lift	Shackle to masthead fitting; Sheave in clew end of boom; 5 1/4" single block fr shackle, becket; Cheek block	5/16 8x19 Plow Steel	3.34T	115	1 3/4"	35'	3150#	
1	Mizen Topping Lift	Shackle to masthead fitting; Sheave in clew end of boom; 5 1/4" single block fr shackle; Shackle	1/4" 8x19 Plow Steel	2.15T		1 3/4"	20'	3150#	
1	Jib Tack Outhaul	Sheave in jib tack slide; Eye to go on bowsprit cone; 5/16 wire; 2" manila; 7" single block eye and thimble; 7/16" wire strap to go on bowsprit cone	7/16" & 5/16" 6x19 Plow St.	7.3T 3.9T	4' 25'	2"	28'	4000#	
1	Main Clew Outhaul	Rose knot soldered; Clew outhaul slide; Sheave; 5" fiddle block fr shackle; 5" single block fr shackle, becket	3/8" 6x37 Plow Steel	5.3T	22'	1 3/4"	55'	3150#	
1	Mizen Clew Outhaul	Rose knot soldered; Clew outhaul slide; Sheave; 5" single block shackle, becket; Cheekblock	5/16" 8x19 Plow Steel	3.34T	18'	1 1/2"	45'	2450#	
1	Spinnaker Sheet & Guys	Snap shackle swivel eye; Sheet 40' — 2"; Fwd guy 75' — 1 3/4"; Aft guy 100' — 2 1/2"				2" 1 3/4 2 1/2"	43' 83' 104'	4000# 3150# 5900#	
2	Lapping Jib Sheet	Shackle; 60'				3"	125'	8200#	
2	Main Boom Guy	Shackle; 5 1/4" single block fr shackle, becket; 5 1/4" single block fr shackle; Wire strop to go on cleat	5/16" 6x19 Plow Steel	3.9T	45'	1 3/4"	60'	3150#	
2	Mizen Boom Guy					2"	50'	4000#	
2	Boom Crutch Tackle	5 1/4 double bl. hook; 5 1/4" single block hook, becket				1 3/4"	130'	3150#	
2	Square Sail Brace	Shackle to yard fitting; 6" single block fr. shackle, becket; 6" single block fr shackle	3/8" 6x19 Plow Steel	5.5T	110'	2"	150'	4000#	
2	Square Sail Sheet	8" single block				2 1/2"	150'	5900#	
2	Yard Topping Lift	Shackle to yard fitting; 8" single block to mast fitting	5/16" 6x19 Plow Steel	3.9T	170'	2 1/2"	90'	5900#	
2	Square Sail Outhaul	Shackle to sq. sail clew; 8" single block shackle to yard fitting; 8" single block	5/16" 6x19 Plow Steel	3.9T	110'	2 1/2"	60'	5900#	

Landfall's Block List is printed on p. 144, and Standing Rigging List on p. 145.

THE TRANSATLANTIC RACE, 1931

On Saturday, July 27, 1931, we set sail from Glen Cove for Newport, our starting point for the Transatlantic Race; and although the wind was light, *Landfall* slipped along quietly and easily throughout the day till sunset, when we took in the mainsail and coated it to keep it dry and free from the night dew.

From 10.00 p.m. till midnight a smart breeze made up, and under her headsails and mizen only, *Landfall* sailed very fast, for during those two hours the wind blew 30 miles an hour. At sunrise we set the mainsail again, and with a light breeze all day, we brought out every sail that *Landfall* had, one after another, dressing her with genoa jibs, balloon staysails, mizen staysails, the most interesting of all being the raffee squaresail, which set well with the wind anywhere from aft to just forward of the beam. After a very pleasant and peaceful sail *Landfall* arrived at Newport, Rhode Island, at 6.00 p.m.

Next morning we towed up to Herreshoff's Yard to complete *Landfall's* fitting out, for although built and completed in Bremen, and after many trials refitted at Glen Cove, the owner still found many things to improve on board. It is always so; an owner can go on perfecting his vessel and her gear for ever, and the only way to stop is to put to sea; so long as a vessel is in harbour there will always be details that can be, and therefore are, altered for the better. At Herreshoff's we saw *Enterprise* and *Yankee* hauled out, and their spars in the building shed. The duralumin mast of *Enterprise*, having a smaller diameter than her wooden mast, must have interfered far less with the wind flowing on to her mainsail.

OLD MAN HERRESHOFF, FATHER OF THE DESIGNER OF LANDFALL, AND WITH HIM PAUL HAMMOND, SMOKING

Although 83 years of age Herreshoff, we found, still made models for which his wife made the sails, and the workmanship of the models was so pleasing to the eye that we were only taken away from them by force. That night his son Sydney towed *Landfall* down to Newport again, where we took in the last of our stores, and cleared decks for action. Our list of stores will be a guide to vessels making long passages.

NON-PERISHABLE FOOD LIST—TRANSATLANTIC RACE, JULY 1931

BEVERAGES

36 cans tall evaporated milk.
3 doz. cans evaporated milk (baby size) cancel.
12 cans condensed milk.
21 cans George Washington coffee.
1 case ginger ale C. & C. pale dry 12½ oz. Canada dry.
1 case sarsaparilla.
1 doz. Nestles cream (baby size).
25 lb. ground carrein (1 lb. tins), best grade 4 A. & P. coffee.
200 tea bags.
4 cans cabin tea (¼ lb. tins).

SOUPS

2 doz. cans tomato (Franco).
2 doz. cans chicken (College Inn).
2 doz. cans bean ,,
1 doz. cans pea ,,
1 doz. cans vegetable ,,
1 doz. cans bouillon ,,
½ doz. cans celery ,,
½ doz. cans asparagus ,,
1 doz. cans Gordon's haddock chowder.
6 cans oxtail (Campbell's).
6 cans mock turtle.

CANNED FRUITS AND VEGETABLES

1 doz. cans corn on cob.
6 cans sugar corn.
1 doz. cans string beans.
2 doz. cans lima beans.
2 doz. cans tomatoes.
1 doz. cans beets.
6 cans carrots.
6 cans asparagus tips.
6 cans strawberries.
6 cans peaches.
1 doz. cans pears.
6 cans raspberries.
6 cans pineapple.
1 doz. cans grapefruit.
1 doz. cans fruit salad
6 cans cherries.
12 cans applesauce.
6 doz. cans plums.
3 pkg. raisins.
6 lb. prunes.
  spinach (cancel).
6 doz. cans corn on the cob.
2 doz. cans green peas (advancer).
  canned sweet potatoes—yams.
½ doz. cans strawberry sauce.
10 lb. evap. apples (sun-dried).
5 lb. evap. apricots.
5 lbs. dried peaches.
3 doz. cans baked beans with molasses.
3 bottles stuffed olives (small).

CANNED MEATS AND FISH

6 cans tuna fish.
6 cans salmon (Iona pink).
6 cans sardines (domestic).
1 doz. cans roast beef.
1 doz. tins sliced bacon 9 oz.
1 doz. roast mutton.
2 doz. corned beef hash (red label).
6 tins Gordon's haddock.
½ doz. cans finnan haddie.
1 doz. cans sausage meat.
1 doz. cans boneless chicken (Charles).
6 doz. cans Canadian boiled dinner.
3 doz. cans fish balls.
3 doz. cans tongue.
3 doz. 9-oz. tins chipped beef.
4 jars Dundee marmalade.
2 box Amer. gruyere cheese.
2 box camembert cheese.
2 Edams cheese.
1 bottle cocktail sauce.
1 bottle chutney sauce.
1 pkg. savita sauce.
1 pkg. Welsh rarebit.
1 doz. canned macaroni.
2 lb. Cheddar cheese.
3 Hormel hams.
3 Hormel chickens.
12 chicken à la King (College Inn).

NON-PERISHABLE ARTICLES TO BE SUBSTITUTED— TRANSATLANTIC RACE, JULY 1931

COOKING EXTRACTS

2 small cans molasses (Br. Rabbit G. Label).
2 1-qt. cans pure maple syrup (in glass 4-pint jars).
4 tins royal baking powder (1 lb.)
2 jars prepared mustard.
2 1-lb. cans egg powder.
2 1-qt. tins pure olive oil (encore qt.).
1 bottle vinegar (A. & P. Cider) 24 oz.
1 nutmeg (ground 2 oz.)
1 cinnamon (ground 4 oz.)
4 pkg. cornstarch (Duryeas).
1 lb. bicarbonate soda.
1 raspberry extract.
1 lb. cream of tartar.

SUGAR

25 lb. gran. sugar in air-tight tins (2 12-lb. tins).
25 lb. light brown sugar air-tight tins (2 12-lb. tins).
10 lb. lump sugar.

CEREALS AND FLOUR

4 cans plain rolled oats.
4 tins Irish   „
25 lb. white flour in tins.
25 lbs. whole wheat flour in tins.
24 pkg. Pep (individual).
6 pkg. triscuits.
6 pkg. Malts breakfast food in cans.
10 lb. polished rice.
10 lb. unpolished rice (cancel).
6 pkg. Aunt Jemima pancake flour.
2 pkg. cornmeal.
6 pkg. farina (cancel).
2 pkg. hominy.
2 pkg. wheatena.
2 pkg. cream of wheat.
12 pkg. grapenuts.
24 pkg. bran.

RELISHES, JAMS, CHEESE, ETC.   (Factory Items)

1 doz. 12-oz. jars sultana strawberry jam.

3 16-oz. jars A. & P. peanut butter.

6 doz. jars honey.

3 8-oz. jars Rajah S.D. mayonnaise.

4 9-oz. jars Rajah mustard.

1 bottle vanilla (red front—pts.).

1 pkg. gelatine (R. small pkgs.).
  Lemon extract (red front—2 oz.).

3 bottles chow chow (C. & B. ½).

3 bottles sweet pickles (Manhattan—qt.).

3 bottles catsup (Q.M.—14 oz.).

1 bottle Worcestershire sauce (Lea Perrin).

4 jars raspberry jam (sultana 12 oz.).

1 bottle Chili sauce.

BUTTER

48 lbs. cabin butter in cans.

122 cans pure lard.

½ lb. black pepper (ground).

3 pkg. table salt (diamond crystal).

1 pkg. paprika 1 lb.

1 doz. cans spaghetti (encore).

12 tins Whitman's chocolate.

12 tins Cadman's chocolate.

5 lbs. assorted nuts.

12 lbs. Maillard's eating chocolate.

3 pkg. cigars.

BISCUITS

6 tins ginger snaps (Kublers).

10 15 oz. Captain's biscuit (Lehmans).

6 cans Graham crackers.

6 cans pilot   „

4 tins oatmeal   „

47 Spratts ships biscuits.

4 boxes thinsies.

PERISHABLE FOOD LIST—TRANSATLANTIC RACE, JULY 1931

BREAD

3 doz. loaves white.

½ doz. loaves raisin.

3 doz. French rolls.

3 doz. white rolls.

1 doz. loaves whole wheat in tins.

1 doz. cans brown (Twitchell & Champlin, Portland, Me.).

Sweibach in tins.

Swedish in tins.

MEATS AND FISH

1 smoked ham.

1 side bacon all sliced in packets of 12 slices in oiled paper, wrapped, packed in salt.

1 smoked shoulder.

10 pkg. yeast.

12 5-oz. pkg. shredded codfish (Beardsley).

FRESH FRUIT AND VEGETABLES

2 bushel new potatoes.

2 bushel dried prunes.

2 bushel dates.

4 crates oranges.

1 crate grapefruit.

1 crate peaches.

1 crate raspberries.

1 crate cherries.

1 crate lemons.

1 crate lettuce.

1 crate celery.

1 crate onions.

The next evening, Thursday July 2, the crews of all the vessels taking part in the Transatlantic Race attended the dinner given by the Cruising Club of America, with Sandy Moffat the commodore in the chair, a very enjoyable function.

Then followed a day of work and play aboard *Landfall* until late afternoon, when all hands went aboard the *Aloha* to tea ; we wandered all over her from her royal yardarms to her keel, for she was most interesting everywhere.

The ironwork and goosenecks of her yards interested me particularly, for with the passing of square-rigged vessels, blacksmiths will lose the art of making them. Yet the time may come sooner than we realise when sailing ships will once more come into their own, for their power, the wind of heaven, is free and their roads, the seas, need no repairs ; the only expense is the cost and upkeep of the ship herself. All that is needed is for fuel, the cost of which has increased so much in recent years, to become scarcer still, and for the people who cruise for pleasure in steamers to realise how damned stupid they are to seek escape from this mechanical world in a ship that is one mass of engines. Then we shall have sailing ships for pleasure cruising and taking odd cargoes, and steamers will carry mails and business passengers only. At least I hope so.

That night I wandered ashore alone to see the Vikings' Tower, which is circular with different shaped arches, and the roof open to the sky. The Vikings, sailing by their Iceland and Greenland route, had discovered America long before Columbus. This night before we sailed seemed a fitting occasion to spend half an hour or so alone inside the tower, thinking over the endurance and seamanship of these old Norsemen sailing their long ships by the cold northern route across the North Atlantic.

LANDFALL'S CREW OF GENERALS

The next morning, July 4, came in with hardly a breath of wind, and George Bonell towed *Landfall* out towards the starting line with his cruiser, the *Old Glory*. Soon the rest of the transatlantic racers were towing after us, all bound to as fine a starting line as one could wish, the *Brenton Reef Lightship*, while the finishing line, Plymouth Breakwater, was 3,000 miles across the North Atlantic.

THE START AT BRENTON REEF. WATER GIPSY, LANDFALL, MISTRESS, DORADE, SKAL, HIGHLAND LIGHT, LISMORE

Noon saw a fine fleet of ocean racers bursting across the line to the gun, for although a good start in a 3,000 mile race may not be so important as in a short race, which would take hours where ours took weeks, every one was eager and keen, and the ten ships went across close together.

Landfall	-	-	-	Paul Hammond -	-	-	60.99 rating	71 ft. O.A.	Scratch
Lismore	-	-	-	W. Rouse -	-	-	59.7 rating	71 ft. O.A.	2.26
Highland Light	-	-	Dudley Wolf	-	-	-	54.51 rating		13.07.50
Mistress	-	-	-	George Roosevelt	-	-	52.21 rating	60 ft. O.A.	18.20.50
Water Gipsy	-	-	Wm. McMillan -	-	-	49.28 rating	59 ft. O.A.	25.27.07
Ilex Dennis H	-	-	Royal Engineers -	-	-	42.72 rating	51 ft. O.A.	44.14.01
Skal -	-	-	T. F. Lawrence -	-	-	42.2 rating	48 ft. O.A.	49.49.24
Dorade	-	-	-	Olin Stephens -	-	-	42.0 rating	52 ft. O.A.	46.28.44
Maitenes	-	-	L. Luard -	-	-	-	40.3 rating	49 ft. O.A.	52.10.26
Amberjack	-	-	P. D. Rust	-	-	-	33.96 rating	45 ft. O.A.	76.55.46

Ten ships well found in gear, men and provisions—the American Cruising Club's rule, requiring every vessel to carry 30 gallons of water per man as a minimum, will give an idea of the thoughtful way in which they approached the problem of satisfying themselves that the racers, as well as being seaworthy vessels, were well found in all respects.

GEORGE BONELL TOWED LANDFALL OUT TOWARDS THE STARTING LINE WITH OLD GLORY

At the outset every vessel was confronted with the question as to which was the fastest course to England. The great circle course just skirting Nova Scotia was my choice, in that besides being two hundred miles shorter, it had stronger, because colder, and more reliable fair winds, and I knew how the *Typhoon*, not a fast boat, had crossed from Cape Race to the Bishops in fifteen days, with a crew of only three. The only thing against this course was the unfavourable Arctic or Labrador current as far as Cape Race.

The more southerly course had only the Gulf Stream in its favour. When I found that we in *Landfall* were going south for the Gulf Stream, I spoke to the skipper of *Maitenes* about the northern route, but he, like the rest of the fleet, was too full of last-minute preparations to be interested. Then to *Ilex*, the other British boat, I suggested the northern course, and even enlisted W. P. Stephens to help me preach my gospel, for he loaned them Bill Nutting's book, the *Track of Typhoon*, with its description of the said fifteen-day passage. And all to no avail, for in the American paper *Yachting* had appeared an article on the best way across to England, which strongly urged the Southern and Gulf Stream course, and the Gulf Stream, with its promise of a free ride, was strong magic, so everyone seemed after the southern course.

The wind at the start was light and easterly, with patches of mist. We all went across closehauled on the starboard tack, with *Highland Light*, a fine cutter, in the lead. *Landfall* was ¼ mile astern after some hours of sailing, the rest of the fleet following roughly according to their size. All day we in *Landfall* tried to catch the cutter ahead, and were unable to; her rig told its tale, as we were close to the wind, and there was not enough of it for our longer length to throw its weight into the scale.

LANDFALL WAS DESIGNED BY FRANCIS HERRESHOFF—   AND BUILT BY RASSMUSSEN

And so the fleet approached the *Nantucket Lightship*, which we reached after 24 hours of sailing at noon, July 5. It bore North by West ½ West, six miles distant. I had watched the rest carefully to see if any were making off to leeward for the northern course, and decided that *Dorade* was, for though a close-winded and weatherly vessel she had not followed in our wake, but had all day sailed along to the northward with her sheets slightly eased, so that I feared she was following *Typhoon's* track. But she was the only one; the rest, including *Maitenes* and *Ilex*, followed in our wake or held to windward of it as the wind freed slightly. There have been, and always will be, arguments as to which is the faster course; but a few more races will prove the general superiority of the northern, for the reasons I have given above.

After a week of sailing *Landfall* was in Latitude 40.50 N. and Long. 51.52 West, with the wind still ahead, sailing along closehauled under genoa jib, balloon staysail, mainsail and mizen, at 8½ knots. To be accurate, she was given a good full, for though we called it closehauled, she was really one point free of that. After a week at sea, we were getting to know her ways; the electric log registered her speed at all times, and had shown us that, closehauled in a jumpy sea, she maintained 8½ knots with her deck some three inches clear of the water, but that as the wind increased and her rail was buried with seas running along her deck, she slowed down to 8 knots; so that easing her of sail when her deck was buried, actually increased her speed. These speeds were not 4 points off the wind but 5 points, one point free, for it is wrong in the middle of the ocean to pinch up within 4 points off the wind, however right it may be for sailing round short courses, where the beat to windward might take half an hour only.

Sunday, July 12, came in with the wind still ahead, and *Landfall* still, after a night of it, doing her 8 knots; but as the day grew, the wind fell away until noon found us becalmed. So while we lay with no weight in the sails, we set to work to adjust our rigging, and found that the only thing that needed setting up was the upper leg on our backstays leading from the top of the mast, for this leg, being longer than the one from the hounds, had stretched more.

The steamer *Tortugero* of Glasgow circled us, gave us a check on our position : Lat. 41.10 North and Long. 48.24 West, and the glad news that *Water Gipsy* was astern of us, which was cheering, for although we had had such light head winds, we wondered if the rest of the fleet had escaped them. After dinner that night a faint air made in from the south-east, and with it a wet fog, so thick that we could hardly see ten yards. During the 7.00 to 12.00 watch some Mother Carey's chickens flew into the mainsail, and dropped on deck unhurt, attracted like moths to the white ghostly loom of our mainsail. This night, after over a week at sea, I made the entry in my diary : " *Landfall* a very happy ship, everyone keen to win, and all thoughtful for the rest on board."

The real reason for that entry was, that our crew was composed of boat owners and so skippers. Our skipper had gathered together a crew of generals, and good ones at that, but we all wondered how we should mix. Paul had, it seems, foreseen all things, and had given each a specific responsibility to fuss and ponder over, as well as watch keeping. The crew of skippers was divided as follows :

FIRST WATCH UNDER THE SKIPPER

Paul Hammond	Owner and Skipper.
Uffa Fox	Sail Trimmer.
John Quincey Adams	Sparks (Electrician).
Waldo Howland	Engineer (Propeller taken off but engine made electricity).
John Hallowell	Sail Maker.
Ben Ames	Navigator.

SECOND WATCH UNDER BRIAN WAITE

Brian Waite	Mate.
Kim Norton	2nd Mate.
Lawrence Pool	Ship's Surgeon.
John Stedman	Bosun and Jack o' the Dust (looked after provisions).
Lawrence Grinnell	Assistant Navigator.
Joe Fredericks	Cook.

The watch system was well thought out, for it gave watches strong enough to carry out any shift of sail, and so ensured that the watch below need never be disturbed. We did not work the English system of four hours on and four off, with the dog watches each evening to change the hours round, for that, while having the advantage of giving short hours on deck, had the disadvantage of short hours of sleep. Instead the Swedish system was worked, and our watches were :

Midnight to 4.00 a.m.	4.00 a.m. to 8.00 a.m.
8.00 a.m. to 1.00 p.m.	1.00 p.m. to 7.00 p.m.
7.00 p.m. to midnight	

The six-and five-hour watches gave time for the watch below to get down to some serious sleep.

The meals were planned to start 15 minutes before, and end 15 minutes after, each watch, thus giving half an hour for meals.

Breakfast	7.45 a.m. to 8.15 a.m.
Lunch	12.45 p.m. to 1.15 p.m.
Dinner	6.45 p.m. to 7.15 p.m.

During meals in settled weather one man only was on deck, and he was steering.

Landfall was designed by Herreshoff, a man of great ability ; she was built by Rassmussen, who was thorough, and her owner had great sailing and sea experience, so as a result of their combined forethought and knowledge, she was very easy on her crew ; every detail had been carefully thought out, and nothing was lacking, for it had already been thought of and placed where it would be needed.

It was no wonder, therefore, that we were happy and contented ; my only care was the thought, which I concealed, of *Dorade* probably on the Northern Great Circle course, for from the very start she had fallen off to leeward and northward, when she could have pointed as high as the rest of the fleet, and would have, had she been after the Gulf Stream. In years to come when these Transatlantic Races become more frequent there will be more rules, and it is very probable that all vessels will have to make a certain Latitude and Longitude one-third of the way across, which will, while taking a great deal of sport out of the game, make it more into a matter of sailing and seamanship, as against the strategy in deciding the course before the start of the race.

Monday, July 13, we made our shortest day's run, 26½ miles, and our position that noon was Latitude 41.36

North and Longitude 47.34 West. Our speed had varied from 1 to 4 knots until 6.00 p.m., when the breeze started to fill in, and it increased to 6 knots with the double spinnaker and the balloon mainsail set. This rig gave us 4,000 square feet of actual sail, 1,000 over *Landfall's* measured area. It had the advantage of not chafing against the main shrouds as it was all set forward of them, but the disadvantage of placing the entire strain upon the top of the mainmast, for the mainsail was set flying like a spinnaker with the tack made fast to the stem-head, the clew through a snatch block through the main boom end, and the head on the genoa jib halyard.

At 8.00 p.m. the wind came on the starboard quarter, south-west, and we set, in addition, the mizen and the mizen staysail, which increased our sail area to 5400 square feet, and as all four sails were drawing we sailed gaily along.

It was so enjoyable that no one wanted to turn in ; fortunately it was our watch from 7.00 p.m. till midnight, so we could enjoy the companionship of the other watch with the cheerful thought that we were losing no sleep, while they were even happier in the knowledge that they were foregoing their sleep for our pleasure, for it is more blessed to give than receive, and so we all yarned quietly and happily till midnight.

Then, as the wind had increased to 20 miles an hour, we started to take off some of *Landfall's* light canvas. We took in the double spinnaker and set the bowsprit spinnaker, then hoisting our mainsail we lowered the balloon mainsail easily and quietly in the lee of it, then set the genoa jib, which with the wind on the quarter pulled well with the bowsprit spinnaker, and finally took in the mizen and mizen staysail. Then we in the first watch turned in, leaving the deck to the second watch.

The next day, Tuesday, noon, our day's run was 190 miles.

The day after was a great day, for it was July 15, and John Quincey Adams' birthday, and we were all busy preparing for the dinner in his honour that night. Joe made an iced cake, and as we had no candles he rigged it

Above : JOE RIGGED THE BIRTHDAY CAKE WITH TWENTY-FOUR MATCHES

Left : WE PUT QUINCEY IN THE STOCKS

with twenty-four large matches, for it was Quincey's twenty-fourth birthday. We put Quincey in the stocks for some time in his birthday suit. A doll was made with oranges, the head orange being cut for the eyes, mouth and nose, and match heads made the eyeballs, a chamois leather coat and the bottom of the skipper's red trousers made the costume. Larry Pool and John Stedman etched *Landfall* under her balloon mainsail and double spinnaker on a copper plate, and by squeezing it in a vice took off twelve prints, using a thick black paint for ink ; the first trial print came out rather like a girl's face, so Brian touched it up slightly with pencil and ink, and pasting it on a box of cigarettes, made it into a special present to Quincey. Two of Quincey's presents were chosen with an eye to his having a few days earlier been constipated. One of these was a necklace of dates from Johnny Hallowell, and the other a small, but beautifully carved, relieving tackle by Waldo. Then there was a horse made from a piece of fairly stiff seizing wire. The skipper gave Quincey a box of chocolate peppermints with three golden ten dollar pieces concealed inside them ; and because it was the first year that Britain and America had been united by racing rules from J. Class vessels to 12-ft. dinghies, I gave him our British Y.R.A. Rule Book with the rules for those and the classes between. And so passed a busy day, for besides our birthday party work, we had to race *Landfall*. She did 6 knots all day till the middle of the afternoon, when the wind starting to freshen, she picked up speed and at 3.00 p.m. reached 8¾ knots, which she gradually increased, till 8.00 p.m. found her doing a steady 9 knots. The watch from 7.00 p.m. till midnight was again our watch, and in the five hours we logged 46 miles, the hourly runs being 9, 9¼, 9¼, 9½, and 9 knots, the wind all this time blowing S.S.W. at 22 miles an hour, and *Landfall* sailing with her genoa jib, balloon staysail, mainsail, mizen staysail and mizen set, for our easterly course brought this wind just abaft the beam.

Thursday, July 16. The second watch from midnight to 4.00 a.m. did 9½, 9¼, 9¼, and 8¾ knots, which made 36¾ miles for the four-hour watch. Our noon position was Lat. 45.43 North and Long. 45.49 West with a day's run of 204 miles. We had logged 214 miles, but there seemed to be a 10-mile drift against us. The best hour's run was 11 knots, which *Landfall* did with dry decks under genoa jib, balloon staysail, mainsail and mizen, for the wind was just one point abaft the beam, and blowing 25 miles an hour.

LANDFALL DOING II KNOTS WITH A DRY DECK

LENANTA, RALPH PEVERLY'S SCHOONER, CAME OUT TO MEET US

Our best run for a four-hour watch was from 8.00 a.m. till noon, when *Landfall* roared along at 10¼, 10¼, 10½, and finished with 11 knots, making 42 miles. There was a great rivalry to see who could put up the best run for a four-hour watch; whenever the wind was over 20 miles an hour, the relieving watch was ready and anxious to take over, for a few minutes either way might have just made the difference.

But soon after midday the wind hauled aft. We set the balloon staysail as a spinnaker, and in the next 24 hours we had logged 193 miles. Then another day's run of 204 miles brought us to Latitude 47.21 North and Longitude 26.24 West. The wind was well aft now, and *Landfall's* heavy mainsail slammed about a good deal in spite of the boom being guyed forward, so we set a light linen mainsail, and took in our cotton one. The change was a great improvement, for the lighter sail was more easily held full by the wind, and having little weight of its own, did not slam about with every roll, so *Landfall* sailed more quietly and easily. And this gave us a chance to do some minor repairs to the mainsail and track. The seizing on the tenth slide had chafed through and this was renewed. Then we found that the screws in the track for 12 feet or so above the boom had broken off, due to two things, the pull aft of the sail just above the track, and the fact that the screws were of an aluminium alloy, which does not really like sea air. The Gulf Stream air is particularly hard on any aluminium alloy, as it is on sails, which although mildew proofed, always feel the effect of its warm dampness. And so, as the man in whose care the spars came, I was hoisted in a bosun's stool and lashed to the mast, and re-fastened the track by drilling fresh holes and putting in extra screws, all of which time *Landfall* logged 9 knots. The moral of that day's discovery was to seize the lower slides on a Bermudian mainsail slack or with the sail set to get length, and not to use aluminium alloys for ocean work.

And so passed Saturday, peacefully and pleasantly, as days at sea do in a well-found sailing vessel.

The day's run ending noon, Sunday, July 19, was not a good one, for although then we were running along at 8 to 10 knots with everything set, we had been becalmed through the hours of darkness, and so 143 miles was all we could chalk up for the 24 hours. But Monday noon saw us with a day's run of 212 miles, in Lat. 48.24.5 North and Long. 18.04 West. The weather was colder, for we were approaching England, and were in a higher latitude than when we started, though it was not the cold, but the damp, that inspired us to light the cabin fires, and they warmed and cheered up *Landfall*, so that we gathered around them yarning when off watch, and there is no doubt that the glow and warmth of a coal fire makes a cabin very cosy.

Tuesday, July 21. The skipper, with the approach to land, was not standing a watch, which really meant that he was in both watches, so we traded Quincey Adams for Kim Norton, who, as second mate, took charge of our watch. The first night watch without the skipper seemed quite sad, for we had all been as so many brothers with him as our father, and we of his watch had looked upon him as in our gang. It was foggy and wet, so Waldo and I were lookouts forward, sitting on the locker and leaning back on the open fore hatch. The time went all too quickly, for we yarned away happily for what seemed 20 minutes when we were called to steer, as we had yarned (been looking out) for two hours and now had an hour each at the wheel to end the watch.

Kim yarned to us about his cruising schooner, which is a small Nina, being 42 feet on the water-line with 1,970 sq. ft. of sail. Three can sail her comfortably, but four make an ideal crew for cruising; and so another night watch passed.

July 22, Wednesday, at noon our day's run was again over 200 miles, being 208½, and we had logged 11¼ for an hour, and during our 4.00 to 8.00 watch we logged 43½ miles, and so put on the best run for a watch so far. The wind was 30 to 35 miles an hour and *Landfall* carried her full sail manfully and easily, but we did take in the genoa jib and set the working jib, as we thought the wind was on the increase. Then the mizen staysail was set. This was a sail I did not like to see set in wind, for the maintopmast backstays went to the mizen top, and as this mizen staysail pulled the mizen mast forward, due to the mizen backstays having no drift aft, it not only threatened to pull that mast down, but also endangered the mainmast; so instead of helping to hoist the sail I stood by the mainmast and watched to see how it would stand. It was a dreadful sight, so the skipper when he looked up the mainmast agreed that the mizen staysail should be stowed, and I breathed again. All due to the fact that the masts were in my care. Had someone else had them allotted to their care I should have probably enjoyed setting that sail, whereas instead I was not happy until it was down and stowed below again.

We were now coming on soundings, and the seas became, instead of the steady majestic seas of the Atlantic, a confused jumble, that broke in all directions. *Landfall* broke and shouldered her way through in grand style and although now and then one would flop on her deck she was generally dry and the fore hatch with its side boards still open. At 5.50 p.m. the *Europa* passed us 10 miles to the northward, bound into the Channel, and this put us exactly on our course and was a good check on our navigation, indicating that we should sight the Bishop's Light at midnight. It was actually only 10.00 p.m. when Larry Pool sighted the loom of it, one point on the port bow. We saw the flashes caught on the low clouds before time, for it was not yet above the skyline.

With daylight a sail was seen to the south and astern, the vessel being hull down. Her sails looked like *Highland Light*, and all morning she slowly gained on us, until noon found her only 2½ miles astern. Then in the same wind and on the same course she failed to gain any more, and so we both made for Plymouth, each vessel striving for the lead. *Landfall* held her lead with her balloon mainsail and double spinnaker pulling her along and across the finishing line, and to a mooring under the lee of Drake's Island.

Lenanta, Ralph Peverely's schooner, came out to greet us with the news that *Dorade* had sailed the northern course, and had been in Plymouth two days, and as we sailed in, there she was out for an afternoon sail. She had, almost all the way across, logged 200 miles a day in the colder winds farther north.

There was no doubt that with her handicap *Dorade* would win, and having beaten *Highland Light* by only 14 minutes across the finishing line we were already third, for her allowance put her ahead of us, and the times at which the others finished would tell us if we still held on to our third position or not. We did not for we dropped back as the others came in, finally settling down to sixth out of ten starters. In a race off the wind it is seldom the scratch boats win, for then the odds are against them; they win with the winds ahead, when because of their size they overpower the smaller vessels.

Lismore, the other vessel of our size, had carried away her main topmast and was the last boat to finish, coming in four days behind us. So all ten racers arrived safely and within twenty-two days of their setting sail from America.

We sailed *Landfall* to Cowes, calling in at Dartmouth for the night on the way up. She sailed along at 8 knots with a 22 mile an hour wind under jib, raffee squaresail, small spinnaker and mizen. This was nice comfortable cruising, and there is no doubt that cruisers with fine fast bottoms have the advantage over slower vessels, as they can go their speed with so little sail set. And *Landfall* came past Portland and through the Needles to Cowes, where she anchored for a week or two before leaving for Bremen and her winter quarters there, ready to cruise the next summer in the Baltic.

· 4 ·

IDEAL PROPORTIONS OF CRUISING YACHTS

"Build me straight, O worthy Master!
Staunch and strong a goodly vessel;
That shall laugh at all disaster,
And with wave and whirlwind wrestle!"

WE accept Venus as the ideal of womanly grace and beauty and her proportions throughout the world are considered perfect to-day, just as they were when the Romans made statues of their goddess of love.

It is fairly easy to discover just what a man admires and loves, for to ask him is to know; but to understand the Ocean's likes and dislikes is far harder. Nicholson, Fife, Mylne, Harley Mead, and Shepherd in this country, and Herreshoff, Burgess, Paine, Alden and Stephens in America, have spent their lives studying the sea's way so that they might design vessels to which the sea would take kindly.

On these graphs are plotted the proportions chosen by the master designers of England and America in their efforts to give to the sea its ideal of grace and beauty. And although they are an effort to reduce the art of designing sailing vessels to a science, this cannot be, for that which is really beautiful comes from the heart, not the brain.

Five years ago, at a dinner in London, given after a meeting at which the rules of a small boat class had been drastically altered, the Chairman, Sir John, called on one designer to describe the boats that would be built to the rule the next year, and upon myself to describe the boats that would be built ten years after. The other designer described a different boat altogether from the one he and I had developed under the old rule, and I said the boats would be practically as they were at that moment in ten years' time, because the wind and sea would remain exactly the same *in spite of the fact that we had altered our rule*, and that although man became weaker through the ages this would not be noticed in ten years.

So the design of my boats has only been refined these five years, and that of the other designer altered and then altered back to its old proportions.

Committees make rules for racing yachts, and when beautiful vessels are designed that come within their rules, they slap their chests and say, "What a fine rule we made to produce such a vessel." They should also slap the designer on the back (not too hard, for designers are all getting old) for it is he that should take the credit for designing a beautiful vessel, not because of the rule, but in spite of it, for the designer is always trying to please the sea.

LOAD WATER-LINE

The load water-line is the line at which a vessel floats when ready for sea, and as water is level and straight (when quiet) measurements are easily taken from it, so the following proportions for vessels are all in relation to the load water-line.

Intelligent yachtsmen describe their yachts as 50 or 60 ft. on the line (mark the line), and at once it gives an impression of speed, sail area, etc.

Others describe their vessels as so many tons Thames Measurement!

A man generally knows just what water-line length vessel he would like, and so by looking at the graphs he can see at a glance just what beam, draught, freeboard, displacement, sail area, and speed his vessel should have. And at the same time he can compare her to existing vessels whose proportions are plotted on each graph, and as most of these have at least one Atlantic crossing to their credit their ability cannot be doubted, while those that have not crossed were plotted on the graph as being for their work perfect little ships.

BEAM

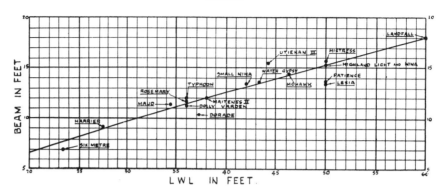

The beam curve plotted might seem a little on the heavy side to Englishmen, as in this country we still feel the influence of the rule that forced designers into producing the narrow plank on edge type, which, although fast under that rule, was as wet as a half-tide rock. The curve plotted is to please the sea, not Englishmen!

FREEBOARD

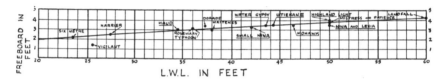

A vessel must have a certain amount of freeboard or every sea will sweep her decks from end to end, but freeboard above this amount, because it pushes the weight of the deck, anchors, winches, etc., in the air, is bad, as it tends to make the boat cranky. And the designers in England and America have arrived at exactly the same proportions of freeboard to water-line length.

The only one above this ideal curve is *Dorade*, and she, because of her narrow floor, had to increase her freeboard for headroom, just two inches.

DISPLACEMENT

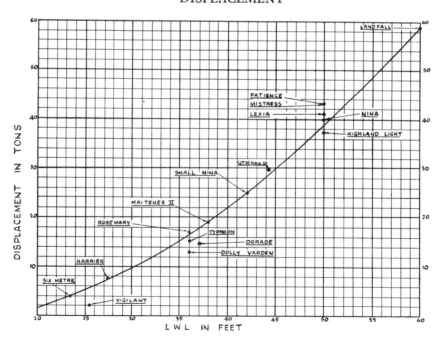

Yachtsmen argue over the ideal displacement far more than any other point in a yacht's design. Heavy displacement is generally looked upon as the cure for all ills in sailing yachts, which is a sad and grievous mistake. The displacement of a yacht, it must be remembered, is the total weight of hull, ballast, spars, sails and all gear, and for any given water-line length there must be an ideal displacement. On most weighing machines will be found, just under the slot where the penny is lost, a table giving ideal weight for men and women in relation to their overall length. If people are below they feed up, and if above they take more exercise or diet. Even if they do not do these things they wish they were just the ideal weight, just as Lady Jane did in *Patience*, whose charms, already ripe, were beginning to decay.

" Fading is the taper waist, Stouter than I used to be,
Shapeless grows the shapely limb, Still more corpulent grow I :
And although severely laced, There will be too much of me
Spreading is the figure trim ! In the coming bye and bye."

The displacement curve drawn is an attempt to show the ideal displacement for each water-line length from 20 to 60 ft., and the aim has been to have 55 per cent. of the displacement in the vessel and gear, and 45 per cent. as lead keel or ballast. Lloyd's scantlings require a certain weight in the wood or metal for all yachts, as they specify sizes for all parts of a vessel, frames, planking, etc. And most yachts are built to these scantlings, so it will be seen that all extra weight through extra displacement goes into lead keels or lead ballast.

But the heavy displacement merchants forget this, and also that vessels are built lighter and stronger than they were, so that a modern vessel, if she were not designed with lighter displacement, would have too great a proportion of her weight in her ballast.

The ideal amount of ballast in displacement is 45 per cent., which should mostly be in the form of a lead keel, where it would in the case of a vessel hitting rocks take the blow. Whereas, if this ballast were stowed inside it would tend to drop through the bottom.

SAIL AREA

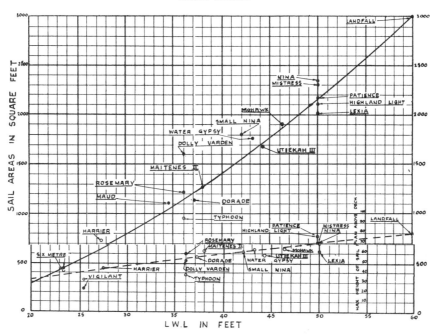

The ideal sail area and its height for yachts of various water-lines is easily read on the graph. It will be noticed that the cutters are usually forced above the ideal height, as all their sail has to be set upon one mast, and that the Americans have generally more sail area, due to the fact that the winds in summer are lighter on the western, which in these latitudes is the weather side of the Atlantic.

Often a yacht is held up as a wonderful hard-weather boat, the only reason for this being that she does not have to reef in strong breezes. The truth is that she is under-canvassed. Being under is almost as great a fault as being over-canvassed. Excessive sail area means over-sparring a yacht ; this was not so detrimental in days gone by, when a yacht could and did reef her spars.

To me, the only fault of the modern Bermudian rig is that while the sails can be reefed the mast cannot, and these tall masts standing up half naked in hard weather look wrong and are wrong.

It will be seen that the curve picks up *Maitenes II.* At one time she had far more sail area and a higher mast ; these proved excessive, and were shortened to those shown on the graph.

DRAUGHT

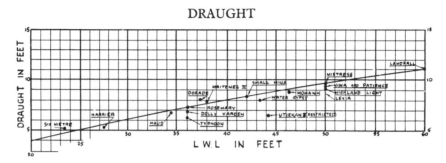

The draught shown is for deep-water work, the open sea, and if a vessel is to be used in districts where the land is high and bold, such as Cornwall, Scotland and Norway, then all is well, for where the land is high and bold the water is deep ; but for districts where the land is flat, the Thames Estuary, Holland, in fact anywhere in the southern half of the North Sea, the draught should be lessened and the beam increased, so that the vessel sails more upright and does not lose any more of her already decreased draught.

A man can tell roughly the depth of the water by the height of the land, for the height of the land is the depth of the water. The North Sea illustrates this ; in the northern half it has the high mountains of Norway and Scotland, and very deep water, in the southern half the flat lands of East Anglia and Holland and shallow water.

SPEED

Owners must praise their vessels, and owners of slow boats praise their comfortable motion in a seaway, quite forgetting that their vessels are comfortable in a sea because they are so slow. A pilot vessel, if driven hard, is very uncomfortable, and so is any sailing vessel travelling at its maximum speed in a sea. It is the speed of a fast yacht that makes her uncomfortable, but as her owner can, by shortening sail, reduce her speed, he has the choice between a fast, but uncomfortable passage, and a slow comfortable one, while the owner of a slow yacht has no choice.

The speeds shown on the graphs are higher than usual, for other people who have studied this maximum speed question have not realised that the overhangs on yachts increase their water-line length in a seaway.

Many times I've heard people say of yachts with moderate overhangs, " Look at her overhangs, she could never stand a sea." Yet the fact remains, that yachts with moderate overhangs are better in a seaway than those without, for it is in rough broken water that the overhangs are most valuable, increasing the water-line length and fore and aft stability, while in smooth water all these overhangs do is to float in thin air and look pretty.

It is not the modern racing yacht's overhangs that prevent her going to sea in strong weather, but her tall mast. For instance, *Britannia*, under her old rig, reefed down her top mast and stormed across to Cherbourg and back ; but now this same vessel (overhangs as well) has to stay at her moorings while little International 14-footers race in the wind that her mast cannot stand.

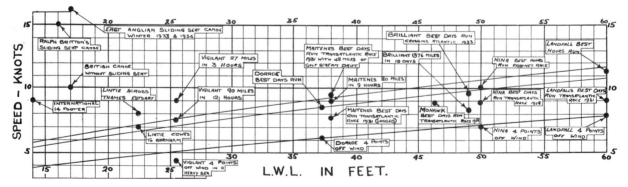

Three different speeds are given for each water-line length, the highest is the speed a yacht can attain under perfect conditions, that is a gale breaking at once after a calm where the yacht could be driven to her utmost before the sea made up, conditions seldom met. In *Landfall*, we could not reach the 11·5 knots shown on the graph, her maximum hour's run being ¼ knot below this; but *Landfall* was a transom-sterned boat, and as her bow lifted on a wave her stern drew down dragging water behind it, thus preventing her reaching the 11·5 knots she would have done with overhangs.

The next speed is one at which vessels could be driven for 24 hours, and *Dorade* is the only one that I know of to do a day's run that puts her upon this line. She has often done such a day's run, crewed by youngsters (as she has always been); she has never wanted for sail, and her long overhangs increase her sailing length in a seaway. *Mohawk's* best day's run in the Transatlantic Race equals *Nina's*, and as she is a shorter water-line vessel she more nearly approaches the line of the maximum day's run for her length. *Nina* is shown with an hour's run of 10 knots, and I do not think, with her very short ends, she could reach the maximum speed allotted for her water-line length, as that allows for longer overhangs.

Brilliant's passage across the Atlantic was remarkably good, for she sailed 230 miles in one day, which gives an average of 9.7 knots and practically puts her upon the line for the best 24-hour run possible for a vessel of her water-line length, while her average speed of 8.33 knots for ten days on end is the best run for that length of time for such a small ship—almost 200 miles a day for 10 days.

Lintie is a six-metre, which two of us sailed from Cowes to Burnham, and her speed across the Thames Estuary double-reefed is ¾ of a knot over the speed I've thought possible for her water-line length, but it must be remembered that these six-metres have no accommodation, so that about 75 per cent. of their total weight is in their lead keels, which enables them to be sailed in hard weather with far more sail aloft than a cruiser could stand, and the average speed of 7 knots from Cowes to the entrance of Burnham River at the Whitaker Beacon is due to this fact plus *Lintie's* overhangs, with their reserve buoyancy and increased sailing length in a seaway.

The third and lowest speed is the speed close-hauled within four points of the wind, so that when tacking a right angle is made to the old course; *Nina*, *Landfall*, and *Dorade* can sail at the speeds for their lengths. My little 22-sq. metre *Vigilant* is shown down below that line; this is not because she was unable to do that speed, but because the only real check I have on her speed to windward was her beat dead to windward across the North Sea from the Terschelling to Lowestoft against a very heavy sea, in weather that kept all our big racing cutters at their moorings in the Solent, and caused all the regattas to be postponed in Norfolk, so it was generally bad, and it was the sea that put her below her mark.

Maitenes did 80 miles in 9 hours, which, falling half-way between the maximum for one hour and the maximum of 24, shows the graph to be about right (that must have been a fine ride). She won the *Pinta's* prize for the best day's run in the Transatlantic Race, but that day she only logged 182, as she had 48 miles of Gulf Stream drift, so both are plotted; the higher figure, of course, should not be shown as this speed graph deals with speed through the water only.

*　　*　　*　　*　　*　　*　　*　　*　　*　　*　　*　　*

Then to show where sailing boats do not conform to these rules, I've plotted very light displacement boats, boats that when driven hard climb out of water and scoot along the top with hardly any wave-making at all. International 14-footers can do 9 knots, and often do when reaching during a race, but the most alarming of all is Ralph Britton's sliding-seat canoe, which was timed at 15 knots over a half-mile reach, the reason for her speed being that he sat at the end of a long slide and his long leverage enabled him to hold his canoe up on her feet. After this, the canoes of England, without sliding seats, look very slow, doing 10 knots, only double their normal speed.

In the summer of 1933 Roger de Quincey and myself took our canoes (sister ships) out to America, where we won the International Canoe Trophy—due to the fact that our canoes were faster in strong winds—so that although while racing out there we did not do 15 knots we felt sure our canoes could do even more than this.

When in October we were once more in England with our canoes, I set to work to improve *East Anglian's* speed reaching: her 120 lb. dropkeel was changed for one weighing 10 lbs., her two masts weighing 30 lbs. were changed for a stayed mast weighing 10 lbs. only, air tanks and heavy keel hoist were taken out so that for trials over the measured mile she was less than half the weight she was when racing, which meant that she was much faster off the wind though not so fast to windward. October, November, December and January were spent with *East Anglian* dashing over the measured mile whenever the winds were right in strength and direction, and after four months she finally did 16.3 miles an hour, a speed that will only be believed by the chosen few who have flown over the water on the end of the six-foot sliding seat of a planing canoe.

The continued effort of those four months was worth while.

My 22-sq. metre *Vigilant* falls just halfway between the light vessels that really plane, and the heavier ones that can never plane. One night, in a full north-westerly gale, we left Kiel in her with full sail up and fairly flew, doing the 27 miles between Kiel and Fehmarnbelt in three hours. That was glorious; we'd plane along with the sea thrown high on either side of us for minutes on end, and then we would strike the back of the sea ahead and drop down to normal speed again, the most exhilarating ride of my life.

The reason for choosing Ocean Racers to illustrate the graphs for ideal cruisers is that: " The best Ocean Racer is the best Cruiser."

· 5 ·

VAMARIE

Length, overall	-	-	-	72 ft. 0 in.	Length, water-line	-	-	54 ft. 0 in.
Beam	-	-	-	15 ft. 3 in.	Draught	-	-	-	10 ft. 4 in.
Displacement	-	-	46 tons	Sail area	-	-	-	2,300 sq. ft.

Owner, VADIM MAKAROFF   *Designers*, COX and STEVENS

IN the autumn of 1933, as I sat writing in the cockpit of *Dorade* in Oyster Bay, a bright varnished ketch came roaring by under jib, mizen, and mizen staysail only, as the wind was strong. Her rig stood well, for a wishbone aloft held the two masts together, thus putting the strains fairly evenly over both spars, so that this vessel combined the handiness of the ketch with the strength of the schooner rig.

VAMARIE PHOTOGRAPHED FROM DORADE

The rig was new to my eyes, and I wondered how it would stand in a strong wind and heavy sea. I was tempted then to ask her designers for her plans to publish in this book, but did not do so, for the rig was unproved and untried.

Months later, as I still sat writing this book, but now on the cliffs of Alum Bay in England, the news came through that *Vamarie* had, in a hard wet drive to windward, won the race from Miami to Nassau. During this race the wind blew 50 miles an hour, and caused nine out of the twelve starters to retire hurt. Sitting on the cliffs, and imagining her plunging and driving through the steep heavy seas caused by that wind, I at once decided that *Vamarie* was worth her salt and place in this book. Then cables flew to Rassmussen in Bremen and Jasper Morgan in New York, and soon I was engaged in redrawing *Vamarie's* lines, accommodation, sail, gaff and gaff fitting plans, and wondering why I had waited until she had proved herself so weatherly, when the impression she had made months ago told me she would be able and seaworthy.

The lines are those of an easily driven vessel, and there is no doubt that they make for a fast, well-balanced and weatherly hull.

The accommodation is unusually planned. The fo'c'sle has three cots, and directly abaft are the galley and pantry. Then there is a single guest cabin to port with a wash room opposite. Next is the saloon, which is very well lighted, even when the 14-foot dinghy is stowed on deck, for the coach roof is cut away on the starboard side to take the dinghy, and though it covers the starboard saloon lights those to port are clear. These are immediately over the saloon table where light is needed, and this unusual arrangement is a good one.

The companionway, as it is abreast the mast, is off centre on the starboard side, and opposite is another wash room, these two dividing the double cabin aft from the saloon. Farther aft is a very fine navigator's cabin, where the chart table is built over the engine and so forms the engine casing. The companionway leading directly on deck to the wheel allows the navigator and helmsman to talk over the course, speed and weather without disturbing the rest of the ship : an admirable arrangement.

Unusual as are the details of her accommodation her sail plan is a new conception of the art of spreading canvas to catch the winds. Although the staysail and mizen are normal, the sails between the main and mizen masts are a new development. The mainsail is shaped like a topsail with a split gaff to extend the clew and allow the sail to take its natural flow, so essential for windward work on either tack. The topsail usually found in

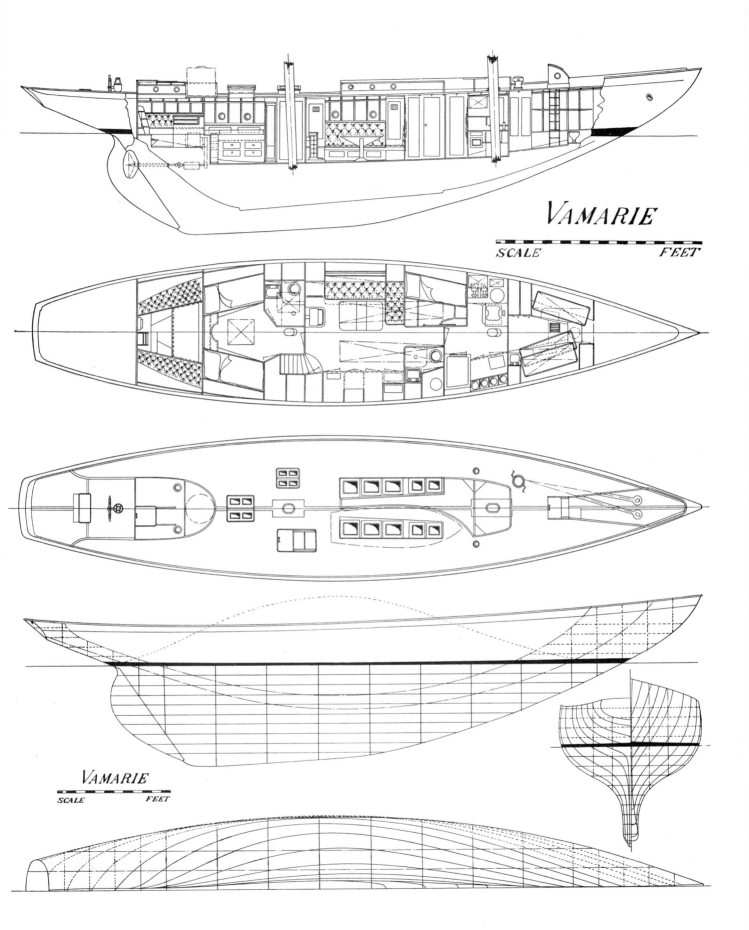

VAMARIE

SCALE   FEET

VAMARIE

SCALE   FEET

gaff-rigged vessels takes a nice curve on one tack, and on the other, because it presses against the peak halyards, is perfectly flat, and so loses its power and drive to windward.

So the fact that a topsail is more efficient on the tack that blows it to leeward of the peak halyards, is generally the cause (unknown to some owners) of their vessel being faster on one tack. If there is a long and short leg to

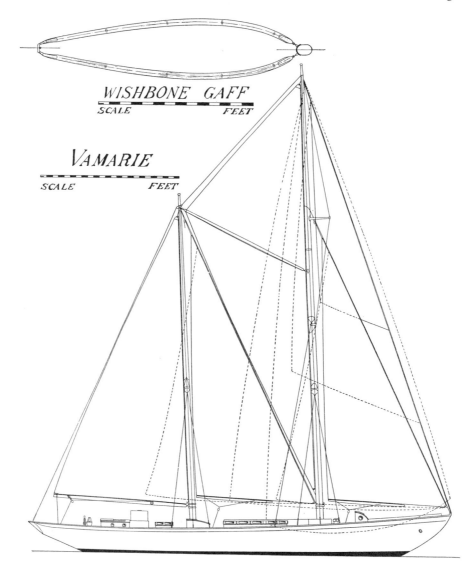

WISHBONE GAFF

SCALE   FEET

VAMARIE

SCALE   FEET

windward the really good skipper of a racer sets his topsail so that it bellies out to leeward on the long leg, and presses against the peak halyards on the short leg. Below *Vamarie's* mainsail the mizen staysail is set, and tacks down on deck immediately abaft the mainmast, thus filling in the rest of the space between the two masts. With her unusual accommodation and sail plan, and her undoubted ability to windward under three lowers in severe weather, *Vamarie* is instructive and well worthy of study.

· 6 ·

NIÑA

Length, overall	-	-	- 59 ft. 0 in.	Length, waterline	-	- 50 ft. 0 in.
Beam	-	-	- 14 ft. 10 in.	Displacement	-	- 40 tons
	Sail area	-	-	-	- 2,500 sq. ft.	

Owner and Skipper, PAUL HAMMOND *Designer*, STARLING BURGESS

BY winning the Transatlantic and the Fastnet Races in 1928, *Niña* proved herself a fast and able ocean racer. Her successful racing career no doubt influenced Vanderbilt to entrust Burgess with the designing of *Enterprise*, with which he successfully defended the America's Cup against *Shamrock V*.

Niña, anchored off Cowes, looked as strange to me as the *America* must have to our seamen in 1851, for both had rigs that were new to England. The *America*, it must be remembered, on August 22, 1851, won the cup pre-

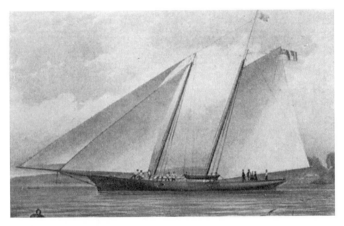

THE AMERICA, ALSO A CHALLENGER FROM ACROSS THE WATER, WITH A NEW SCHOONER RIG

sented by the Squadron for a race round the Isle of Wight, six years later giving it to the New York Yacht Club, since when it has been known as the America's Cup.

Before her visit, schooners in this country did not use the triatic stay (from mainmast head to foremast head above fore gaff), both masts being stayed independently of each other, which allowed the foretopsail to remain set when tacking. Besides introducing the triatic stay, America changed our racing sails from flax to cotton.

Niña and *America* were alike in that they were both invading yachts with strange new rigs, both winning cups for America from England, thus putting these National cups on the higher plane of International cups.

Her short ends are the result of the American Ocean Racing Rule, otherwise it is certain *Niña* would have had longer overhangs fore and aft. The result would be a shorter bowsprit, would make reefing the mainsail easier, as well as giving stability, steadiness, and speed in a seaway.

Sweeping buttocks, easy diagonals, and waterlines, high, firm, yet not hard bilges, all combined make as sweet a set of lines as could be wished for. No wonder Burgess gave *Enterprise* the same sections and buttocks.

Niña's lines I've always admired (excepting the short ends), the hull hauled out and the model in the owner's home being pleasing to my eye. With her small amount of wetted surface she is easily driven, while the outside lead ballast enables her to stand up to hard weather.

The staysail schooner rig is quite new ; *Advance* started it some six years ago in America. For windward work it is unquestionably faster than the ordinary schooner rig, and while it never can be as fast, it makes for an easier

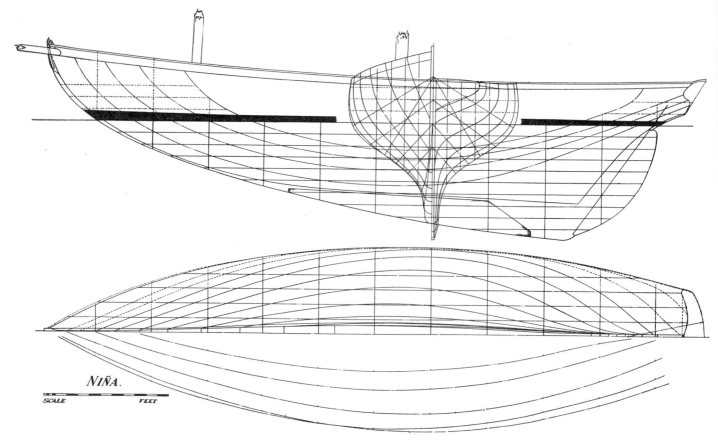

NIÑA.

SCALE · FEET.

NIÑA.

SCALE · FEET.

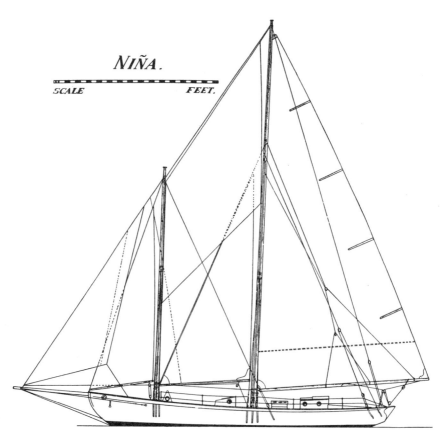

handled vessel than a cutter, with its sails split up into so many small pieces. In effect the rig is a cutter with a small mainsail and a large fore triangle.

Some years ago I made many experiments, endeavouring to discover the best proportion of headsail to mainsail for the cutter rig, one rig having such a small mainsail and large headsail that friends asked me which of the two was the mainsail. Those experiments showed that the smaller the jib and larger the mainsail the faster the boat to windward at a sacrifice of speed off the wind, while the boat with the large headsail was faster off the wind but slower to windward, always using the same total area.

NIÑA'S HEADSAILS LIFT RATHER THAN DRIVE

So as *Niña* at the best is a cutter with a small mainsail and a large foretriangle, she cannot expect to hold a similar hull with a cutter rig of normal proportions to windward, for besides the proportions of her headsail to mainsail being wrong for windward work, she has the weight and windage of her foremast.

Reaching she would be faster than a cutter, and there is no doubt headsails, loose footed and sheeted at the clew, lift rather than drive a vessel along. Dead before the wind she could not hold a cutter, as then she loses one-third of her sail area, her spinnaker boom setting on the foremast, while the sails between the two masts hang lifeless. I'm very fond of the schooner rig for three reasons: both masts are stayed together, so strong and reliable, the main topmast or fisherman's staysail set aloft catches the light airs there, and under foresail alone a schooner will heave to when the wind is strong enough for her to put her head under her wing.

So when I first beheld *Niña* I looked at her rig to see just how it affected the things for which I loved a schooner. The staying of the mast first of all dropped a point, for the triatic stay led down to the deck at the foremast instead of to the foremast head, this making a backstay necessary from the foremast head.

The fisherman's staysail was much easier to handle and could be carried to windward even in short tacks, for it did not have to be lowered and reset each tack. *Niña's* fisherman's staysail was easier to hoist and take in, for, running on a tramway and stay, it was under control the whole time. The old type set flying was a brute to take in during a squall. The ease with which the fisherman's staysail can be handled more than makes up for the extra work setting up the foremast backstay.

In the autumn of 1922, in a small schooner, we hove to under foresail alone until an onshore gale eased enough to allow us to carry on under staysail, foresail and main trysail. Although the wind was onshore, that little schooner, with her foresail sheet started a little and her helm a-lee, slowly but surely fought her way to windward, clear of the dangerous shoals to leeward, while hove to. That foresail's work impressed upon me the usefulness of the schooner rig.

In *Niña* the foresail is replaced by a main staysail with about two-thirds a foresail's area, and I wonder if she would heave to as well under this as under a foresail.

THE STAYSAIL SCHOONER RIG SETS LITTLE CANVAS WHEN DEAD BEFORE THE WIND

SET FROM THE JIB-BOOM TO THE MAIN TOPMAST THIS BIG REACHING JIB MAKES BLACK ROSE ALMOST A CUTTER

The great advantage of the staysail schooner rig is its elasticity, for it can be either a hard racing or an easy cruising rig. For racing a wonderful assortment of sails can be set forward of the mainmast, from the three small lowers to the great bowsprit spinnaker, setting on the bowsprit and running past the foremast head to the main topmast head, so filling the whole space forward of the mainmast, while the jib, fore and main staysails, with a three-quarter-sized mainsail, make a very easy and simple cruising rig.

Some years ago I bought the Yankee jib topsail of one of our large racing cutters, and setting it on my old schooner's jib boom end found it reached past the main topmast head, so it was cut to fit, and with one halyard at the foremast head and another at the main topmast head we used it racing, improving *Black Rose* enough to win Lord Gort's Cup.

It was disappointing to find that *Niña* on the other side of the Atlantic had a similar sail, it being so gratifying for a man to think that he invented a sail.

In this country (England), where schooners are scarce, the staysail of a cutter is often wrongly called the foresail. Friends aboard my schooner often lowered the staysail when asked to stow the foresail, whereupon I would say : " . . . The foresail is that gaffsail set on the foremast."

The staysail schooner rig with its elasticity and speed is so pleasing that if I were building a small schooner she would be staysail rigged, provision being made for the triatic stay and a fore topmast, enabling her to be easily and cheaply altered into an ordinary fore and aft or a topsail schooner, if desired, later.

For her first ocean races *Niña* had no bulkheads at all, having just one large cabin, in which her crew lived rather like men in a bell tent. Where there are no ladies this is quite a good arrangement, giving far more light,

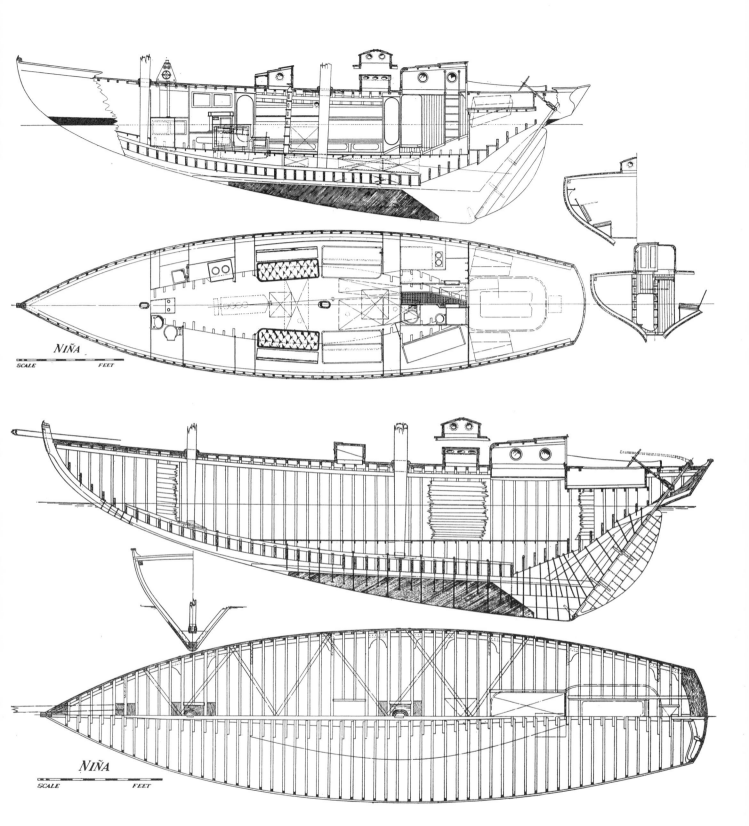

NIÑA

SCALE   FEET

NIÑA

SCALE   FEET

air and space below than that usually found in small vessels. *Typhoon*, in which I cruised to America, and *Cayuse*, a small edition of *Niña*, were fitted this way, and life aboard both was very comfortable. *Niña's* owner later altered her accommodation to that generally found in a cruiser of her size.

In order to win a race across the Atlantic a boat must feed and house her crew in comparative comfort, otherwise they would not be fit enough to sail their vessel to the best advantage in all weathers.

My reason for holding up ocean racers as examples for cruisers is that being first and foremost a cruising man I have done just enough racing to understand that the ideal ocean racer is the ideal cruiser. Yachtsmen are generally divided into two groups, purely racing and purely cruising men, neither being able to see the merits of the other vessel. These ocean racers are cruisers as developed by racing men. Combining, as they do, the knowledge of cruising and racing men, they are interesting and instructive, and besides this, they have to face every sort of weather in their races across wide oceans.

Ocean racers have done a great deal of research work for cruisers, they have proved the ability of the tall Bermudian mast to stand. Indeed, if we take the facts of races it would be considered stronger than the ordinary main and topmast rig, for records show that while many topmasts have carried away the Bermudian rig has stood.

The cutter rig is the fastest yet evolved, but for cruising, where ease in handling sails is of more importance than speed, the canvas should be split into smaller and more easily managed sails. This generally means a two- or three-masted rig. (Sometimes as many as seven masts being used.)

Niña's staysail schooner rig, offering, as it does, almost the speed of the cutter with the ease in handling of a schooner, is very tempting.

·7·

PATIENCE

Length, overall, - - - 68 ft. 0 in.		Length, water-line - - 50 ft. 0 in.
Beam - - - - 13 ft. 10 in.		Draught - - - - 9 ft. 4 in.
Displacement - - - 43½ tons		Sail area - - - - 2,180 sq. ft.

Owner, H. E. WEST   *Designer*, CHARLES NICHOLSON

PATIENCE was built as a fast cruiser in 1931, and after a successful summer of cruising and racing entered the Fastnet Race of that year against sixteen American and English Ocean Racers. By leading such a strong and fast fleet round the Fastnet from Cowes and back to Plymouth, *Patience* showed her ability and weatherliness against the sloppy seas encountered in the English Channel.

PATIENCE

There is no doubt that easy water-lines and diagonals, combined with easy section and narrow beam as in *Patience*, make for a vessel that will forge ahead through the Channel seas all the time, for such a vessel has little wetted surface, which tells heavily when the sheets are hauled down hard for a long thrash to windward.

PATIENCE.

SCALE   FEET.

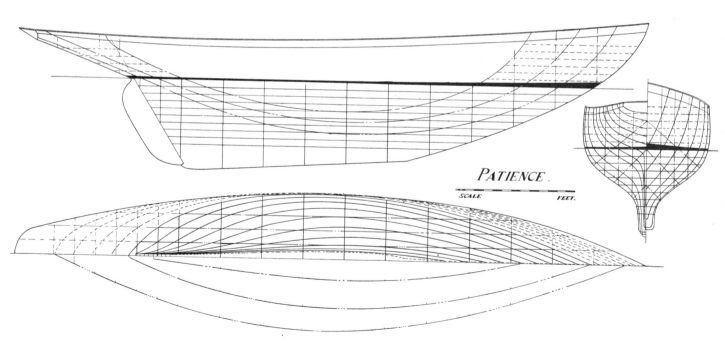

PATIENCE.

SCALE   FEET.

Her Bermudian cutter rig is without doubt the best for windward work, as apart from the efficiency of the sails there is a minimum of windage in spars and rigging aloft, and it must be remembered that every wire, block, or spar that goes aloft means that much extra windage, a simple fact often lost sight of. The counter enables the boom end to be reached from the deck, and this is a comfort on dark nights with a sea running, as it makes for ease in reefing.

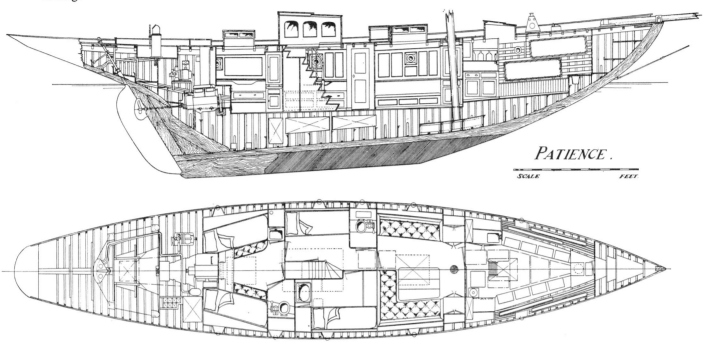

PATIENCE.

SCALE   FEET

Her accommodation is good; she has four folding cots in the fo'c's'le, abaft of which is the saloon, and to starboard under the deck house is the owner's stateroom, opposite which is a single cabin, while further aft is a double cabin. The lighting and ventilating is arranged so that it leaves the deck clear for setting and taking in sails.

Patience with her speed, weatherliness and comfort is a fine example of our cruising vessels.

· 8 ·

LEXIA

Length, overall - - - 60 ft. 0 in.		Length, LWL. - - 50 ft. 0 in.		
Beam - - - - - 13 ft. 6 in.		Draught - - - - 9 ft. 0 in.		
Displacement - - - 41 tons		Sail area - - - 2,000 sq. ft.		

Owner, Lt.-Col. T. P. Rose Richards   *Designer*, Frederick Shepherd

*L*EXIA'S owner, being unable to buy a second-hand cruiser to suit him, asked Shepherd to design him a ship in December 1930. In January the design was complete ; work was commenced on her at the Lymington shipyard, and July saw her under way. The next month, August, she entered the Fastnet Race, and although not

LEXIA IS WELL AND TRULY BUILT

built to the Ocean Racing Club's formula, she managed to be the first British yacht on time allowance, *Dorade*, from America, winning the race.

In February 1932 she sailed from her home port, Chichester, to Madeira in 11 days 8 hours, in spite of the fact that she was hove to for sixty hours.

She started with a fine easterly wind down channel, which after three days developed into a gale in the Bay, and although still running comfortably *Lexia* was hove to with her mainsail rolled down to within three mast-hoops of the gaff jaws and lay quiet for two nights and days. Then the lacing along the gaff gave way, and *Lexia* was run off before the gale till this was renewed, when she was brought once more into the wind ; but she shipped a green sea, which, breaking into the mainsail, practically submerged her, although the only damage was a sprung boom, which was seized with wire and gave no trouble.

LEXIA : HER SMALL AREA IS MADE UP FOR BY OVERLAPPING HEADSAILS

Because the lacing of the gaff chafed through, *Lexia* has since used stops, a separate one at each eyelet, so that even if one does break the rest hold, whereas, if one part of a lacing chafes, the whole of the sail lacing on the gaff is adrift. Chafe is a great danger on long passages in fore-and-aft vessels, as generally a long distance is sailed with a fair wind, when the mainsail is eased on to the shrouds, whereas a square-rigged vessel has her sails forward of the mast and shrouds and so free from chafe.

Then again, take the different shrouds and stays set up by lanyards ; the smaller the lanyard, the more parts it has and the neater it looks, and when new a small lanyard is as strong as a large one ; but because it has three times the number of parts, it has more chance of chafe and each part is more easily chafed through, so it is not so good for its job.

A reef lacing has the advantage that it adjusts itself to the strain, and so pulls evenly all along the row of reef eyelets, and is thus less liable to tear the sail. Reef points all tied separately are unable to adjust themselves, and so often tear the sail at a point which, through being tied too tightly, takes more than its fair strain. But the reef lacing has the disadvantage of letting go everywhere once one part chafes through, although this again is an advantage in shaking out a reef in a hurry, when a slash with a knife at once frees all eyelets, and the tack and clew earings being released, the sail is ready for hoisting in a much shorter time than if it had had reef points. It follows that for racing lacings are best, and for cruising, reef points. *Lexia*, however, had neither, as her Woodnutt reefing gear enabled her to reef with her boom broad off, and the sail full of wind. This is how a roller sail should be reefed, as then the wind smooths out all wrinkles and a clean reef is taken in. A roller reefing boom should be

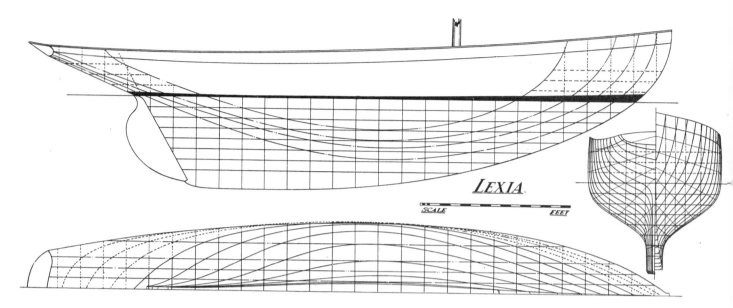

LEXIA.

SCALE   FEET

larger on its outer end, so that more sail is rolled up at this point, thus keeping the boom out of water. The topping lift takes the weight of the boom whilst reefing.

Lexia's original boom was 8 in. diameter, but because it was sprung, she had a new 9 in. boom made in City Island when she reached America. I think a boom 8 in. at the inner end and 9½ in. at the outer end would have been ideal.

From Madeira she sailed to Las Palmas and to Trinidad, taking 23 days on this last passage of 3,000 miles with a trysail and trysail topsail set on one hand, and a masthead spinnaker on the other, a comfortable and easy rig. From Trinidad, she visited Grenada, St. Lucia, St. Kitts, St. Thomas and the Virgin Group, and then

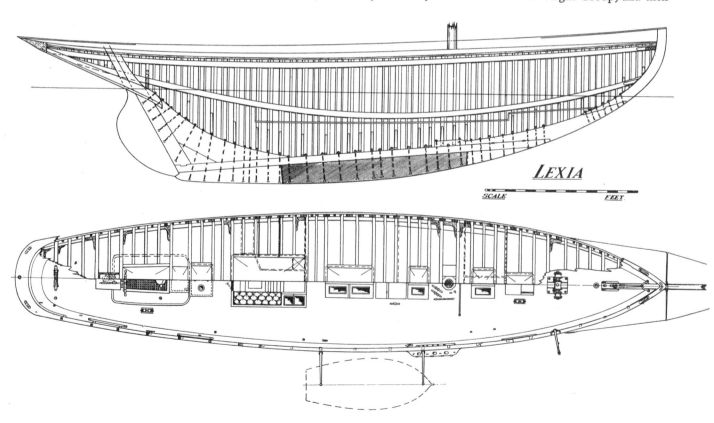

LEXIA

SCALE   FEET

on to Nassau, Miami, Charlestone and Norfolk. As she was earlier in America than anticipated, *Lexia* visited Boston before refitting in Long Island Sound for the Bermuda Race. This race was a reach and *Lexia* finished ninth against a fleet of 28 starters, taking 79 hours from Long Island Sound to Bermuda.

A day or so later she sailed for home, making the Lizard 20½ days out from Bermuda, and after a night in the Channel picked up her moorings in Chichester Harbour, which she had left six months previously.

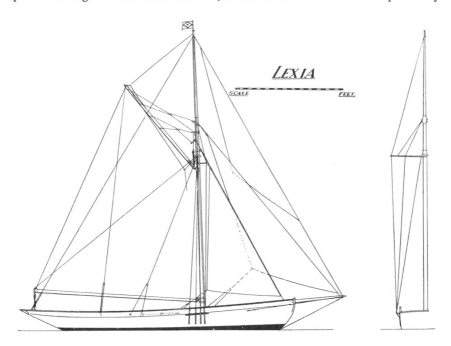

In 1933 she made an eight-day passage to Gibraltar, cruised to Morocco and home again via Cadiz, Lisbon and Oporto. She has proved herself a comfortable and sturdy cruiser, able to steer herself, heave to and make good passages.

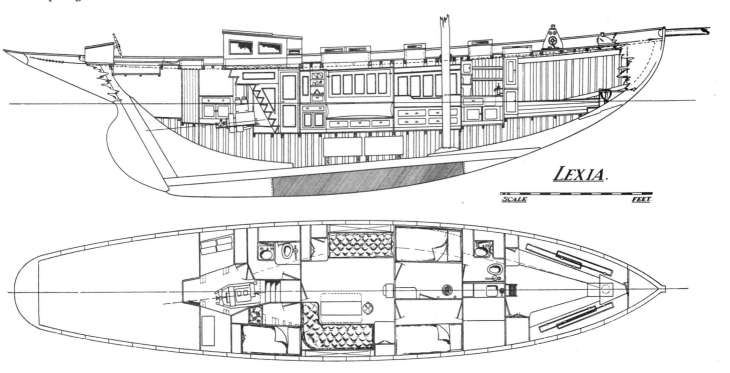

Her lines show her wide garboards, which give her such good floor space and accommodation below. Her " V " counter is just right for cutting rather than slamming down on a sea left after a gale has died away. These conditions are the only ones I know of when a counter is bad, but happily they are seldom met, for it is most uncomfortable to be pitching, tossing, rolling and jumping about in a seaway with no wind. Practically all her ballast is outside in the lead keel, and *Lexia* is most comfortable in a seaway in spite of the fact that many people think outside ballast makes for discomfort.

GOOD SAILING WEATHER

The comfort of her accommodation is rather astonishing, and her owner finds difficulty in living ashore, because *Lexia* is so cosy aboard, but one always expects to find a vessel designed by Shepherd roomy and cosy. Years ago it seemed to me he must design his vessels to a scale one inch to the foot, and then for the accommodation use a three-quarter scale, and I have still that impression, for he seems able to put a quart into a pint mug.

THE SPINNAKER BOOM, SOCKETED INTO A GOOSE-NECK, SQUARES
THE TRYSAIL OFF BEFORE THE WIND

Her small sail area, to balance her rather narrow beam, is made up for by her overlapping headsails, which in light weather increase her sail area without increasing her sail measurement, or making her spars too long for hard weather. *Lexia's* trysail, when dead before the wind, is squared off with the spinnaker boom shipped into a socketed goose-neck, which has a saddle round the mast, and the clew is hauled out by an outhall. Generally a trysail is useless dead before the wind, but with this simple affair, it is quite good, and even if a gybe occurs no damage can be done. A topsail set above the trysail increases the sail area, while still keeping a rig easily worked during a winter passage across the Bay.

· 9 ·

FLAME

Length, overall	-	-	-	63 ft. 6 in.		Length, water-line	-	-	48 ft. 0 in.
Beam	-	-	-	12 ft. 0 in.		Draught	-	-	-	8 ft. 3 in.
Displacement	-	-	-	32 tons		Sail area	-	-	-	2,100 sq. ft.

Owner, CHARLES NICHOLSON   *Designer*, CHARLES NICHOLSON

THE first time *Flame* impressed herself upon my mind was one Monday morning many years ago, when, rigged as a yawl, she came bursting into Portsmouth Harbour before a strong south-westerly wind, and with a flood tide under her, seemed to be going 14 knots over the ground. *Flame* has sailed our seas since 1900, when, as a young man, Charles Nicholson designed and superintended the building of her.

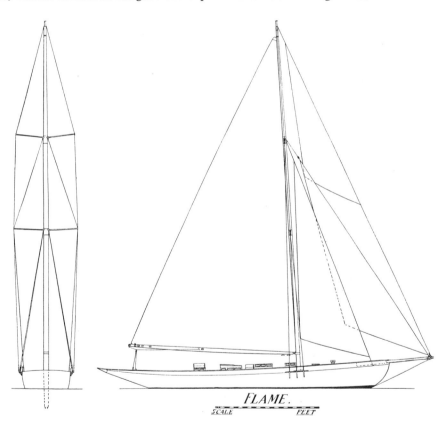

FLAME.
SCALE   FEET

The second time was the summer of 1933, when she was to be England's hope against the American *Dorade*, for although there were four others in the Fastnet Race, these two were the fastest vessels. Strange though it may sound, our hopes were high with *Flame* matched against *Dorade*, for *Flame* had her owner as skipper and Bobby Somerset as navigator, and a pretty good crew as well on board, and she is very much the same type as *Dorade*; or rather *Dorade* (for she was designed 30 years after *Flame* was built) is very much the same type as *Flame*. They

69

are alike in that they are both 3 tons under the normal displacement for their water-line lengths, both are less in beam for their length than the average cruiser, and both have easy bilges and water-lines.

To compare their lines is to see how close the resemblance is between one of the most remarkably fast cruisers of these times and one built during the reign of Good Queen Victoria; and it is a pleasing thought that the likeness conjures up. It shows that if a vessel is well designed and well built, she will not only last a man's lifetime, but will hold her own against much younger vessels; and because of this, it is wise to go to the best designers and builders.

The 1933 Fastnet Race, then, was between two vessels with easy lines and sections, and little wetted surface as a result; and *Flame* with a new Bermudian rig stood a good chance of being the winner. But because of the reputation of the Fastnet Race (previously held in August) for strong winds, *Flame* was measured for sail area to her jib halyards only; and though saving 3 hours of time allowance, she lost her jib topsail, yankee jib topsail and topmast spinnaker, and this was her undoing, for the race was in the fine month of June, and it is not until August that our strong south-west monsoon weather sets in.

All the way round the course the Fastnet racers had light fine weather, and though *Flame* beat the fleet she did not save her time on two boats, for when the allowances were made she came in third to *Dorade* and *Grenadier*, with *Brilliant*, *Lexia*, and *Ilex* behind her.

Had she not cut her area down, she might have won in spite of her age; as it is, her performance is startling, for to

FLAME WAS MEASURED FOR SAIL AREA TO HER JIB HALYARDS, AND SO WAS NOT ALLOWED HER JIB TOPSAIL

lead a fleet of modern vessels for 720 miles at the age of 33 is no small achievement. And to design and build such a vessel as a young man, and then to lead the fleet in her round such a long course so many years later, speaks well of the design and construction of both *Flame* and her owner.

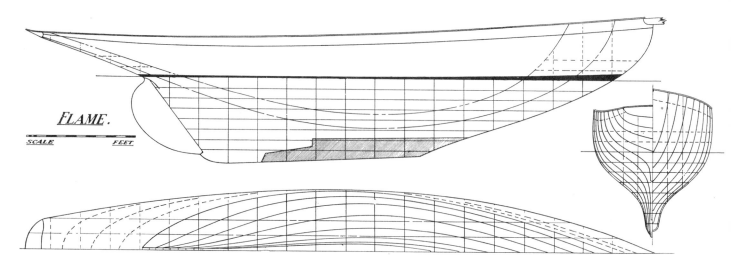

FLAME.

SCALE   FEET

· IO ·

BRILLIANT

Length, overall	-	-	-	61 ft. 6 in.	Length, water-line	-	-	49 ft. 0 in.
Beam -	-	-	-	14 ft. 8 in.	Draught -	-	-	8 ft. 10 in.
Displacement	-	-	-	38¼ tons	Sail area	-	-	2,082 sq. ft.

Owner and Skipper, WALTER BARNUM   *Designer*, OLIN STEPHENS

FOR hard cruising off soundings Walter Barnum wanted a vessel, not only strongly rigged and masted, but also sturdily built, and *Brilliant* is, as a result of these requirements, a boat that can be driven hard without fear of anything falling down from aloft, or a sea straining her deck.

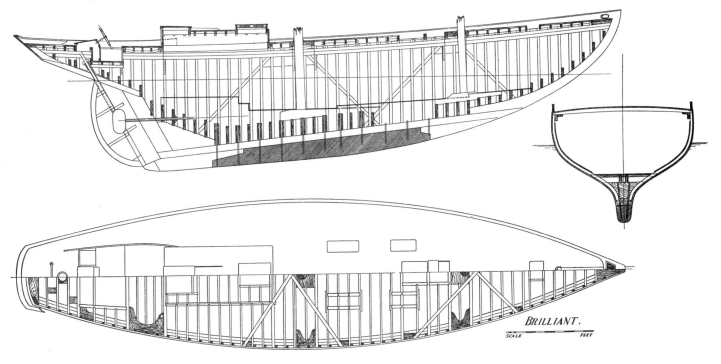

BRILLIANT.

Yet in spite of this she is fast when conditions are right for her, as her passage across to England in June 1933 shows. Most people when they look at heavily built and powerfully lined vessels think that their best speed is in a gale of wind. Under such conditions they appear fast because of the spray flying, but practically every vessel makes its best speed with winds from 25 to 35 miles an hour; above that weight of wind reefing becomes necessary on account of the sea, and if a sailing vessel has not reached her maximum speed when it is blowing 30 miles an hour she is under canvassed.

And although *Brilliant*, to American ideas, seems to have little sail area, to our ideas this is not so, the difference being between the weather and leeside of the Atlantic. American vessels generally have more sail than the English, due to the fact that our winds are generally stronger than those of America in summer. In the faintest of airs heavy vessels will sail and ghost along at an astonishing rate, for at such low speeds their full lines do not hinder them at all. The finer lined vessels show up to advantage when the wind freshens, as their maximum speed is more easily reached.

Brilliant must have had weather to her liking across the Atlantic, for she made the ocean part, from Block Island to the Bishops, in half an hour under 16 days. And the whole from City Island to Plymouth in 17 days 18 hours.

Her best run for five days was made with a southerly wind abeam blowing 25 miles an hour, and in those five days she sailed 1,077 miles; if not the best ever done by a boat that length, it is the best recorded. Averaging over 200 miles a day for five days is seldom the lot of small ocean-going yachts, for conditions must be right, as if

BRILLIANT. THE FASTNET RACE WAS HELD IN JUNE, SO THE WINDS WERE LIGHT

the wind increases so that heavy seas make up steeply then the vessel has to be slowed or hove to, or if the wind falls away she slows up for want of it. The wind has to blow consistently between 20 and 40 miles an hour.

Dorade's best five-day run in the Transatlantic Race of 1931 was 1,013 miles, another average of over 200 a day, which shows that a fine-bottomed craft has a higher speed, or rather more easily reaches her highest speed, for *Dorade* is only three-quarter the length of *Brilliant* on the water-line, and as both were designed on the same drawing board it can be assumed that the lines are of equal merit, the difference being that one set is finer than the other.

Brilliant had sailed across for the Fastnet, but this race was in June and the weather therefore light, when her heavy rig was against her, as was *Lexia's*. Neither of these did well.

On September 3 she sailed for home via Madeira and the North East Trades, and getting winds to her liking reached Madeira in 8 days, averaging 185 miles a day. As, in light weather, we had taken 14 days over this same course in *Diablesse*, the news of this startled me, for I was in America and on Long Island at the time; and bursting into Olin's office at City Island I breathlessly (having run miles) asked him for *Brilliant's* plans for this book, as I was trying to collect the very best designs for it. And he said, " Yes."

From Madeira she took 3 days to Tenerife, and 23 days from there to Bermuda and another six from there to City Island, experiencing good weather all the time, only having to stow her foresail and topsail for six hours in the Gulf Stream, but at Montauk Point she picked up the weather she revelled in, and finished the passage in 10 hours, passing Montauk at 9.30 p.m. and picking up her moorings off City Island at 7.30 a.m. Just 10 knots, a Brilliant end to *Brilliant's* Brilliant cruise.

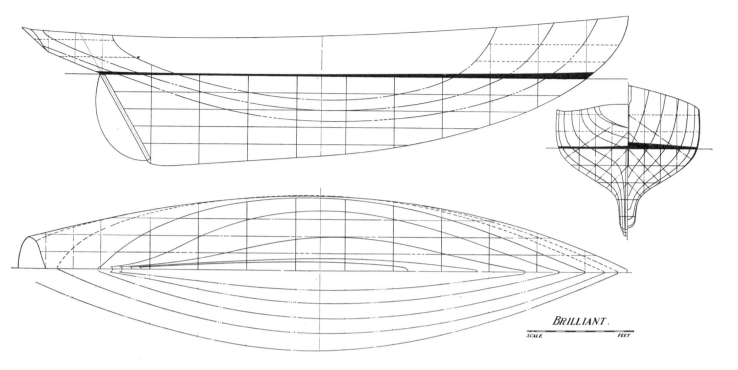

The lines are those of a fast yet very weatherly cruiser, with clean easy buttocks and powerful sections standing out from the rest. These two combined make a fast reaching vessel, the sections giving power to carry sail and the easy buttocks making for high speeds. Her best day's run, when she logged 230 miles, which averages 9·58 knots, was made with a beam wind and shows her ability reaching.

Dorade with her easy sections is at her best to windward and running, all her remarkable days' runs being made with the wind well aft. These records show the effect of the difference between the two sets of lines.

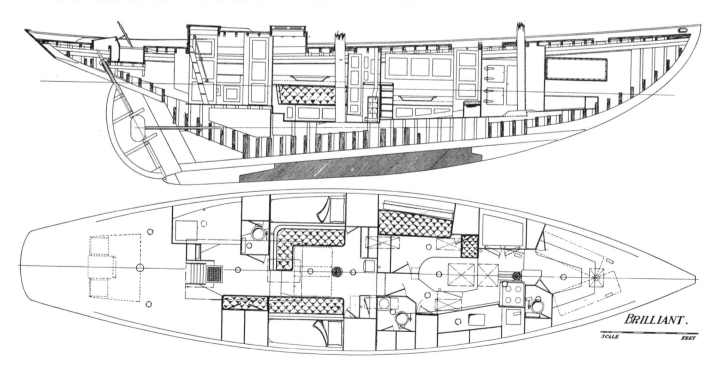

Brilliant has a chart room aft on the port side, a useful and unusual thing in such a small vessel, opposite which are oilskin lockers and a seat. The saloon is forward of this, then comes a single cabin to port, and the wash room to starboard, and the galley divides this from the fo'c'sle.

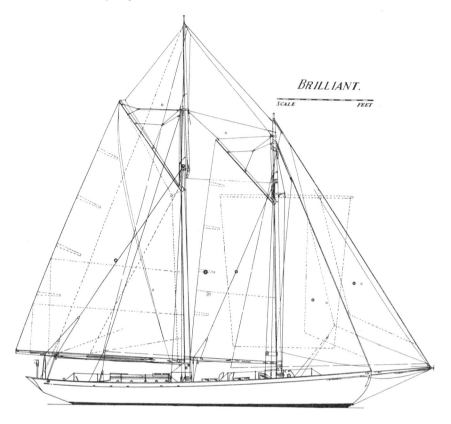

Her area of sail is normal, but divided into a snug and strong schooner rig, which makes her look very seaworthy and workmanlike. Such a rig makes one wish to cruise round the world in *Brilliant*, for any one of her spars could be replaced, in almost any part of the world, although it is very unlikely that any would carry away.

· II ·

GUINEVERE

Length, overall - - - 64 ft. 9 in.		Length, water-line - - 46 ft. 8 in.
Beam - - - - - 14 ft. 0 in.		Draught - - - - 8 ft. 9 in.
Displacement - - - 31¼ tons		Sail area - - - - 2,000 sq. ft.

DESIGNED by Harley Mead as a fast cruising schooner, *Guinevere* looks seaworthy as well as fast, and the buttocks, water-lines and sections all blend together naturally without any hardness. Looking at the sections one sees them changing from the bow to midship and finally to the after sections without any effort or appearance of change ; so when built *Guinevere* will be fast and easy at sea.

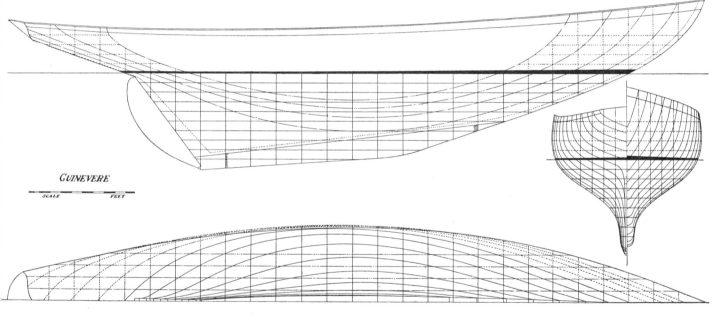

GUINEVERE

SCALE   FEET

Her 12·9 ton lead keel, just 41 per cent. of her displacement, is a nice proportion, and gives power to carry sail without making her stiff and uneasy in her motion, for while outside keels and ballast are undoubtedly right for sailing vessels that go to sea, it must be remembered that one can have too much of a good thing.

The sail plan is that of a strong and fast rig, and this type of schooner is probably the best two-sticked rig with which to go to sea, for in light winds a cloud of canvas can be set from the bowsprit to the main topmast, while in hard weather with the staysail, foresail and main trysail set, the largest sail (the foresail) is the middle one and easily handled, so that the rig has the advantage of a ketch in really bad weather. In a heavy gale *Guinevere* could tuck her head under her wing, and lay quiet under her foresail only with its sheet slightly eased and the helm a-lee, all of which time, because the two masts are stayed together, there is little fear of either carrying away, for they support each other.

The accommodation is excellent. In the fo'c'sle there are two pipe cots, and the W.C. brings to mind the fact that in tending the oil bags on her quarters one of the crew of *Maitenes* was washed overboard in a gale of wind and that a large schooner caught by a heavy gale in the Bay pumped oil through her forward W.C. to damp down the seas. These two things suggest to me the idea that any small vessel intending to use oil for calming the waves in a gale should fit a pair of oil tanks forward, one under the deck on either bow and one under the deck on either

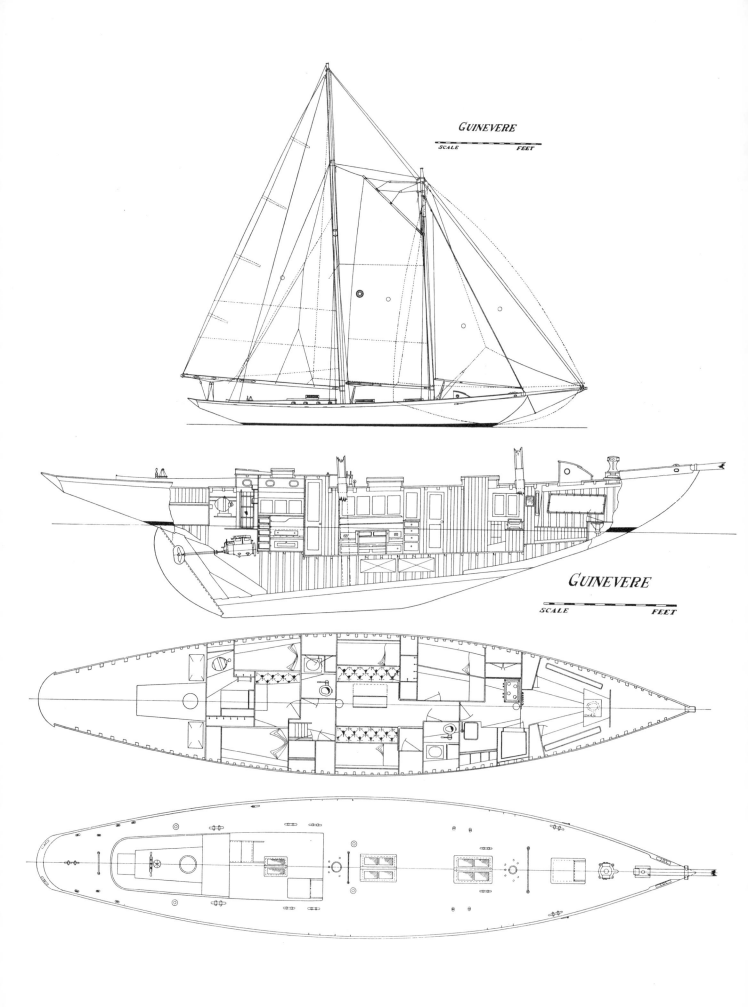

GUINEVERE

SCALE   FEET

GUINEVERE

SCALE   FEET

quarter. Then with a suitable tap the oil would flow quietly for days if needed, as if the tank did run dry it could be refilled from the inside, so that the man doing the job could not be swept overboard. The filling pipe would lead towards the centre of the boat where it could be reached, though the shorter the pipe the less liable to damage and leakage. In *Typhoon* we pumped oil and bilge water (mostly oil) out through the bilge pump as we were heaving-to to our drogue, but the waves took no notice of the oil at all.

Abaft the fo'c'sle is the galley, the full width of the ship, and then comes a single-berthed cabin to port with a wash room to starboard, and the saloon extends from this to the mainmast. The saloon has two settees and built-in berths at the back of them, which is a very comfortable and serviceable arrangement. The companionway, with its oilskin lockers to starboard and another wash room to port, divides the saloon from the double cabin aft, so that *Guinevere* is very comfortable and roomy below decks.

On deck all is clear, as she is flush except for the coach roof aft, which besides giving headroom to the after cabin protects the helmsman in the watertight cockpit.

Altogether, *Guinevere* is a fine little schooner with good lines, well planned, and has a sail plan and rig suitable for all weathers from a calm to a gale.

· 12 ·
DORADE

Length, overall - - - 52 ft. 0 in.	Length, water-line - - 37 ft. 3 in.
Beam - - - - 10 ft. 3 in.	Draught - - - 8 ft. 0 in.
Displacement - - - 14¾ tons	Sail Area - - - 1,100 sq. ft.

Owner and Skipper, OLIN STEPHENS   *Designer*, OLIN STEPHENS

AT least Olin was skipper till 1932 when, having to race his 6-metre *Nancy* in England, he handed *Dorade* over to his brother "Rod", who with her won the Bermuda Race for her class that year. This year he sailed her from America to Norway, down to Cowes, England, and back to America after winning the Fastnet Race.

DORADE

The first time I met *Dorade* was just two days before the start of the Transatlantic Race, 1931, at Newport, Rhode Island. That night we all attended the Dinner given by the Cruising Club of America, and there George Roosevelt, in yarning to me, said that he did not think the club should allow such fragile boats as *Dorade* to race across the Atlantic. As this was only my third visit to America it seemed wrong to disagree with a name like Roosevelt, especially when its owner had a big black mistress, so I said yes and no at what I judged to be the right

78

moments.   Three weeks later, when we all arrived in England, we found this fragile vessel there to meet us. *Dorade* had beaten all her larger rivals, including *Mistress*, by days, so had won the Transatlantic race without calling upon her time allowance.   After this she won the Fastnet Race (1931) almost as nicely, and the sympathy towards the smaller boats began to turn to understanding, and when she sailed across the Atlantic to win the Fastnet again last year (1933) she convinced Committees that smaller boats, well sailed, are far faster than their handicap supposes.   In the light of this understanding it is probable that handicaps will be readjusted.

In looking at the lines of *Dorade* it is well to pause a moment to think of her remarkable record, almost a possible (as we'd say on a rifle range).   1930 second in the Bermuda Race for her class, 1931 won the Transatlantic Race and the Fastnet Race, 1932 won the Bermuda Race for her class, 1933 sailed across the Atlantic, won the Fastnet Race and then sailed back to America.   Her greatest achievement, however, is her return voyage to America this summer : Cowes, England, to Larchmont, America, in 26 days 15 hours.   (This remarkable passage to windward across the Ocean is dealt with in chapters on the North Atlantic.)   Off the wind *Dorade* is as fast as a 10-metre, and to windward half a minute a mile slower, and reaching across the Sound this summer in a smart breeze the 12-metres had difficulty in dropping us astern.   So *Dorade* is fast beyond all doubt, all possible doubt whatever.

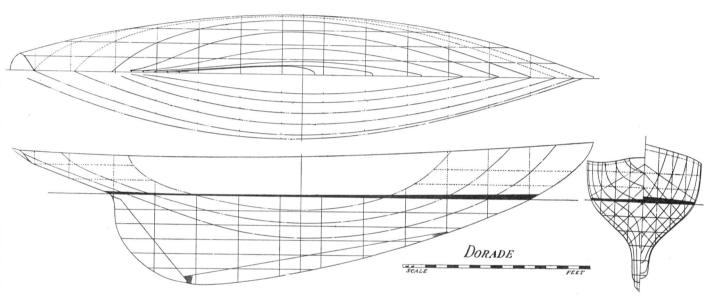

DORADE

SCALE   FEET

It is said that " success is the reward of toil."   I wonder if Olin whilst designing *Dorade* smiled across at his brother, and said, " Rod, we'll alter that to ' Success is the reward of ease.' "   For *Dorade* is easy throughout, her easy sections made for ease in draughting her lines, this in turn made for ease in building, the final result being an easy seaboat, one easily driven and easy on her gear.   She was even more easily driven than her designer anticipated, for after the first year, when she was only second in the Bermuda Race, Olin cut down her mast and rig, thus perfecting *Dorade*, since when she has proved unbeatable with her understanding and seamanlike crew.

The sections are rather like those of our yachts of about 1900, and, to my eye, they appear to be between those of *Flame* by Nicholson of that year, and the old 20-tonners by Mylne.   For some years I owned an old schooner with a section similar to *Dorade*'s in that her rise of floor amidships was 45 degrees, and that she was also a narrow vessel.   So that when I first sailed aboard *Dorade* I felt quite at home, being used to a narrow easy-sectioned boat that fell over to a certain angle easily and then became stiff ; the likeness ending here, for my schooner was slow.

Dorade's ends are not chopped off, the bow and stern being the natural ending of her lines, and these overhangs help in a seaway when they increase her effective length from 37 to 52 ft., thus increasing her natural speed and fore and aft stability.   Her deep draught partially compensates for her narrow beam, and is an advantage to windward.

Dorade does not come to the ideal proportions for cruisers, as given in the chapter on that subject, and so is very instructive.   Her narrow beam is balanced by her deep draught, her light displacement by a small sail area, and her narrow floor space forces her freeboard higher, for headroom.

The yawl rig was chosen for handicap purposes ; without her mizen *Dorade* would still rate the same, so as, under the rule, the mizen with its staysail is free, it is well worth having.   Such a mizen is of little value dead before the wind, for besides spoiling the clean run of wind into the mainsail and spinnaker, it tends to drive the vessel into

DORADE IN THE TRANSATLANTIC RACE, 1931

JULY 15, 1931; DAY'S RUN 205 MILES
From the pictures by R. F. PATERSON)

the wind; while to windward, because it is in the dirty wind off the mainsail, it has to be sheeted so tightly that it has little forward drive. However, reaching in light to strong winds, the mizen, with its staysail, is a great driver, and when the wind is really strong *Dorade*, with her mizen stowed, will steer far more easily than a cutter, for her boom is so short.

The double headsail rig makes for ease in handling in hard weather, for by hauling the staysail to weather *Dorade* will slow down, and her crew, waiting till her speed has dropped to 3 knots, quietly change jibs or do

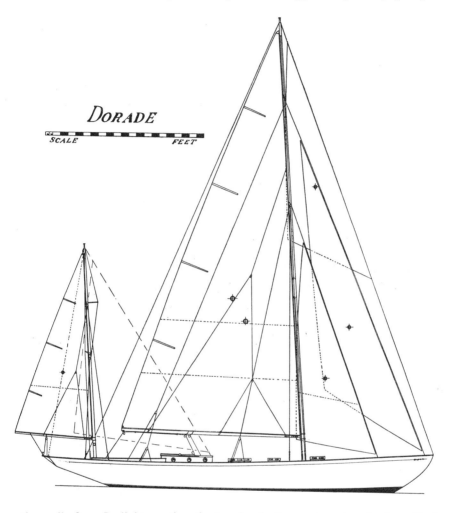

whatever the weather calls for. In light weather the two headsails are stowed and a large Yankee jib topsail set from the stem to the masthead, thus filling in the whole of the fore triangle. This sail was the only unhandy thing aboard *Dorade*, for in tacking we had to pass it between the jib and the jibtopsail stays, where there was only 18 in. of space on deck. About 1860 our square-rigged merchantmen changed from large single to double topsails, as they were so much easier to handle if split in two. *Dorade's* double headsails do for her what the double topsails did for the square-rigged merchantmen. Not only is it easier to set two, sheet two, or change two smaller sails, but a boat is often able by simply stowing one small sail, to carry on through a squall and re-set it immediately afterwards. The ease with which *Dorade* is handled was impressed upon me last summer, when standing ashore at Oyster Bay, I saw Rod sail her in single handed, pick up his mooring, stow sails and jump into the International 14-footer *Arrow*, which his confederate, Porter Buck, had meanwhile sailed out alongside, all within 8 minutes. And to crown this, the *Arrow* won.

Although merchantmen the world over adopted the double topsail our Men-of-War did not as, having ample man power, they did not have to study ease in handling sails.

Dorade rolled when running, but this was largely cured last summer, before she left Cowes for America, when a balance reef was put in, running from the tack to 3 ft. above the clew; this must have kept her mainsail from going forward of the mast aloft when the main sheet was eased, for she rolled much less. It also prevented the boom from tripping in the sea when running, and Rod thinks this reef might even have been 4 ft. deep at the clew.

The mainsheet leading off the centre of the boom tends to prevent it lifting when the sheet is started. The fault of the modernised Bermudian rig lies in the fact that when the sheet is started, instead of the boom squaring off as it does in the gaff rig, the sail aloft falls away, and it is usual to see this tall rig with the mainsail squared off on to the crosstrees, while the main boom is still at 45 degrees. (For weight of canvas see Chapter on Sails.)

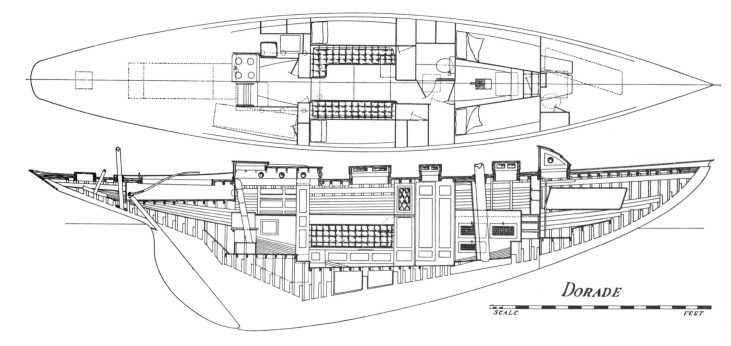

DORADE

SCALE   FEET

Her mast is well rigged fore and aft, forward there are three stays, jibtopsail, jib and staysail, and there are three backstays each straining aft from the points on the mast where the corresponding stay pulls forward. The drift of the backstays aft is good, that taking the pull of the staysail being the same distance abaft the mast as the forestay is forward. The jib and jibtopsail backstays have even more drift aft than the base of the foretriangle, and so it is that *Dorade's* mast stands perfectly straight no matter how hard she is pressed. This in turn gives head-sails with luffs that stand and a nicely-setting mainsail.

Wire halyards and winches did away with the necessity for setting the halyards up every watch, and winches taking the load off the sheets enable one man to trim sheets down instead of three; she had twelve winches all told. The same cruising yachtsman who scorns the winches on an Ocean Racer admires and praises the handiness of a Thames barge, losing sight of the fact that it is only the winches aboard that enable two men to handle these 100-ton vessels.

The fo'c'sle with its single cot is used as a sail room, as *Dorade* has always carried an all-amateur crew; abaft this is the fore-cabin with two berths, which are faced with plaited gratings for ventilation. A wash room to port and a locker and bookcase to starboard divide this cabin from the saloon, which has two sleeping berths with settees in front. The saloon table at one time had its legs upon the floor, which with *Dorade's* narrow floor-space (2 ft. 8 in.), gave little leg-room for the crew. This year the table legs were inverted and made fast to the deckbeams, turning the tables upon the swing table, for it altered it from an unstable table into a stable table, the legs down from the deck forming perfect life rails.

Abaft the saloon to port is the galley, in its right and proper place on a small boat, for here it is near the centre of the see-saw, where the motion is least. Opposite the galley is the chart table with its electric log and compass, enabling the navigator to tell exactly the course and speed without enquiring of the man at the helm. This log is also easily read from the tiller, and it gave my vanity a nasty shock, for, before steering *Dorade* with her tell-tale log, I fondly imagined that I took a boat quite nicely to windward. The art of steering to windward lies in holding the boat high yet footing fast; *Dorade's* best was four points off the wind and just over 6 knots. And sitting steering her, I saw that log dropping down as low as $5\frac{3}{4}$ knots without my feeling that I was starving her of wind, or the compass showing that I had pinched her above her best course.

That fine point where the last ounce is coaxed out of a boat to windward is very difficult to define. Hence it is, no doubt, that boats go some days better than others : the helmsman is able, without effort, to hit off this point exactly and sail a wonderful race. On other days, instead of winning he comes in well down the list, quite

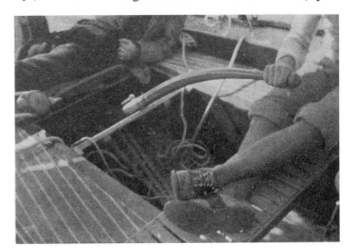

Above : DORADE'S TILLER LOCK

Left : DORADE DID NOT HAVE A PIANO,
" ROD " SUPPLIED THE MUSIC.

convinced that something is wrong with his boat. How often we hear the expression " My boat would not go to-day," when it should be " I could not get my boat to go to-day." Yacht owners, who claim the credit when they win and blame their boats when they lose, remind me of my young days, for when I was naughty my father would say to mother, " That nipper of yours ——," but when I won medals he'd say, " My son, etc., etc."

Dorade's small tiller shows that she is easy on her helm, and proves her to be a well-balanced boat. The tiny lever seen half-way down the tiller locks and unlocks it in an instant, and the duckboard stretched across the cockpit

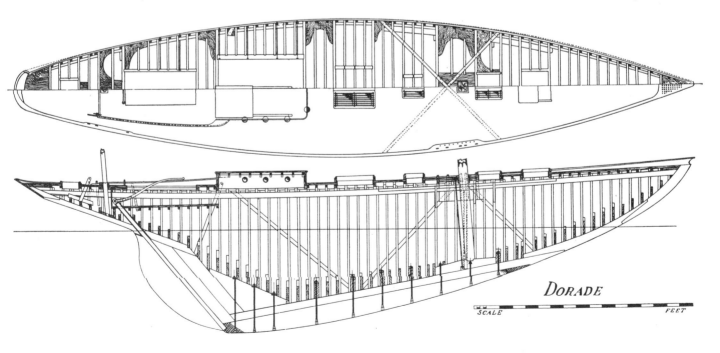

DORADE

SCALE   FEET

makes steering an easy job. The tiller has a rather surprised expression as it peeps out from under the deck upon the world. This is caused by the mizen mast, which forces the rudder post to be cut off short, as can be seen from the plan.

This year *Dorade's* ventilators were improved, for where they originally led directly below, they now lead into a box on deck, from which the air is taken below by another pipe standing several inches above the deck. When a wave is taken down the ventilator it partly fills the box and escapes through tiny scuppers, without rising above the level of the pipe leading below. Therefore water cannot find its way below unless two seas are shipped down the ventilator in rapid succession, and this, so far, has not occurred.

The beams run right across under the skylight, making the deck very strong and easy to keep watertight. Farther aft, however, the deck beams cannot run clear across, as the coach roof is built here to give headroom in the galley and protect the helmsman in the cockpit.

" ROD " LOOKING BACK. MIZEN STOWED

In this description of *Dorade* I have tried to make it clear that her ability and success does not lie so much in any special point, but in the perfection of every detail. The comfort of the helmsman, his being able to read on the log directly he starves her on the wind, the position of the galley, the ease with which the navigator can work, the staying of the mast all help to make *Dorade* such an able little ship. And she has always had a crew to match this perfection.

· 13 ·

ROSEMARY

Length, O.A.	-	-	-	52 ft. 0 in.	Length, L.W.L.	-	-	36 ft. 0 in.
Beam -	-	-	-	12 ft. 0 in.	Draught -	-	-	7 ft. 0 in.
Displacement	-	-	17 tons	Sail area -	-	-	1,400 sq. ft.

Owner and Skipper, ISAAC BELL   *Designer*, WILLIAM FIFE

THE race round the Isle of Wight on June 17, 1933, held by the Island Sailing Club, showed me that *Rosemary* was beyond all doubt a fast and seaworthy vessel, for she won this race under her trysail after her mainsail had been blown away.

ROSEMARY WINNING UNDER TRYSAIL AFTER BLOWING AWAY HER MAINSAIL

The start was at 8.00 a.m., with the wind W.N.W., strong enough to cause quite a sea, as it was against the ebb tide ; and the fleet started under shortened sail for the beat to the Needles.

As helmsman of *Daedalus*, a sixty-year-old cutter, of the Itchen Ferry type, sturdy, but slow to windward in a lop, I gazed with envy and admiration at *Rosemary* sailing a point higher in the wind and travelling three miles to our two, as she sailed out from under our lee and was soon hull down ahead, never expecting for a moment to see her again till we had finished our fifty-four mile race, and were safely back at Cowes.

We had a full mainsail, staysail and jib, and although no topsail, had all the sail we could carry, but in spite of this *Daedalus* seemed slow, for every time her bow rose to a sea her stern dropped and dragged dead water. She would have travelled faster through the water under the North Shore where the tide was less and so the sea calmer, but not so fast over the ground, so we kept her to the Island side of the Solent, where the tides run stronger and seas steeper.

The tides round the Island play an important part in navigation, whether racing or cruising, and they cannot be studied too much. In the matter of speed they are twice as important as they seem at first; for instance a boat sailing at 6 knots with a 4-knot tide with her is travelling over the ground at 10 knots, but if she is going at 6 knots against a 4-knot tide she is only doing 2 knots, which makes 8 knots difference in speed over the ground, double that at first supposed.

Out in the Channel the flood tide runs to the east and the ebb to the west, and so it is in the Solent, but through Spithead, between Bembridge and Cowes, there is a different stream, for the last part of the ebb and the first half of the flood run eastward, while the last of the flood and the first of the ebb run to the westward.

As everywhere else in the world, the tide is weaker along the shore; most bays, if deep, have eddy tides running directly opposite to the main tide, and for this reason the tide turns an hour or two earlier in these bays and near the shore. Because the tides are so strong and regular, a yacht sailing round the Isle of Wight has no need of an engine, for if worked properly these tides will take her where she would go without any fuss or effort. For instance, a small yacht could drop out of Yarmouth Harbour on the last of the ebb, which, taking her out past the pier would put her into the young flood, and this taking her to Cowes at 3 knots would save any engine work at all in a calm.

The block of tidal charts will illustrate the direction of the streams but not the strength. The general strength is 3 to 4 knots, but past headlands and through the narrows of Hurst, the speed is naturally increased, yet nowhere to above 6 knots, although the streams boiling and tearing through Hurst and past St. Catherine's and the Needles seem to be travelling at double that speed.

Rosemary too worked this strong tide, but her overhangs were of the greatest help to her in the sea, holding her steady fore and aft, for as soon as she tried to drop her bow and stern her sailing length increased and prevented her doing so.

And so we fought our way down to the Needles, where there was such a steep sea running over the Bridge and through the Needles Channel that in *Daedalus* we eased our main sheet right off, and sailed her at about 3 knots with only the headsails drawing, as charging into the steep seas she seemed intent on bursting both headsails, for she dipped them into solid water. *Mermaid*, a much larger vessel than *Daedalus*, alongside and to windward, did not ease anything; she buried her jib in a sea heavier than most, and away went both jib and bowsprit. So she had a fine mess to clear up forward. For the bowsprit, held by the wire shrouds and bobstay, tried hard to punch holes in her bow, and it was with great difficulty and a certain amount of danger of being swept overboard, that *Mermaid's* crew at last tidied up the broken gear as she ran back into the Solent.

The *Enid*, some ten minutes astern, plunging into the steep breakers off the Needles Channel, burst open her garboards, and was at once filled above her floorboards. She turned back and ran into Alum Bay, whilst her crew bailed hard with buckets in order to keep her afloat. They just managed to get into the bay before she foundered in 15 ft., where she lay with her spars showing above the water until the seas battered her to pieces.

This was at 10.00 a.m. In *Daedalus* we rounded the Bridge Buoy and squared away for St. Catherine's, only to find that the strong ebb on our bow pushed us seawards, so we had to gybe to get into the easier tide of Brook Bay; all the crew were against this manœuvre because of the sea, but we were racing, and as I had the tiller there was little hesitation or argument, for they were too busy with backstays to talk, and we were soon in the slack water under the land and gaining rapidly on everyone, even *Rosemary*, for we were the only boat to gybe and take advantage of the slacker water. Off shore the strong ebb would run for at least another two hours, so whilst we in *Daedalus* were foaming along at 7 knots with a fair tide of 1 knot, thus travelling 8 knots over the ground, *Rosemary* was doing 9 knots against a 3 knot tide, and thus only 6 knots over the ground. In addition to this we had the wind and tide together, and so could carry a spinnaker, though when it was set I had to call for help on the tiller.

So we came to St. Catherine's, *Daedalus* being second to round with only *Rosemary* in front. We were well within our time allowance, and would have felt very sprightly had the wind shown any sign of shifting S.W., and so altering the beat from Bembridge Ledge to Cowes into a reach, for with that long beat against the tide we knew that *Rosemary* would lose us again. On the run across to St. Catherine's, *Guenora*, who not only had her topsail stowed but also two reefs in her mainsail, showed how easily a boat could run if not driven, for although a much faster vessel, she was now only travelling at our speed and sailing along as quietly as a lamb, whilst we in *Daedalus* had two men on the tiller all the time our spinnaker was set.

On the reach across Sandown Bay *Rosemary* and *Otter* sailed away from us, and we rounded Bembridge Ledge third, with that dreaded beat in front of us, during which we knew *Daedalus* could not do well against the boats with overhangs, which would aid them in a seaway.

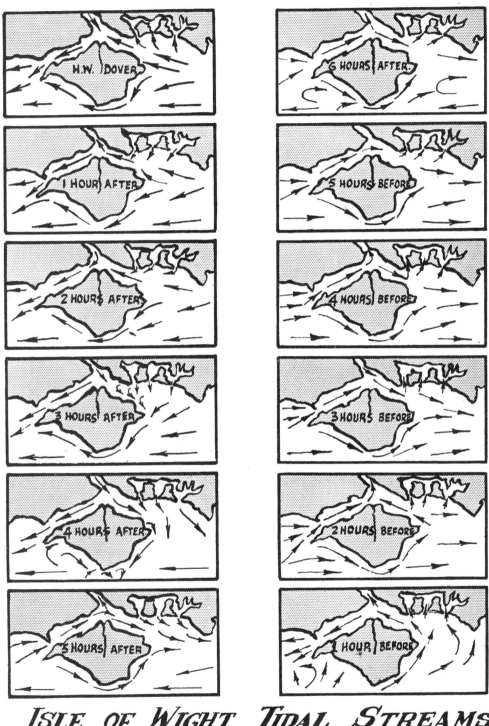

ISLE OF WIGHT TIDAL STREAMS

By the time we were beating through the Forts *Rosemary* was off Ryde Pier, and down came the strongest squall of the day ; it split *Rosemary's* mainsail right across from luff to leach, blew in half *Guenora's* jib just to leeward of us, but did not affect *Daedalus* except to stun her, for instead of going faster in the increased wind she slowed. This was probably due to the fact that watching the water to windward, we had seen this squall bearing down on us, and were ready, so when it struck us I sailed *Daedalus* along as fine as possible, starving the sails of wind as much as I could without letting them shake, for one shake and a sail would have split in that wind, just as it would have done if given the full weight of it.

ROSEMARY.

SCALE   FEET.

Slowly we tacked very short boards all along the sands, and weathering Ryde Pier were able to ease the tide, and making better progress finished fifth to *Rosemary, Felise, Otter,* and *Guenora.*

We had the satisfaction of knowing that in such strong weather the four ahead were all much faster vessels, as were many astern of *Daedalus.*

Rosemary had won a wonderful race, and the fact that she was able not only to hold but to increase her lead under her storm trysail, which she had set after her mainsail had split off Ryde Pier, shows the strength of the wind and also the ability of *Rosemary.*

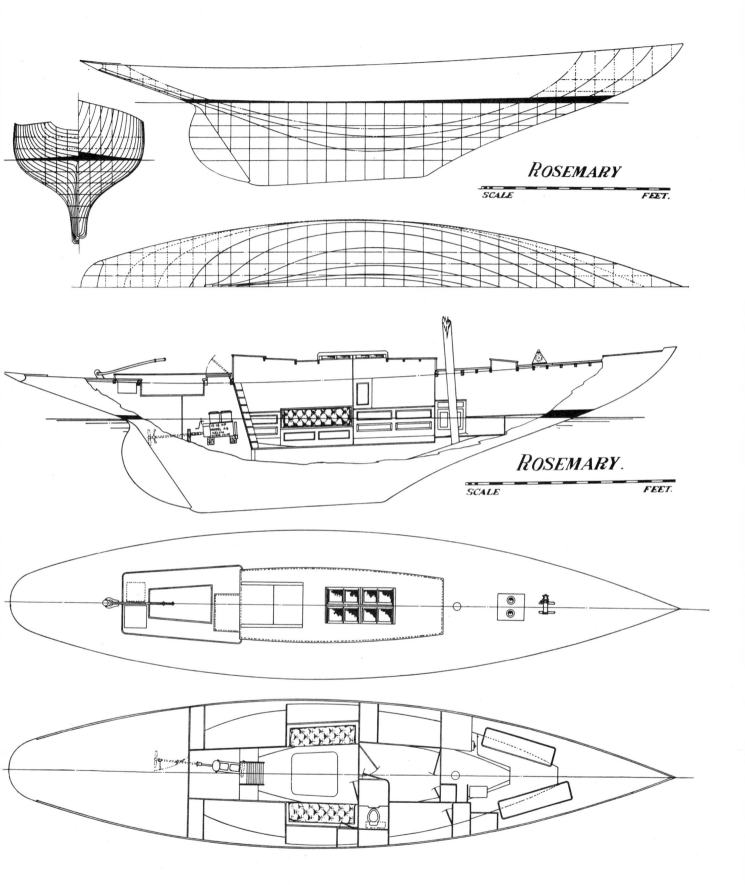

ROSEMARY

SCALE   FEET.

ROSEMARY.

SCALE   FEET.

Rosemary's lines are perfectly balanced, as are all Fife's designs, and looking at them it is easy to understand why *Daedalus* had two men on the tiller, whilst one man was steering *Rosemary* with the greatest of ease, though she was farther off the shore in a steeper and heavier sea, and travelling through the water at nine knots.

These lines are the only example of Fife's work in this book, and coming from such a great designer's board they are interesting and instructive. With no rule to hamper his brain, Fife has turned out a beautiful vessel, and one that, besides having grace and speed, is very seaworthy. Soon after this race round the island her owner asked me aboard as crew for a long distance race, and I found *Rosemary* a very easily handled and most comfortable vessel at sea.

In the fo'c'sle she has two pipe berths and the galley, next abaft this is a double-berthed cabin, and the wash room, then comes the light and airy saloon, which is very roomy, and aft of this are two sleeping berths.

Her sail plan is very simple and effective, for the single headsail is very easy to control and the main boom, coming inside the end of the counter, gives a mainsail that is easily set, reefed, gybed or taken in.

The decks are fairly clear and free from gear with such a simple rig, for every sail and mast put into a sailing vessel means so many more halyards, sheets, shrouds and other gear, and *Rosemary's* two sails reduce all these things to a minimum.

Altogether *Rosemary* is a fine example of the designer's and shipwright's art.

· I4 ·

ETAIN

Length, overall	-	-	-	46 ft. o in.	Length, water-line	-	-	31 ft. o in.
Beam	-	-	-	9 ft. o in.	Draught	-	-	6 ft. 6 in.
Displacement	-	-	10 tons	Sail area	-	-	-	814 sq. ft.

Owner, MARJORIE GOODSON   *Designer*, LAURENT GILES

AS it is so seldom that a Naval Architect designs for a lady owner, such a design is bound to be out of the ordinary and therefore interesting, for although we poor men think that generally women have no idea of what they want, they most often not only know what they want, but get it. And in *Etain* Miss Goodson has exactly what

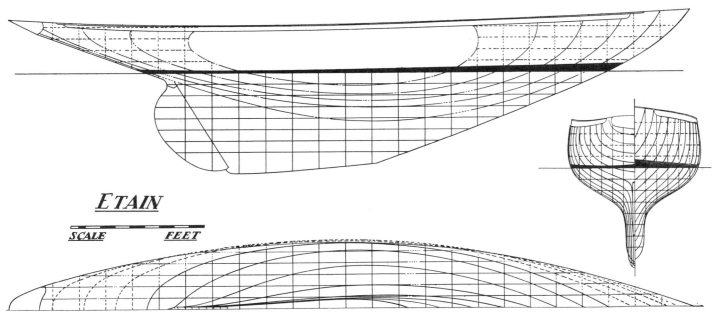

ETAIN

SCALE   FEET

she desired; for she explained to the designer that, having ridden blood horses, she was not going to sea in a hack, and that the 8-metres designed to the International Yacht Racing Rule appealed to her, but having first of all considered converting an 8-metre into a cruiser she thought a far better result would be obtained by designing a cruiser right away on those lines.

And so we see a young lady with very definite ideas and proposals approaching an architect, and there is no doubt that when owners have such a clear and sharp picture of their vessel it is a great help to the designer, for in this case he knew that he had to design a seagoing 8-metre with good accommodation, a fast, easily handled, and weatherly vessel.

The lines show how well the idea was carried out, for *Etain* is a cruising 8-metre, and with her liveliness and responsiveness is delightful to sail. The sail plan, with 524 square feet in the mainsail and 390 in the fore triangle, making a total of 814 square feet, is so well balanced that *Etain* will sail herself, and as the mainsail is within the strength of one man she is an ideal singlehander for the man who wants a thoroughbred, with the speed of the racer blended with the accommodation of a cruiser.

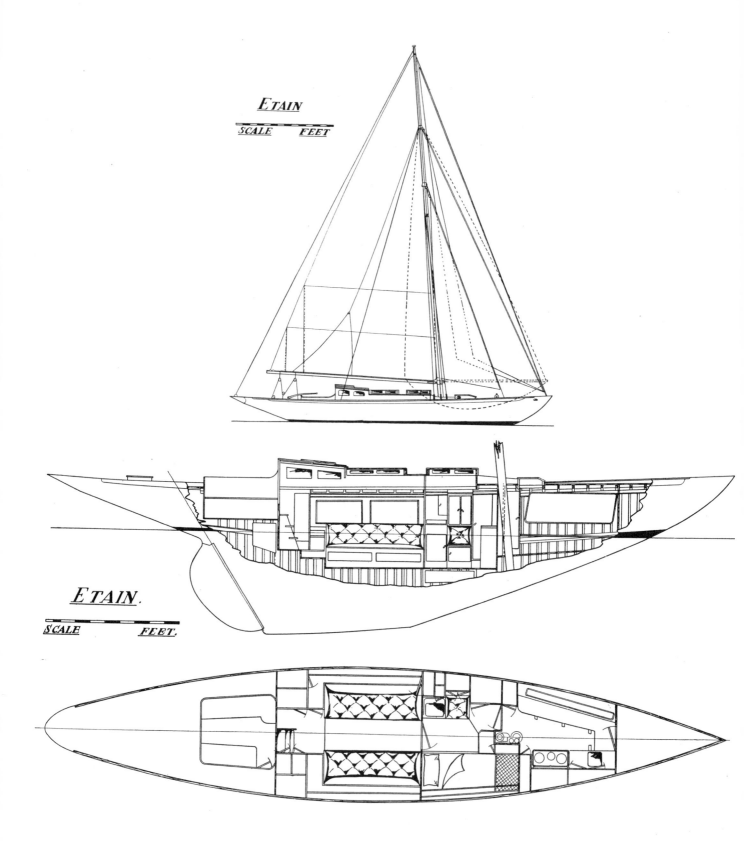

ETAIN

SCALE   FEET

ETAIN.

SCALE   FEET.

The fo'c'sle has a single folding cot and also the galley, and practically has the mainmast too. In the days gone by the fo'c'sle always had the mast, but owners and designers generally now shift the bulkhead forward, so that the mast comes into the fore cabin or saloon, the extra room thus given there making up for its squeaks and groans when the vessel is driven hard or rolling in a seaway becalmed.

Abaft the fo'c'sle is the owner's stateroom the full width of the vessel, and bearing in mind the lady owner, one expects to find this very cosy and stately, and it is, being complete in every detail, bunk with drawers under, two wardrobes, dressing table, book case, lockers, a wash basin and a W.C. skilfully hidden under the seat alongside the wash basin.

ETAIN

At sea *Etain* has proved comfortable as well as fast and able to look after herself, in spite of the fact that so many look upon such a vessel as useless for cruising. Many cruising men think that the heaving to is a question of forefoot, whereas it is really a matter of sail balance, for when on a passage in a 6-metre and in *Vigilant*, both of which have far less forefoot than *Etain*, I have hove them to for an hour or so while cooking and eating a good hot meal, and this in quite a strong wind and heavy sea. Generally if a vessel will sail herself she will heave to for she is balanced, in hull and rig.

Etain looked upon as a cruiser must give a shock to many, but if they can read the chapters on *Vigilant's* cruise to Sweden and back they will then come back to *Etain* and think what a comfortable vessel; with the galley shifted aft *Etain* would make even more comfortable passages at sea.

· 15 ·

DRIAC

Length, overall	-	-	-	40 ft. 0 in.	Length, water-line	-	-	30 ft. 6 in.
Beam	-	-	-	10 ft. 0 in.	Draught	-	-	6 ft. 3 in.
Displacement	-	-	13½ tons		Sail area	-	-	870 sq. ft.

Owner and Skipper, A. G. H. Macpherson   *Designer,* Charles Nicholson

IN 1931 the Royal Cruising Club awarded their Challenge Cup to *Driac* and her owner for her cruise of 5,000 miles from Portsmouth to Malta and along the shores of the Mediterranean and home to Portsmouth and so acknowledged that this was the best cruise of that year.

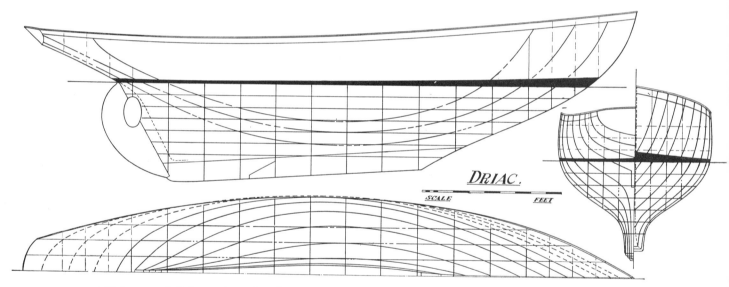

DRIAC.

SCALE   FEET

This proved *Driac* to be a fine little cruiser, seaworthy and weatherly, for she met strong winds and gales generally ahead, and had it not been for her good windward qualities she would have spent almost twice the time she did on the cruise. Off Ortegal (Spain) she weathered on September 19 the gale that farther north did so much damage to the French tunny fleet, many of them foundering; and the tunny fishermen have fine great wholesome ships, designed and built to fish off shore, in the Bay of Biscay, one of the worst spots in the world.

Driac's lines, like those of *Patience* and *Flame*, also by Charles Nicholson, are easy and sweeping without any hardness, and she has the same full garboards of these two vessels, which besides cutting down wetted surface (which tells so much in beating to windward) give good floor space, so necessary to good accommodation. Her beam, as it naturally should be, in a smaller vessel, is greater in proportion to her length than her larger sisters, for a smaller vessel requires more stability and power from her section; but generally her lines are very like those of *Patience* and *Flame*.

The Bermudian cutter rig, with 483 square feet in the mainsail, is just about as large as could be handled by one man in all weathers; for although a man could handle a larger sail in moderate weather he could not in a gale. The bowsprit following the sheer line steeves upwards, which besides looking pretty is a good thing, for when driving into a head sea a sailing vessel takes heavy water into her headsails, and this, apart from putting heavy and unfair strains upon the mast and sails, often carries away the bowsprit, which, pounding against the bow, might easily punch a hole before it could either be stowed aboard or cut adrift. The wind flogging the jib and bowsprit about,

DRIAC.

SCALE   FEET

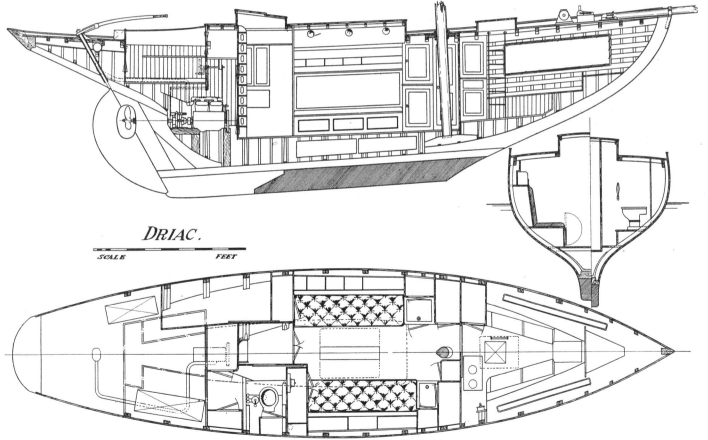

DRIAC.

SCALE   FEET

and the seas helping to liven things up might easily turn such an accident into a tragedy. When sailing through the Needles Passage on one occasion I saw a sailing vessel carry away her bowsprit, and after trying in vain to stow it on a wind, she ran back before the wind, and then was able to, for the jib was becalmed behind the mainsail. There were very steep seas running at the time, and I had slackened the main sheet right away in the boat I was steering, and even with only her jib and staysail drawing she went too fast into those seas for my liking, for I was afraid of the bowsprit going. When I looked astern at this other vessel I knew that I was right in coaxing this large cruiser through those seas, as though she had been an open dinghy. Once clear of the Needles the seas were longer and easier.

Below decks *Driac* has a fo'c'sle with two cots, and abaft this a fine saloon, and a single cabin aft on the port side opposite the wash room. The steering is by tiller, and the helmsman sits in a deep cockpit, *Driac's* owner preferring the shelter of the latter to the safety afforded to the ship by the shallower self-draining cockpit, out of which the helmsman might easily be washed or pitched overboard.

And there is much to be said for both cockpits.

There are no skylights to leak, as light and air are let in through ports in the side of the square coach roof, and as these are upright the water does not lay on them and soak through.

DRIAC

When hove to for gales generally only the close-reefed mainsail or trysail was set. She rode out one gale off Falmouth under her close-reefed mainsail only, when the wind recorded at Falmouth was 70 miles an hour ; so *Driac* and her rig are well worthy of study, and the time will soon be here when we shall look upon the tall efficient Bermudian rig as the normal rig for hard-cruising vessels, in spite of its tall naked look when close reefed. At the moment, although I've crossed the Atlantic with tall hollow Bermudian spars, I am not at all sure of their ability to ride out a long heavy gale at sea, for a collapse of any one member, a shroud or crosstree, might easily lead to the whole lot carrying away.

However, *Driac's* designer, her owner, and she herself help us all in our search for the ideal cruiser and rig, as she is so near to perfection, with her seaworthiness, comfort and speed.

· 16 ·

TWILIGHT

Length, overall - - - 28 ft. 0 in.		Length, water-line - - 27 ft. 6 in.	
Beam - - - - - 9 ft. 0 in.		Draught - - - - 5 ft. 10 in.	
Displacement - - - 7 tons		Sail area - - - - 670 sq. ft.	

FALMOUTH Quay Punts are without doubt weatherly vessels, for, as they were designed as handmaidens to the sailing ships calling at Falmouth for orders, they had to brave the wind and sea, summer and winter, between the ship and the quay, and when without a job they went seeking a ship away down channel.

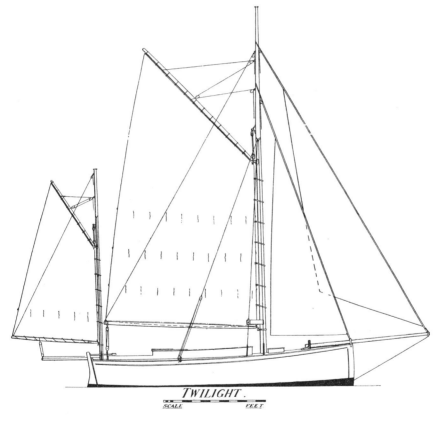

TWILIGHT.
SCALE   FEET

Their mainmasts were cut off at the upper peak halyard block, to enable them to clear the yard arms of the ships they served. The lines and sail plan of *Twilight* illustrate the characteristics of this type of vessel.

So Spot and I, journeying to Norway to sail *Twilight* home to Cowes, had no fears as to her seaworthiness and ability to take what came in the way of weather, although some Norwegian friends, not used to this type of vessel, were doubtful of her ability.

On the way to Norway our steamer met a heavy gale from the north-east, which delayed her some hours, and as this gale was still blowing when we arrived at Kristiansand, we waited three days for it to ease down, for whereas at sea a small vessel manfully rides it out, it is wrong to start out in a gale, and Marine Insurance Companies of small vessels would, I think, be within their rights if they refused to pay insurance on a small vessel that, without just cause, put to sea in a full gale.

And so we waited, and on Thursday, April 29, 1926, put to sea at 5.00 p.m. with three reefs in the mainsail, a reef in the staysail, and our jib and mizen unrigged and stowed below in the fo'c'sle. The driving sails are those in the centre, and not at the ends of a vessel, and even with this small amount of sail *Twilight* had all she could carry, for there was still plenty of weight in the wind, and a high sea running from four days of a hard gale that was only just starting to ease.

In the first 24 hours we travelled 125 miles, and considering the sea running and the overall length of our vessel, this pleased us. Day followed day, and still it blew hard and cold from the north-east, and coming down to the Dutch coast we headed in for the *Terschelling Light Ship* on Saturday afternoon to check our position. The sunset looked wicked, and fearing an on-shore gale from the north-west, I let her go on out to sea again without sighting the *Terschelling*, so that, when the gale arrived, we should be able to drive away before it for days if necessary without fear of that lee shore.

We drove and drove her out towards the centre of the North Sea. Besides the three reefs in the mainsail the gaff jaws had been lowered on to the main boom, so that we only showed a small triangle of mainsail and the stay-sail. Even with this small amount of sail we were travelling so fast that *Twilight* trembled throughout as she rushed down the face of the seas.

At 3.00 a.m. Spot yelled for help, as he could not hold her on her course, and jumping out of my bunk to his assistance, I was just in time to see a huge sea curling in over the stern the height of our mizen mast. We were pooped, and very heavily; I was knocked backwards into the cabin but not hurt, and was soon on deck stowing the rest of the mainsail, after which *Twilight* with only her staysail set was easier to steer.

Turning in again I left Spot at the helm, still fighting to clear the Dutch coast. Later that night, with only the staysail on her, she started pulling seas aboard again over her transom, so we streamed the drogue out aft, and, lashing the tiller, let her drive very slowly before the gale, which was fortunately due north, so that we could by now drive the full length of the North Sea from the north of Holland to France without fear of land.

We took turns watching for ships that might run us down till daylight, when we both turned in for the day. That heavy sea we had taken aboard had, in spite of her self-bailing cockpit, filled her above the level of the bunks, but we slept in wet clothes and bedding without harm, although it was bitterly cold. After laying to our drogue for 24 hours, during which time no really heavy water came aboard, we were able to haul it in and drive on under staysail only for some hours, when the wind easing still more allowed us to show the peak of our mainsail.

In a gale of wind a small vessel can either heave to under sail or lay to a drogue, generally referred to as a sea anchor by yachtsmen, but always as a drogue by our lifeboatmen, who look upon it as the most important part of their equipment. In days gone by the sea anchor meant the anchor to seaward and the shore anchor the anchor nearest the shore; but yachtsmen all over the world have adopted, rightly or wrongly, the words sea anchor for drogue, and so throughout this book the words sea anchor mean drogue.

Aboard *Typhoon* in November 1920 we tried to heave to bow on to a sea anchor, putting a terrific strain on the warp without once laying head to wind. It is easy to understand why a boat will not lay bow on to a sea anchor, for in the hull there is far more windage forward through higher freeboard, and there is also far more windage in spars and rigging aloft forward, both tending to blow her bow off, while under water she has a deep heel aft, her fore foot is generally cut away, so everything is against her laying head to wind.

Typhoon's behaviour convinced me of the folly of trying to heave to head to wind and sea, and I decided that the next time I was caught in a fair gale and unable to run on before it any longer I would stream the sea anchor astern. And *Twilight* justified my convictions, laying quietly with hardly any strain upon her sea anchor, beside which the warp over the stern was clear, and so had nothing to chafe on, such as bowsprit and bobstay.

To my mind in a gale ahead a vessel should heave to under sails when she will, however slowly, proceed on her course, while with a gale astern she should stream a sea anchor aft when the gale will drive her on her way.

Later on the wind eased enough to allow us to set our three-reefed mainsail, and once more we sailed gaily for Cowes. On Tuesday afternoon we reckoned to sight the South Foreland in half an hour, and we saw it within twenty minutes. After five days at sea this seemed good, but navigation in the North Sea in clear weather is not difficult, and we had been able to take a noon sight for latitude every day but the one on which the sun had not shown through, and as we had not seen any land since Norway we knew we must be running near the middle of the North Sea.

Shooting the sun with a sextant requires two hands, one to hold the sextant and the other to work the vernier, and generally in a small vessel one man holds the navigator, and this leaves his hands free. But as we were only two and Spot was steering, I had to take sights alone, and found it difficult. Years ago leadsmen had a platform in the chains from which to heave the lead, and such a platform, easily rigged in the main and mizen shrouds of a small vessel, would enable the leadsman or navigator to use both hands for the lead or sextant, as it would have a device for gripping him round the waist.

It was cheering to see the Foreland, as it seemed that now we should storm along to the Wight in smooth water under the lee of the land. Just before the noon sight the wind had eased enough to allow us to carry full mainsail, and soon after the spinnaker was set, but this was only for an hour, for a squall out of a clear sky hit us, bursting the spinnaker and springing the boom. The remains were sadly gathered in, and the wind continuing to freshen forced me to take in one reef after another until all three were in again, and we could do no more but lower the gaff jaws on the boom again.

After rounding the Foreland we re-set the three-reefed mainsail and tore along the coast in fine style, thoroughly enjoying the comparatively smooth water of the Channel after the steep tumbling seas of the North Sea. The reason for the seas breaking so badly in the North Sea with northerly gales, is that the seas running south are always running into shallower water and so are tripped up, just as the large Atlantic seas roaring in on the Continental Shelf cause the chops of the Channel.

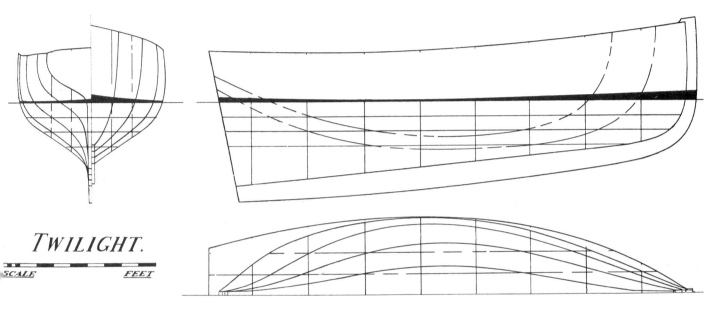

TWILIGHT.

SCALE   FEET

All went merry as a marriage bell till we were half-way between the *Royal Sovereign* and the *Owers*, when we were suddenly and unexpectedly becalmed, almost within sight of the Wight. During this calm the mizen was bent and rigged and the jib also brought up from the fo'c'sle and set, and we attempted to sail without wind, about as sensible as trying to skate without ice. For twenty hours we lay idle, watching the reflection of the sails, which seemed to go down under the water for miles.

As suddenly as we had been becalmed the wind came again as strong as ever. We stowed the jib, but not before the leach had blown away, and then took in the mizen, and for a time forced *Twilight* to carry her full main, but it was too much for her, so the three reefs were tucked in one by one very reluctantly, for after the calm we did not like the thought of shortening sail.

The wind was still fair, and we chased away before it past the *Owers*, to the Island through the long dark hours. Our course through the Forts and Spithead was a wild rush, and we arrived off Cowes at dawn. The wind was north, so as we steered south up the Medina we brought it aft, and half a mile from our anchorage we stowed all sails. Even then we had far too much way on when we arrived, which gave us an idea of the wind's strength.

We had arrived after a 6½ days' passage from Norway, one day of which was spent hove to, another becalmed, so in 4½ sailing days *Twilight* had made the passage from Norway to Cowes under a three-reefed mainsail, and at times only a staysail. Damage sustained : carried away topping lift, sprung spinnaker boom, burst spinnaker, and blew away leach of jib.

During the run down through the North Sea the breaking seas were so full of phosphorescence that they lit the sails, and the effect those dark nights was that of lightning, and so tiring that we could at times only steer for 1½ hours at a stretch.

Twilight, designed and built in 1904 by W. E. Thomas of Falmouth, is a fine example of a Quay Punt, and is a credit to her designer and builder, for she withstood the gales of the North Sea manfully and inspired us with confidence throughout our stormy passage.

Many people consider that the Quay Punts are heavy displacement and cumbersome vessels, but this is wrong, for evolved for service in the heavy seas found off the coast of Cornwall, they are normal and natural in all their proportions. Indeed *Twilight*, excepting for 10 square feet of sail and an inch of draught extra, is exactly to the ideal proportions for cruisers given in the chapter on that subject, although I had not considered her when I drew these graphs, as they were made from vessels designed for pleasure and not work. I hope that *Twilight's* passage, and this description of her, will dispel the fallacy that Quay Punts are unwieldy vessels.

· 17 ·

HARRIER

Length, overall - - - 30 ft. 6 in.			Length, water-line - - 27 ft. 3 in.	
Beam - - - - - 9 ft. 0 in.			Draught - - - - 4 ft. 11 in.	
Displacement - - - 7·8 tons			Sail area - - - - 720 sq. ft.	

Owner, CHRIS. RATSEY   *Designer*, HAROLD LIDSTONE

A PEACEFUL WEEK-END

THE average story of the sea and sailing is of strong winds and mountainous seas, with the vessel rushing wildly along seemingly with the bit in her teeth, heedless of the control of her crew. And it has been so since the beginning.

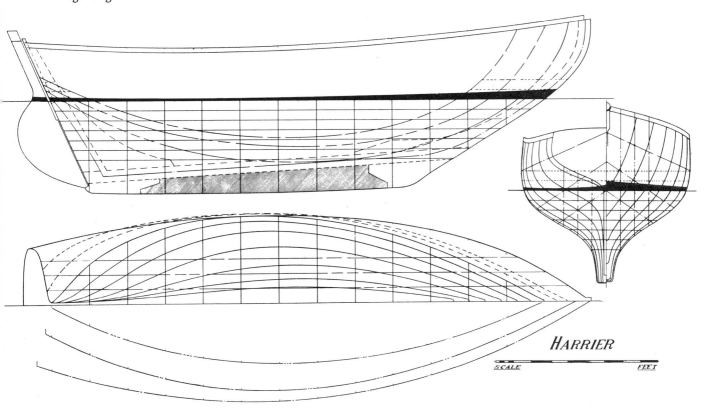

HARRIER

SCALE   FEET

Noah, the first cruising man with his crew, were the sole survivors of the bad weather encountered 2,500 years B.C. I am unable to reproduce the lines of his vessel, the Ark, but her dimensions are as follows : length overall 300 cubits, beam 50 cubits, and depth 30 cubits. A cubit is the old standard of linear measurement, being the length of a man's arm from the elbow to the end of the middle finger, about 18 inches. So the Ark was quite a large cruiser, being a three-decker, 450 feet overall with a beam of one-sixth of the length.

Later, 1,050 years B.C., in the Psalms, we read of the sea as a place where " They are carried up to the heaven, and down again to the deep ; their soul melteth away because of the trouble. They reel to and fro, and stagger like a drunken man : and are at their wit's end."

Another 50 years later Homer describes Odysseus, or Ulysses, coming ashore with his heart broken by the brine.

And the reason for all this is, that these strong winds and heavy seas impress themselves more upon a man's brain than the soft soothing winds that smooth the furrows of care and worry from his face.

WE CROSSED THE STARTING LINE

So in order to save the reader of this book from feeling that he has to wear oilskins throughout its pages, and to hold on for fear of being swept away by a heavy sea, this story of a pleasant and quiet week-end is written. It is of a September Race to Poole Harbour, where we stayed the night, the next day sailing on to Lulworth, and back to Cowes, all in calm, peaceful weather.

THE REAR-COMMODORE'S BOREAS SUNK AT HER MOORINGS

HE HOISTED HIS FLAG ABOARD VIGILANT

With a light easterly wind we crossed the Island Sailing Club's starting line. The three flag officers were racing, the Commodore in *Dolly Varden*, the Vice-Commodore in *Moby Dick*, and as the Rear-Commodore's *Boreas* had been sunk at her moorings, he hoisted his flag aboard *Vigilant*. *Lo III, Suzette, Freya, Daedalus, Petrel* and *Harrier* made up the fleet of nine starters.

Although the wind was light it was fair, and combined with the fair tide, enabled us to sail the 27 miles in fast time, the Parkstone Sailing Club timing us in across the line between Old Harry and Poole Bar Buoy three hours after the start. *Suzette* won, with *Moby Dick* second, and the smallest boat, *Petrel*, third on time allowance.

Then we sailed into Poole Harbour, moored and cooked our evening meal, while the day quietly and peacefully turned into night, when *Vigilant's* crew, Doctor Cooke, myself and James Damant, who was helmsman, turned in.

Early next morning, *Harrier* set sail for Lulworth Cove, and made a pretty picture, as her tanned sails stood out against the easterly light. Designed by Lidstone for Chris. Ratsey in 1926, she has sailed winter and summer for eight years, only being hauled out for a month each winter to rest awhile, and has proved a sturdy little ship. Her sections are particularly good, combining as they do power with ease, and giving 6 ft. 6 in. headroom on a 27-ft. water-line boat, are really fine.

After watching *Harrier* out of sight, we cooked and thoroughly enjoyed our breakfast before making sail and following her.

The light fickle wind was easterly until we were past Old Harry, and then it shifted into the west, and in order to cheat the flood tide we made short boards close under the steep cliffs between Peverel Ledge and St. Albans Head. Once past St. Albans we stood into Chapman Pool, and easing the tide still more, soon arrived off Lulworth Cove.

Lulworth Cove is extremely difficult to discern from the sea, but *Harrier*, anchored inside and rolling gently to the swell, enabled us to pick out the Cove without any effort. We sailed in, and luffing alongside *Harrier*, made fast astern, and stowing our sails went ashore in our dinghy.

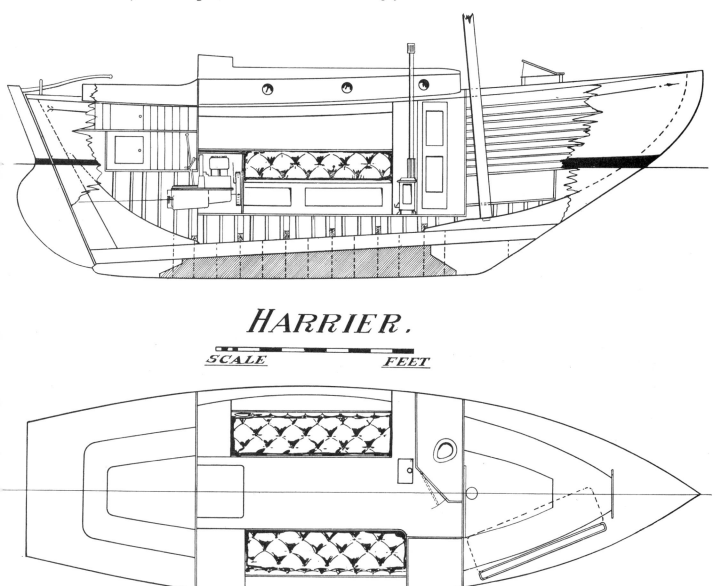

HARRIER.

SCALE   FEET

We joined *Harrier's* crew in a ramble over the hills round the Cove, then aboard for a bathe and lunch.

The light wind was now northerly, so sailing out through the narrow entrance, made narrower by the ledges under water, was quite simple, and once outside we were able to lay our course to St. Albans and the Needles in smooth water with the wind off shore.

The wind was so light, that aboard *Vigilant* we set an extra jib forward and the fo'c'sle hatch cover as a mizen, from the topmast backstay to the mainsheet horse and sheeted to the dinghy's keel on our stern.

Harrier and *Vigilant* kept close company till Hurst was reached, where *Harrier*, going into Keyhaven for the night, left *Vigilant* to carry on for Cowes and Home.

LULWORTH COVE IS DIFFICULT TO DISCERN FROM THE SEA

It had been an enjoyable week-end, with enough wind to take us to the haven where we would be, and not enough to cause any thought of reefing. In the evening light we landed the Rear-Commodore on the green of Cowes with ten minutes to spare for his dinner party, while the doctor and I quietly sailed up the Medina to Kingston, and so ended this delightful peaceful cruise. We had been away 32 hours, and had sailed practically 100 miles under ideal conditions, gentle breezes and calm seas.

HARRIER.

SCALE   FEET

· 18 ·

VIGILANT

Length, overall - - - 34 ft. 6 in.			Length, waterline - - 25 ft. 6 in.	
Beam - - - - - 6 ft. 4 in.			Draught - - - - 4 ft. 3 in.	
Displacement - - - 2 tons			Sail area - - - - 236 sq. ft.	

Designer, Owner and Skipper, UFFA FOX

PRACTICALLY every small sailing vessel with outside ballast and a deck is able to stand far more hard driving than her crew of human beings, and this fact, among others, accounts for so many different types being held up as ideal for cruising, where gales have to be weathered at sea. If man were able to stand more than small ships, in the way of hard weather, we should soon arrive at the ideal sailing vessel, and cruisers would all be alike just as the international racing class boats are.

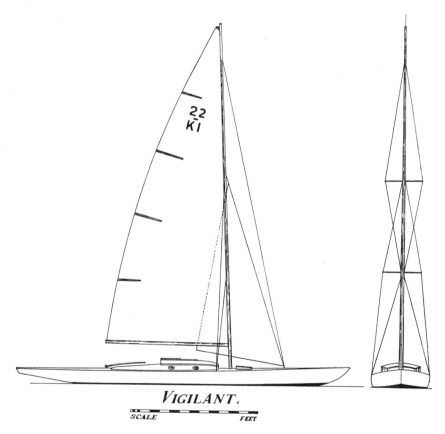

VIGILANT.

SCALE   FEET

The cruise described in the following pages was made by a boat of the type that is generally looked upon as being quite unsuited to the open sea. She is Bermudian rigged, with a mast longer than her hull, the halyards and luff rope of the mainsail run up inside this hollow spar, while her displacement to length is so light that the " Q " class, which races on the Solent, refuses to let her compete. Compared to the international 6-metre yacht, she is of about the same size, with half the sail area and half the displacement. Without holding this extreme type of racing boat up as ideal for deep water work, I should like to point out that *Vigilant* made her cruise to

Sweden and back to Cowes in a summer noted for its strong winds, and five different times encountered wind of gale force—registered ashore, not by her crew.

While chasing away before three of these gales, she seemed to tear along at twice her natural speed, which suggests that her press of sail was three times as much as she should carry.

Vigilant did not suffer at all through this harsh treatment, except that the paint came off her seams under water near her entrance, which would have happened to any new vessel, and is the reason for not coppering a new ship until she is a year or so old, and settled down in life.

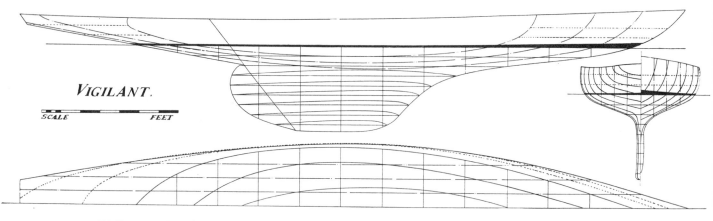

Vigilant was launched, had two spins to air her new sails, and was then loaded up with food, spare sails and other gear for her cruise to Sweden, leaving Cowes at 6.30 p.m. on Monday, June 30.

We were a crew of three. Dr. R. T. Cooke, who is the owner of the 5-tonner *Enid*, and is grandson of the famous E. W. Cooke, R.A., Bob Dickerson, one of my old sea scouts now grown up to a man-sized engineer, and myself, owner.

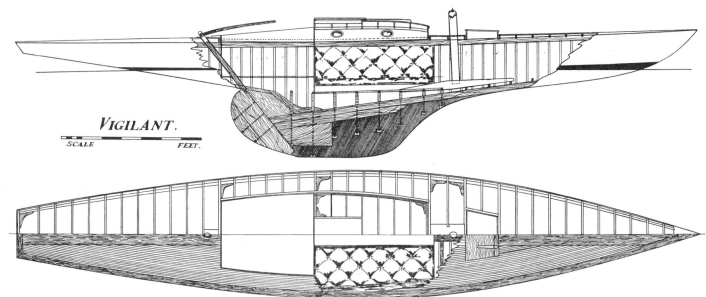

The weather report looked as though we were in for a dead beat in a jump, as it stated " wind 30 miles an hour S.E.," but as we beat through the Spithead forts, heavy rain squalls from all directions, with violent thunder and lightning, knocked the wind down to faint airs from all points of the compass. With hardly a breath of wind we sailed up Channel past the *Owers, Royal Sovereign* and *South Goodwin Light Vessel*, taking three days to do what we could have done in one with a decent breeze, and at 9.45 p.m. July 2, with the *North Goodwin Light Vessel* close abeam, we set our course for the *Terschelling Light Vessel*, 180 miles away N.E. ¾ E. On July 3, at 6.00 p.m. Latitude 52.06, Longitude 2.50 E., we were passed by the *Bremen* close to leeward, which showed we were right on our course.

The *Bremen* seemed to have some purpose in life, as she roared by with her wave high up her stem, and another right over her propellers. Her model spent six months in the testing tank at Hamburg, and the reason for the bulge in her stem below water is to bring the crests of the waves along her side half a wave forward, so that

MODESTY IS ONLY A SENSE OF
PHYSICAL IMPERFECTION

VIGILANT RUNNING BEFORE A FIFTEEN M.P.H. BREEZE (BOOM SEEN SQUARED OFF).
BREMEN TRAVELLING 21 KNOTS BRINGS THIS WIND AHEAD AT SIX MILES AN HOUR

one is right over her propellers. This form of forefoot has no greater resistance than the ordinary entrance, but in the *Bremen's* case has the advantage of increasing propeller efficiency. For although it is obvious that on a paddle steamer the paddles must work in the crest of one of the waves she makes along her side, it is not quite so evident

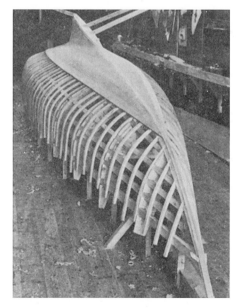

VIGILANT TIMBERED OUT

VIGILANT HALF PLANKED

that a propeller, to do its best work, should be under the crest of one of these waves. A paddle wheel would be seen spinning round in thin air if in the valley of the wave, while a propeller slipping just under the surface would be unnoticed.

That night dinner consisted of gin and vermouth, soup, mackerel (just caught), beef, spaghetti, fruit, cider and port ; we usually fed well.

A day from the log will illustrate our lazy life, not fully, as we swam several times a day when there was little wind, and generally amused ourselves.

"July 4. 3.45 a.m. Sunrise, although yellow, has the appearance of forecasting a nasty day. Not an air of wind since midnight, and the boom has slammed about, as the lop from the old wind is only just settling down. Noon. Still without a breath of wind, no sights to-day, as clouds blot out sun. Day's run, noon to noon, 60 miles, all done in 10 hours yesterday. Set up all standing rigging this morning ; although *Vigilant* is a racer she has

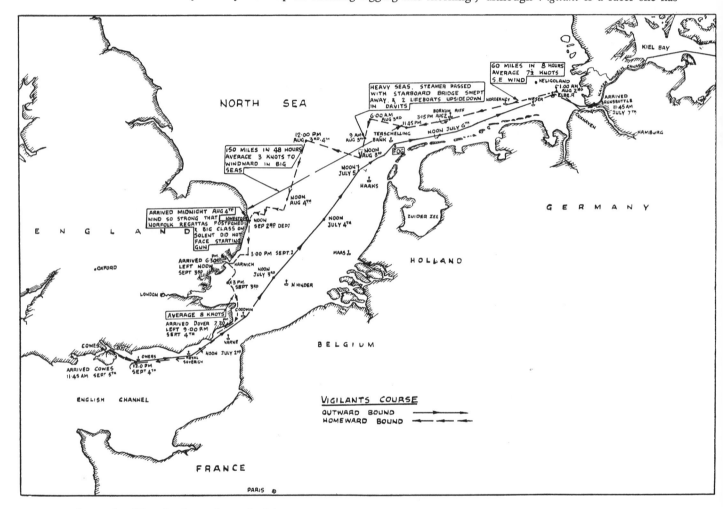

lanyards of Russian hemp instead of the usual rigging screws, as I have old-fashioned ideas on the subject. Racing people have admired the way the halyards and luff rope of the mainsail work inside *Vigilant's* mast, which is stream-lined for efficiency to windward, and then have been startled to find it supported by Russian lanyards. 1.00 p.m. Faint air, N.E., steering N. on starboard tack, speed 1 kn. 2.00 p.m. Rain squall kills wind, all hands go below ; quite cosy in cabin, doctor snoring peacefully. 4.00 p.m. Felt something about to happen, so went on deck ; only there two minutes, when a sudden squall of wind and rain came from the N., and away went *Vigilant* N.E. at 5 kn., close hauled on the port tack.

It is dark, the sea is smooth, as the rain is heavy enough to prevent even this weight of wind from making a ripple, everything quiet and unnatural, and a feeling in the air that something is coming.

4.30 p.m. Very heavy squall, and I can only see 100 yards. 5.00 p.m. Squall eases, we have never reefed, so have a dress rehearsal, rolling down two reefs, and then shaking them out, all is well. 6.00 p.m. Wind strong, and *Vigilant* is sailing fast for so small a vessel on a wind ; we are doing 6 knots in a N.E. direction generally, the wind shifting from N. to N.E., so we tack often, to keep on the course nearest to N.E.

6.40 p.m. Wind eased, doing 1 knot. 7.10 p.m. Wind shifts again, and freshens. Doing 5 knots, N.E. ½ E.

Since 4.00 p.m. we have done 15 miles N.N.E., and sailing as we are, we should sight the *Haaks Light Vessel* in four hours, but visibility bad, so do not suppose we shall pick it up this side of midnight. 12.45 Midnight. *Haaks Light Vessel* bearing E.S.E., light just above skyline, so about 10 miles off."

We had had a fresh wind from 6.00 p.m. till midnight, when it eased away, and then we were becalmed from 4.00 a.m. till noon, when a faint air came, which gave us a speed of 1 knot. *Vigilant* impressed us well with the way she walked along on a wind, and seemed very manly indeed when the sea made up after an hour or two of a fresh wind. At 4.30 p.m. on July 5 we sighted the light tower on the N. end of Texel Island, when the faint air that had carried us since noon left us, and we were becalmed till 9.30 p.m. when another enabled us to work our way towards the *Terschelling Light Vessel*.

VIGILANT LIFTED OUT OF WATER AND SCUDDING ALONG AT TEN KNOTS

July 6. I woke to find Bob steering with a light N. breeze with a thick fog. We sounded and found 16 fathoms, dead low water.

The tide was running N.N.E. so we steered E. to get inside steamers. This fog meant two on deck, and we sounded every fifteen minutes, getting 16 to 18 fathoms. At 3.00 a.m. we sighted the light tower on Terschelling island bearing E.S.E., but dared not approach closer than 3 miles to the land, as shoals run out that distance. A night at sea with fog means extra work, and as so many ships pick up the *Terschelling Light Vessel* and pass outside it, we went inside, where we might have run ashore. This would not have mattered with the light wind we then had, but often a fog is the precursor of a gale in which a ship would break up if unfortunate enough to be ashore. The fog, after lifting a few minutes for us to fix our position, shut down again, and we sailed on parallel to the coast, sometimes at 5 knots and sometimes at 2 knots as the wind was patchy. The rising sun burnt up the fog and the wind too, and we slowly sailed past the Frisian islands at an average of 2 knots. At 9.00 p.m. we were off Borkum with a light wind N.W. that was freshening fast, which looked as though the breeze foretold by the fog would be a N.W. one, a bad wind for this coast, but a fair one for us to the entrance to the Kiel canal. At midnight we were off the island of Juist, the breeze getting stronger and looking like a gale before daylight.

July 7, 7.15 a.m., we left the outer *Elbe Light Vessel* to port, having averaged 7 knots since midnight, which is good going for so small a boat. She did this without any effort, as although the seas were steep, both Bob and the Doctor had slept since I took over at 1.00 a.m.

Vigilant fairly smoked up the Elbe, doing the 36 miles from just outside the outer *Elbe Light Vessel* to Brunsbuttelkoog in 4½ hours, exactly 8 knots. We gybed twice, because of the bend in the river, the first time off *Elbe 4 Light Vessel* in quite a sea, as the wind was right in, and we were not up to any land yet, although we had sailed 17 miles from the outer *Elbe* in less than 2 hours.

Gybing in wind of that strength appears asking for trouble, so I had better explain how we did it. It must be remembered that our rig was Bermudian, and that there was no heavy gaff aloft; our boom was short and hollow, so it settled down to simply getting the sail across, not so bad. We did not touch the sheet, simply put the helm up hard, with the boom right off, the wind had to be almost on the beam before the mainsail would blow across, and then it flipped over with a rush, but the wind being abeam, or even forward of the beam, the sail was aback when across, with no wind in it at all; then we bore away and tore off on the new gybe. We reached Brunsbuttelkoog at 11.45 a.m. and were stowed at noon, waiting to enter the canal.

It cost about £2 to go through, I forget the exact amount. In the lock they said that we must tow through, but the Lord was good, and Lauriston Lewis, who was locking through, also bound to Sandhamn with his 12-metre, which was afterwards rammed by *Lulworth* and sank off Cowes, kindly said that he would tow *Vigilant* as well as his racer. As we were first to sail out of the lock (showing papers, Customs and locking through took an hour and a half) we thought we might as well sail on, as we had a fair wind, so we did, and were quite delighted to observe that our speed by the kilometres marked along the bank was 10 miles an hour. We tore along for 17

VIGILANT

miles, then the canal took a turn to windward, so that we could not lay the course, and the *Marjery*, towing *Lucilla*, caught us; we had a good 100 yards start at the lock, as we were smaller and easier to get under way.

They took us in tow and we went through alongside the 12-metre. It was fine going when the wind came ahead. As we locked through at Holtenau, they told us it was blowing a N.W. gale, and it would continue, so that it would be best for us to stay a day or two in Kiel. We sailed clear of the lock, and tied up to Bellevue Bruick for our stay. We carried no dinghy, and always reckoned to tie up, as when in harbour I like to feel I am ashore.

For July 8 and 9, the weather report was N.W. gale and sea rough; so we stayed moored to our pier very comfortably. When entering strange harbours, I usually sail round leisurely first, looking for the best berth, and then have only to moor once.

July 10. The weather report still talked of gales from the N.W. but was more cheerful, so we decided to have a shot at it, and left our cosy pier at 8.15 p.m. To *Kiel Light Vessel* we were on a wind, but in the shelter of the fjord Bob and the doctor made supper, in spite of the fact that we were almost on our beam ends in the puffs. We fed before clearing the land, having taken $1\frac{1}{4}$ hours to sail close hauled the 8 miles down the Kiel fjord. We passed close to the *Kiel Light Vessel* at 9.30 p.m. seas going clean over us, not spray, but solid water, as we were on a wind and sailing fast.

At the Lightship we bore away on our course for the *Fehmarnbelt Light Vessel*. This was East and brought the wind on our port quarter. We flew along now, planing, with the sea thrown high each side of our bow, then the mad rush would be checked as we climbed up the back of a wave, and quite often we would be swept by heavy seas, a glorious ride. A gale is exhilarating until it tires a man out, and this was really fine, rushing headlong while we were planing, and then losing speed and coming down to normal as a huge sea swept our boat. Then *Vigilant* would recover her breath and strength, and away we would go again. After two hours of this, my arm ached so that I could not hold *Vigilant* properly, so Bob came alongside me and put his weight on the tiller at the times when she wanted treating roughly. So we rushed on until off the N.W. point of Femern, where our jib sheet parted ; we put her in the wind, took in the jib, reefed the mainsail, so that the head of the sail was half-way between the hounds and deck, and rove off another jib sheet, then carried on on our course. We had done 27 miles in 3 hours ; Dixon Kemp at one time said the speed of vessels was the square root of L.W.L., but after the *Sappho* sailed her record-making passage across the Atlantic he increased it to the square root of the L.W.L. × 1·45, and Froude and his tank tests rather proved this ; so our speed, according to theory, should have been only $7\frac{1}{4}$ knots.

It always amuses me to hear overhangs regarded as useless and dangerous (as they always are) in a seaway, for then is the only time they are of value, increasing the effective water-line length and fore-and-aft stability. The only time they are a nuisance is in a calm immediately following a blow, for then there is an old sea left over and the counter banging down on this shakes the boat from end to end. This is easily cured by giving the counter a sharper " V " section. But then under those conditions any vessel is very uncomfortable and miserable, helpless, and flung about in all directions. Thank heaven those conditions are seldom met, and when they are, they are not long lasting.

We now squared away more for the Geydser shoal, and averaged 6 knots for the next 30 miles, with only 14 sq. ft. of mainsail showing, the rest being rolled up ; this will show the weight in the wind. Rounding the Geydser Reef we made for Hesmaes, a small harbour, 18 miles to windward. Although our small sail was all right running, we needed more than we could safely carry to drive us to windward, so we made sail, and with our mainsail a foot below the hounds and jib, we had 100 sq. ft. showing, and at times were buried to the top of our coach roof. We made good time and averaged 4 knots to windward, the best we ever did, but it was not quite a true beat, more of a long and short leg.

We arrived at Hesnaes at 11.00 a.m. July 10, a pretty harbour, and stayed almost 24 hours, leaving at 10.00 a.m. With full sail, we averaged 6 knots till 6.30 p.m., when the wind, which had been easing down all day, only gave us about 5 knots. Measuring the height of the sea as best I could with angles, it appeared to be 20 ft. from crest to valley. By midnight we were becalmed 10 miles due S. of Sandhammaren Point, having sailed almost 80 miles in $13\frac{1}{2}$ hours, and so ended a N.W. gale, which started while off Borkum ; if we'd only been as manly as the boat we should have been in Stockholm, but being weak, we wasted this wind by going into two harbours.

From midnight till noon the next day July 12 we had only sailed 10 miles, and by 5.30 p.m. were only another 5 miles on our way. However this was a fine day, spent swimming, varnishing deck, etc. At 7.30 p.m. with a fair wind, we had sailed 12 miles in 2 hours, the wind being just strong enough to make little white caps all round.

This was pretty going, with Bob and the doctor cooking the dinner, and all was peace within. At 8.30 p.m. the wind had gone abeam, so we took in the spinnaker as the wind was now W.N.W. instead of S.W. Next morning at 3.30 a.m. we were abreast Ut Klippan (meaning Uttermost Point) practically becalmed. Everything seemed very dismal, low heavy clouds were coming from the N.E., rocky islands and rocks were all around, altogether a dismal place with the appearance of a gale coming again. The wind soon shifted from the light air, W.N.W. to N.E., with rain, but after two hours the rain cleared, and it blew hard out of a clear sky with a steep sea. A German yacht of about 20 tons came up from astern soon after rounding Ut Klippan, and as it was blowing about 25 miles an hour she passed us beating to windward, both of us being Bermudian cutters and carrying full sail.

As she passed, she hoisted her ensign, and we hoisted ours in reply, hoping that the wind would either decrease or increase, for in that smart breeze she was definitely faster. Later in the day the wind did increase, so I was routed out of my warm bunk to give battle to the enemy, now two miles or more ahead and dead to windward. We eased our main sheet away instead of reefing, and started in on the job of beating the larger vessel.

By now it was blowing 35 miles an hour, and the sea was very steep and breaking, and taking a small vessel like *Vigilant* to windward in it was a real pleasure. The method I adopted is one which I had learnt in open boats, that is, to sail them on their course in the valleys of the waves, but instead of luffing into the crest bearing away and taking the sea broadside. So manœuvred, the boat does not lose her way at every sea, neither does she rush into the sea, for the breaking crests slide under or over her broadside with only their own force, the boat being neutral to them. Sailing *Vigilant* in this way to our great joy we soon started to overhaul our enemy, and finally sailed past her, she having three reefs in, and we with full sail. Soon she stowed her mainsail and, turning tail, ran back before it round Ut Klippan to shelter under the land she had just left.

All day we beat to windward with full sail, and at 3.00 p.m. were hove to off the Garpen Lighthouse, making sure of the way into Bergqvara, as if we hit the rocks with this sea it meant Good-bye *Vigilant*. Having satisfied ourselves that the marks agreed with the different compass courses, we sailed in, the course twisting about to clear rocks, submerged and awash, and found ourselves in a pretty natural harbour. We sailed round about looking for the best spot, then shot into a small sort of dock, square, about 50 feet by 50 feet, with an entrance about 18 feet wide, and moored inside. In entering tricky harbours it is as well to have a good look from the outside before going in, unless racing, for even if you jump up and down in a seaway outside for two hours deciding the best way in, it is better than wrecking the ship, and as you have really come for a sail, you should be in no hurry

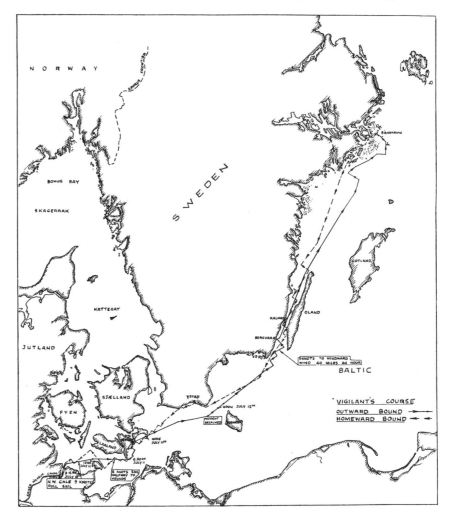

to go into port. We went to a dance that night, and I thoroughly enjoyed polkas, waltzes, two-steps and human music, instead of wails from such untuneful instruments as play in England. Surely the waltz will return before those of us who have learnt waltzing die.

July 14. The Skipper of the salvage tug which had towed in a ship of timber abandoned in yesterday's blow said it was the hardest wind they had had since the winter. The survey people could not work, and yet we had driven *Vigilant* through the steep sea with full sail, doing 30 miles in $9\frac{1}{2}$ hours, which is better than 3 knots dead to windward. At noon we left Bergqvara with a light S.W. wind, and sailed up to Kalmar, which is 19 miles, in 3 hours, just over 6 knots. After walking round the town for $2\frac{1}{2}$ hours we left at 5.30 p.m. for Sandhamn. The wind was very light but fair and by 9.00 p.m. we were becalmed off Skagganes. Then we were towed by a trader at 3 knots till 2.00 a.m.—5 hours.

July 15. 2.35 a.m. sunrise. Wind east off Runo Rodskar, just south of Oskarhamn, steering N.E. by N. for Almas Grundit off Sandhamn 140 miles away. 6.15 a.m., end of the island of Oland abeam. Noon, Lat. 57.42.09. Long. 17.19.10 E. And by midnight we were another 35 miles on our way.

From the log. "*July 16th.* 2.20 a.m. Becalmed, and sun rises clean out of the sea, just as it sank. So light have been able to read all night. 2.45 a.m. Wind N.E., very light. Close hauled, can just steer. N. wind shifted and steering N.E. 5.30 a.m. Sight Lighthouse to the W., which must be Landsort. 8.15 a.m. Tack ship off Soderskar rocks, about 6 miles N.E. of Landsort, and steer close hauled on port tack parallel to the Islands. Noon. Off Lagland, a small rock. 5.30 p.m. Hufvudskar Lighthouse abeam, doing about 2 knots N.E. by E. for Almas Grundit, 20 miles off. 8.30 p.m. No wind, but *Vigilant* fanning herself along, so as to give us steerage way. Seals around us ; they have heads like smooth-coated retrievers and are friendly but shy."

July 17. 2.20 a.m. Sunrise. Quite light all night, so we could read and *Vigilant* still fanned herself along in the calm. 5.00 a.m. Wind came ahead, steering E. $\frac{1}{2}$ S. 7.00 a.m. Tacked, steering N. by E. for *Alma Grundit Light Vessel*, which is visible. We all washed and shaved and smartened ourselves up as it is much nicer to arrive spick-and-span. 9.00 a.m. till 10.00 a.m. Hundreds and hundreds of racing yachts appeared from out behind rocky islands, so we were right for Sandhamn and the races. We arrived at the Committee boat between two starts, and asked for a programme ; they told us to get " to hell out of it," and threw us a programme, all of which was not easily understood. However, we started off with our class, 30 in a race, and ended up last, the boat next to us being the winner of King Oskar's cup a few days ago. The wind shifted when we were to windward of the fleet and put us to leeward.

We had arrived at Sandhamn in time for the last four days of the European Meeting of all Nations, which began on July 2 and ended July 20. This was remarkably well arranged by the Royal Swedish Yacht Club, to celebrate its hundredth birthday, and consisted of banquets and racing with 500 yachts from all nations both at sea and on the fjords, and showed the value of international building and racing rules.

I wonder how long it will be before the ocean racing rule becomes international with a meeting of say 100 boats in the Solent, from which place they race to Madeira, where they feast and then race back again.

On July 18, the doctor, Bob, and myself had breakfast ashore ; rather a sad meal, as the doctor had to return home by aeroplane, because of his job. I imagine that a doctor has a hard life, being called at all hours to perform his duty to mankind, who seldom fully appreciate what is done. The doctor gave us a hand to get under way, and out to sea we went, both Bob and I feeling sad, as we knew that when we returned after the race he would be on his way to England, so that only Bob and I would race *Vigilant* and sail her home.

We raced out at sea with the rest in a flat calm. We were all in one place for 4 hours, so Bob and I cooked and had a decent meal, then shaved and dressed ready for the dinner and dance at the Royal Swedish club house. People were quite surprised to find our evening clothes in good order after such a trip in a small boat. We finished last in the race.

We had a fine breeze for the race on July 19. At the start we were sailing nicely down the line, close hauled on the starboard tack, and just before the gun we had about 18 boats port tack. The rule gave us the right to put them all about, but instead I eased the main and jib sheets, and stopped *Vigilant*, letting them all past on port tack, and started last. For had we charged them, as we had the right to do, there would have been a dreadful mess, as there was a smart breeze blowing.

We had sailed 1,200 miles to be at Sandhamn and the sea had washed us of all petty things such as taking advantage of rules at the expense of so many other racers, so although we had manœuvred for this advantage we did not take it.

After beating to windward some time we were still a bad last, so we looked at the rest of the fleet. There they were with everything sheeted harder than seemed sensible, and as we had no winches, we had to shoot *Vigilant* in the wind, to sheet flat. Then we started to go up through the fleet, but we had wasted half the beat, so only reached fourth place by the time we were at the weather mark. On the run we gained on the boats ahead and those behind, without passing any, then the reach home came and three boats passed us. Then we altered our sheets, and started to gain on them, but did not catch any, and finished seventh. Fine dinner and dance that night.

July 20. We raced this day on Kanholms Fjord. When the gun went we were head to wind on the line with no steerage way; disgraceful ! So as usual we started last. It was a reach to the first mark, and once we were away we passed boat after boat, rounding the first mark fourth. Then came the run, the rest of the fleet set great reaching sails to leeward, and by putting the spinnaker boom in the ordinary jib and booming it out to windward, they filled this huge jib, and several passed us. We, not knowing how far and where the next mark was, did not set a spinnaker, but we imagined we would beat them going to windward. The Y.R.A. rule bars a contrivance for rigging the jib outside the boat, and we thought the using of the spinnaker boom in the clew of the jib counted as a contrivance, so when one boat passed us I waved our bow in over her cockpit every time it lifted on a sea, which made the crew angry. As we pretended *Vigilant* was taking charge, they sheered off to leeward and dropped two places. On the beat we did not shine and finished eighth, but still there was quite a fleet behind us. This day there was a smart breeze too. That night the prizes were presented after dinner, and I was surprised, but delighted, when they presented me with a handsome cup—not for my racing ability, but for the cruise over, and to remind me of Sandhamn. I do not think there was any weed on *Vigilant's* bottom, although she had been overboard a month ; I raced badly, being used to 14-footers, which are quickly about and away. It was not until the last race that I realised that we lost so much each time we tacked, and I had been tacking far too much, and never in my life have I made a good start. We were up against the finest of helmsmen, and what more could a man desire ?

July 21 at 5.30 p.m., we sailed past the Royal Swedish Yacht Club, and dipped our ensign in farewell, a rather sad performance as everyone had been so kind and nice. The wind was very light from the N., and we reached along slowly through the narrow channel to Kanholms Fjord, where we had raced yesterday, as we intended sailing down inside the islands to Landsort. We had hardly started when the wind came west with rain, and we had to turn to windward through pretty islands each side until we came to the Lighthouse on Yxhammarkubb, when our course became S.W. We could lay it with very small islands close aboard to windward, and larger ones beyond, while close to leeward was the island of Runmaro. These islands, we were told, were very pretty, but in this S.W. wind and rain in the twilight they looked dismal, so when we came to Styrsvik, about 2½ miles from the north end of Runmaro, we thought we would go in for the night as it was 9.00 p.m., and hoped the morrow would bring sunshine. We had no chart of this small inlet ; but sailing in places like Norway and the West of Scotland had taught me that in such countries if you steered clear of everything you saw you were safe ; so we went in and tied up ashore to the rocks, quite snug.

When cruising if you remember that bold high land and hills have deep water right up to the shore, and you can therefore put your boat ashore without touching bottom, and that flat land means shallow water for miles out to sea, you will seldom come to harm. Generally the height of the land is the depth of the water. But there are exceptions.

July 22. Styrsvik. After a night's sleep we woke to find a smart wind from the N. and bright sunshine, had a walk over the island, breakfasted, and left at 7.00 a.m. Doing about 6 knots we sailed the 15 miles to Dalaro in 2¼ hours. We landed here and looked over the town for over an hour, leaving again at 10.30 a.m., passing Landsort, and out to sea at 3.45 p.m. (30 miles in 5¼ hours is almost 6 knots.) At first we made better than 6 knots, our average over the 45 miles being 6 knots good.

It had been delightful sailing, 6 knots being a comfortable speed, unfolding the view, giving us time to enjoy it, then bringing fresh islands along before we tired of the last. My entry in the log will have to explain or I'd take three pages of description. " Fascinating islands all around, some eight miles long, others simply rocks 3 ft. across, with all sizes between, some covered with grass and firs, others bare rock and trees, some rock and grass and some bare rock, but all with character, some inviting and others forbidding, as were the low rocky ones with the waves sweeping clean over them. A cruiser's paradise. Out at sea we continued to average 6 knots until 6.30 p.m. when the wind died right away, and we were only doing 2 knots.

July 23. Noon. Becalmed, Lat. 57.45.50, Long. 17.12.10, having sailed along at about 2 knots since about 6.30 p.m. last night."

Soon a light air made S.E. by S., and we stood inshore on the port tack until we came to the outlying rocks over which the swell surged even on such a fine day. Then we came about and tacked down along these rocks, as they were interesting, and at 7.00 p.m. we were off Blackan Rock, when we tacked and stood across for the north end of the island of Oland, tacking close inshore at Byxelkroken at 9.00 p.m. Midnight we were 3 miles S. of Jungfrun, having made 10 miles to windward in the last three hours.

July 24, at 7.30 a.m., we were at the Island of Skaggenas, having breakfast. We had sailed 28 miles to windward in the 7½ hours since midnight. We beat the other eight miles to Kalmar in two hours, and went ashore at 9.30 a.m., leaving again at 1.00 p.m. with the wind just a faint air, dead ahead. All afternoon we had no breeze, so thought we would spend the night ashore at Morbylanga, but when off there at 5.30 p.m. a breeze came east so we carried on. At 7.00 p.m. we were to the east of Utgrunden, and doing 6 knots with a smart breeze that was rapidly freshening into a gale.

At 9.35 p.m. we passed Stengrund buoy, simply flying along. The wind had shifted from E. to N.E. and howled through the mast and rigging. By 11.10 p.m. we were abreast Ut Klippan light, but as I thought it could not possibly be the light, we carried on out to sea, for I said to Bob, " It is impossible for this boat to do such a speed, as it is 18 miles from Ystengrund buoy to Ut Klippan." We held on our course another half-hour, but nothing else showed up, so we brought the wind on the quarter and headed for Sandhammaran Point.

Although there is no tide in the Baltic the wind affects the water, and blowing it into a corner causes it to be above the normal level there, and this then runs back to find its true level, so that at times currents are felt. Such a current must have been under *Vigilant* at this part to enable her to sail almost 12 knots.

July 25. 2.00 a.m. We reefed down until we had 49 sq. ft. in the mainsail, and our full jib 51 sq. ft., making 100 sq. ft. of sail with which we did 6 knots. The sea was running very steep, and as far as we could judge was 30 feet from crest to valley. It was rather fun when *Vigilant* was poised on the top for a moment before she rushed headlong down the face of the wave. At 11.00 a.m. Sandhammaran was abeam, and we decided to have a spell ashore, so headed her up for Ystead. On rounding the point we saw no less than 10 three-masted schooners anchored in the lee of the land, rolling their decks under. We sailed through this fleet, and entered Ystead, mooring up at 1.00 p.m., exactly 24 hours from Kalmar, having sailed 150 miles in that time, most of it reefed to the bone. The reason for reefing was that both our crosstrees had bent double, and this was also our excuse for going into Ystead and wasting a fair breeze.

The next day the shipyard owned by the harbour repaired our crosstrees, and we had a very enjoyable yarn. They had just built the latest Swedish life-boat, so we talked of weatherliness in small vessels and such things. We left Ystead at 11.00 a.m. with the wind W., so made long and short legs along the south coast of Sweden, which is very pretty though low lying. By 2.15 p.m. Smygehulk point was abeam. We had sailed 18 miles in 3¼ hours which equals between 5 and 6 knots, good going, as we had a smart breeze. Then we steered for Moen Lyn (Denmark) close hauled, making 5 knots good. By 6.00 p.m. we had done 20 miles of the 40 across to Moen Lyn, and the wind having been very light for an hour had now come S.W., so we had a dead beat. 7.00 p.m. brought

WEATHERBOUND, CUXHAVEN.
WIND FORCE 8 N.N.W. AT BORKUM AND
FORCE 8 N.W. AT HELIGOLAND

THE GREAT NUMBER OF SAILING SHIPS IN THE BALTIC SHOWS IT IS
IDEAL FOR SAILING

a heavy squall, wind howling, and steep sea, but the wind was more W. and so we were able to lay S.W. At 10.00 p.m. Moen Lyn was abeam, and the wind ahead, so we stood offshore and then in, all through the night.

July 27. 10.00 a.m. We cut through the Geydser Reef, beating to windward in a fresh breeze, heeled right down, and doing 5 to 6 knots through the water. The Geydser Reef extends 10 miles to sea, but both on the outward and homeward passage it paid us to take one of the cuts through it about two miles off-shore, keeping a lookout for breakers over rocks, an easy job as each time there was plenty of wind and sea. We stood off-shore 3 miles and then came about, making good time till 12.30 p.m. (noon) when our speed dropped to 2 knots as the wind eased up. Soon after rounding the Geydser, we saw a fine three-masted schooner ahead and to windward, but we beat her easily, sailing higher in the wind, and going faster through the water, conditions being ideal for us, as we could just carry full sail, but ought to have had a reef in. At 7.45 p.m. we just made the S.E. point of Femern Island, and coming about could lay up along a weather shore, which gave us smooth water for dinner, the wind being fresh again with a jumpy quick sea. The 8 miles of smooth water gained by tacking, especially for it, gave us nice time for a comfortable meal. Once clear of the island, we began bucking the seas again, and had a lively night.

The next day, July 28, at 11.00 a.m., we passed *Kiel Light Vessel*. We had had a strong wind all night, which fell away, and had been light since 8.00 a.m. We were still beating to windward, as we had been since we left Ystead on the south coast of Sweden. At times we had hard squalls of wind with rain, then the wind eased again. At 2.00 p.m. we moored outside Holtenau entrance to the Kiel canal, and at 4.00 p.m. entered the lock. Raining hard. We were in luck's way for a tow through, as in the same lock was *Solaz* owned by A. M. Symington, who had cruised in her from Spain to Norway via Scotland, and had just come down through Denmark. She is a motor cruiser of 100 tons, so we towed through the canal behind her in style, tying up for the night at Brunsbuttelkoog.

July 29 we passed through the locks at Brunsbuttelkoog with the *Solaz*. It was blowing a gale N.W. and the tide was against us, so her owner thoughtfully suggested towing us to Cuxhaven, another 15 miles down the river, where we could wait till the weather was better. We took off most of our clothes, as it was a wet passage, being towed 9 knots into a short sea. We found the 160 tons schooner *Amphitrite* in Cuxhaven ; she had just been out to the outer *Elbe Light Vessel* and returned as the N.W. gale was playing up old gooseberry on the bar.

Wednesday and Thursday were spent exploring Cuxhaven, as the weather signals said N.W. wind force 8, which is a fresh gale. A trading schooner came in ; two of her people had been washed overboard at the bar ; how she recovered them I cannot think, but one was dead and the other in hospital, so we were content to stay.

On August 1 the glass was up, and wind dying away, so we got away on the tide at 7.45 p.m. (It seemed strange to have to deal with tides again after being in the tideless Baltic.) It was a dead beat out to the entrance, and we were at the outer *Elbe Light Vessel* at 12.30 midnight. Although the wind had died right away, there were still some steep waves rolling in, and at times we shipped them solid, so imagined what it had been like here during the gale. (The Channel race round the *Sovereign*, Havre and back to Cowes, started that day and only one ocean racer, *Spica*, survived the course.)

August 2. 1.00 a.m. After being becalmed, the wind shifted from N.W. and came out of the S.E. in a sharp squall, and then settled down and enabled *Vigilant* to sail well till 9.30 a.m., by which time we were to the north of Borkum, when the wind eased away. At 3.15 p.m. we sailed sedately past *Borkum Riff*. This Light Vessel is to the west of Borkum. By 6.00 p.m. we were becalmed again 12 miles to the west of *Borkum Riff* for a while, then the wind came again light from the south, working S.W., and pushing us to the N. of our course. Finally at midnight it came W.S.W. right ahead, and began to blow hard. We were 16 miles E.N.E. of Terschelling, heading W.N.W. doing about 5 knots ; as yet there was not a heavy sea, but everything pointed to a hard beat to windward of 150 miles to Lowestoft, where we were bound, as *Vigilant* had been entered for the races during the Royal Norfolk and Suffolk Sea Week.

At 6.00 a.m. on August 3 we tacked ship after sailing 30 miles W.N.W., and could lay S.S.W. on the starboard tack. I intended working to the north of our course to Lowestoft, as a S.W. wind usually finishes up N.W. and I like to be to windward when this happens and able to take advantage of it. At noon, we went about on the port tack after sailing 30 miles. Towing a log stops a boat, and although we carried two aboard, we did not use either, as we could judge our speed quite well. 9.00 a.m. The next morning a steamer passed us with her starboard bridge swept away, and her two starboard lifeboats almost upside down in the davits ; she had evidently shipped a heavy sea ; I called Bob up to see this cheering sight, and it was nice to know that we were not the only boat taking water aboard. The wind eased at times, so our average speed of 5 knots dropped to about 4 knots, and we carried on for 12 hours on the port tack, coming about again at midnight.

On August 4 the wind was still dead ahead ; at times it eased right down, and then it was fierce for an hour or so. All the fishing smacks we had passed had had a reef and topsail, and I have been told by owners of these that that means the wind is about gale force. Noon. The glass had been going down ever since we left Cuxhaven. We could not see it, but reckoned we were about 10 miles W. from *Smith's Knoll Light Vessel*. The log reads: " Glass down 7 tenths and going down fast ; becalmed in a sea that simply jumps straight up like pyramids, as seen in very early paintings, before artists realised the shape of waves. Looks dirty, have managed to stick full sail till now, but decide to reef, as there is a feeling in the air that there is trouble about." We had just reefed her down, showing about 100 sq. ft. of sail, with full jib and well reefed main, when the wind jumped at us from the N.E., and we started to rush along ; it then blew from all round the compass, in hard short squalls, and finally settled in the N.N.W. and blew very fiercely while we tore along. It was now Bob's watch, so I went below and turned in. Soon after I get below the wind came ahead, so of course we slowed down to 5 knots against a steep sea. Bob tacked her after we'd gone 10 miles S.S.W., and he had rather a strenuous time. The helmsman, besides having to steer, had to pump hard to keep pace with the water shipped, as we had not a self-bailing cockpit, and *Vigilant* often dipped her cabin top and the sides of the cockpit in her efforts to defy what must have been a gale. At 4.30 p.m. the wind eased, so we gave her full sail again, and by 9.00 p.m. were 5 miles N.E. of Lowestoft, which was plainly visible. The wind now fell right away, and those last 5 miles took us 3 hours to sail, so we did not arrive till midnight, having sailed 150 miles dead to windward in 48 hours against a heavy sea, an average of 3 knots, and very good for a small vessel. The Customs came aboard and we had a tea-party, the tea in this case being rum ! They told us that all the regattas on the Broads had been postponed for weather that day, that *Britannia* and her class had not faced the starting gun in the sheltered Solent, that most of the boats in the Channel race had given it up, so we drank to the weatherly qualities of *Vigilant*.

To bed on August 5 at 3.30 a.m. after the tea-party, and were up again at 6.00 a.m. after 2½ hours' sleep. At 7.30 a.m. we left Lowestoft and sailed up to Oulton Broad, where we had to wait for the railway bridge. We moored up on Oulton Broad off Wooden's yard at 9.00 a.m. and soon cleared everything out of *Vigilant*, and Bob came home by train, while I stayed to race in the dinghies that afternoon.

The next day I caught the train to Cowes, had a yarn in London to break the journey, and arrived home at tea time. I saw the rest of Cowes Week, and was very sorry to hear of the *Lucilla* being sunk in Cowes Roads after her cruising to Sandhamn and back without any harm ; which shows that the open sea is no more dangerous than a crowded roadstead. After Cowes Week I returned to Oulton Broad and Lowestoft for the racing there.

Then at noon on September 2 *Vigilant* sailed out of Lowestoft bound for Cowes. On board were Peter Brett, a hefty youngster still at Oxford, myself and Mollie, my wire-haired terrier. Our animals are long suffering; the only real joy in life for Mollie is rabbit shooting or killing rats, and yet she sailed with us to Cowes without any complaint, not even when she fell overboard.

12.30 p.m. Off Pakefield, there was hardly a breath of wind. Tom Thornycroft bound to Cowes with *King Duck*, his wonderful new motor cruiser, took us in tow. On board *King Duck* he had his international 14-footer *Golden Eye* with which he had just won the Prince of Wales Cup, and also his son's 14-footer. At 3.00 p.m. having towed us at 10 knots we cast off at the *Shipwash Light Vessel*. 3.15 p.m. The tide would soon turn against us, the wind was light and dead ahead, so we decided to go for Harwich. At 6.25 p.m. we were inside Harwich Harbour, having sailed 18 miles in just over 3 hours, an average of 6 knots, the wind having freshened after we had headed for Harwich.

At noon, September 3, we left Harwich. The wind had shifted to E.S.E., and we had it ahead when first out of the harbour, but after clearing some shallow patches we were away down Barrow Deep through Fisherman's Gat, past the North Foreland, and into Dover at 7.20 p.m.

September 4 at 9.00 a.m. we left Dover, with a foul tide, and a nice breeze from the S.E., doing 6 knots through the water. 1.15 p.m. found us off Dungeness, 6.00 p.m. off Beachy Head, and by midnight we were at the Owers, having had a nice breeze all day.

September 5. 3.00 a.m. The wind had fallen away to a calm, so after passing the Warner we tied up to Seaview pier, as the tide was foul. We had taken 18 hours from Dover, making our average 6 knots, which is good, as we had had two foul tides and one fair tide, while only at times had the wind been strong enough to make *Vigilant* plane. I took Molly for a walk and then turned in ; we still had no need for a dinghy. It was fun sailing the *Vigilant* round inside the inner harbour at Dover, and beating her out through the lock gates.

A SMALL VESSEL MUST NOT LOAD HERSELF WITH USELESS GEAR, SO THE SEXTANT MIRROR WAS USED FOR SHAVING

At 9.00 a.m. we were under way for Cowes, as the tide had turned with us. We had no wind, but somehow we sailed along past Ryde, and entered Cowes Harbour at 11.45 a.m. While we were in Osborne Bay the wind came from the west, so the last part of our cruise ended in another turn to windward. The previous day the clouds, high up, had been coming from the west and the falling glass had foretold the west wind. We sailed up to Kingston, moored up to the pier we had left, and so ended a very enjoyable cruise which showed *Vigilant* to be a boat with a remarkable turn of speed for her length, and for her size, and considering the smallness of her crew, a very able sea boat. I had gained a stone in weight while on the cruise, and would advise anyone run down to get a small manly boat and go for a cruise ; there is very little worry with a small boat, for you can reef her under almost any conditions in 10 minutes if she has only 236 sq. ft. of sail, which divided into two makes the sails very small indeed. Then, too, with such a small boat there is no need to have a dinghy with all its worries.

Cowes to Sandhamn, 17 days.
Sandhamn to Lowestoft, 14 days.

· 19 ·

CRYSTAL

Length, overall - - - 30 ft. 6 in.		Length, water-line - - 22 ft. 0 in.
Beam - - - - - 8 ft. 6 in.		Draught - - - - 4 ft. 3 in.
Displacement - - - 4·9 tons		Sail area - - - - 479 sq. ft.

Owner, DAVID ANDERSON   *Designer*, FREDK. SHEPHERD

CRYSTAL is one of the best, if not the best cruiser of her size and type ever designed, for although only 22 ft. on the line she has 6 ft. of headroom for a length of 10 ft. with a 2 ft. 9 in. floor space, and this on a very pretty set of lines.

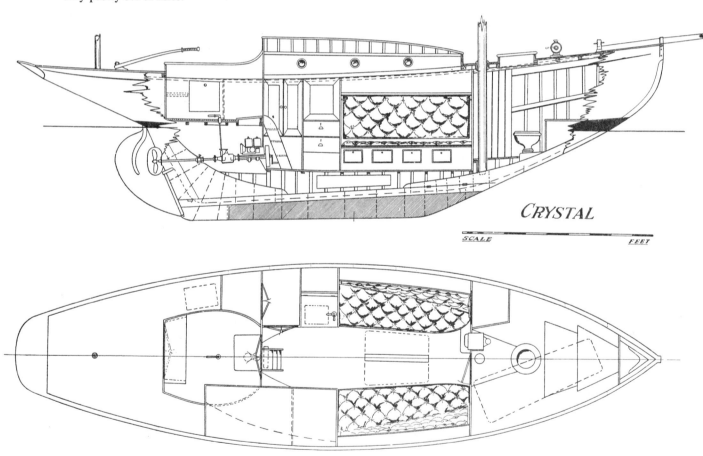

CRYSTAL

SCALE   FEET

Generally such headroom in so small a vessel is only obtained through distorting her lines and proportions, so that she sacrifices her sailing qualities for her accommodation, but here accommodation, beauty of line and proportion are nicely blended.

The lines are powerful, and although firm, the bilge is not hard and harsh, and in looking at it it must be remembered that the smaller the boat the more powerful should be her sections generally.

Her accommodation is well thought out, and she can sleep four, one in the fo'c'sle, two in the saloon, where the backs of the settees fold down and so make beds at night, while during the day they fold the bedding back out of sight, and the fourth in the berth abaft the saloon on the starboard side. This in time of peace is a sideboard.

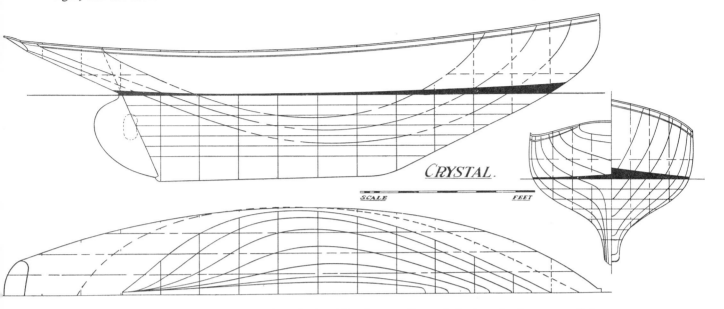

CRYSTAL.

SCALE   FEET

Opposite this berth is the galley, well aft, as it should be in a small vessel, for here in the centre of the seesaw the motion is least, the cook can stand up, for there is 6 ft. headroom here, and also the smell and fumes from the cooking and stove are soon out of the sliding hatch.

The coach roof 2 ft. 9 in. wide, as is the floor space, gives full headroom over the floor, and being so narrow does not interfere with the deck space at all, so that the 305 sq. ft. mainsail can easily be set or reefed or taken in.

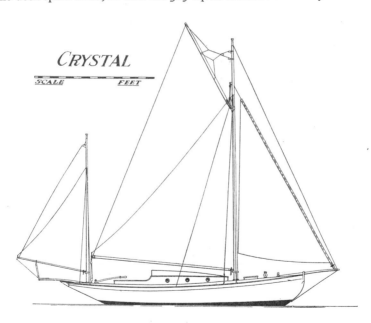

CRYSTAL

SCALE   FEET

· 20 ·

EEL

Length, overall - - - 21 ft. 0 in.		Length, water-line - - 19 ft. 0 in.
Beam - - - - - 7 ft. 0 in.		Draught (without C.B.) - 2 ft. 0 in.
Displacement - - - 1½ tons		Sail area - - - - 200 sq. ft.

Designer and Owner, GEORGE F. HOLMES

THE Humber Yawl Club, starting life fifty years ago as the Eastern Arm of the Royal Canoe Club, and finding that the 30-inch beam Rob Roy Canoes were too damp for the steep tidal waves of the Humber, developed a larger and more powerful canoe known as the Canoe Yawl, the Club changing its name accordingly.

After a number of years the larger canoes reached their natural limits, and *Eel* is a good example of the yawls. She was designed by her then owner for his own use. The canoe yawl has developed into quite a different type of vessel from the Rob Roy canoe, and there is no doubt that the *Eel* is the logical conclusion of a departure from the light canoe.

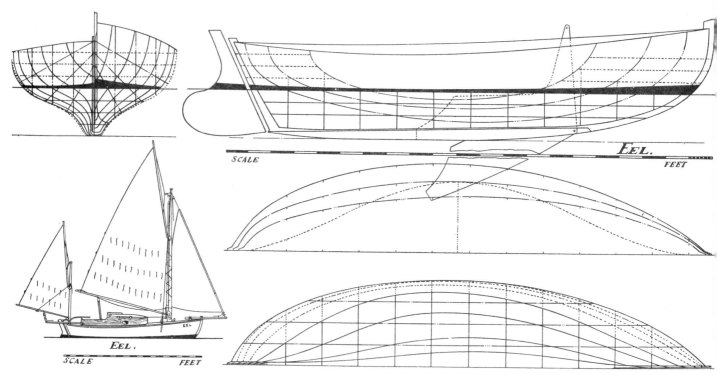

The charm of a canoe is its lightness and portability, and once these two things are passed, as they are bound to be with size, the natural end is a canoe large enough to live and sleep aboard, and one with power enough to stand up by itself in its battle with the winds and seas ; in other words a small centerboard cruiser with a canoe stern.

Eel's owner is an artist, whose etchings have for years brightened the pages of England's yachting publications ; and when an artist takes to designing sailing vessels the result is bound to be pleasing to the eye. Generally through life that which is pleasant to look upon is found to be near perfection. A fact borne out by our newspapers, for an item to become news must be unusual. Now a man usually chooses his wife in the first place by her looks or rather by the way she appears to his eyes, and the newspapers report divorces (in this country at least) as items of news, and never does a happy marriage appear in print unless in the local papers, which record the fact in a roundabout way, for they say Mrs. So-and-so died at the age of 75, and then a week or a month later Mr. So-and-so, who, tired of life without his mate for fifty years, joined his wife.

And so whenever an artist designs a sailing vessel or house or almost anything the result is generally very near perfection, for it must be remembered that in order to please the eye an artist has to be first of all most observant, and able to discern in life the essential points in order to pick them out and portray them to the world. Generally a man likes things without in the least saying why or being able to say why. One man admires a scene, another a house, but the artist, in order to paint these things, must know why he admires them, and so when any artist designs a sailing vessel the result is generally all it should be. The only fault ever seen by myself in the many designs by artists is the softness of line; they are rather inclined to soften up every line, and *Eel's* sections will illustrate my point; for such a tiny boat firmer bilges would, I believe, have helped.

Eel's owner and skipper had a different boat every year for fifteen years, and then when he had built *Eel* he remained steady and steadfast for fifteen years, which does not show stagnation, but that he had at last arrived at the ideal vessel for the Humber, and that the development of the canoes to Humber yawls was complete.

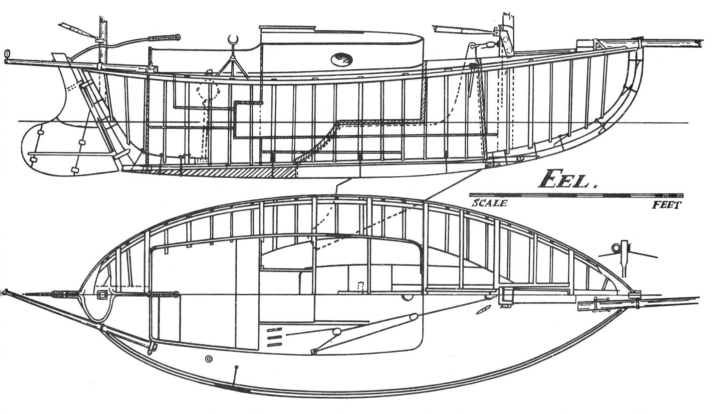

The Humber yawls were designed light enough to be taken on the deck of a steamer so that the owners could cruise in foreign waters, for their whole holiday would be taken otherwise sailing the boats to distant parts. And *Eel's* wanderings have taken her into many countries, for with her hull draught of 2 ft. increased at will to 4 ft. by her centerboard, she could cruise in waters barred to the ordinary cruiser on account of her draught. The L-shaped dropkeel or centerboard is the best type of all, as it cannot play the tricks of the ones that are hoisted by chains or wires. If *Eel* grounds and a stone jambs in her slot, the board can be forced down with the lever on deck. There is no wire or chain to break, only the tackle to the tabernacle, and if this carries away the board will not be lost, as it will fetch up with on its shackle at its maximum draught of 4 ft., when the tackle can be easily replaced, and the board hauled up again.

The mainmast lowers aft on its tabernacle for bridges, allowing *Eel* to explore waters 2 ft. 6 in. deep with bridges across if she so wishes. When in 1912 after fifteen years her designer-owner thought out another vessel he passed *Eel* on to his club mate Ernest Oliver, who has sailed her this last twenty years continuously, and the fact that *Eel* has had only two owners in her thirty-six years of life shows how discerning is the eye of an artist.

· 21 ·

VALHALLA'S WHALEBOAT

Length	-	-	-	-	30 ft. 6 in.	Beam	-	-	-	-	5 ft. 6 in.
Depth (amidships)		-	-	2 ft. 6 in.		Weight (stripped hull)	-	850 lbs.
		Sail area (dipping lug)	-	-	-	192 sq. ft.

" O'er the glad waters of the deep blue sea
Our thoughts as boundless and our souls as free."

OUR boat was a whaleboat off the *Valhalla*, and she was swift and seaworthy, climbing the waves as easily and gracefully as an ocean bird. Those who have not sailed in a lightly-built whaleboat have missed one of the greatest joys of sailing, for such a boat fills one with the buoyant hope that springy turf imparts on a sunny day. We had sailed our boat summer and winter for three years, and she filled us with the confidence of a tried and trusted friend, as she should, for the whaleboat is the finest sea boat ever evolved by man.

Developed for over 300 years in the hardest service of the seas, she could be nothing less than perfect. In her work she hung in davits high above the water in the heat of the sun, ready to be lowered with a rush whenever a whale was sighted. She was filled with 1,000 lbs. of gear, harpoons, and line besides her crew of seven men, making the weight this light boat had to carry in action with the whale close upon one ton. Away the boat would chase after the whale, rowing or sailing according to the weather; the whale harpooned (it sometimes weighed 80 tons) she might be towed by it at about 15 knots often dead to windward into the steep sea of a rising gale with night coming on.

The whale killed, the whaleboat would lay moored in its lee till daybreak, when she would probably be found by her parent ship, which had all night beaten to windward searching for her, and all would be well.

Or, as frequently happened, the whaler would be unable to find her boat, and after the latter had waited as long as it dared, she would make sail for the nearest land, which would probably be an island many miles away; and many whaleboat voyages of over a thousand miles are recorded.

Such was the breed of our boat, so no wonder she filled us with buoyant spirits, which I hope, and believe, all of us Cowes Sea Scouts, who learned sailing and seamanship in *Valhalla's* whaleboat, will retain till the end.

After three years of cruising along the coast between Beachy Head and the Start, we decided to sail across the Channel to Havre, and up the Seine if possible to Paris and return to Cowes, all within our two weeks' summer holiday.

With a rising glass we left Cowes in the last fling of the strong S.W. wind which had been blowing some days, and, with a fair tide, beat down the Solent on the morning of Saturday, July 29, 1921. The day before, I had sailed from Lymington to Hamble aboard a friend's schooner under her foresail only, and had then beat in my canoe across to Cowes against a wind that was strong enough to dismast three of the four 6-metres in the American team racing for the first time against Britain off Ryde.

We went ashore for the afternoon in Colwell Bay, just inside the Needles; for the flood tide, running up Channel all the afternoon, would be setting our whaleboat to leeward, and with her small drop keel and dipping lug we could not afford to start out with a lee-going tide; so we spent the time wandering over the hills at the west end of the Isle of Wight.

At 7.20 p.m. we set sail for France, and in two tacks cleared the Needles with the young ebb pushing us to windward; at 8.30 p.m. we were clear of the Island heading South by East, close hauled on the starboard tack, for Havre 100 miles away. With a crew of ten we divided into three watches of three, the jobs being look-out, main sheet man and bailer, with an hour on each job, so that each man did an hour at each job during the three-hour watch. Being Scoutmaster, I missed the watches, but steered all night, so, with four on, and six off watch, we settled down for the night.

The sunset promised a fine night, and although there was still enough wind and sea left to keep the bailer occupied, there was nothing alarming in the spray flying aboard all the while, and the six off watch slept soundly enough under oilskins and tents, which kept them fairly dry.

After steering all night, early dawn is generally depressing, but on this occasion the light stealing over the waters revealed the watch below, who had been invisible all night. The chaps were funny enough to make me laugh till I cried. Two pairs of feet sticking out from under the dodger forward were all that could be seen of the two stowed in there, two more were hung like hammocks with their necks on one thwart and the backs of their legs on the next. One of them, with his head driven well inside his sou'wester, looked so miserable as to be absolutely comic. Charles, who was 6 ft. 2 in., took up most of the foot board running down the centre of the thwarts, Bob

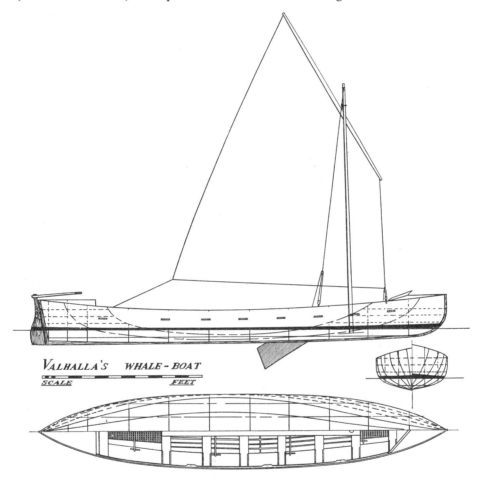

VALHALLA'S WHALE-BOAT
SCALE   FEET

had one arm round Charles, while the other was hanging loosely in the bilge water. We put the look-out man to sleep as it began to get light, so that the only two awake, besides myself, were Bill on the mainsheet and Spike bailing. I had to laugh again when one of the sleepers developed cramp and woke with a jerk, only to drop off to sleep again as quickly. At 8.00 a.m. I turned in after an enjoyable breakfast, giving instructions to be roused for trouble only, as the boys otherwise called me out of sheer kind-heartedness when they made coffee or tea. Napoleon used to leave orders, when turning in, that he was only to be called to hear bad news, and his example should be followed by everyone in command, for upon the brain of the man in charge of an army or a ship depend success or failure, and he must rest whenever possible, so that his brain is energetic and sparkles when needed, for often the time arrives when he can have no rest for perhaps 24 or 48 hours. And this he can endure, if he has not been tired out by unnecessary duty.

At 4.00 p.m., after eight hours of peaceful sleep, I woke to find the water no longer flying in fine spray over the weather bow, but instead much quieter, with the gentlest of airs, giving steerage way, but no more ; and within half an hour of waking there was a flat calm. But as it was hot we put off rowing until the cool of the evening. Then at 8.00 p.m. we split into two watches for rowing, my watch taking the first four hours. A 15-ft. oar, even if it is spruce, seems long and heavy for a fifteen-year-old boy to row with for four hours, but they were all used to it, and took these shifts as a matter of course.

By 11.30 p.m. the two lights ahead, which had before only been visible when we were on top of the swell, were in full view, so Ivan called their flash while I timed them. They were Cap la Heve, every 5 seconds, and Cap Antifer, every 20 seconds, so we were just where we should be, 25 miles off, for they are 390 feet above sea-level. We kept rowing along at 3 knots with five oars, knowing that we only had another half an hour before the other five took our places.

At 4.30 a.m., half an hour after my watch had started on their second spell of rowing, they were delighted to hear me call " Spellho ! " for a breeze was making from the S.W. ; and setting our dipping lug to port we sailed south on the starboard tack close hauled, not quite laying our course. All the gang turned in, leaving myself to steer, tend to the main sheet, look-out, and to think and dream alone, yet with nine of the best within call.

So for three hours I was very happy with my thoughts, and I tried to fathom the mystery and fascination of the sea. Here we were, ten youngsters from 14 to 23 years of age, our second night at sea in an open boat, quite contented and perfectly happy, when we should have been full of anxiety and worry. We knew and respected the mighty power of the wind and sea, for we had been out when steamers had been anchored in St. Helen's Roads to shelter from strong S.W. winds which according to papers had blown 60 miles an hour. In one storm we had rowed with all seven oars hard at it on a lee shore just holding our own for 6½ hours till the wind eased and backed a couple of points. In a long calm we had run out of water and learned the meaning of, " Water, water everywhere, nor any drop to drink." So it was not ignorance of the sea, but knowledge of her ways, that brought us happiness, and that sense of security necessary for the handling of open boats in a seaway.

The fog that came with dawn suddenly lifted at 7.30 a.m., and the high land ahead caused me to yell "Landho," at which all the nine woke up for their first glimpse of the France we had started out for. We sailed on, and came about fifty yards off the beach, 2½ miles to leeward of Cap de la Heve, the tide and wind having set us that distance off our course.

It was not till 10.30 a.m. that we rounded the cape and saw Havre for the first time, a small bay with a clean beach and houses, and beyond, the town itself. So we washed, and smartened ourselves and our whaleboat up, and sailed through the breakwaters, entering Havre Harbour at noon.

We had taken 40 hours from the Needles into Havre, an average of 2½ knots, but none of us minded that at all, as we had come for a sail, and had we maintained the speed at which we started, about 7 knots, we should have been wet through and bailing hard all the way across, instead of basking in the sunshine. Cruising and sailing is surely pleasure in all weathers. If calms prevail there is the warm sunshine and fresh air to enjoy, if hard strong winds there is the pleasure and exhilaration of high speeds and a fast passage, while moderate winds have the charms of middle-aged people, who have put behind them the follies and recklessness of youth, and have not yet the ills of old age.

We wandered along the sea-front and then round the town of Havre, during the hottest day there of the year. Presently we heard Spike and Harry laughing, and when we went back we too laughed, for Charles had collapsed with the heat, and Spike and Harry were dragging him along to a grog shop to give him some cognac. Charles is 6 ft. 2 in. overall and fairly beamy, so quite heavy for two small chaps like Spike and Harry, who were weak with laughter. However, we gave him a drink and he came round in a minute to collapse again as suddenly, but within a short time was as right as rain again. Small chaps are generally tougher than large ones, and in the case of growing boys this must always be remembered by the man in charge ; boys who have outgrown their strength must also consider this.

At 6.30 p.m. that evening we left Havre, and, sailing W.S.W. to the outer Seine buoys, bore away before a smart breeze and ran up the river with a strong flood tide. The channel between the sands at the mouth of the Seine is continually shifting, but, with our small draught, we found no difficulty in following its winding course, for there were red buoys to port and black buoys to starboard, and we were soon inside the sands, for the tide was running at about 6 knots. The tide was nearly high, so this part of the river, that till now had been idle of shipping, swarmed with steamers, and was very busy, as a river leading to the capital of any country should be.

We reached La Roque breakwater at 8.30 p.m. and tied up for the night. Some slept in a mud hut ashore, which seemed the home of thousands of rats, others were under our sail stretched over a fence, and I had the whaleboat.

Next morning (Tuesday) at 7.30 we awoke, and piling everything into the boat, were soon being carried towards Rouen with the strong rushing flood tide, and, after a wash, cooked and ate our breakfast. We then settled down to row, as there was no wind ; but at 8.30 a strong breeze abaft the beam enabled us to hoist sail, and soon we were tearing along in fine style, though the wind was very uncertain due to the winding river and its high banks.

At 10.30 tramp steamers passed us, some outward and some inward bound. Owing to the bar at the mouth of the river, they can only sail at certain times, reminding us of wild-fowl flighting at sunrise and sunset, for suddenly there are dozens of steamers, and then no more for another twelve hours. Noon found us off Duclair, and the tide turned against us, so we tied up to its tumbledown pier, and visited this small market town. After a feed we arranged some sports amongst ourselves, and spent that afternoon at tug-of-war, boxing, wrestling and relay racing, as well as sprinting and racing longer distances. To wind up with the gang set upon their unfortunate Scoutmaster and forced him to eat grass. At 9.30 p.m. the first of the flood made, so we left for a four-hour row, mooring to a small island at 1.30 a.m. for our night's sleep. Seven of us landed and turned in on a lawn in front of an old house. We were soon wrapped in our blankets and asleep, having left the other three in the boat. We were not far from Rouen, and our reason for choosing this island was that in Rouen we should find no place to pitch a tent and sleep. We always took tents with us, but never pitched them unless it rained.

ROWING

At 7.00 a.m. the owner of the house, which we had thought empty, came out, and so did his wife. Thinking that perhaps the seven sleepers in brown blankets might not improve the lawn, to his or his wife's eyes, we turned out, and taking the whaler to the end of the island, turned in again till 11.00 a.m. Then we made for Rouen with the young flood, reached there 45 minutes later, tying up alongside the small London steamer, *Leelee*, and set out to explore one of the most historical cities of Europe.

We saw in the market place the tablet marking the spot on which Joan of Arc was burned, and, wandering into the museum, saw a queer old tiller of which no one knew anything, some very interesting armour, and also a sword and medal given by Napoleon to one of his officers.

On our way to the cathedral we walked through St. Romain Street and saw the big clock and fourteenth-century houses. We climbed the 812 steps to the top of the cathedral spire, and there met the Manchester Grammar School land scouts. They were walking to Paris from Havre, averaging fifteen miles a day carrying all their kit, which seemed pretty good going for youngsters. While at the top of the spire, we felt it swinging, for there was a hard wind blowing at that height, and we were told that it actually swung 6 feet, being 510 feet above the city. The solid, heavy-looking sky-scrapers of America looked ugly to my eyes when I first saw them, for I was so used to seeing the tall slender spires of European cathedrals and churches, which swing like trees to the wind.

After tea we set sail and were soon bowling along at 6 knots before a strong wind. Catching up with a tug towing at 4 knots, we lowered sail and tied on astern, for while in one bend of the river we could sail 6 knots, we could hardly do 2 at the next, so that it was easier to tow at a steady 4 all the while, and the river folk were very pleasant company. At 6.30 p.m. the tug moored up for the night, so we sailed on to one of the small islands, and went ashore to cook our evening meal. After an hour ashore we set sail once more, finally turning in for the night on an island about nine miles above Rouen, and as there was no rain we could continue to have the sky full of stars for our roof.

Not pitching tents makes for ease in getting under way each morning, and this was useful, for at 6.00 a.m. the tug which had towed us the previous day came abreast and, sighting us, blew his whistle. We were up, piled our blankets into the boat, and, rowing out into the river, caught the fourth and last of the barges she was towing, by the time it was abreast of us. We washed and dressed while we were being towed at 4 knots towards Paris.

At 9.30 a.m. we came to the first lock, and entering, rose 8 feet before continuing on our way. This lock only took three-quarters of an hour to pass through, but the next took three and a half hours, as there were so many barges and tugs waiting bound up or down the river. While in the lock, we almost lost Bevvy for ever, for although he reckoned to speak French well, he had to fall back on a *French-English Dictionary*, and the match he asked for was a love affair instead of a thing with which to light a stove. However, we rescued him with shrieks of laughter, and continued on happily. In that lock we rose 15 feet, and gaining height, the river became more beautiful, though this seemed impossible, so lovely had it appeared below Rouen. At times the river wound round a hill, and then away for miles would stretch a scene that might have been part of dreamland.

As our tug finished towing at 7.00 p.m., we rowed on to the next lock, arriving there at 1.00 a.m. We tied up to the second fleet of barges from the lock, for we wanted a tow through behind the first fleet when they started, so did not wish to disturb their sleep and annoy them now, for ten cannot turn in on a 30-ft. open boat without a certain amount of noise.

At 5.45 a.m. wild shrieks from three tugs' whistles awakened us with a jerk. All the gang seemed irritable, and no wonder, for it is hard on the nerves to be wakened suddenly by piercing shrieks from three steam whistles; I think everyone prefers to be awakened by a cup of tea, two biscuits, and a charming voice, saying:

> " Awake, for morning in the bowl of night
> Has flung the stone that puts the stars to flight."

We moved close to the lock, and as soon as the fleet of barges had formed two deep inside, we squeezed in, and tied to the last barge for the day's tow. The gang turned in, leaving myself to watch our boat through the lock, and steer her till the next one.

At 10.30 a.m., as we were about to enter another lock, I woke the gang, who by now had had nine hours' sleep. We had quite a lot of fun at each lock, for then the gang went shopping, and Spot brightened us all up this time by buying a tin of baby's food instead of jam, and, not to be defeated, spread it on his bread and butter. At 3.30 p.m. we came to another lock, and had a swim whilst the fleet packed themselves in. Leaving at 4.30 p.m. we towed until 6.00 p.m. when the fleet moored to the bank for the night, two miles below an imposing town with a cathedral which from that distance looked similar to Westminster Abbey.

We made sail, and reached along with a nice breeze, soon arriving at the town, which was Mantes. We visited the cathedral, and, after filling our beakers with water from the fountains, had a bathe, and then continued our way to the next lock. As we passed under the town bridge a Canadian canoe with two men rowing attempted to race us. At first we went easy to take their measure, and then opening out soon left them behind. We rowed on, and finally tied up just below a weir with its roaring water. There was a strange charm about these night journeys under oars, tiring though they might be. The trees and banks reflected in the calm waters of the river gave everything an unaccustomed and weird appearance.

At 5.50 a.m. two Frenchmen came alongside to see who we were, and we discovered that our fears of the night before were correct, and that we had come up a blind alley to the weir. Although the lock was only 100 yards on our starboard hand we had to row three miles to reach it. So back we went, and then doubling once more, rowed to the lock. Here we enquired the distance from Paris, and found that it was 70 kilometres by the river although only 45 by road.

We walked into Meulan to talk things over during breakfast, for our money was getting low, and as we had been a week reaching this far, we should take a week to retrace our steps, by which time our holiday would be ended. So we reluctantly decided to return home without reaching Paris.

All the way we had not seen a single steamer bound for Paris. We had hoped to be able to tow at 8 knots or so behind some small freighter, which would only take minutes to go through locks where the tugs with their barges took hours. However, it is always sad to think what might have been; and at 10.15 a.m. we made fast astern of the last of a string of five barges just leaving the lock, bound for Rouen at a steady 4 knots.

At 2.30 p.m. a motor barge with only two barges in tow caught us, and, as she was doing 6 knots to our 4, we let go our barge, and rowing at about 5 knots dropped alongside her. Jammer made a wild leap aboard the second barge, which was high out of water because it was so light, and making fast our painter on her bollards, slid down the rope into the whaleboat quite neatly. After towing us for three-quarters of an hour, the tug sheered towards the bank just above a lock, and paying out more of our towing line, we were able to sheer still more towards the bank, and Spot leapt ashore to see if the steamer blowing astern was British. She turned out to be the *Swallow* of Grimsby, so we rowed over to the lock which was a small one. Directly she was in, we squeezed in astern. The *Swallow* drew 8 feet of water and travelled at 8 knots, and her skipper volunteered to tow us. She was in a hurry, as her sister ship was held up in the Channel by heavy weather, the two trading between Paris and London with general cargoes. Towing at 8 knots with the banks so close each side gave us an impression of great speed in our boat, but not so much to the five of us who, being aboard the *Swallow*, were higher above the water. At 10.15 p.m. the *Swallow* tied up just above Amfreville Lock, and we turned in for the night on her after-deck. At 8.30 a.m. we moored alongside the quay at Havre and bought in the market place enough food to take us home to England, and stowed it all aboard the whaleboat.

The *Swallow* was unable to leave till Monday, so we continued where we left off with our exploration of Rouen.

We looked over the tower in which Joan of Arc was imprisoned, another in which she was tortured, and saw the doorway through which she was led to the market place to be burned. Then we saw the crypt in which William the Conqueror was buried, and visited various other places of great historical interest.

In some of the streets the houses were very very old, and leant across the street farther and farther with each storey until they practically met at the top, and so shut out the sunshine and fresh air.

On the way back we met Sir Percy Armitage, who, besides being Commissioner of Scouts for Cranford, was Gentleman Usher to the King, and we had a most interesting yarn, for he had raced and sailed in all sorts of boats from *Britannia* downwards.

At noon on Monday, August 8, we left Rouen homeward bound astern of the *Swallow* at 8 knots. A steamer like the *Swallow* is forced to take three pilots up the Seine; the first takes her through the shifting sand-banks at the mouth of the river, the second from Havre to Rouen, and the third from there to Paris. So it is with a steamer outward bound, and we lost our lively Albert at Rouen for another pilot with no energy at all.

By 7.30 p.m. we were at the entrance of the Tankerville Canal, and as there was far too much sea, due to strong N.W. winds, for the pilot to take the *Swallow* out, she anchored and we tied up to the piles alongside the lock gates awaiting high water, for we hoped to go through the canal and so save the dusting we should get in the Seine estuary.

On the way down we had shipped quite a lot of spray, for we had been towed against that strong wind at 8 knots with a fair tide and in some of the reaches of the river where the wind was dead ahead there was quite a sea.

At 10.15 p.m. we pushed off from the piles, for the young flood in the Seine rises so rapidly that if our boat had been caught for thirty seconds only under a notch in a pile, she would have filled. The Seine bore, of which I had been rather afraid, only shows itself during the spring tide of the equinox; but it is far better to be sure than sorry, and on our way up the Seine we always waited till the bore should have passed before getting under way. A wall of water, 8 feet high, travelling at 10 knots, is not a thing to take chances with in an open boat with nine youngsters, whose mothers looked to me for their safe keeping.

At midnight we entered the canal, and here for the first time we were expected to show ship's papers, passports and so forth. We had none, so I signed the book "Cowes Sea Scouts" and all was well.

At 6.00 a.m. the two tugs that locked through with us got under way for Havre, and as we had carefully tied up to one before turning in we started away for Havre with the gang still asleep, while I steered. At 8.00 a.m. I routed them out, and we cooked and ate breakfast. Then several of them washed in the canal, and held forth on the virtues of cleanliness until we passed a brown and white dog blown up like a balloon with its four legs pointing skywards, doing, we reckoned, half a knot under bare poles, when we who had not washed laughed loud and long at the expressions on the washed faces.

After arriving at the Havre locks and dropping 14 ft. we took half an hour to reach the breakwater entrance and, passing through, started away for Cowes. After a while we tied up to a bell buoy about three miles off Cap de la Heve, for the strong N.W. wind of the night before had faded away, although it was still in the same direction, and so dead ahead, and too light for our small sail area. There was still a heavy swell rolling in, which occasionally broke, and after laying to that lurching buoy for 1½ hours our warp carried away. We therefore set sail, for the wind had veered to north, so that we could lay our course within a point.

The relief of sailing after being tied to a rolling bell buoy can hardly be described, and we were all very happy and contented to be at sea once more, with our boat just flicking the tops off each wave. At 7.00 p.m. we were 16 miles away from Cap de la Heve, then the breeze veering still more, and freshening, sent us along gaily for the Island. Sunset was most inspiring; at 8.30 p.m. the sun, looking like a great red ball of fire, just touched the horizon, and we quite expected to see great clouds of steam arise from it. At this time the clouds were wonderfully red at the top and golden below; the changing colours of a sunset at sea are one of the wonders of the world, and beyond the powers of any pen to describe.

In that night's sunset the mackerel clouds overhead were a cold blue and a warm red, and where the sun sank the clouds were red with golden curls, giving the promise of a fine night. Although a dawn at sea is often lovely it is not so grand as sunset, for red in a sunset means a fine night, but red in a dawn gives warning of strong winds, and thus has a sinister appearance. At sunrise and sunset the Lord tells those who understand the weather for the day or night.

At 9.30 p.m. Cap de la Heve light was under the skyline, so we were twenty-five miles on our way, and the flash of St. Catherine's, seventy-five miles distant, was visible in the sky. This is only a sixteen-mile light, as it stands fairly low, but being the second most powerful light in the world its beams caught the clouds above strongly enough to be visible almost across Channel. This was a great help to me, for steering all night looking into a compass is trying to the eyes, whereas steering all night at distant flashes in the sky was nice and easy. From 10.30 p.m. till 1.30 a.m. we had a strong wind and slid along at 7 knots; with the wind came a ghostly mist, so that at midnight everything looked unreal. The bellying sail, the mast, the eight sleepers and the one bailing, all seemed airy and misty forms, and even the sides of the whaleboat seemed flimsy, and not at all solid. But at 1.30 a.m. the wind died away, so that we had only just steerage way, and with the wind went the mist.

The sunrise was a fiery and angry red, which meant wind before the day was out, perhaps more than we needed, so I routed out Bill to take charge while I had some sleep before it came. The calm continued meanwhile, so at 9.00 a.m. we started rowing, and after two hours sighted the Island, looking like a low bank of clouds on the skyline. We rowed quietly till 4.00 p.m. when the promised wind came with a rushing squall ; we then stowed oars and, setting sail, were just able to lay N.N.W. close hauled, which, with a weather-going tide, would just take us into Brooke Bay.

With the ten of us sitting out to windward we were only sailing at about 5½ knots, for sheeted down hard we were too close to the wind for our boat to show her speed.

At 7.00 p.m. we eased sheets, having decided to spend a night at Ventnor, for, by the time we reached Brooke, the flood would have made, and our whaleboat would not beat against a 3-knot tide to the Needles' Channel and home. In landing at Brooke we should ship water, and so soak all our blankets, but Ventnor, in the lee of St. Catherine's, would have fairly smooth water. With the wind abeam our speed jumped from 5½ to 8½ knots, and at 9.00 p.m. we landed at Ventnor for the night, to be anxiously asked by the coastguards what ship we were from, as they had been watching us in the sea running outside for hours through a telescope, and thought we were a shipwrecked crew. The gang turned in on the beach, while I slept in the boat. The next morning, Thursday, August 11, we left Ventnor with a fair wind and tide for Cowes, and rounding Culver Cliff came upon the *Britannia* and the other large yachts racing without their topsails. When *Britannia* races without a topsail the wind is quite strong. Arriving at Cowes we went aboard *Diablesse*, to find that her owner and his wife were aboard H. Fiennes Speed's yacht, so we went there too for a yarn. Then we sailed on up the river to our club room, and home to tea, after thirteen days of strenuous but enjoyable voyaging on sea and river.

Our whaleboat had made her first voyage across channel successfully, and although we planned in future years to cruise down to Spain, she never sailed that far, for we never had long enough holidays. In later years she twice crossed the Channel, her best run being from Cowes round Bembridge Ledge to Cherbourg in twelve hours, the distance being 84 miles. Her average speed on that occasion was 7 knots, which is quite a high average for a 30-ft. open boat to maintain for such a distance, especially when it is considered that her crew were growing boys. Her days are ended, but she will always remain in the memory of her grateful crew as the best sea boat in the world.

· 22 ·

GADGETS

M OST owners have little trick arrangements aboard their vessels, ranging from such things as a jack inside the cabin door to take off sea boots, to a guide on the topmast, which saves a man going aloft to thread on the topsail hanks ; and this chapter is of such contrivances. For when these things have been worked out and perfected by their owners, they make life easier (or they should) aboard.

A BOOT JACK

LANDFALL'S ROUND HOUSE SEAT

The sea boot jack reminds me that few people realise that the reason sea boots are at times difficult to take off, is because the feet have become hot and swollen inside them ; but if they are dipped for a minute, either over the side or in a bucket of water, they cool down and shrink, when the boot slips off easily. (If the water is not cold enough to shrink the foot there is no need to wear sea boots.)

A V or U cut in the end of a piece of wood 12 inches long and 4 inches wide, with a short piece underneath to raise it 4 inches off the deck, will make a good boot jack, if well fixed at the bottom of the companion way ; for generally on a small boat when sea boots are needed, it is nice to have two hands to oneself, and this jack will pull off boots without even the necessity of bending down. . . . But it must be fastened down firmly and out of the way or people stub their toes on it.

    *   *   *   *   *   *   *   *   *   *   *   *   *

If continued cheerfulness is a sign of great wisdom, dolefulness is a sign of constipation, and *Landfall's* round house seat was the finest aid to cheerfulness I have ever met. It clipped on the rail aft, and on this a man could sit in the sunshine and fresh air and . . . ruminate. *Landfall* had three W.C.s below, but once we set sail from America these were cut off, and never used until we were moored in Plymouth Harbour. The sanitary arrangements aboard small vessels generally leave much to be desired, but not so *Landfall's* seat on the stern.

    *   *   *   *   *   *   *   *   *   *   *   *   *

Dorade's tiller-lock is one of the most useful gadgets that I have met, for it locks the tiller in an instant, and releases it as fast. The drawings illustrate its working. Underneath the tiller is a beam, which supports the tiller

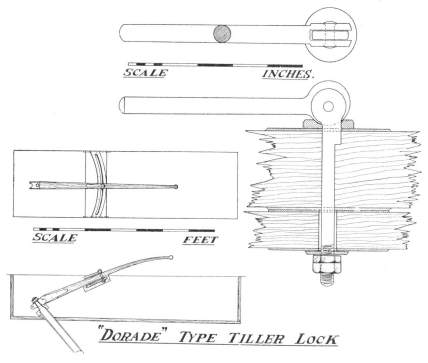

"DORADE" TYPE TILLER LOCK

and saves the rudder head a lot of strain, for most helmsmen, without realising it, press down hard on the tiller at all times, which wrings the tiller head. There is a slot in this beam, in which the locking bolt works ; this bolt passes through the tiller, and at the top has an eccentric lever, so that whenever the lever is lifted it locks the tiller

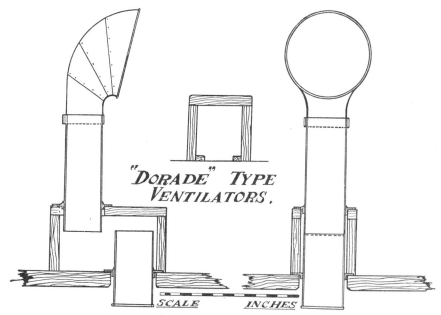

"DORADE" TYPE VENTILATORS.

in an instant to whichever part of the beam it is over at that moment. It is so simple and effective that the wonder is it has not been invented before ; and this is said of all good ideas, for they are so good that other people always wonder they have not thought of them themselves.

Any vessel fitting this to an existing tiller should strengthen the tiller where the bolt goes through, otherwise the hole might weaken the tiller.

Dorade's other gift to the sailing world is her ventilator. When seas are flying over small vessels their hatchways have to be closed down, so that just when fresh air below is most important, there is none, with the result that going off watch is not looked forward to as it should be, for there is a damp fug in the cabin. *Dorade* spent two years like this, and then her owners invented their water trap, the same ventilators were used, and the existing holes through the deck. A short tube was fitted in the old holes, to stand several inches above the deck, then a box was fitted over this tube and through the top on one side of this the ventilator led, so it will be seen that water shipped down the ventilator is trapped in the box and has to rise above the level of the intake pipe before it can get below ; and as the box is fitted with scuppers to let the water away on deck, it never rises above the level ; the only way it could do so would be for two waves to be shipped in rapid succession down the ventilator, a thing that has not so far happened, although *Dorade* has twice crossed the northern part of the North Atlantic with them. The steady flow of air these ventilators give makes them well worth while. The extra cost is only that of the short tube in the deck, and the wooden box on deck. The drawings and the scale in inches show exactly how they are made and fitted.

*   *   *   *   *   *   *   *   *   *   *   *   *

To anchor well and truly the anchor and cable must be under perfect control from the order " Let go " until the right amount of cable has been paid out and the vessel is riding nicely to her anchor or anchors, and yet it is

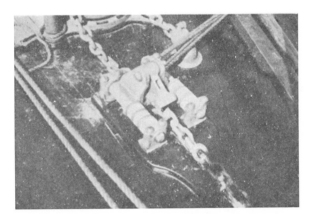

COMMODORE GOODERHAM'S COMBINED CABLE BRAKE

. . . AND STOPPER

very seldom one sees any braking device on small yachts ; unless the cable is under full control when running out it will run too fast and, piling down on top of the anchor, tend to catch a turn round one of the flukes and so render the anchor useless when most needed . . . (in strong winds).

While cruising and racing on board Commodore Norman Gooderham's schooner *Yolanda*, I met the most effective cable brake and stopper for small vessels imaginable. Norman with his sailor's instinct had invented a very simple and powerful brake ; swung forward, it only needed the pressure of a man's foot to brake and actually stop the cable flying out through the hawse pipe, and then swung backwards it became a pawl that locked the chain securely, while the rubber buffers of the stopper relieved *Yolanda* of most of the shocks a small vessel is subjected to when snubbing at her anchor in a seaway. It was thought at first that a lever would be needed to give the brake enough power, and the slot for the lever can be seen in the top of the brake ; but in practice the pressure of a man's foot was found to be enough and so the lever spends its life in the fo'c'sle in case it is ever needed. *Yolanda* is 44 feet on the water-line and has tall spars, so the brake and pawl are worth while ; and Canada's greatest racing man has no waste gear on his cruising schooner which he races so successfully.

*   *   *   *   *   *   *   *   *   *   *   *

Space on small vessels is most valuable, for a man in his house can give more room for his front door mat than he can afford for the whole of his saloon, in which he spends some four months of the year as compared to the few moments spent greeting people on his doormat. So *Landfall*, by using a small piano as the lead weight in the saloon table, besides giving a new idea, stresses the fact that things serving a dual purpose, because they halve space, double the room aboard small vessels. A large piano is not needed when a small one will easily fill with sound a small vessel. *Landfall's* tiny piano easily filled her saloon with sound. The table top had several hinges in it, so that it could be folded back to form a music rest, and having more slope than the average piano rest, held the music better ; bottles even, as in the photograph, rested on it safely.

*   *   *   *   *   *   *   *   *   *   *   *   *   *

Many years ago, in England, the position of the salt on the table was of great significance, you either sat above or below the salt according to your rank ; but on *Landfall* we all sat below the salt, for above the swing table was a smaller edition of it, suspended from the deck, with a rail round. This was a two-decker, and held mustard, salt, sugar, knives, forks, spoons, in fact every instrument and aid for eating which civilisation has forced upon the races under its sway, all handy and easily reached from the table. These things lived there always when not in use, a far better and easier plan than stowing them away in dark cupboards. The only improvement to *Landfall's* swing

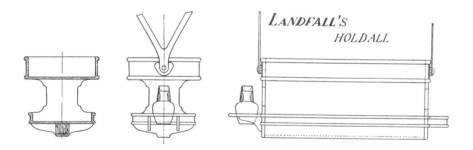

LANDFALL'S HOLDALL

table and double decker above that I can think of, would be one good stanchion from the deck to the floor at each end to hold both. Such a stanchion would be stronger, and would also form a deck stanchion to strengthen the deck. Moreover it would make a safe rail to hold when approaching the swing table in a seaway, with a heaving and pitching cabin floor.

*   *   *   *   *   *   *   *   *   *   *   *   *

The Rear-Commodore of the Royal Thames has invented many useful things for sailing vessels, and as some of these are for racers they appear in that half of the book ; but the backstay lever, which J. S. Highfield has thought out and tried with great success aboard his 15-metre *Dorina*, is simple and effective, and because it always sets the backstays exactly, is very suitable for cruisers, for otherwise in the night watches it is difficult to know just how the backstays are set up after tacking or gybing. The lever is really a channel bar, and when it is pushed right down it is over its centre, therefore the greater the strain the less chance it has of lifting. In fact it is impossible to lift it by the pull of the backstay, but because some rope catching under it might do this, it should have a locking catch, which would prevent a rope finding its way under.

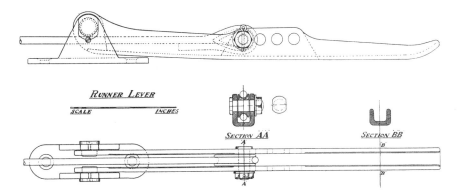

It would seem that there is little power in this lever at first sight, but a second thought will bring home the fact that as it begins to arrive at the spot where it is dragging home the last few valuable inches of the backstay, it is becoming increasingly powerful. *Dorina* fitted one of these on one side, and still left the ordinary backstay gear the other side; and the proof as to which was the better and easier, as well as the surer method, can be gauged

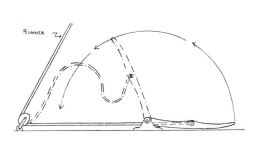

DIAGRAM SHOWING HIGHFIELD RUNNER
LEVER IN ACTION

IT IS DIFFICULT TO KNOW HOW BACKSTAYS
ARE SET UP, IN THE DARK

by the fact that her crew schemed and aimed to work the lever, and the unfortunate one worked the ordinary backstay on the other side. Time will see the use of this backstay lever increased in racing and cruising vessels, for it has power and adjustment combined with the advantage that the backstay is set every time to its exact tautness, there being no rope parts to stretch and give, all the power being in the lever, whose length never varies.

On racers with twin headstays these levers can be used to slack up the stay on which no sail is set. Thus all the weight is thrown on the luff of the headsail, causing it to stand much better.

· 23 ·
MASTING AND RIGGING

THE earliest illustration of which I know, showing details of the masting and rigging of vessels, is one in the Science Museum, a picture of an Egyptian ship of the Vth Dynasty (2,600 years B.C.).

The sail was set on one large mast formed by two spars joined at the top and spread the width of the ship at the bottom, the mast having the appearance of a tapered ladder. The illustration shows the mast lowered aft into a crutch, and the crew rowing.

At first sight one does not realise how clever this rig is, but then with a rush thoughts flood the brain of a naval architect, fill him with admiration for the old Egyptian ship designers, and make him wish he could dig them up to congratulate them on their job. Iron, except in the form of meteorites, was unknown to the ancients, so they must have said, " To do away with the constant stretch and shrinkage of rigging we will use a mast made like unto sheer-legs, and it was so." Then all they needed was a stay rope fore and aft. That they knew as much as we know of rigging, is seen by the truss rope running fore and aft to support the overhangs of the ship, as this runs over struts in exactly the same way that we now stay our tall masts, the only difference being that the rope is a vegetable fibre (flax), while our rigging is steel, and that they have used a Spanish windlass instead of a rigging screw. Lacking wire rigging and steel rigging screws, they were forced into the double mast.

It is only in recent times that iron and steel wire have enabled rigging to become important, for with the constant stretching of hempen rigging, the masts had to take the greatest part of the work in supporting sails, but now the rigging is becoming more important than the masts, which are only members, though still important ones, of a carefully planned structure.

The reason for going back to the beginning of things is to try and stop people ploughing ground, already not only ploughed but sown and reaped, for it is so easy to keep running round in small circles. Even Curry, the author of that excellent book, *The Aerodynamics of Sails*, fell down by using an ancient Egyptian mast, and, claiming it to be new, said that it was the fastest rig yet to windward. However, our little canoes, with the inefficient rig forced on them by the American rule, sailed one point higher and footed as fast as the Curry racer, which had the same sail area.

The more civilised a country becomes, the easier it is for it to run round in circles. We elect a government, and strangely enough put in with them an opposition party, and, odd though it may seem, do this year after year ; yet when a rugger team is chosen to play against another nation, no one would dream of putting in a few extra players, whose duty it was to run along and trip up our own players. But we do just that with our parliamentary team. Perhaps one day this country will see how futile this is, and then, whichever party wins the election, that party will go in alone ; there will be only just over half the Members of Parliament, which will mean twice as much work, as there will be only half as much talk. Ah me ! And to think that otherwise intelligent men expect me to get interested and excited over politics, and waste time voting.

*   *   *   *   *   *   *   *   *   *   *   *   *

The four usual rigs of small vessels are, cutter, schooner, ketch and yawl, and these four different rigs are illustrated in this chapter, the boats chosen being *Lexia*, *Niña*, *Landfall* and *Dorade*. There is no doubt that a careful study of these different vessels' spars will be good for everyone, for Lexia has, amongst other cruises, twice crossed the Atlantic. *Niña* won the Transatlantic Race and the Fastnet Race in 1928, and *Landfall* has raced across the Atlantic, while the little *Dorade* has three times crossed the Atlantic, putting up record runs, one from America in 17 days, when she won the Transatlantic Race, and her crossing in 1933 to America in 22 days, which was most startling. So there is no doubt that these four rigs have been tried and tested.

LEXIA

Lexia's cutter rig is shown first, as it is naturally the rig chosen or given first thought, for its simplicity, strength and efficiency.

Her mast is 10 inches in diameter from deck to hounds, and tapering away to $6\frac{3}{4}$ inches at the upper peak halyard block, is there the same size as the heel of the hollow topmast, which has a 10-inch housing. This 10-inch housing brings the thought that a mast should not go through the deck at all, but should sit on the deck, when it would be as the jib of a crane, which, being free to take up any position it wishes, can be treated as a strut under compression ;

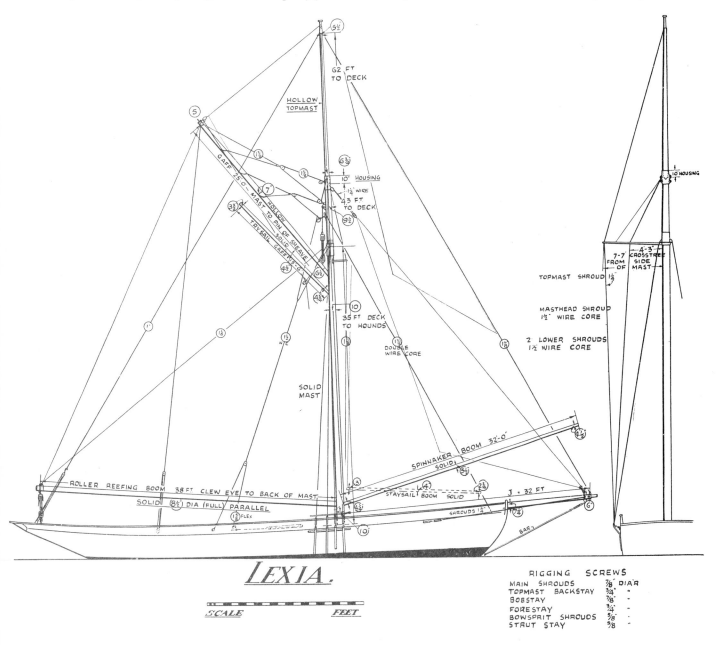

but because a mast is stepped through the deck, it is bound for a certain part of its length, and so is bent, and this increases the strain. My first boat, a canoe, had the mast stepped on the deck, and my latest boat, also a canoe, has just the same, and, as these little boats generally lead the way in thought, I am going to be bold enough to prophesy that in the years to come, first the racers and then the cruisers will all step their masts on deck, when even if a shroud does carry away the mast will not, for it will simply fall over the side. Years ago, tent poles were stuck in the ground, a few pegs would pull out, away to leeward went the tent and the pole broke, which meant that it could not be reset. Sometimes because the tent pole was earth-bound it broke because the guys slacked off and allowed the top to sag to leeward, and then, when bent, the pole was unable to stand its load and crumpled up. But now tent poles sit on the ground, and in the future masts will sit on the deck. This will happen gradually, and be all the better for it; and it is quite easy to see why tiny vessels like canoes lead thought, then the racers and finally the cruisers follow, for experiments in small boats like canoes cost little, and racers can experiment, because, racing in sheltered waters, they have only expense to consider. The cruisers hardly experiment, they want a thing tried and proved before they make use of it, for besides expense, they have another consideration, because they sail off-shore, and that is the danger that the carrying away of gear involves. Not only do they risk the loss of their vessel, driving ashore on a rocky coast, but they also risk starvation, for a sailing boat off shore might easily run out of food if dismasted, before she could rig a jury mast and make a port.

The hollow topmast of *Lexia* is tapered from its 6¾ in. at the heel to 5½ at the top, while her only other hollow spar, the main gaff, is 6½ in. diameter at the throat, 7 in. in the middle and 5 in. at the top.

Lexia's solid boom, 8¼ in. in diameter and parallel, was sprung when a heavy green sea broke into her mainsail, and practically submerged her, on her way to America, where she had a new one made, 9 in. in diameter, which has stood well, but is too heavy. For roller reefing, the boom should be larger at its outer end, since with every turn the diameter increases greatly at the tack, where the luff rope rolls down on top of the under roll, while at the outer end, because of the cut of the sail, the leach rope comes inboard at each roll in a spiral, and so with every turn more sail is rolled up at the luff than at the leach, and results in the boom dropping into the sea at its outer end. Had *Lexia's* new boom been made 8 in. at the mast and 9½ at the outer end, this would have been avoided, for whenever we make a roller reefing boom, we make it hollow with a greater diameter at the outer end, and as I said before, the little boats lead the way in thought and gear, because an experiment in them costs so little.

The spar plan and list of rigging will illustrate *Lexia's* cutter rig which, excepting for its 8¼-inch boom, stood everything it was called upon to stand in two Atlantic crossings, two Fastnet Races, a Bermuda Race, a cruise to the Mediterranean and the Brittany Coast. And there is much to be said for her sturdy cutter rig, with the only hollow spars, topmast and gaff, which in the event of their carrying away would not cripple her, for her trysail could be set till such time as her main gaff was fished. *Lexia's* is a simple, strong and effective rig with little to get out of order.

BLOCK LIST FOR 40 TONS CUTTER *LEXIA*

Name of Block	No.	Kind	Size	Sheave	Description of Block
Main Throat halyards - -	1	Treble	5″	Patent	Eye and shackle to take main halyard strop.
,, ,, ,, - -	1	Double	5″	,,	Eye and shackle to take gaff ironwork.
,, ,, purchase - -	1	Double	4½″	,,	Eye and shackle.
,, ,, - -	1	Double	4½″	,,	Eye and shackle.
Peak halyards (to have steel cheeks)	2	Single	4½″	,,	Solid eye and thimble shackle for gaff spars (wooden shells with steel cheeks).
Peak halyards - - -	3	Single	4½″	,,	Eye and shackle for mast head ironwork.
,, purchase - - -	1	Double	4½″	,,	Eye and shackle.
,, ,, - - -	1	Single	4½″	,,	Eye and shackle and becket.
Topsail sheet - - -	2	Single	3½″	Common	Bows and thimble (gaff end and mast heads).
,, ,, tackle - -	1	Double	4″	Patent	Eye and shackle.
,, ,, ,, - -	1	Single	4″	,,	Eye and shackle and becket.
,, whip - - -					2 whips, no blocks.
Main runner tackles - -	2	Double	6″	,,	Eye and shackle.
,, ,, ,, - -	2	Double	6″	,,	Eye and shackle and becket.
Main sheet - - - -	1	Treble	8″	,,	Eye and shackle for boom end.
,, ,, - - - -	1	Double	8″	,,	Solid eye to take buffer shackle.
,, ,, - - - -	2	Single	7″	,,	Swivel eye and shackle leads.
Staysail boom sheet - -	1	Double	4½″	,,	Eye and shackle boom end.
,, ,, ,, - -	1	Single	4½″	,,	Solid eye and shackle for horse.

Name of Block	No.	Kind	Size	Sheave	Description of Block
Staysail boom sheet - - -	2	Single	4″	Patent	Swivel eye and shackle leads.
,, tackle - - -	1	Double	4″	,,	Eye and shackle.
,, ,, - - -	1	Single	4″	,,	Eye and shackle and becket.
Topmast stay tackle - -	1	Double	4½″	,,	Eye and shackle.
,, ,, ,, - -	1	Single	4½″	,,	Eye and shackle and becket.
Staysail halyards - - -	1	Single	4″	,,	Eye and shackle for mast head.
,, ,, fly block -	1	Single	4″	,,	Standing jaw and screw pin for head of sail.
,, ,, purchase -	2	Single	5″	,,	Eye and shackle.
Jib purchase - - -	1	Double	4½″	,,	Eye and shackle.
,, ,, - - -	1	Single	4½″	,,	Eye and shackle and becket.
,, sheets - - -	2	Single	5″	Common	Bows and thimble.
Topsail tack tackle - -	1	Double	4″	Patent	Eye and shackle.
,, ,, ,, - -	1	Single	4″	,,	Eye and shackle and becket.
Jib sheet tackles - -	2	Double	4½″	Common	Eye and shackle.
,, ,, ,, - -	2	Single	4½″	,,	Eye and shackle and becket.
Preventers backstays tackle -	2	Double	4½″	Patent	Long loose hooks.
,, ,, ,, -	2	Double	4½″	,,	Eye shackle and becket for deck bolt.
Spinnaker halyards - -	1	Single	5″	,,	Bow and thimble.
,, tack - -	1	Single	5″	,,	Rope strop.
,, after guy whip -	1	Single	4½″	,,	Rope strop.
,, boom lift - -	1	Double	4″	,,	Eye and shackle.
,, ,, ,, -	1	Single	4″	,,	Eye and shackle and becket.
Jib topsail halyards - -	1	Single	4″	Common	Bow and thimble brass lined for wire.
,, ,, tack tackle -	1	Single	4″	,,	Eye and shackle.
,, ,, ,, ,, -	1	Single	4″	,,	Eye and shackle and becket.
,, ,, sheet ,, -	2	Single	4″	,,	Eye and shackle.
,, ,, ,, ,, -	2	Single	4″	,,	Eye and shackle and becket.
Main boom topping lifts -	2	Single	4″	,,	Eye and shackle brass lined for mast head.
,, ,, ,, purchase	2	Double	5″	Patent	Eye and shackle.
,, ,, ,, ,,	2	Single	5″	,,	Eye and shackle and becket.
Trysail sheets tackle - -	2	Double	6″	,,	Eye and shackle.
,, ,, ,, - -	2	Double	6″	,,	Eye and shackle and becket.
Deck leads - - - -	2	Single	6½″	,,	Swivel eye and shackle.
Snatch blocks - - -	2		8″	Common	Swivel hooks.
Deck tackles - - -	2	Double	5½″	,,	Loose hook.
,, ,, - - -	2	Single	5½″	,,	Loose hook and becket.
Dinghy falls - - - -	2	Double	5″	Patent	Eye and long bolt for davit head.
,, ,, - - - -	2	Single	5″	,,	Swivel hook and beckets.
Cutter ,, - - - -	2	Double	6″	,,	Eye and long bolt for davit head.
,, ,, - - - -	2	Double	6″	,,	Swivel hook and beckets.
Steel Blocks					
Peak halyard blocks to have steel cheeks.					
Trysail sheet deck blocks -	2	Single	5″	Patent	To take eye bolts on quarter.
Main runners - - -	2	Single	5″	Solid	Double lug and screw pin.
Jib halyards - - - -	2	Single	4″	,,	Eye and shackle for mast head ironwork.
,, ,, - - - -	1	Single	4″	,,	Standing jaw and screw pin for head of sail.
Staysail tack - - -	1	Single	3″	,,	Double lug and screw pin.
Jib topsail tack - - -	1	Single	3″	,,	Eye and shackle.
Thimble shackles - - -	2				For main runners spans.
Long hooks and thimbles -	2				For main runners for deck eye bolts.

STEEL BLOCK LIST FOR 40 TONS CUTTER

Name of Block		Size of Wire	No.	Kind	Size (Diam.)	Sheave	Description of Block
Main throat halyards	Steel	$1\frac{1}{2}''$ cir.	1	Treble	5″ sheave	Patent	Bow eye and shackle to take main halyard strop.
„ „ „	Steel	$1\frac{1}{2}''$ cir.	1	Double	5″ sheave	Patent	Bow eye and shackle to take gaff ironwork.
Peak halyards - -	Steel	$1\frac{3}{8}''$ cir.	2	Single	$4\frac{1}{2}''$ sheave	Patent	Solid eye with sheave and span shackle for gaff spans. (Steel shells, wood cased.)
Peak halyards - -	Steel	$1\frac{3}{8}''$ cir.	3	Single	$4\frac{1}{2}''$ sheave	Patent	Eye with sheave and shackle reeved for masthead ironwork.
Topsail sheet - -	Steel	1″ cir.	1	Single	$3\frac{1}{2}''$ sheave	Common	Bows and shackle (gaff end).
Staysail halyards -	Steel	$1\frac{1}{4}''$ cir.	1	Single	4″ sheave	Patent	Eye and shackle for masthead.
„ „ fly block	Steel	$1\frac{1}{4}''$ cir.	1	Single	4″ sheave	Patent	Standing jaw and screw pin for head of sail.
Main boom topping lifts	Steel	$1\frac{1}{8}''$ cir.	2	Single	4″ sheave	Common	Eye and shackle brass lined for masthead.
Trysail sheet deck blocks	Steel	$1\frac{1}{2}''$ cir.	2	Single	5″ sheave	Patent	To take eye bolts on quarter.
Main runners - -	Steel	$1\frac{5}{8}''$ cir.	2	Single	5″ sheave	Solid	Double lug and screw pin.
Jib halyards - -	Steel	$1\frac{1}{4}''$ cir.	2	Single	4″ sheave	Solid	Eye and shackle for masthead ironwork.
„ „ - -	Steel	$1\frac{1}{4}''$ cir.	1	Single	4″ sheave	Solid	Standing jaw and screw pin for head of sail.
Staysail tack - -	Steel	1″ cir.	1	Single	3″ sheave	Solid	Double lug and screw pin.

N.B.—One hundred blocks : Do we realise the weight and cost of any vessel's blocks ?

RIGGING LIST

Standing Rigging	Cir.	Kind	Running Rigging	Cir.	Kind
Main shrouds - - - -	$1\frac{1}{2}''$	Wire core	Main throat halyards - -	$1\frac{1}{2}''$	Flexible
Cap „ - - - -	$1\frac{1}{2}''$	„	„ peak „ - -	$1\frac{3}{8}''$	„
Main topmast backstay - -	$1\frac{1}{4}''$	„	„ sheet - - - -	$2\frac{1}{2}''$	Best rope
Etc., etc.			Trysail sheets - - - -	$1\frac{1}{2}''$	Wire
			Staysail halyards - - -	$1\frac{1}{4}''$	„
For topmast stay - - -	$1\frac{1}{8}''$	„	Jib sheets - - - -	$1\frac{1}{8}''$	„
Forestay double - - -	$1\frac{3}{4}''$	„	Main runners tackles - -	$1\frac{5}{8}''$	„
			Staysail boom sheet - - -	2″	Hemp
FLEXIBLE STEEL WIRE			Other purchase ropes to suit blocks.		
Topsail halyards - - -	$1\frac{1}{8}''$				
Jib topsail „ - - -	$\frac{7}{8}''$				
„ „ tack - - -	$\frac{7}{8}''$				
Staysail tack - - - -	1″				
Jib sheet pennants - - -	$1\frac{1}{8}''$				
Spinnaker after guy pennant -	$\frac{7}{8}''$				
Main boom topping lifts - -	$1\frac{1}{8}''$				

NIÑA[1]

The schooner is the best rig for strength, because the two masts stayed together, as in *Diablesse*, support each other, so that the schooner rig is stronger than a cutter. In the early days of aeroplanes the pioneers always endeavoured to build monoplanes, for they rightly went to nature for their lessons. A friend of mine, a retired Captain of His Majesty's Navy, was once stationed with Bill Cody. Cody went away north on the American continent and shot birds, then spreading them out, with their wings in the positions he wanted, allowed them to freeze, when he flew them as kites and learned his lesson that way. But because of the materials used these monoplanes of his were not strong enough, and so he made a biplane to get the strength of a girder, and flew successfully. His ideas on monoplanes were right, because now that we have improved our materials, monoplanes are made once more, as they are more efficient. The schooner rig, with both masts braced together, can be likened to the girder effect of a biplane's wings.

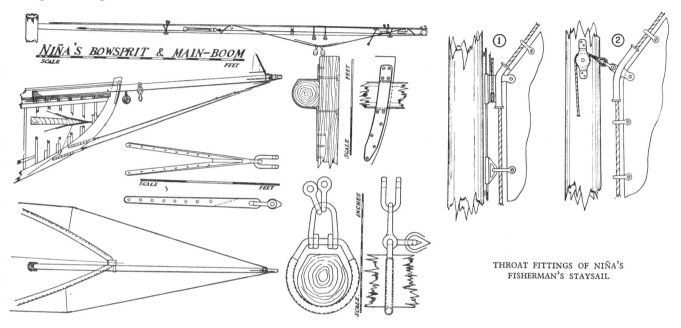

THROAT FITTINGS OF NIÑA'S
FISHERMAN'S STAYSAIL

Niña has proved her spars and rig, and if they stand in her schooner rig, where broadly speaking the two masts are stayed independently of each other, they would stand more securely with the gaff foresail and triatic stay rig of *Diablesse*.

Hollow spars for off-shore work are new, and little is known of them in consequence, so these detailed drawings of *Niña's* spars are both interesting and instructive, as they have been tried and proved by *Niña* winning the Transatlantic and Fastnet Races of 1928, then cruising to Nova Scotia and down to Bermuda.

The International Yacht Racing Rule for yachts up to 12 metres, which generally race during daylight in sheltered waters, calls for the wall of hollow spars to be at least one-fifth of the diameter, yet Burgess has given *Niña*, an ocean racer, a mast with a wall of only one-sixth its diameter. When we consider the stresses and strains that *Niña's* rig must have been subjected to during the night sailing on her long passages, we appreciate her designer's work.

Niña excelled in windward work, which shows that her masts stood well, as it is impossible for a vessel to go to windward with spars that bend, and so distort the sails set on them, and allow those set on stays to sag away to leeward.

The mainmast is 82 ft. 6 in. overall × 13½ in. × 9½ in., with walls 2 in. in thickness, tapering to an inch wall at the top, and is oval in section from trunk to heel. A mast, for strength, can be tapered at the top to half its maximum diameter, and *Niña's* is just under this, being 6 in. × 4¾ in. at the top.

To support this mast athwartships, three sets of shrouds are used, the upper two running over the two sets of spreaders, the lower shroud doubled each side, running straight to the deck.

The lower spreaders are 7 ft. 8½ in. × 6¼ in. × 2½ in., and the upper spreaders are shorter and smaller, being

---

[1]See page 56 for *Niña's* sail plan.

6 ft. $3\frac{1}{2}$ in. × $4\frac{1}{2}$ in. × $1\frac{7}{8}$ in., and the accuracy of detail in *Niña's* rig can be gauged by the fact that these spreaders have the section and angle of incidence of an aeroplane wing.

In designing racing and cruising craft, I have always used main shrouds with a breaking strain equal to the displacement, and topmast shrouds one-third of this strength, and this is a simple and effective rule, for as the main shrouds are strong enough to lift the vessel clean out of water, she is unable to carry them away sailing.

Niña's lower and intermediate shrouds on main and foremast combined break at 44 tons, and as this is 4 tons over her displacement I feel more confident than ever of this simple rule.

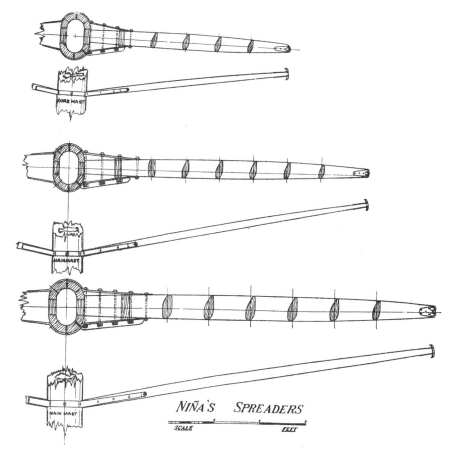

NIÑA'S SPREADERS

The strength of the two lower shrouds combined is 40,000 lb. Because it is neater and easier, it is a temptation to pass the wire round the mast, so that both ends are on deck, and to make the eye by a seizing at the mast, when the strength of these shrouds lies in the weak seizing wire. Since losing a mast in a gale off the Azores through this method, I have always insisted on a separate eye spliced in each shroud.

The intermediate shroud going over the lower spreader has a breaking strain of 20,000 lb., being the same sized wire as the lower shroud.

The topmast shroud from the topmast head to the deck, over the upper spreader, breaks at 11,800 lb.

Forward there are only two stays, the topmast leading to the foremast head, and the mainstay leading down to the lower part of the foremast, and upon these two stays are set the fisherman's (or maintopmast) staysail and the main staysail, and to hold the luffs of these two sails taut the two backstays, from the points where their luffs intersect the mast, lead as far aft as possible.

The foremast is 51 ft. overall, oval-sectioned 12 in. × 8 in., tapering to half this size at the top, and the walls taper from $1\frac{5}{8}$ in. to $\frac{7}{8}$ in. at the top. Being shorter, this mast has only one set of spreaders at about two-thirds its height above the deck, and they are 4 ft. 5 in. × 4 in. × $1\frac{1}{2}$ in.

The lower foremast shrouds, breaking at 28,000 lb., fasten to the mast just below these spreaders, while the cap shrouds, breaking at 11,800 lb., lead over the spreaders to the deck. From the foremast head the jib stay runs down to the bowsprit end and the forestay to the stem head, and upon these two the jib and staysail are set.

Besides the main- and foremasts being hollow, the spinnaker boom and squaresail yard are hollow, for, having to be handled at sea, it is necessary for these spars to be light for ease in working.

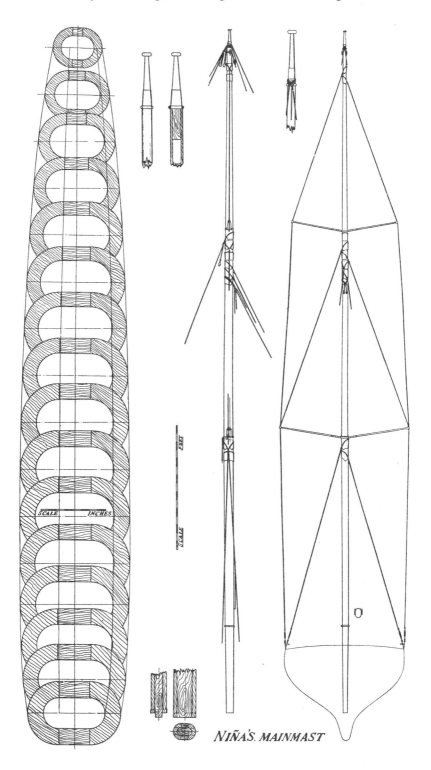

NIÑA'S MAINMAST

The spinnaker boom is 25 ft. overall × $5\frac{1}{2}$ in. diameter in the middle, tapering to 3 in. at the end, and has $1\frac{1}{8}$-in. walls in the centre and $\frac{3}{4}$-in. walls at the ends.

A solid, 2 ft. long, is left in the centre of the squaresail yard, in way of the scotsman, which is seized on by wire. This spar is 28 ft. overall × $7\frac{1}{2}$ in. diameter, tapered to $3\frac{1}{2}$ in. at the ends, with a $\frac{3}{4}$-in. wall throughout.

The main boom is a solid spar, 33 ft. 6 in. overall × $7\frac{1}{2}$ in. diameter, tapering to 5 in. at the mast. The bowsprit is also solid, $6\frac{1}{2}$ in. diameter, 21 ft. 6 in. overall, 14 ft. of which is outboard, the double bobstay being worthy of note.

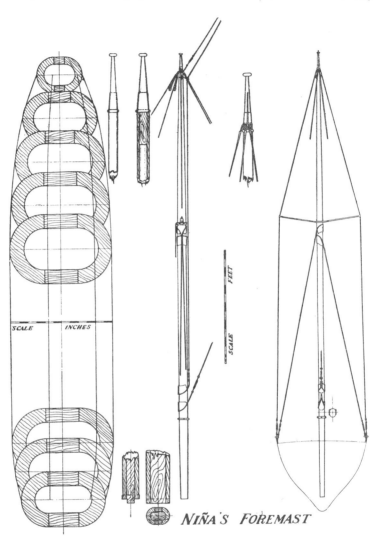

NIÑA'S FOREMAST

SIZES OF STANDING RIGGING

MAINMAST		FOREMAST	
2 lower shrouds each side	$\frac{1}{2}$ in. dia. (each side)	2 lower shrouds - -	$\frac{7}{16}$ in. dia. (each side)
1 intermediate shroud - -	$\frac{1}{2}$ in. dia. (each side)	1 upper shroud - -	$\frac{3}{8}$ in. dia. (each side)
1 topmast shroud - -	$\frac{1}{2}$ in. dia. (each side)	1 jib stay - - -	$\frac{7}{16}$ in. dia.
		1 forestay - - -	$\frac{9}{16}$ in. dia.
1 topmast stay - -	$\frac{5}{16}$ in. dia.	1 backstay - - -	$\frac{7}{16}$ in. dia. (each side)
1 main stay - - -	$\frac{9}{16}$ in. dia.		
		BOWSPRIT	
1 topmast backstay - -	$\frac{3}{8}$ in. dia. (each side)	2 bobstays - - -	$\frac{3}{4}$ in. dia.
1 lower backstay - -	$\frac{3}{8}$ in. dia. (each side)		

LANDFALL [1]

A ketch rig should be treated for staying as though the mainmast stood alone, for looking at *Landfall's* main topmast backstay to the mizen, it will be seen at once that little support can be given to the main topmast from the mizen, for there is no pull after to the mizen backstay, as this has no drift abaft the mast, owing to the short stern. Whenever *Landfall* set her mizen staysail she pulled her mizen mast forward, which in turn let the main topmast head forward to the great discomfort of my brain, as I was in charge of the spars during the Transatlantic Race. The only thing, in fact, that caused me worry crossing the Atlantic in *Landfall* was the fact that the mainmast was not treated as a cutter's mast, and stayed independently of the mizen.

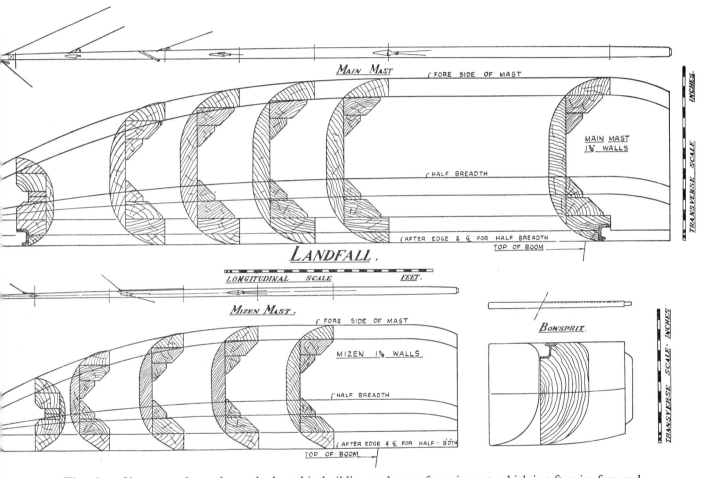

The plan of her spars shows the method used in building up her 92-ft. mainmast, which is 1 ft. 4 in. fore and aft × 1 ft. 1 in. athwart ships, with 1¾-in. walls, while the mizen mast is a 68-ft. spar with walls 1⅜ in., and is 12 in. fore and aft by 9 in. athwart ships. Both masts are made up of thirteen different segments, such a construction being possible by the strength of glue, for the glue is so strong that generally when a hollow glued mast carries away the wood splits rather than the glued joint.

Landfall's list of blocks and rigging will prove helpful, for they are those of a ketch on which great pains were taken to ensure strength as well as lightness, the whole of her rigging being of stainless steel, and no part failed on its job. Although crossing the Atlantic we did not encounter any dirty weather, *Landfall* several times logged 11¼ knots, which shows that she was being driven, and generally speaking the heaviest strains come upon a mast when the vessel is being driven along at her maximum speed just before reefing, for once sail is shortened the strains are relieved from the topmasthead, and being lower on the mast enable the rig to stand against them more easily. So it may be said that *Landfall's* rig stood up to its work well and would always do so, for she has cruised along the Atlantic coast, raced across the Atlantic, cruised in the Baltic and it has never failed.

[1] See page 29 for *Landfall's* sail plan.

LANDFALL'S BLOCK LIST

Item of Rigging	Location	No Required	Size	Kind	Wire or Rope	Fittings
Main Halyard	Main Sail Head Board	1	9"	Single	W & R	Upset Front Shackle
~~Main Halyard~~	~~Jig~~	~~2~~	~~5¼"~~	~~Double~~	~~R~~	~~1 with Front Shackle, 1 with Front Shackle & Becket~~
Mizzen Halyard	Head Board	1	8"	Single	W & R	Upset Front Shackle
Jib & Fore Staysail Halyard	Head Board	2	8"	Single	W & R	Upset Front Shackle
" " " " "	Mast Fitting	2	8"	Double	W & R	Front Shackle
MizzenStaysail Halyard	Mast Strap	2	5¼"	Single	R	Front Shackle
" " "	Tack Tackle	2	4"	Single	R	1 Upset Side Shackle & 1 Front Shackle & Becket
Spinnaker & Balloon Halyard	Mast Fitting	2	8"	Single	W & R	Front Shackle
Gantlines	Masthead	2	4½"	Single	R.	Front Shackle
Main Sheet	Boom & Deck Padeye	5	9"	Single	R	4 Front Shackle, 1 with Side Shackle
" "	Traveller	1	9"	Double	R.	Front Shackle
Mizzen Sheet	Boom	1	8"	Single	R.	Front Shackle
" "	Boomkin & Boom	2	8"	Double	R.	Front Shackle
Staysail & Jib Sheet Leader	Deck	12	5¼"	Single	R	Screw Eye Deck Plate 10 Spare Deck Plates
Staysail Sheet	Sail	4	5¼"	Single	R.	Pair on Shackle
Jib Sheet	Pennant	2	5¼"	Single	R.	Rope Strap
" "	Jig	2	4½"	Double	R	Front Shackle
" "	"	2	4½"	Single	R.	Front Shackle & Becket
Main Backstay Runner	Backstay	2	7"	Single	W	Jaw
" " "	Deck	2	7"	Single	W	Front Shackle
" " "	Jig	4	6"	Single	R	2 with Front Shackle, 2 with Front Shackle & Becket
Mizzen Backstay Runner	Backstay	2	5¼"	Double	R	Jaw
" " "	Chain plate	4	5¼"	Single	R	2 with Front Shackle, 2 with Front Shackle & Becket
Main Topping Lift	Runner	2	5¼"	Single	R	1 Front Shackle & 1 Cheek Block
" " "	Jig	2	4"	Single	R	1 Cheek Block & 1 with Front Shackle & Becket
Mizzen Topping Lift	Runner	2	4"	Single	R	1 Front Shackle & 1 Cheek Block
Jib Outhaul	Bowsprit Strap	1	7"	Single	W & R.	Eye & Thimble
Main Clew Outhaul	Jig	1	5¼"	Single	R	Front Shackle & Becket
" " "	"	1	5"	Fiddle	R	Front Shackle
Mizzen Clew Outhaul	Jig	1	4½"	Single	R	Front Shackle & Becket
" " "	"	1	4½"	Single	R	Cheek Block
Main Boom Guy	Jig	4	4"	Single	R	2 with Front Shackle & 2 with Fr Sh & Becket
Boom Crutch	Tackle	4	5¼"	Double	R	Loose Hook
" "	"	4	5¼"	Single	R	Loose Hook & Becket
Square Sail Brace	Jig	4	6"	Single	R	1 with Front Shackle, 1 with Fr Sh & Becket
Square Sail Sheet	Sail	2	5¼"	Single	R	Front Shackle
Yard Topping Lift	Mast	2	5¼"	Single	W & R	Front Shackle
Square Sail Outhaul	Yard	4	5¼"	Single	W & R	Front Shackle

N.B.—78 blocks. Shewing a saving of blocks as compared to *Lexia's* Gaff Rig, as a ketch generally has double the blocks of a cutter.

LANDFALL'S STANDING RIGGING

No Required	Item	Details	Diameter	Construction and Material	Approx Strength in Tons or lbs	Length required with allowance for Splicing etc
1	Jib Stay	Solid Thimble Both Ends — Sheave in Bowsprit — 95'-0" — 5/8" Turnbuckle on Deck	7/16"	6x7 Blue Center Steel	7.9T	103'
1	Fore Stay	Solid Thimble Both Ends — 62'-4" — 5/8" Turnbuckle to Deck Fitting	9/16"	6x7 Bl C Steel	13.0T	73'
2	Fore Span Stay	Solid Thimble Both Ends — Strut — 28'-7" — 7/16" Turnbuckle to Mast Fitting	5/16"	6x7 Bl C Steel	4.5T	75'
4	Main Lower Shroud	Solid Thimble Both Ends — 27'-2" — 5/8" Turnbuckle to Chainplate	5/8"	6x7 Bl C Steel	16.0T	150'
2	Main Intermed Shroud	Solid Thimble Both Ends — Spreader — 49'-10" — 5/8" Turnbuckle to Chainplate	5/8"	6x7 Bl C Steel	16.0T	120'
2	Main Upper Shroud	Solid Thimble Both Ends — Spreader Spreader — 70'-0" — 5/8" Turnbuckle to Chainplate	7/16"	6x7 Bl C Steel	7.9T	186'
2	Main Backstay	Solid Thimble to Mast Fitting — 58'-0"	1/2"	6x19 Bl C Steel	10.8T	132'
1	Spring Stay	Solid Thimble Both Ends — fitting — 89'-3" — 1/2" Turnbuckle to Mast Fitting	5/16"	6x19 Bl C Steel	4.5T	97'
4	Mizzen Lower Shroud	Solid Thimble Both Ends — 22'-4" — 5/8" Turnbuckle to Chainplate	7/16"	6x7 Bl C Steel	7.9T	126'
2	Mizzen Intermed Shroud	Solid Thimble Both Ends — Spreader — 37'-7" — 5/8" Turnbuckle to Chainplate	7/16"	6x7 Bl C Steel	7.9T	92'
2	Mizzen Upper Shroud	Solid Thimble Both Ends — Spreader Spreader — 51'-5" — 1/2" Turnbuckle to Chainplate	5/16"	6x7 Bl C Steel	4.5T	118'
2	Mizzen Backstay	Solid Thimble to Mast Fitting — 34'-6"	3/8"	6x19 Bl C Steel	6.3T	84'
1	Bobstay	Solid Thimble Both Ends — 16'-6"	1 1/8"	6x7 heavily Galv Iron	17.2T	87'
2	Bowsprit Shr	Thimble & Shackle — 18'-10" — 3/4" Turnbuckle	1/2"	6x7 draw steel	9.0T	47'
2	Boomkin Shroud	Thimble & Shackle Both Ends — 8'-6"	1/2"	6x7 heavily Galv Iron	3.57T	30'
2	Bowsprit Footrope	Thimble & Shackle Both Ends — 15'-0"				

" Because things seen are mightier than things heard," this list by Herreshoff is good, as besides being a check by drawings it helps the rigger to carry out the designer's ideas.

The list of *Landfall's* running rigging is printed on p. 36.

VAMARIE [1]

In *Vamarie's* rig there is the great point, that when it really blows hard and the mainsail is stowed, her two masts are almost perfectly rigged, for the wishbone gaff is made fast to the mizen topmast, and while she is slogging in steep angry seas, her masts are held rigid by a stay from the stem head over the main topmast head to the mizen topmast head and down aft to the deck on the end of the counter, and this combined with the wishbone gaff makes as strong a system of bracing and staying as it has so far been my lot to see. And there is no doubt that sailing along in hard weather, or jilling along lazily in moderate weather under her three lower sails, *Vamarie's* rig would cause nothing but ease of mind to her skipper. The sails are so split up, that even on a vessel 54 feet on the water-line, the mainsail has only 670 sq. ft. in it, and though this wishbone rig is a ketch rig, the mizen is so well in from aft, that its position almost makes *Vamarie* a schooner.

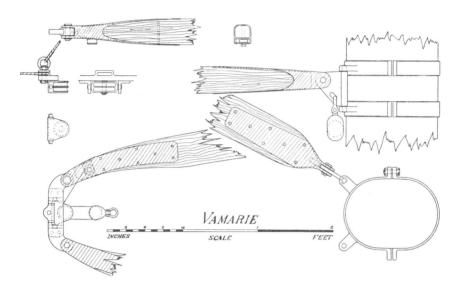

The detail drawing illustrates the wishbone gaff, which is shown above the sail plan, and it will be seen that it is a very ingenious arrangement, and a spar that will probably in the future be used more and more, for it allows the sail set by it to take its natural curve. Anyone who contemplates using such a spar should carefully study the details shown, for Abeking and Rassmussen have developed them so thoroughly that they would be difficult to improve upon, although, as with all things mechanical, time may bring slight modifications.

The rig is new, but *Vamarie*, by winning the race from Miami to Nassau in wind blowing fifty miles an hour dead ahead, proved its ability to stand in hard strong weather. Its great points are the ease in handling the sails in all weathers, and its strength when the wind is strong enough for her to carry her three lowers only. Time alone will tell just how good this rig is ; if it is as perfect as it seems, all ketches in the future will be rigged as *Vamarie*.

DORADE [2]

Dorade's mainmast may be looked upon as though she were a Bermudian cutter, as both her masts are stayed and rigged entirely independently of each other. Her mainmast, its scantlings and rigging, may be taken as ideal for either a cutter or a yawl of her dimensions. When *Dorade* first came out her mainmast was 59 ft. 6 in. above the deck, but after one season this was cut down to 56 ft., and as she was greatly improved by this change the height might be considered as exactly right. The mainmast is a round spar with $8\frac{3}{4}$ in. diameter and $1\frac{3}{4}$ in. walls in its largest place, tapering to $5\frac{1}{4}$ in. at the top, where the walls are $1\frac{1}{4}$ in., and as this spar has three times crossed the Atlantic

---

[1] See page 54 for *Vamarie's* sail plan.   [2] See page 81 for *Dorade's* sail plan.

without showing any signs of weakness, it has proved its strength and ability. It should not be forgotten that, although the strength of a mast is in its rigging, it must also be strong enough itself to withstand the compression strains put upon it by the rigging.

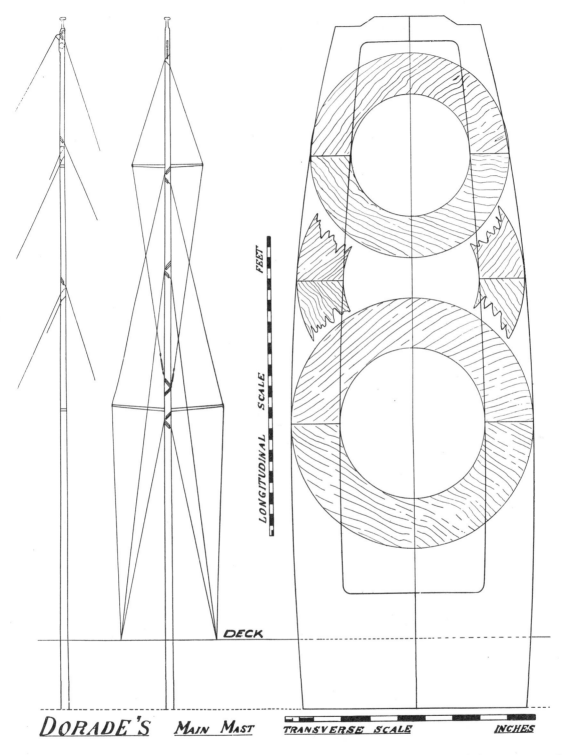

DORADE'S MAIN MAST   TRANSVERSE SCALE   INCHES

The noticeable thing about *Dorade's* rigging is that each of the three backstays is entirely separate, and that they are all as far, or farther, aft of the mast as the corresponding stays are forward of it. The staysail backstay is as far aft as the forestay, the jib backstay is farther aft than the jib stay is forward, and the topmast backstay is farther aft than the topmast stay is forward, and this is as it should be. As the topmast backstay is made fast aft near the mizen mast, it never needs tending when tacking, as the others do.

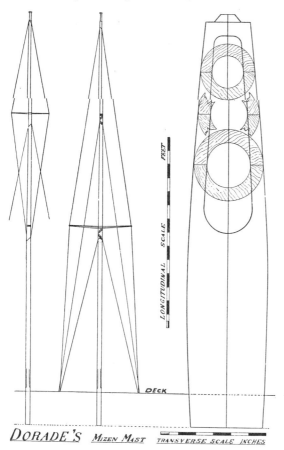

DORADE'S MIZEN MAST   TRANSVERSE SCALE INCHES

The mizen mast is a neat little spar, and with its two shrouds well spread fore and aft is well stayed too. The dotted mizen staysail is not carried in strong winds, when a smaller one, reaching to the fore end of the cockpit only, is set, and the mizen backstay is far enough aft to hold this sail fairly well.

The plans illustrate *Dorade's* masts, and the accompanying list describes her standing rigging. It is all of 19 strand wire, which is stronger though no lighter than the ordinary 6 × 7 strand, for the 19 strands lay so close and well together, that the wire is a true circle instead of having six corners like the 6 × 7, and so the diameters should be increased for the usual stranded wire. In America they measure wire by the diameter, and in England we measure by the circumference, and ours is the more exact method, for the circumference of a circle is roughly three times its diameter, and so three times greater in accuracy.

Dorade has won one Transatlantic Race, and two Fastnet races, and having three times crossed the Atlantic has proved her rig, for in the Transatlantic Race day after day she sailed 200 miles in the 24 hours, which shows that she was being driven hard; indeed her young crew have, in order to win their races, always pushed *Dorade* to the limit, so that her spars and rigging may be looked upon as the best yet devised for such a vessel.

DORADE'S STANDING RIGGING

All 19 strand wire

MAINMAST

Lower shroud	-	-	-	-	$\frac{7}{16}$ in. dia.	Jib stay	-	-	-	-	$\frac{5}{16}$ in. dia.
Mid shroud	-	-	-	-	$\frac{3}{8}$ in. dia.	Forestay	-	-	-	-	$\frac{5}{16}$ in. dia.
Main shroud	-	-	-	-	$\frac{3}{8}$ in. dia.	Topmast backstay	-	-	$\frac{1}{4}$ in. dia.
Topmast diamond shroud	-	-	$\frac{1}{4}$ in. dia.	Jib backstay	-	-	-	$\frac{1}{4}$ in. dia.
Topmast stay	-	-	-	-	$\frac{1}{4}$ in. dia.	Staysail backstay	-	-	-	$\frac{1}{4}$ in. dia.

MIZEN MAST

Lower mizen shroud	-	-	-	$\frac{3}{16}$ in. dia.	Mizen topmast diamond stay	-	$\frac{1}{8}$ in. dia.
Mizen shroud	-	-	-	$\frac{3}{16}$ in. dia.	Mizen topmast backstay	-	-	$\frac{1}{8}$ in. dia.
Mizen topmast shroud	-	-	$\frac{1}{8}$ in. dia.			

NOREEN

Cruising men should study the rig which H. M. Crankshaw has given *Noreen* ; it is an effort to combine the speed of a cutter with the smaller and more easily handled mainsail of a schooner. One plan shows *Noreen's* rig with her mainmast 3 ft. abaft of midships, whilst the other shows it superimposed upon *Niña's* rig, both boats being drawn to the same scale.

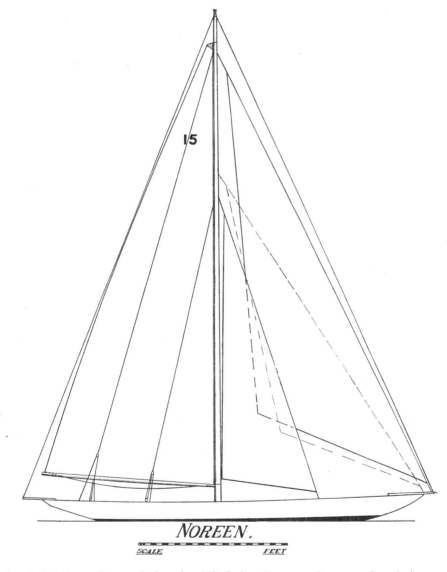

NOREEN.

SCALE   FEET

Noreen's rig, while being as fast to windward as *Niña's*, has the great advantage of not losing any sail dead before the wind, for her spinnaker boom setting from her mainmast reaches as far as the jib tack, whilst *Niña's* is the length from her foremast, on which it sets, to her jib tack, so she loses all sail area between her main and foremasts when running dead before the wind. Under rating rules this is levelled up by the one rating as a cutter and the other as a schooner.

I met *Noreen's* rig at its birth, for I was with H. M. Crankshaw when he bought *Britannia's* topmast and jack-yard for *Noreen's* new mainmast and topmast, these two hollow spars being joined 52 ft. above the deck. At that time I did not appreciate *Noreen's* rig, and it is seldom that new ideas are appreciated, for they are not understood. The advantages of her rig are many, her mainsail is small, so easily set, reefed or taken in, her staysail can be lowered in strong winds, and she is still perfectly balanced under jib and mainsail, for although the staysail is a great driver it is a neutral sail aboard *Noreen* as far as balance goes. Such a large foretriangle enables a great variety of sails to be set forward of the mast, the result of this being that the small mainsail seldom needs reefing. When really blowing she would be well balanced with her working staysail set forward of the mast, and another staysail abaft the mast as a trysail, for such an easily driven hull requires but little sail to drive it.

The windage of her mast so far aft would probably enable *Noreen* to lay reasonably quiet with no sail set heading into the sea during a gale. Large, light sails set on the stays forward of the mast take *Noreen* along quietly in the lightest of zephyrs. The following list of *Noreen's* gear is of interest, for besides showing the strength of the rigging required for such a rig, it also shows the size of *Britannia's* topmast and the jackyard for her topsail.

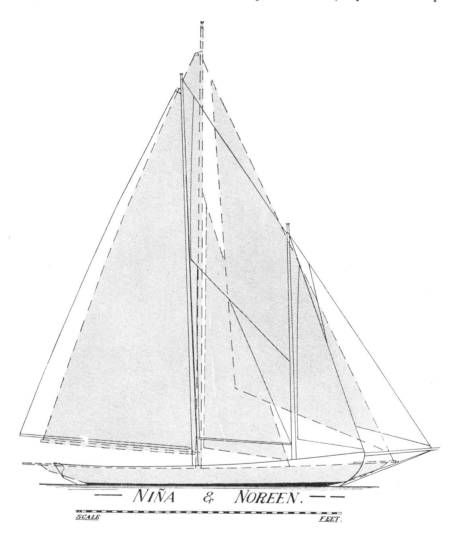

— *NIÑA & NOREEN.* — —

SCALE   FEET.

SPECIFICATION OF *NOREEN'S* GEAR

Mainmast.—Diameter at deck, $11\frac{3}{8}$ in. ; diameter at cap, $8\frac{1}{2}$ in.

Topmast.—Diameter at heel, $7\frac{1}{2}$ in. ; diameter at top, $4\frac{1}{2}$ in.

Main Boom.—Diameter at outer end, $6\frac{3}{4}$ in. ; diameter at inner end, $5\frac{1}{4}$ in.

Spinnaker Boom.—Diameter at outer end, $3\frac{1}{2}$ in. ; diameter at middle, $5\frac{1}{4}$ in. ; diameter at inner end, $3\frac{1}{2}$ in.

Top Shrouds.—1 in. cir. plough steel ; topstay, 1 in. cir. plough steel.

Second Shrouds from Top.—1 in. cir. plough steel ; second stay, $\frac{7}{8}$ in. cir. plough steel.

Cap Shrouds.—$1\frac{1}{4}$ in. cir. plough steel ; runners, $1\frac{1}{4}$ in. flexible steel ; two forestays, $1\frac{1}{4}$ in. cir. plough steel.

Main Shroud.—$1\frac{1}{2}$ in. cir. plough steel ; preventers (not yet used), $\frac{3}{4}$ in. cir. plough steel.

Main Halyard.—1 in. cir. flexible steel ; purchase, $1\frac{5}{8}$ in. hemp ; whip, $1\frac{3}{4}$ in. hemp, 1 in. flexible steel tailed on ; two double 4 in. internal iron-bound blocks.

Main Sheet.—2 in. hemp, 5 in. I.I.B. blocks.

Staysail Tack.—$\frac{5}{8}$ in. plough steel; fall, $1\frac{1}{8}$ in. Manila. One double 3 in. block; one single and Becket ditto.

Spinnaker Boom Left.—$1\frac{1}{4}$ in. hemp, 2 × 4 in. I.I.B. blocks.

Staysail Sheets.—$1\frac{3}{4}$ in. hemp; tackles, $1\frac{1}{2}$ in. Manila; 2 × 3 in. I.I.B. blocks; pennants, 1 in. flexible wire, $2\frac{1}{2}$ in. bulleyes.

Jib Topsail Sheets.—$1\frac{1}{2}$ in. hemp; jib sheets, 2 in. hemp; pennants, 1 in. flexible steel, $3\frac{1}{2}$ in. double and single blocks.

Spinnaker Guys.—$1\frac{1}{2}$ in. hemp, 1 in. flexible steel leg, $4\frac{1}{2}$ in. rope strop block.

Jib Halyard.—1 in. flexible steel, $1\frac{1}{2}$ in. hemp, downhaul, $1\frac{1}{4}$ in. hemp, purchase, 1 double, 1 single $3\frac{1}{2}$ in. I.I.B. blocks, 2 × 4 in. single wrought-iron blocks.

Fore Halyard.—1 in. flexible steel, $1\frac{3}{8}$ in. cir. hemp fall, 1 only 4 in. wrought-iron single block, 1 only 5 in. I.I.B. block for whip.

Jib Topsail Halyard.—$\frac{3}{4}$ in. flexible steel, $1\frac{1}{2}$ in. hemp, fall, $3\frac{1}{2}$ in. I.I.B. block.

Jib Topsail Tack.—$\frac{5}{8}$ in. flexible steel, 1 in. hemp, fall, 2 × 3 in. I.I.B. block.

Runner Tackles.—Legs 1 in. flexible steel, falls $1\frac{3}{4}$ in. hemp, 1 on each leg, $4\frac{1}{2}$ in. wrought-iron block, 1 on each leg, $4\frac{1}{2}$ in. triple I.I.B. block, 1 on each leg, double and Becket I.I.B. block, 1 on each leg, $4\frac{1}{2}$ in. single I.I.B. block, 1 on each leg, $\frac{5}{8}$ in. galvanised iron hook.

* * * * * * * * * * * *

Cruising men should feel, as I do, grateful to Fred. Shepherd, the Lymington Shipyard, Burgess, Herreshoff, Cox and Stevens, Abeking and Rassmussen and Olin Stephens, as well as to the owners of *Lexia, Niña, Landfall, Vamarie* and *Dorade* for their open-heartedness in giving me the plans and details of the masts and rigs of the vessels in this chapter, for such a collection of plans have not before seen the light of day. They must therefore be of the greatest value to cruising owners; that is to say, to designers, to builders, and through them to the owners, who are the first and last creators of their vessels. For an owner first thinks and dreams his vessel, he then takes his ideas to a designer who, after he has sorted them out and perfected them, hands them to the builder, who in turn hands the owner the cruiser he dreamed of some months previously.

· 24 ·

SAILS

SAILS are made of flax or cotton, and of these flax is the stronger and more enduring, and is generally used for storm sails, for besides its strength it is also easier to handle when wet, for then cotton becomes very hard. Cotton, however, does not stretch as flax, and holding its shape always, is chosen for racing sails ; so that generally speaking flax is better for cruising and cotton for racing. In England sail cloths are measured by weight, and given numbers, and for some strange reason flax is one number different from cotton, a No. 1 flax being equal to a No. 2 cotton, and so on, and these numbers really give the weights of canvas, as will be seen by looking at the readings on the left-hand side of the graph. For there, in the right-hand column, will be found the weight in ounces of a yard of canvas 18 in. wide, and to the left of this the cotton number and the flax number.... So reading along the graph it will be seen that *Harrier* has a storm trysail 8 oz. a yard in weight, and a mainsail of No. 12 cotton, which is $5\frac{1}{4}$ oz. a yard in weight, while her light sails are of 2 oz. per yard material. The English material is 18 in. in width,

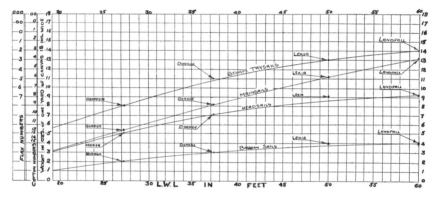

but in America the weight of canvas is taken at 24 in., which must be allowed for, as a 12 oz. canvas 18 in. wide is equal to a 16 oz. canvas 24 in. wide. Plotted on the graph will be found the sail weight for *Landfall*, *Lexia*, *Dorade* and *Harrier*. All these weights were given me by Ratsey and Lapthorn of Cowes, together with the numbers and weights of the different details of the cloths. The reason I went to them is, that besides being the king of sail-makers, they make the sails for the King, and that is as high as it is possible to go in this world.

In this country practically all sails, whether for racing or cruising (for then racing and cruising could be done in the same vessel), were loose footed and of flax, with a lot of flow in them, until 1851, when the renowned *America* came over and won the Squadron Cup for the race round the Isle of Wight. The *America* had rather flat and laced foot sails of cotton ; and—our sails then changed to cotton and were made flatter, probably too flat, and are now once more being made fuller. Then fairly soon after the *Britannia* was built the vertical cloths of the mainsails were changed in racing vessels to horizontal cloths, for they ran in from the leech instead of parallel to it, and though sails made this way are better for racers, as the seams run with the flow of the wind along the sails, they are not so strong, and therefore not so good for cruisers.

But because the racers set the fashion, as will be seen by looking back through the history of pleasure sailing, the cruisers follow the racers. Even when the racing rules produced the narrow plank-on-edge boats, which were as wet as half-tide rocks, and again when the racers' sails were cut square instead of parallel to the leech the cruisers followed the fashion. I believe the cloths parallel to the leach to be better for the cruiser, for in *Typhoon* our mainsail split from leech to luff, while in our sea-scouts' whaler, whose mainsail had vertical cloths, a similar accident only resulted in losing the after cloth of our sail, for when the tear came to the first seam it ran along parallel to this, and the rest of the sail held. Then battens need not be used at all in mainsails with vertical cloths, and battens are without doubt a curse, fouling topping lifts and backstays, and tearing the sails. They should never find their way into a cruiser's mainsail.

But the greatest advantage of a " vertical mainsail " is the strength it gives along the reef points, for these can be placed in each seam so that their pull is taken where the sail is twice as strong, and so well able to take the strain, while in a cross-cut mainsail the points come generally upon a single part of the sail where it easily tears.

When the cloths are square to the leach a cruising vessel should have a leech rope fitted, for strength, the whole length of the leech, so that the sail is entirely roped in, by the luff, head, leech and foot ropes. One frequently sees drawings showing the cloths in sails, which are not parallel or square to the leech, and such drawings are wrong, for unless the cloths are either square or parallel to the leech the sail quickly loses its shape, for the strain is not coming directly down the warp or the weft threads.

ULERIN, 1890

A MAINSAIL WITH VERTICAL CLOTHS SETS WELL WITHOUT BATTENS.   AS THE SEAMS ARE VERTICAL THERE
IS NO STRAIN ON THEM, AS IN A CROSS CUT MAINSAIL WHERE THE STRAIN COMES ON THE STITCHES

The best illustration of this is a man's necktie, which in going round his neck and tying in a knot, has to stretch out of shape, and so, because its job in life causes it to be twisted and turned about like a weak-minded man, it is cut on the bias, which is shown by the stripes running diagonally across it at 45 degrees. So when a sail has to be shortened on the foot, we will say two feet, instead of this being cut off the leach, as might at first be supposed, it has to be cut off the luff, otherwise the leech is cut on the bias as a necktie, and soon the sail is useless. This cutting off the luff lowers the boom end, so the foot has to be cut up at the clew as well, and this explanation will probably help owners to realise the work involved, and the reason the cost of such cutting is twice what they thought it might be, for there is about four times more work to do than they realise. This is true of all good work, for good workmen are good only because from their knowledge they know the value of, and so pay the greatest attention to, the smallest details.

Tanning a sail takes away its strength, and when new an untanned sail is much stronger. This is true of tarring ropes too ; a heavily tarred rope loses 25 per cent. of its strength, and this is easily understood, for a vegetable fibre being subjected to hot tar, must lose its virtue, but once having been soaked with tar, it remains at about that strength, as the tar preserves it from the weather, while the untarred rope gradually loses its strength due to weather until it becomes weaker than the tarred rope. And this is so with sails ; when new the tanned sail is weaker, but with the passing of time it becomes stronger, for it remains much about its original strength, while the untanned sail slowly loses strength. How slow may be gauged by the fact that the Ratsey sails of my old 20-ton schooner were still serviceable after 30 years, and during the years I had her they never came off the spars summer or winter, as I used her more during the winter than the summer. The mildew proofing to which all sails are at present subjected is not perfect, but a new process is just coming into being, and when this is perfected, white sails will undoubtedly be far superior to all others for strength and durability. The one thing against white sails is their power to reflect the sunshine, but as men do not as yet pluck their eyebrows, their eyes are fairly well protected from the light above, as in addition to the protection eyebrows give, the eyes are also recessed under the forehead. It is the reflected light that hurts the eyes, for as men now shave their faces, any glare from below strikes right into the eyes, and a beard on the cheeks would parry this upper cut of light reflected from water or snow.

So generally speaking white sails are better for cruising as well as racing, because of their strength, while the glare off them in daytime might well prove a blessing at night, when a light flashed on the sails would show far better than a light directed to an overtaking steamer, as without losing much power it is spread over a large area, besides showing the steamer that it is a sailing vessel he is overtaking, and exactly how she is headed.

Because the track on which it runs (the ocean) and its power (the wind) need no repair, the sailing vessel has only herself to maintain, and as she takes nothing from the earth's resources in her voyages across oceans, the time must arrive when she will once more come into her own, for the coal and the oils in the earth cannot last for ever, and when these fuels are used up the world will be grateful to those who, for pure joy, built and navigated small sailing vessels, and so not only kept alive, but also improved the art of sailing.

And this time may be here earlier than we expect, for *Dorade's* two Atlantic crossings, 17 days from Newport to Plymouth and 22 days from Cowes to Larchmont, show the possibilities of sail, for a 400-ft. vessel has three times the inherent speed of *Dorade*, which would bring those passages down to six and eight days, times which compare favourably with the fastest liners. So when sailing ships come back again, they will be far faster than the clippers of the last glorious age of sails. And this improvement, in design of hull, masting and rigging, sails and sail-making, is entirely due to those whose greatest joy is to sail.

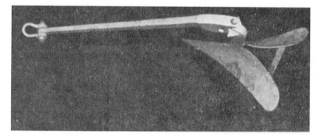

THE C.Q.R. PATENT (PLOUGHSHARE) ANCHOR

(*See page 155*)

HERRESHOFF ANCHOR
NOTE TIPS OF PALMS TURNED OUTWARDS

(*See page 155*)

A Ploughshare Anchor quickly bites in, and once in, there is nothing above ground for the cable to take a turn round; whereas the ordinary anchor has three points (the upper fluke and the two ends of the stock), a turn round any of which means a foul anchor, which is a delusion and a snare.

· 25 ·

ANCHORS

"ANCHOR, Hardy, anchor ! . . . do you anchor, Hardy." Captain Hardy then said, "Shall we make the signal, sir ? " " Yes," answered Nelson, " for if I live, I'll anchor." Nelson's last command was an entreaty, and coming from our greatest seaman and fighter, whose foresight and judgment were never at fault, it should have been carried out, for had this dying command and wish been obeyed, we should have had, as a result of Trafalgar, nineteen prizes instead of only four. The rest foundered or were driven ashore by the gale that came on.

Nelson, with his seaman's instinct, knew that a westerly gale was brewing, and that our fighting ships and prizes would have so much of their rigging shot away that they could never hold off the shore sailing. It is a known fact, that once these ships shortened sail they did not make an inch to windward because of their enormous windage. The state of the fleet can be gauged by that of the *Africa* (64 guns), which had her main topsail yard shot away, and her bowsprit, while her three lower masts were so badly hit that none of the latter could afterwards stand. Her remaining masts and yards were more or less injured ; her rigging and sails cut to pieces, and her hull, besides its other serious damage, had received several shots between wind and water.

To add to the peril of our fleet and their nineteen prizes, the ships were in thirteen fathoms of water with the shoals of Trafalgar a few miles to leeward. Four prizes, all 74-gun ships, weathered the gale that came on. Of these the *San-Ildefonso*, the *Swiftsure* and the *Bahama* anchored and rode out the gale, while the *San Juan-Nepomuceno*, which was not disabled, was safe in the offing before the gale reached its strength.

So Nelson's dying command, " Anchor, Hardy, anchor ! " shows that these ships could, and did, rely on their anchors, to hold them off a lee shore in the teeth of an onshore gale. From my youth up I've looked at the *Victory* with her enormous windage, and then at her anchors, and have wondered that such small things could hold such an amount of masts, spars and cordage, against a gale.

Anchors indeed, from the earliest times, have been used to hold vessels off a lee shore in a gale of wind, for when Saint Paul was shipwrecked in the stormy seventh month of A.D. 62 the ship was driving ashore before a gale at midnight, when " they cast four anchors out of the stern, and wished for the day." After laying to these anchors safely all night they hauled them in, and setting sail, ran their ship ashore, in an endeavour to make a certain creek ; but running aground " the forepart stuck fast and remained unmoveable, but the hinder part was broken by the violence of the waves."

So it is easy to understand why the anchor became the symbol of hope, for to the old sailing ships caught on a lee shore by a gale of wind, anchors were their last and only hope of holding off, and their anchors received great attention. To me it seems, that with the weatherliness of sailing vessels such as in this book, the dread of a lee shore has gone, and with it the attention that was paid to anchors, for with her windward ability a modern fore-and-aft vessel can generally claw off a lee shore even in a gale, and so although till now throughout the ages anchors have been relied upon, under such conditions they are no longer.

With the changing of hemp shrouds to wire came a great saving of windage, and with the saving in spars, through more efficient sails cutting down the sail area, and with her fine lined hull, the modern vessel is more easily held off a lee shore by her anchors when her sails are stowed. But even so, these must be given a great deal of thought, for the time comes to almost every vessel, when her anchors alone stand between her and destruction, and then it is that they are found to be symbols of true or false hope to the vessel's crew for ever after.

The illustration shows the Herreshoff anchor, which is very similar to the Nicholson, and these are the two best anchors so far in England and America, and although these are more expensive than the other types they are worth while because they are so good.

An anchor's efficiency may be gauged by its holding power for its weight, and working along the lines of a ploughshare, that has through countless generations been evolved from the old wooden hand plough to the modern steel share to cut into land, G. I. Taylor, F.R.S., a cruising man, has produced an anchor that is really a double-bladed ploughshare with a long shank.

Tests with a 50 lb. anchor of this type proved it to have a holding power of sixty times its own weight, which is three times as great as the ordinary type, and six times as great as the stockless anchor. So this anchor appears in this book, not as a tried and trusted anchor such as a Nicholson or a Herreshoff, but as a new and untried anchor, that will probably in the years to come halve the anchor work on sailing vessels, and my recommendation is for cruising and racing men to use one-half the weight of their ordinary anchor, but to take their ordinary anchor stowed away below until the new one has proved itself.

Normal stockless anchors do not find their way into this book at all, for holding only half as well as the Nicholson or Herreshoff, they need to be twice their weight and should only be used in power vessels, where the extra weight is balanced by the fact that an engine hauls it up. Being stockless it stows into a hawse pipe by itself—its only virtue.

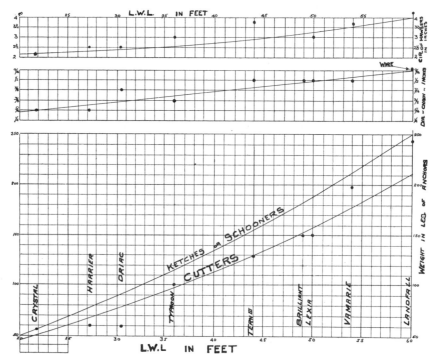

The graph is an attempt to show at a glance the weight of anchors required by any sailing vessel from 20 to 60 ft. water-line. Above it in the same block is the size chain for the same vessels, and above this the hawsers. The anchor weights are given in lbs., the diameter of chain in fractions of an inch, and the circumference of the hawsers in inches.

As the anchors, cables and hawsers of existing vessels are plotted on this graph, they serve as a comparison to the weights and sizes suggested.

Although Lloyds in their tables do not specify heavier anchors for schooners and ketches, they need them owing to the extra windage of their two masts, and on this graph a special line is plotted for these rigs.

It will be noticed that *Tern III*, a vessel that is not in this book elsewhere, is plotted on the graph, and the weight of her anchor influenced me in drawing the line for cutters' anchors more than that of any other vessel, for her owner, Claud Worth, has studied cruising vessels and their equipment probably more than any other cruising man in this country.

His little " Cherub," a weight slid halfway down the chain cable, is a most excellent dodge, for, acting as a spring or damper, it stops a vessel snubbing at her anchor in a seaway.

This brings the thought of a wire cable, as *Landfall* uses. In hauling the anchor with a chain cable 50 per cent. of the load is in the links grinding through the hawse pipe or over the roller fairlead, and in a wire cable this is reduced to 10 per cent., so wire, besides its lightness, has less friction in hauling aboard, and stowing on the winch as it comes aboard, is far easier to handle. However, because of its lightness it has no weight in itself to act as a spring and so help the anchor to hold the vessel riding to it, and therefore it is not so reliable.

But a combination of Professor G. I. Taylor's double ploughshare anchor, a wire cable and Claud Worth's " Cherub " might easily halve the anchor work in the future.

And so this chapter concludes with an appeal to cruising and racing men to study the anchor problem deeply, so that in future everyone will rest secure in the knowledge that their anchors and cables will hold when on a lee shore in a gale, and the order comes, " LET GO ! "

· 26 ·

NORTH ATLANTIC

" Wouldst thou "—so the helmsman answered—
" Learn the secrets of the sea ?
Only those who brave its dangers
Comprehend its mystery."

AN army, invading a strange country, sends out scouts in advance to report on roads, swamps, forts and the forces of the enemy, but a vessel invading the sea cannot send out scouts to report on the conditions that she must meet, neither does she need to, for these have all been reported and charted clearly by the Hydrographic Office of America, which publishes a wind and current chart of the different oceans for every month of the year.

And just as the field marshal plans the routes and the time his army will advance from the reports of his scouts, the captain of a ship plots the course of his vessel from these pilot charts, which are founded upon the researches made by Lieutenant Maury of the United States Navy about 1850. He collected all the knowledge and data possible from every captain, and plotting their voyages with the winds and currents experienced, on charts, was able to produce charts and books with the experience of 1,000 voyages over different parts of the ocean. So a young captain, taking a ship for the first time over a strange ocean, had knowledge that would have taken him a lifetime to discover, already plotted for him on charts. So Maury saved shipping companies time and money by shortening voyages through the knowledge of winds and currents, besides saving the risk of shipwrecks through unknown currents.

In 1853, there was an International Conference in Brussels, at which France, England, Norway, Holland, Denmark, Portugal and Sweden all agreed upon the usefulness of ocean research, and so the whole sailing world with its thousands of ships was engaged in the study of the winds and currents of the sea. Consequently, voyages were shortened everywhere by days, and Australia was brought one-third of the distance nearer to England by Maury's dream, or rather the results of the research which followed it. A master mariner has all this knowledge in the twelve charts illustrating these chapters.

The Hydrographic Office of America kindly gave me a set of their North Atlantic pilot charts for the year 1933, and from these I have drawn the twelve monthly charts for this book, and have only shown the winds and currents. The small Atlantic chart shown in the middle of *Africa* gives the percentage of gales for the different parts of the Atlantic, an average of twenty years being taken.

The tracks of *Typhoon, Diablesse, Landfall, Dorade, Brilliant and Niña* are plotted on these charts, as they will show the courses taken by these vessels, and help the navigator in choosing the course for his ship.

If she will not go to windward, then a course giving a fair wind must be chosen, a great circle from America to England, or by way of the N.E. Trade Route from England to America. If the vessel is weatherly and will go to windward well, then she has an alternative course from England to America as illustrated by *Dorade's* remarkable run in 1933, North about. This fast passage of 22 days to windward across the Atlantic, being the first of its kind in a small boat, is historical. Perhaps for fifty years sailing vessels have not improved in their maximum speed through the water, but all the while they have been improving in their weatherliness, laying closer to the wind and footing as fast or faster as the years go by. They have at last reached the stage, as proved by *Dorade's* western passage, where it is quicker to go directly across the Atlantic against the westerlies than to go south about through the fair winds in the N.E. Trades, so now an owner has two courses open to him going westward across the Atlantic.

* * * * * * * * * * * *

The currents of the N. Atlantic generally run the same direction as the wind, and there is no doubt that a steady wind like the N.E. Trade affects the surface of the water, blowing it along with it, much like a man blowing a plate of thin soup would blow the top layer across to the other side. So it is easy to imagine the warm water of the equator being blown between the West Indies at about 3 knots into the shallow Gulf of Mexico, where it is heaped up and heated still more, from whence it runs along the coast of America aided by the prevailing S.W. wind, which drives it across to the British Isles, where it gives the S.W. part of England a climate warm enough for tropical trees to live. If easterly weather sets in at the latitude of New York the Stream slows, and ceases to run on the surface, so for days in easterly weather a small sailing vessel will receive no help from the Stream, but when the wind turns westerly she will often have a lift of as much as 50 miles from the Stream in one day. Running down the Labrador coast is the cold Arctic Current, which in warm summer months brings icebergs from the frozen north. These bergs reach the Grand Banks of Newfoundland, where they are very dangerous, for here the cold Arctic Current and the Gulf Stream meet, and as many as 50 days out of 100 are characterised by thick fog caused by the meeting of the cold and warm air over these currents.

Farther south between the N.E. Trades and the Westerlies, where there are calms, is situated the Sargasso Sea, a spot in the N. Atlantic Ocean with neither wind nor current, that often figures in sailing ship stories, that tell of old ships that are imprisoned by thick masses of weed, wherein dwell monsters of the deep, who carry off members of the crew at night. All of this is of course very much exaggerated, but having sailed through this sea, I can quite imagine how writers of sea stories would increase the heat of the place, and thicken the weed (which is really no thicker than dried grass thrown on the water) into great masses of weed which would imprison a ship. What really happened most likely was that towards the end of perhaps a long voyage from England to America a ship would bend up out of the Trades too soon, and be a prisoner in this area through lack of wind sufficient to drive her onwards into the region of the Westerlies.

The N. Atlantic wind system is divided into the Westerlies above Latitude 35 and the N.E. Trades below Latitude 30, with a calm belt between the two entirely different winds, and also a calm on the equator between the N.E. Trades and the S.E. Trades, all of which the various pilot charts show clearly.

A great circle course is the shortest distance across oceans, the reason being that the world is a sphere, although drawn flat on charts and maps, so the straight and shortest line is a curved line on the flat chart, just as a straight line on an orange would take a curve if the peel were flattened out truly.

The steamer tracks between England and America are plotted on these charts, and it will be noticed that they are curved. However, instead of taking a direct great circle course steamers first of all make a point south of the fogs and icebergs of the Grand Banks of Newfoundland.

This is the result of the sinking of the *Titanic*, for she hit an iceberg in the fog ; so now, all the foremost passenger liners clear the Banks with their fog and icebergs.

Prevailing winds and calms are shown by the wind rose in each 5 degree square. The arrows fly with the wind, the length of the arrow from the centre of the circle measured on the scale in the lower left hand corner gives the number of times in each 100 observations that the wind has blown from or near the given point.

The number of feathers shows the average force on the Beaufort Scale.

The number in the circle gives the percentage of calms, light airs or variable winds.

THE BEAUFORT SCALE

FORCE	WIND SPEED IN MILES PER HOUR	DESCRIPTION
0	0	Calm
1	3	Light air
2	6	Light breeze
3	10	Gentle breeze
4	16	Moderate breeze
5	21	Fresh breeze
6	27	Strong breeze
7	33	Moderate gale
8	40	Fresh gale
9	47	Strong gale
10	55	Whole gale
11	65	Storm
12	above 65	Hurricane

So a glance at the July chart will show that while just above Latitude 50 the Westerlies blow generally at force 5, or 21 miles an hour, and that just below 50, the winds are force 4, or only 15 miles an hour, the percentage of gales is about equal, and as 25 miles an hour with the wind just abaft the beam is the ideal sailing breeze, the best way across from America is just above Latitude 50 on a Great Circle course, and *Dorade* has shown it to be the best way back as well.

Sixty-four years ago the British Schooner *Cambria*, racing from Queenstown to New York, beat the American Schooner *Dauntless*, which was twice her size, for although the *Dauntless* was the faster vessel, the *Cambria* under cover of the darkness tacked to port, and sailed the northern course, and so won from the larger and faster vessel.

Her time was 23 days 5 hours, and though only a tenth of her tonnage, *Dorade* beat this time by some 12 hours. The fact that *Dorade* took her departure from The Bishop's, while the *Cambria* took hers from Queenstown, makes her record passage all the more remarkable, and shows beyond all doubt that the designing, building and handling of sailing vessels is improving with the advancing years, so that vessels now have the choice between making a passage across oceans with a fair or a foul wind, whereas in days gone by they could only sail with the wind.

A study of these charts, and of the Atlantic and other oceans themselves, will further improve sailing and seamanship.

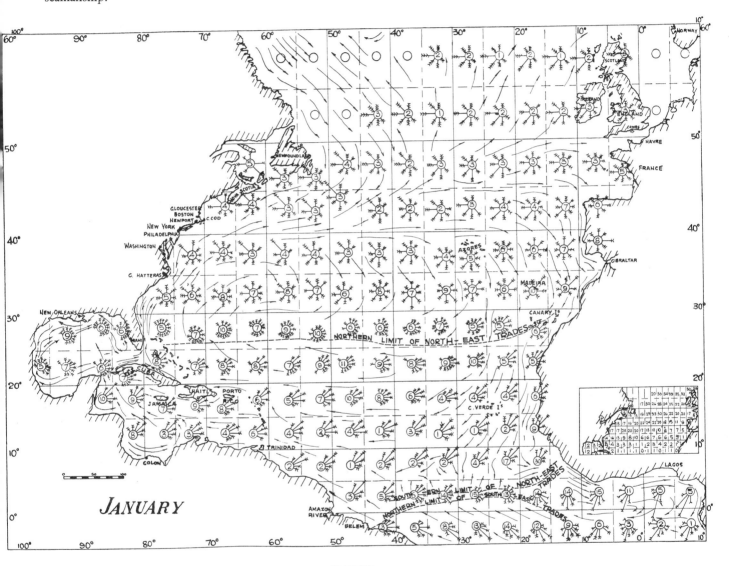

JANUARY

GALES

January and December are the two stormiest months of the year, as the following list of gale percentages taken in the middle of the North Atlantic on the latitude of Newfoundland from the small chart inserted in Africa will show :

January	-	-	-	-	-	30%	July - - - - - 5%
February	-	-	-	-	-	25%	August - - - - 5%
March	-	-	-	-	-	22%	September - - - - 10%
April -	-	-	-	-	-	18%	October - - - - 14%
May -	-	-	-	-	-	13%	November - - - - 18%
June -	-	-	-	-	-	6%	December - - - - 30%

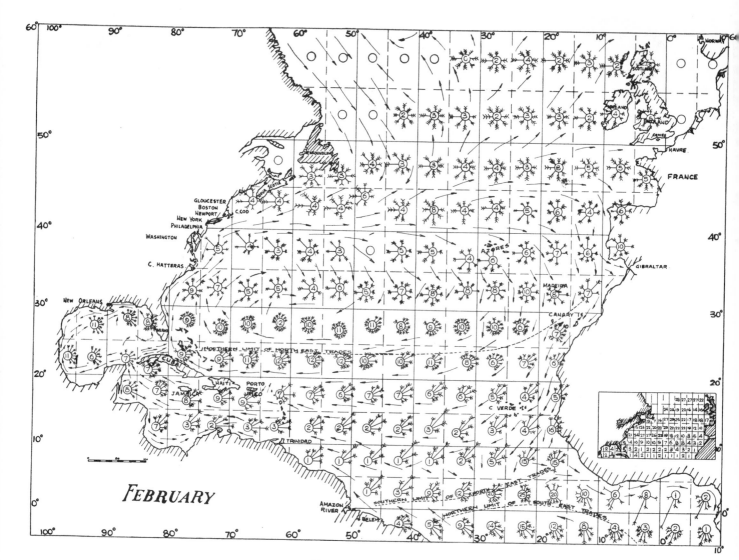

HOW TO READ CHART

A study of the wind rose off the coast of Ireland for February will show the usefulness of these charts, as by taking the length of each wind arrow and measuring it with the percentage scale in the lower left-hand corner, it will be seen that the month's winds are as follows (the number of barbs on each arrow giving the force) :

West	-	-	-	25% force 6
North-West	-	-	-	19% force 6
South-West	-	-	-	19% force 6
South	-	-	-	14% force 6

North	-	-	-	9% force 4
North-East	-	-	-	6% force 4
South-East	-	-	-	6% force 6
Calms	-	-	-	2% force 0

The arrow-heads show the Gulf Stream running in a northerly direction off shore. The gale chart inserted in Africa gives winds of force 8 and over off Ireland, a percentage of 19 for February. So from the above any seaman can judge fairly accurately the weather to expect in February off the west coast of Ireland, and with a little study of these charts the weather anywhere any time in the North Atlantic.

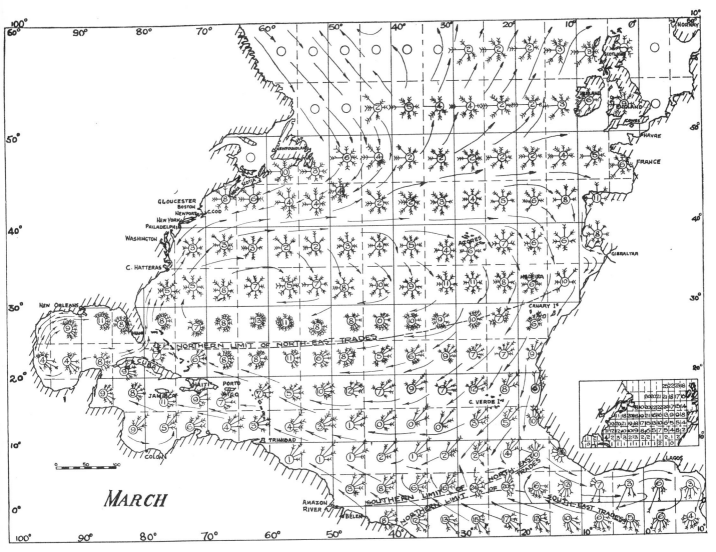

MARCH

OCEAN CURRENTS

The arrow-heads show the direction and flow of the North Atlantic Currents, which might be likened to mighty rivers. The greatest of these, the warm Gulf Stream, starts in the Gulf of Mexico, and after running a little way up the American coast spreads out in a fan, which extends from Spain to Greenland, while to the west of Greenland the cold Arctic Current runs south between the Gulf Stream and Newfoundland as far as Cape Hatteras, getting narrower and narrower until it finally disappears at Miami.

From Spain the Gulf Stream bends southward and then curves backward to the Gulf of Mexico, where, in cooling that heated part of the world, it gets warmer and starts out once more on its round trip to Spain and West Africa. That these currents are affected by the wind is proved by the fact that an easterly wind slows up and then stops the Gulf Stream drift entirely by the time it has reached the latitude of New York, where much of its power has been lost.

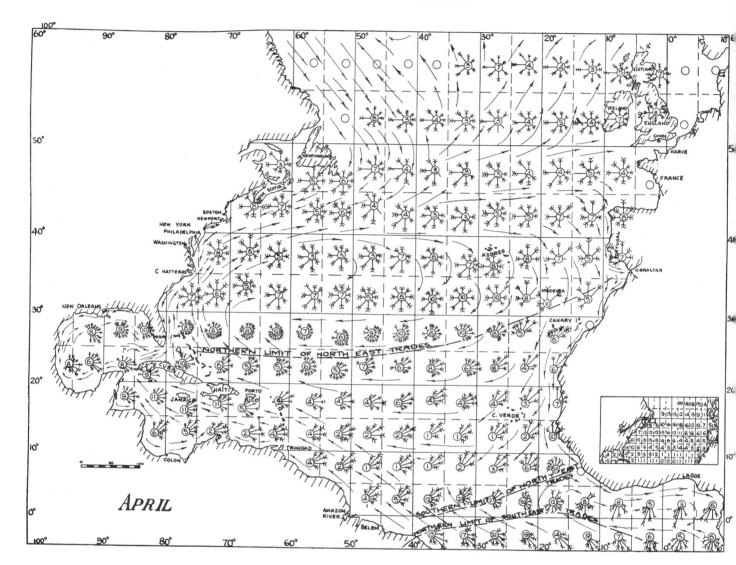

APRIL

FOGS

June is the month of fog off Newfoundland, as the list of fog percentages for each month will show. These percentages deal with the fogs off Newfoundland only, caused by the meeting of the warm Gulf Stream and the cold Arctic Current.

PERCENTAGES OF FOG

January	-	-	-	30% to 35%
February	-	-	-	30% to 35%
March	-	-	-	40% to 45%
April	-	-	-	40% to 45%
May	-	-	-	40% to 45%
June	-	-	-	60% to 65%
July	-	-	-	50% to 55%
August	-	-	-	40% to 45%
September	-	-	-	30% to 35%
October	-	-	-	30% to 35%
November	-	-	-	30% to 35%
December	-	-	-	30% to 35%

The reason for the percentage of fog being higher in midsummer it would seem is because then the Arctic Current is bringing down icebergs set adrift from the frozen north by the summer sun, and these on meeting the warm Gulf Stream off Newfoundland cause fogs. Countless ages of melting icebergs have probably formed the Grand Banks, for undoubtedly when they break away they bring pieces of land with them which they deposit when they finally melt, and on this land is probably frozen moss and food for fishes. So the icebergs besides causing the Grand Banks of Newfoundland also make its fogs and feed its fishes.

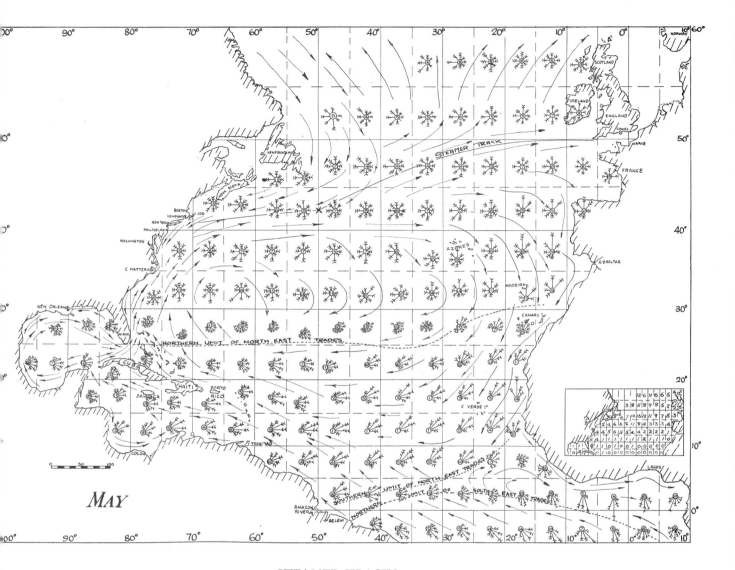

MAY

STEAMER TRACKS

The steamer track from the English Channel to New York is shown on this chart, and it will be seen that instead of taking the shortest (great circle) course to New York it first of all makes a point marked with a cross to the south of Newfoundland clear of the icebergs and practically clear of the fogs. For shipping companies realise that their greatest advertisement is safety at sea, and that it would be foolish to have their passengers living like fighting cocks all the way across the Atlantic only to perish by an iceberg off Newfoundland. The reason for the curve in the track is that though the earth is round it is shown flat on maps and charts, so that a straight line on the curved earth's surface becomes a curved line when the earth's surface is laid out as a flat plane. Just as a straight line in the skin of a tennis ball would become curved if the ball were skinned and the skin laid out flat.

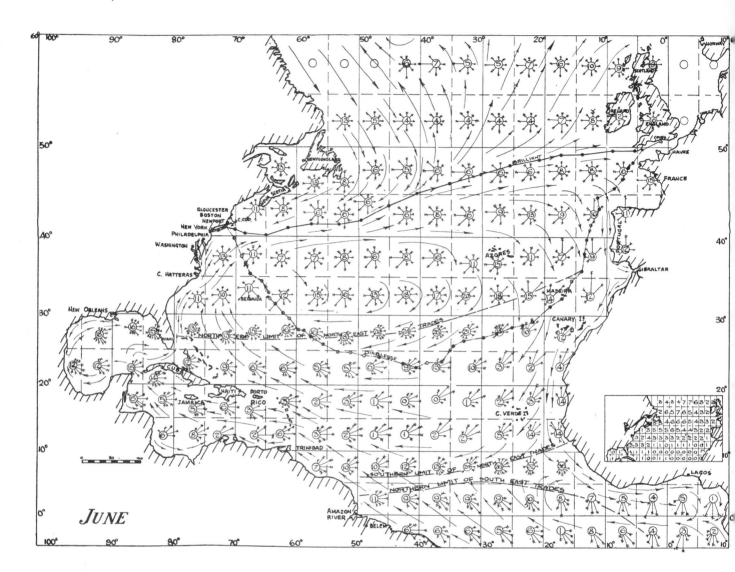

CALMS

The number in the centre of each wind rose gives the number of days in one hundred which are calm, and this list of percentages taken in the middle of the Atlantic on the latitude of Newfoundland will show that the Atlantic is seldom calm. June, July and August are the months with most calm weather, and then only 6%, exactly the same as the interest on my overdraft at the bank, and as I've great difficulty in living on this interest, I consider it small.

PERCENTAGE OF CALMS

January	-	-	-	-	-	3%	July -	-	-	-	-	6%
February	-	-	-	-	-	4%	August	-	-	-	-	6%
March	-	-	-	-	-	2%	September	-	-	-	-	4%
April	-	-	-	-	-	4%	October	-	-	-	-	2%
May	-	-	-	-	-	4%	November	-	-	-	-	1%
June	-	-	-	-	-	6%	December	-	-	-	-	2%

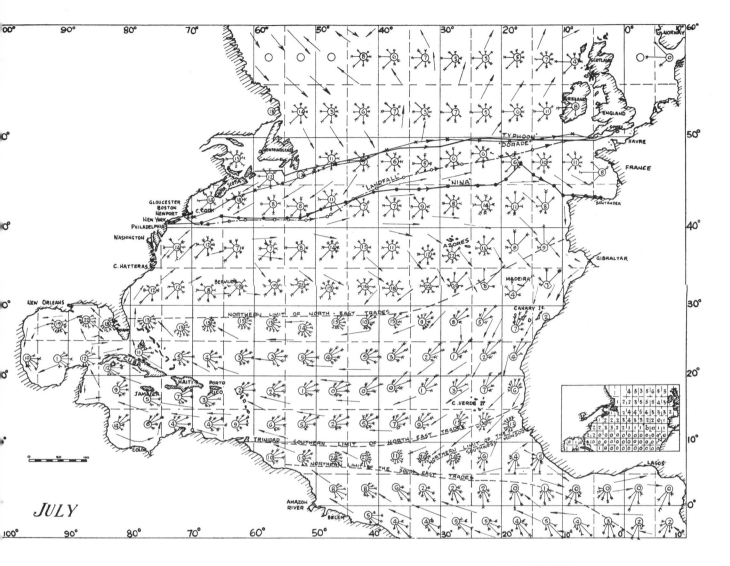

JULY

COURSES ACROSS THE NORTH ATLANTIC FOR SMALL SAILING VESSELS

Typhoon, Niña, Dorade and other small yachts have shown that it takes (for such craft) 15 to 16 days only to cross from Newfoundland to the south-west of England in July if they keep on a great circle course close to latitude 50 as they did, or north of it.   The reason is seen by studying the winds on this July chart, for 80 to 90 per cent. of them are westerly or north and south, which means a fair or a beam wind, and as these vary from force 4 to 6 (16 to 27 miles an hour) they are ideal for fast passages, these wind speeds being enough to drive a small sailing vessel along at her maximum speed and yet not enough for reefing as they are abaft the beam.   Farther south the winds are warmer, and though of the same speed they have not the power and drive of the more northerly and so colder winds as the warm air is not so dense.   On this chart are plotted four yachts' tracks.   *Typhoon* in 1920 had a fair wind all the way across the Atlantic.   *Niña* in the 1928 Transatlantic Race had a fair wind until she reached Long. 20 West, when, as will be seen by her course, the wind came dead ahead and she first of all stood north-east before putting about and sailing south-east for the north-west of Spain.

Dorade and *Landfall* in the 1931 Transatlantic Race could just lay the course close hauled at the start as the wind was south-east, but after this it remained astern and never forward of the beam all the way across.

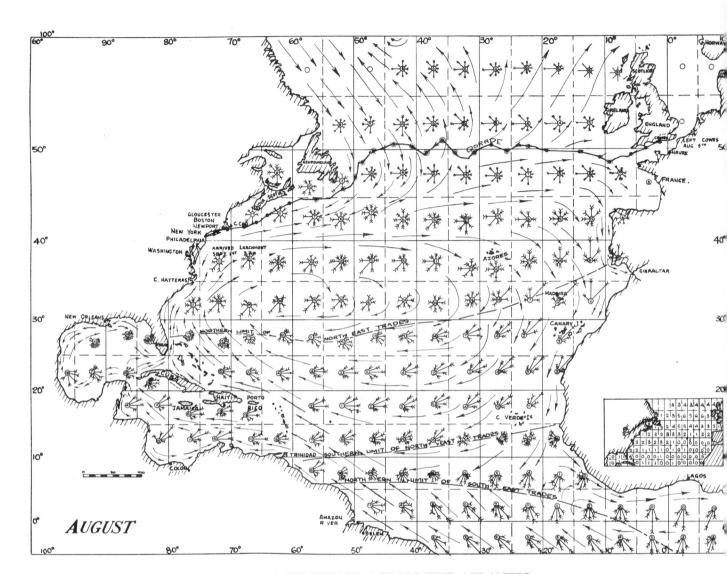

AUGUST

TO WINDWARD ACROSS THE ATLANTIC

On this chart is plotted *Dorade's* passage to windward across the Atlantic of 22 days 15 hours from the Scillies to Pollock Rip, and on this passage she had to reef and also drive along with her trysail set instead of her mainsail on more than one occasion, for though the gale chart shows 6% and 5% of gales, a head wind of force 6 will often cause a small vessel to reef, unless she is undercanvassed, for she is driving into it, and so increasing its power and the power of the seas.

So *Dorade* reefed often and at times took in her mainsail and set her trysail in her passage to windward across the Atlantic in August.

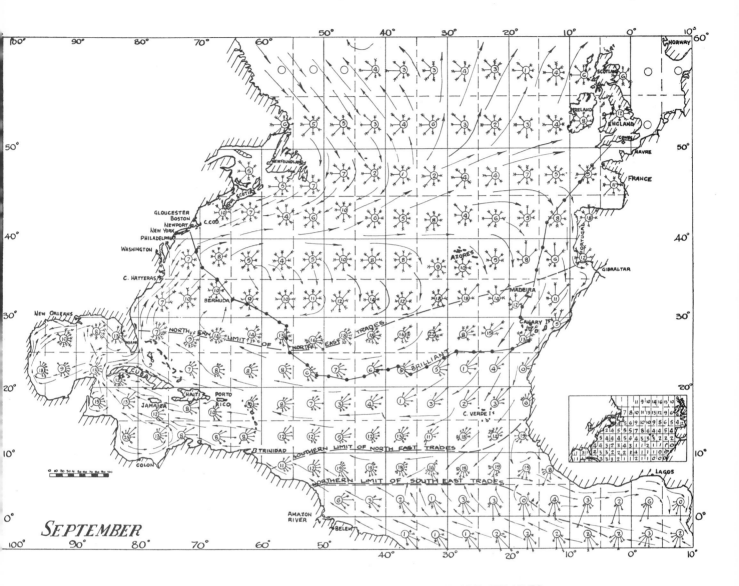

SEPTEMBER

FROM ENGLAND TO AMERICA THROUGH THE N.E. TRADES

Brilliant's track shows the way to America from England by the North-East Trades, a fair wind passage. *Brilliant* followed fairly closely the route recommended to sailing ships, her only difference being that she started to bend up north out of the Trades at Long. 50 West instead of Long. 60 West, and there is no doubt that a passage through the Trades in a sailing vessel is one of the finest things that can happen to any man, for there life is pleasant, the fair wind generally blowing at about 20 miles an hour is enough to keep the ship fairly cool in spite of the fact that she is almost directly underneath the sun. The northern and southern limits of the Trades are marked on each chart, and also the northern limit of the South-East Trades is shown as they come above the Equator, and between the two trades are the doldrums, 20% calm and the rest variable winds.

Brilliant's track takes her down the eastern edge of the Sargasso, and then running along south of it in the Trades, she bends up north and so skirts through the western end of this sea, which is without current or winds worthy of the name, but which for all that is full of marine life, weed with the tiniest crabs on it, and fish.

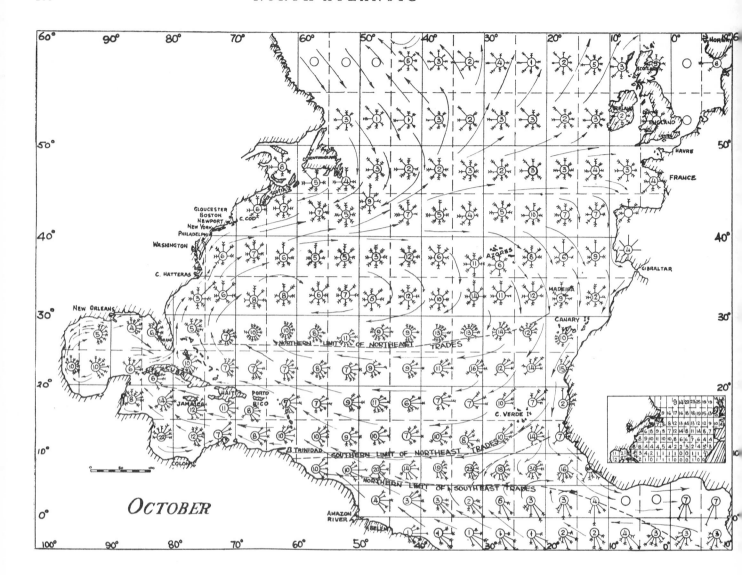

OCTOBER

DOLDRUMS

During this month the percentage of calm in the doldrums has increased from 19% in September to 23% and 30% for October, and so points out that a careful study of these charts which show winds, calms, gales and ocean currents, is well repaid by anyone making long passages, for they give a clear idea of the weather to be expected. Running along the northern edge of the North-East Trades on this chart will be found calms varying from 14 to 10 days in every hundred, and though to people in a moderate climate like this England these do not sound dreadful, they are, for being almost directly under the sun (the sun is north of the line in summer) the heat is oppressive. We had several days of this in *Diablesse*, and everything on board was warm, excepting the water from an eastern jar, which was hung in the slight draught running through the ship, and this was icy cold.

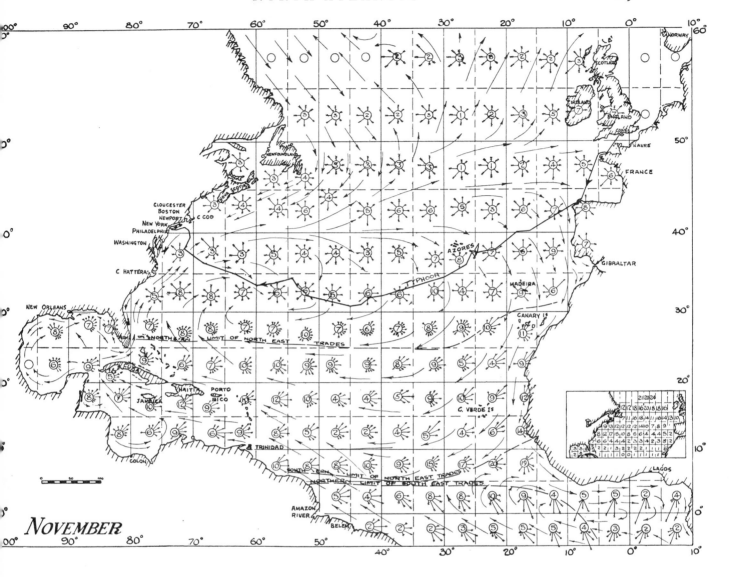

November

WINTER STORMS

The tiny chart inserted in the middle of Africa seems very insignificant until one is in a boat that in the ocean seems even tinier than the chart showing the percentage of gales, and then that chart becomes all-important. So it was aboard *Typhoon* in November 1920 when we had bent up out of the Trades and our course took us through areas marked 17% gale.   On the chart this was said to be winds of force 8 and over (no given top limit), and these were an average taken over ten years 1897 to 1907 so were accurate, and while we did not mind a gale of force 8, 9 or 10, we feared we might get even more, and we did, for the gale we met was so strong that you could not breathe looking into the wind, and I've not met such wind (thank Heaven) since.

So the tiny chart in Africa is probably the one to study most by owners of small vessels making long voyages. On all steam boilers there is a steam gauge with a red mark on it, and the stoker watches that mark, for if his steam increases beyond it he endangers the boiler, himself and his ship or train, though the boiler will stand and has been tested to a higher pressure.   So it is with a sailing vessel, winds 60 miles an hour and over are dangerous, and it should be every navigator's aim to keep his vessel in winds 50 miles an hour to 10 miles an hour, the ideal being 25 miles an hour with the wind aft and 15 to 20 miles an hour with it forward of the beam.

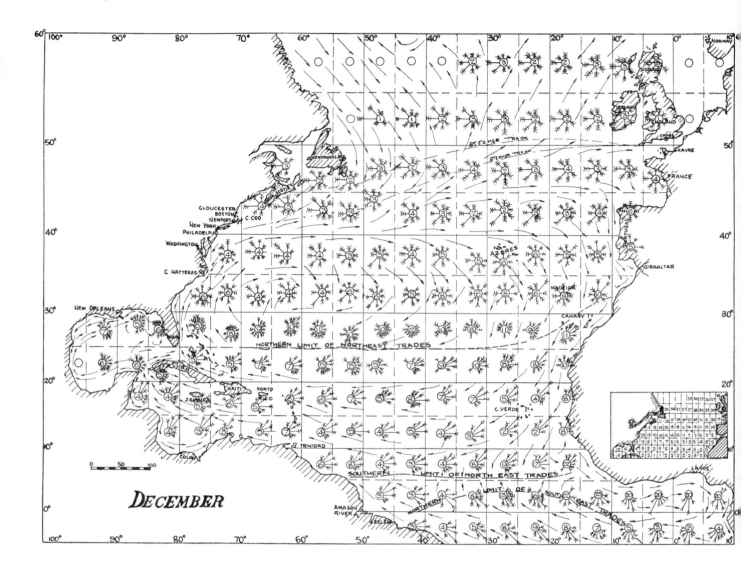

CHRISTMAS CONDITIONS

    This chart shows the limit of the South-East and the limit of the North-East Trades almost touching—the doldrums being very small this month.

    The Hydrographic Office of America, Washington, D.C., which kindly gave these charts to me to copy for this book, welcome information such as will aid them in keeping these monthly weather charts correct, for it must be remembered that it is from the reports of seamen that these charts are made, so anyone by reporting to them their observations of winds, weather, currents, fogs and icebergs, etc., will be helping all who go down to the sea in ships.

PART II
RACING

CRUISING men will probably sigh when they come to this part of the book, and will not wish to read the accounts of races and the descriptions of the racers and their gear, but they should, for by so doing they will perhaps increase their knowledge, and, better still, they may decide to race for perhaps only a season, but that season will improve their sailing and understanding of their cruiser so much, that their cruising will be all the better for their having raced. And when they are cruising, and come upon a fleet of racers they will avoid them if they can, or interfere with them as little as possible ; and though perhaps only half the racing fleet will at the time show appreciation of their understanding kindness, they will all remember them in their prayers that night as they turn in.

For the cruising man must bear in mind that practically every improvement in his cruising vessel is thought out, developed, and perfected by the racing man before it is adopted for cruising, so that he owes the racing man something always. The competition in racing forces all racers to study their boats and gear at all times, and points out at once with no uncertain finger mistakes, as well as improvements, in hull and rig, and also in sailing and seamanship. These chapters on racers and their gear, as well as races, will (it is hoped) add to the knowledge of all who read and understand.

· I ·

BRITANNIA

Length, overall	-	-	122 ft. 0 in.	Length, water-line	-	- 87 ft. 0 in.
Beam	-	-	- 23 ft. 3 in.	Draught	-	- - 15 ft. 0 in.
Displacement	-	-	- 153½ tons	Sail area 10,797 (1893) and 9,235 (1933)		

Designer, G. L. WATSON   *Owner*, HIS MAJESTY KING GEORGE V

" *Britannia* the pride of the Ocean,
Beloved by the brave and the free.
The Shrine of a Sailor's devotion
What ship can compare unto thee ? "

WAS ever a vessel better named, designed, built and raced than *Britannia*? Her very name, it seems, inspires everyone to his greatest effort, and when the fact that she was designed and built for the late King Edward VII when Prince of Wales, and is now owned by our present King, is added to such a name, it can easily be understood that everyone aboard while racing puts forth his utmost.

BRITANNIA REACHING THROUGH COWES ROAD AT HER MAXIMUM SPEED

It is a great honour and a privilege to be able to commence these chapters on racing vessels with the greatest racer of all time, and also a great pleasure. For *Britannia* enables me to point out to the pessimistic yachtsman (who stresses the fact that the *America* won a cup given by the Royal Yacht Squadron in 1851 for a race round the Isle of Wight, and that though over 80 years have passed we have been unable to win this cup back in spite of many attempts), that twice since then America has sent over large cutters, *Navahoe*, 1893, and *Vigilant*, 1894, and that *Britannia* beat the pair of them fairly comfortably, for she always finished ahead of *Navahoe*, while out of 17 races, in which *Vigilant* took part, *Britannia* won 11, *Vigilant* won 5 and *Satanita* 1.

BRITANNIA AS SHE CAME OUT WITH VERTICAL CLOTHS IN HER
MAINSAIL

BRITANNIA FITTED WITH DEEP BULWARKS FOR CRUISING

BRITANNIA WITH HER MARCONI TOPMAST

BRITANNIA UNDER HER PRESENT BERMUDIAN RIG
NOTE THE TWO BROKEN BATTENS

FOUR PHOTOGRAPHS DEPICTING *BRITANNIA*'S LIFE-HISTORY

Since then America has not sent over to Britain a large racing cutter, but when she does she will still find the old *Britannia* ready to give battle. So these chapters on racers do not start, as do most of our racing stories, with a picture of Britain with her tail down.

 *   *   *   *   *   *   *   *   *   *   *   *

Britannia brings home many lessons. She proves that beauty is a matter of education, for when she first breasted the waters forty years ago she was considered ugly to a generation educated to admire the hollow clipper bow, while to-day she is held by all as a model of grace and beauty. " Handsome is that handsome does."

SIR PHILIP AT BRITANNIA'S HELM. NOTE HOW EASILY WATER RUNS OFF HER DECK
SINCE BULWARKS WERE CUT DOWN IN 1934

Her life-history is instructive to designers, builders, owners and rule makers. For she points out to these, that what is good for one is good for all, as each depends upon the other. If the designers of a class design bad boats, that class is a failure, if builders do not put in the best of work and workmanship the same applies, while if the rules are bad the class is bad, and these three things affect the owner, for he owns the result. The rule makers spoilt the large class in 1897, and it was not until 1920 that it was strong again, when the rule makers again encouraged vessels similar to the old *Britannia*.

Now the rule for the large class is the universal rule of America, for America has adopted the European rules for classes from 12 metres downwards, and we have adopted their rules for the largest class, the " J " Class, so that as the large racers are now designed to an international rule, their position is stronger than ever before.

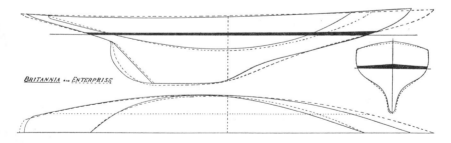

BRITANNIA and ENTERPRISE

Britannia's lines are wonderfully fair and sweet to the eye, and looking at them one ceases to wonder at the fact that even though forty years of age, she still is as fast as the best, for the sections, water-lines and buttocks could not be improved upon to-day. This is borne out by the plan of *Britannia's* profile, quarter buttock, deck water-line and midship section, with that of *Enterprise* dotted on it, for in 1930, *Enterprise*, after defeating the best of the American cutters, defeated the best of the British, namely *Shamrock*, in the *America's* cup contest. And the likeness between *Britannia's* lines and those of *Enterprise* is very startling. I have brought *Enterprise* to *Britannia's* size for comparison, for it must be remembered that *Enterprise* is 7 ft. shorter on the water-line, being 80 ft. on the line.

This plan, while showing that great minds think alike, is also a great tribute to the brain of G. L. Watson, for besides showing that his lines can hardly be improved upon to-day, it proves that the proportions and shape he

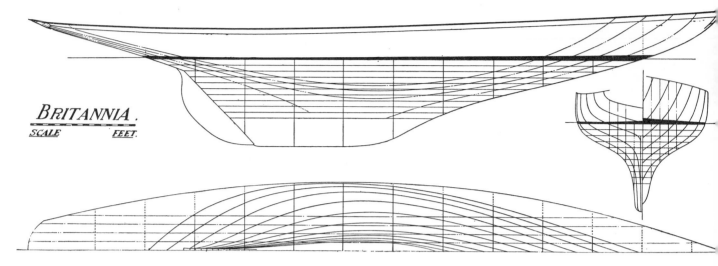

BRITANNIA.
SCALE   FEET.

gave *Britannia* are considered ideal after all these years, for it must be remembered that he did not have to consider quarter beam, length, displacement and draught, as the designers of to-day are forced to do. But when these restrictions were added to the rating rules they encouraged practically the same hull as *Britannia's*.

Her accommodation plan shows that half of the accommodation length is given over to the crew and the galley.

Next abaft of this is her saloon, which, extending the whole width of *Britannia*, is spacious and airy, and is most cheerful with its pictures. Farther aft, abreast each other, are two state rooms, the owner's being to starboard, and in this the dressing-table is the most noticeable thing. For in its two upper corners are carvings showing thistles, roses and shamrocks all flourishing on one stem, pointing out that Scotland, England and Ireland should for each other's benefit dwell together in unity and peace, while in the two lower corners are the most striking carvings of all, *Britannia* with her shield and trident. How well the carver loved his work, and the hours spent at it one can only imagine, for this age, with its acceptance of articles stamped out by machines in thousands, has lost one of the greatest joys of life—the joy of working quietly with the hands and brain alone.

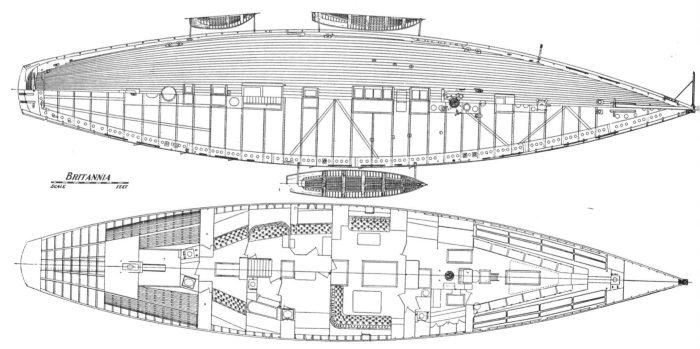

BRITANNIA
SCALE   FEET

Right aft of the accommodation is the ladies' cabin, separated from the rest of the accommodation by the companionway and bathroom. The counter, as in almost all the large racers, is used as a sail locker, and although roomy there is need for all this space as the sails are large and their area makes them heavy to handle.

The thin counter, looked at in profile, appears too weak to stand up to the strains put upon it by the mainsheet and the backstays, but inside it is carefully braced by a light but well thought out steel girder throughout its length.

The sail plan shows her original rig, with the Jack yard topsail and reefing topmast in dotted lines, and in solid lines the Bermuda sail plan given her in 1931. The noticeable thing is the increased height and reduced base of the sail plan.

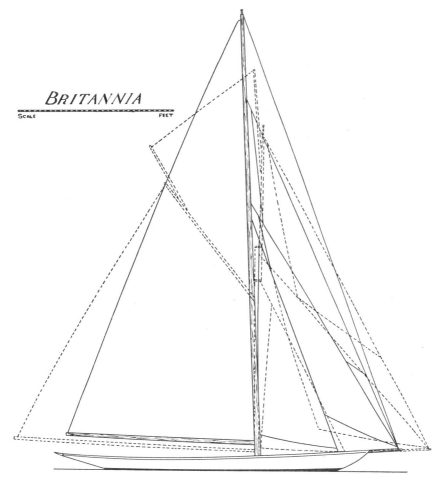

BRITANNIA
SCALE   FEET

Her gaff with all the halyards and blocks attached to it is gone, and her mainsail has now a parabolic curve from truck to boom, whereas before it was flattened at the gaff, and the topsail on one tack was flattened as it was pressed against the peak halyards. So, with the saving of weight aloft and the increased efficiency of the mainsail, *Britannia* is far better to windward now than she was. But as so often is the case in this world, a gain in one direction is a loss in another, and it will be some years before the tall Bermudian rig on these large cutters will be properly understood, and until such time we shall not see *Britannia* able to storm across Channel at 12 knots in a nasty sea as she did in 1893 against the American *Navahoe*.

And those who, like myself, sigh over the loss in hard weather ability must be patient, and remember that in *Britannia's* early days the large cutters sometimes carried away their short mainmasts, which showed that they were not properly understood then, so the time will come when these tall Bermudian spars will be as strong or stronger than the old short gaff cutter mainmasts, for with increasing years comes increased knowledge and improved materials.

May that time come soon, for these large cutters are sturdy and strong, and fit for any weather in every detail excepting in their masting and rigging, and when the day dawns that sees their one weakness strengthened every lover of the sea will rejoice.

· 2 ·

S A T A N I T A

Length, overall - - 131 ft. 6 in.		Length, water-line - - 93 ft. 6 in.
Beam - - - - 24 ft. 6 in.		Draught - - - - 14 ft. 10 in.
Displacement - - - 126¼ tons		Sail area - - - - 10,093 sq. ft.

Owner, A. D. CLARKE   *Designer*, J. M. SOPER

THE larger a sailing vessel the sweeter her lines generally, for a man's height remains the same whether he is on a small or a large vessel, so when his full headroom has been obtained there is little need to go into deeper buttocks or higher freeboard than necessary for the ship's sake. But in small vessels, lines have to be distorted, freeboard raised and coach roofs built to get headroom, so one generally expects sweeter lines, and finds them, in larger vessels.

SATANITA.
SCALE   FEET

And *Satanita's* lines are long and easy, and it is not to be wondered at that she could, and did, do 16 knots, on a reach between the *Warner* and the *Owers*, which is the record for yachts. She is the longest (water-line) cutter ever built, and was designed to race against *Britannia*, *Valkyrie* and *Caluna*, all built on the Clyde.

A yacht designer must love his work, in fact any man must be a lover of his work to excel at it, and so, when on Christmas morning in 1892 J. M. Soper received the order to design *Satanita*, he regarded it then, and still does, as the finest Christmas present he had received in his life, even if he did work all through the holidays to design his masterpiece, so that the workmen could start on her hull after their Christmas holidays.

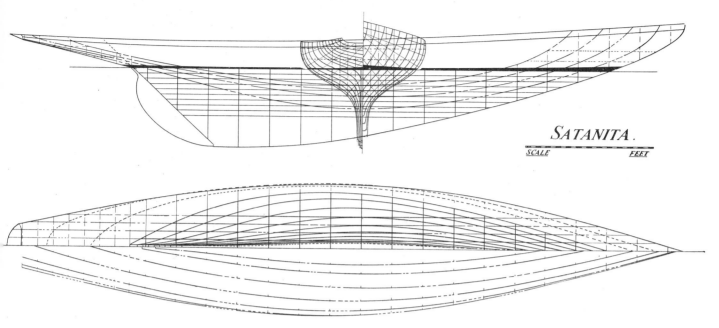

SATANITA.

SCALE   FEET

Satanita was built in record time and competed in the Southend to Harwich Race when she came in second to *Valkyrie,* and considering that she carried away her throat halyards and reset her mainsail by using the trysail sheets, this was a good start.

Because of her length, she was at her best in strong winds, and beat all records over the Squadron Courses. She was timed at over 16 knots in slack water between the *Nab* and the *Owers* lightships. (The Nab is now a tower in a slightly different position.) In her second year, she averaged 13·7 knots on the Thames from Gravesend to the *Mouse* light-ship and back, a broad and a close reach. Because they could reef their topmast and had a low rig compared to that of the present day, these old vessels never failed to start, no matter how hard it blew, and in spite of the enormous sails they spread. *Satanita's* sail area was 10,093 sq. ft., Y.R.A., and her main boom 91 ft. long.

The difference in values in forty years is interesting : *Satanita* was built for £8,500 and such a boat to-day would cost £30,000, three times that amount due to increased wages and costs ; this is one argument in favour of building yachts, because they are made by hand practically throughout and increase in value rather than de-crease with the passing years.

The old Solent one-designs built forty years ago for £175 are now worth £200 and change hands at this price. This seems strange until we look at the records of old churches, when we find the finest workmen getting $\frac{1}{4}$d. an hour, and

SATANITA'S LENGTH MADE HER THE FASTEST RACING CUTTER YET BUILT

because as the years roll on, artisans, that can work well with their hands, will become more and more scarce, and so worth more, the value of their work will increase. Machine-made articles can never be as beautiful as those made by a hand guided by a loving heart and clever brain.

· 3 ·

NYRIA

Length, overall - - - 112 ft. 0 in.		Length, water-line - - 72 ft. 6 in.
Beam - - - - 20 ft. 0 in.		Draught - - - 13 ft. 9 in.
Displacement - - - 114 tons		Sail area - - - - 7,418 sq. ft.

Owner, ROBERT YOUNG   *Designer*, CHARLES E. NICHOLSON

*N*YRIA, designed and built 28 years ago, is very interesting, as twice in her life she has led the way in design and construction. At the time of her birth, competition among the large classes had become so keen that designers had forced each other to cut down the scantlings so fine, that the hulls threatened to become useless as cruisers after their racing life had ended.

NYRIA WAS THE FIRST LARGE CUTTER TO ADOPT THE BERMUDIAN RIG

However, Charles Nicholson asked *Nyria's* owner to have her a racer in shape, but a cruiser in construction to Lloyds' highest class (20 A 1). The year after *Nyria* was built the I.Y.R.U. were wise and adopted Lloyds' scantlings for the large racers, and although *Brynhild*, *White Heather* and *Shamrock* were not to such a high class at Lloyds and were lighter in hulls than *Nyria*, it was a step in the right direction, followed ever since over here

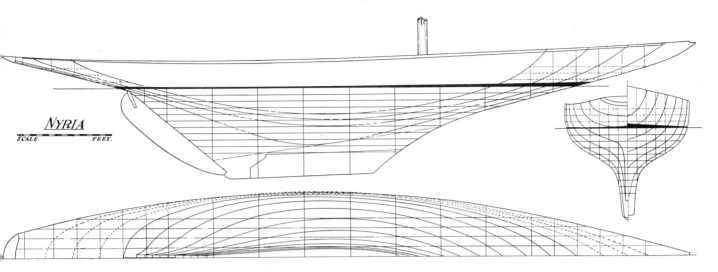

NYRIA
SCALE   FEET.

and now in America. Her lines show the cleanness that can only be found in large yachts, the raking stern post is very noticeable, and there is no doubt that it does cut down wetted surface neatly and easily. Being so easily driven, *Nyria's* lines cannot be improved upon to-day, excepting to get something out of a rule, for the wind and sea remain the same always, and only rules alter designs.

Steel masts are considered new, but *Nyria* had one when she was first built, and of the same unusual principle in construction as now built for British " J " class yachts, although, unfortunately, she carried it away off Ostend.

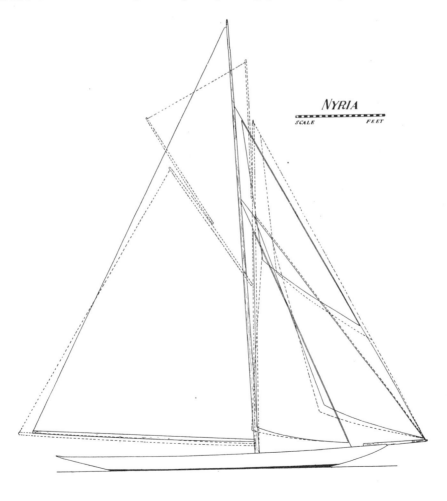

NYRIA
SCALE   FEET

However, by way of a record, within a week she was racing with the Royal London Yacht Club on the Solent with a complete new set of spars and rigging excepting for her bowsprit and spinnaker boom. This record could not now be approached with present-day rigs. In 1921, after the war, Mrs. Workman brought her up to date, and the lowering of the lead keel, as shown on the plan, together with a Bermudian rig, improved *Nyria* beyond belief. She was the first large yacht to have this tall rig, and was much talked of in 1922, everyone saying what a mistake it was, yet soon afterwards all large yachts followed her lead. Now all racing vessels, from the largest to the smallest, have Bermudian rigs, for there is no doubt that it is the fastest to windward yet evolved, and racers stand or fall according to their ability to windward. So *Nyria* has twice led the way for the largest classes ; at her birth, by being built to Lloyds' highest class, and twenty years afterwards by being the first large yacht with the Bermudian rig.

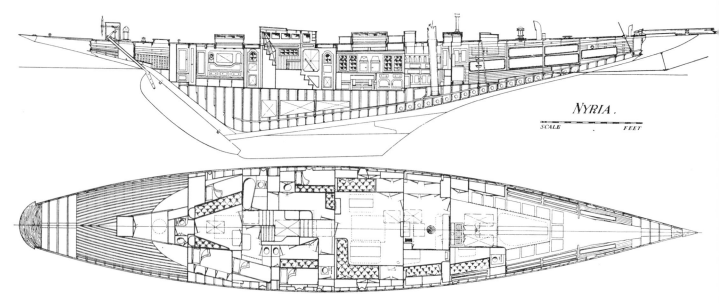

Nyria.

SCALE   .   FEET

During the last few years she has sailed in the Mediterranean, her rig having been altered from a Bermudian cutter to a ketch. Her teak planking and construction is almost as sound to-day as when she was built about thirty years ago.

The accommodation plan gives an idea of the ease and comfort to be found aboard such a fast and able vessel.

· 4 ·

WEETAMOE

Length, overall	-	-	125 ft. 9 in.		Length, water-line	-	-	83 ft. 0 in.
Beam	-	-	20 ft. 0 in.		Draught	-	-	15 ft. 0 in.
Displacement	-	-	143 tons		Sail area	-	-	7,560 sq. ft.

Present Owner, F. H. PRINCE   *Designer,* CLINTON H. CRANE

(Built for a syndicate headed by George Nichols and Junius S. Morgan.)

DESIGNED and built as a possible defender of the *America's* Cup in 1930, *Weetamoe* came very very near to being the chosen ship, as the list of races won by the four built in America to the " J " class rule that year will show :

Enterprise (80 ft. Lwl.)	-	-	won 14 races
Weetamoe (83 ft. Lwl.)	-	-	won 12 races
Yankee (84 ft. Lwl.)	-	-	won 7 races
Whirlwind (86 ft. Lwl.)	-	-	won 1 race

As these races ranged over three months, June, July and August, all weather conditions from strong winds to heavy calms were experienced, so *Weetamoe* may be looked upon as an excellent example of a yacht to the " J " class rule,

WEETAMOE CLOSE-HAULED ON HER WAY TO THE STARTING LINE

for even when the rule calling for heavier masts was made after the 1930 contest, because of her length and displacement *Weetamoe* was still able to win races, while the shorter *Enterprise* was not fitted to the altered rule, as it was thought that she would not be powerful enough to win races with a 5.500 lb. mast (1,500 lb. heavier than her 1930 mast) plus the 7 tons of internal accommodation the altered rule demanded, for all the extra weight would have to be taken from her lead keel.

One is struck by the ease of each of *Weetamoe's* lines, and how very like its neighbour each one is, for there is no sudden change in the diagonals, buttocks or water-lines. But in the sections a change can be seen, which at first sight is startling, for the bow sections above and on the water-line are sharp, and then one notices the first four sections abaft the fore end of the water-line are rounded in rather quickly at the bottom after which they become sharp again. This rounding is not to cheat any rule but an effort to cut down wetted surface, and a glance at the fore endings of the water-lines will show that those above the water-line are sharp and gradually get fuller and fuller till down at the lead keel they resemble the bow of a torpedo.

That *Weetamoe's* designer studies every detail very carefully I know full well, for he taught another youngster and myself archery. The two of us shot against him, but his patience and ability to note the tiny details generally unseen soon saw our combined scores so great that he could not equal them though generally all his arrows but one would be in the gold, and that one only just out. And so looking at *Weetamoe's* lines I can picture him quietly and carefully perfecting the unusual underwater bow of *Weetamoe*.

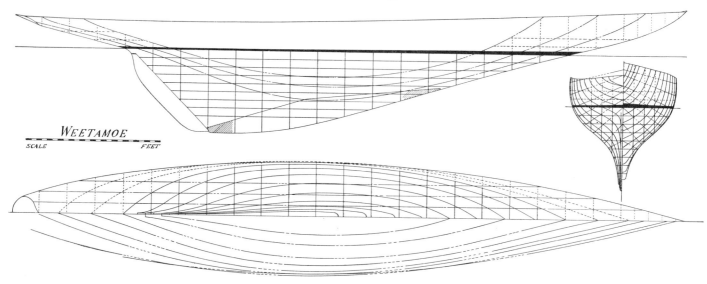

WEETAMOE

SCALE   FEET

In 1930 *Weetamoe* had a three headsail rig very similar to *Britannia's*, as did all the large cutters, but the rule forcing a heavier mast and the knowledge gained in the next three years enabled her to be rigged with two headsails for the 1934 season. This is a more efficient rig, for there is no doubt that the middle headsail of the three disturbs the after one (staysail), and with the knowledge increasing years will bring there is little doubt that these large cutters will all have single headsails in spite of the difficulty in staying a mast to support them and the harder work in handling such a sail.

The two backstays are as they should be, entirely separate, and while the one taking the strain of the fore stay is the same distance abaft the mast as the foot of the fore stay is forward of it, the one taking the jib strain is not as far aft as its corresponding stay is forward. The reason for this, it would seem, is to keep this stay forward of the helmsman, for the sound of a wire backstay twanging in a breeze behind a helmsman might easily disturb his peace of mind, and so take his attention off the race.

Two things are noticeable in this mast. Due to its size it needs no topmast stay or topmast backstay, a saving in windage of 300 ft. of wire, but, more than this, the absence of the topmast forestay puts all the pull of the main sheet directly upon the fore and jib stays, which means that they must be taut on a wind. We successfully rigged the 6-metre *Nada* this way some time back. The thing against such a strong mast is its size and windage, for *Weetamoe's* mast is 2 ft. 6 in. fore and aft, and 1 ft. 6 in. athwartships, and such a spar must disturb the luff of a mainsail directly behind it unless it revolves, which the rules will not permit.

The other clever point of *Weetamoe's* rig is the hook at the masthead to take the head of the mainsail; this relieves the mast of half the compression strain due to the main halyard. The mainsails of these large cutters weigh about three-quarters of a ton, so there must be that same strain on the halyard to hold it up, making a total strain of 1½ tons, without taking into consideration the extra strains put on to stretch the luff taut and those set up when the mast shortens under compression and then straightens out in going about. That hook halves some of these loads and entirely frees the mast of the others. In England a wire strop is fitted to the masthead, and one of the crew goes aloft to shackle the mainsail headboard to this, but *Weetamoe's* masthead hook does away with this entirely. The masthead hook is solid and does not move, but looking at the sail plan it will be seen that the main halyard block on the headboard has an eye worked into its upper part; this is lashed towards the mast when the sail is hoisted (for it must be remembered that such a mainsail shakes and flogs about a great deal when being hoisted in a breeze).

When the mainsail is just above the hook the halyard is eased down and the lashing takes the eye over the hook, for the race or cruise.

To lower the sail the mainsail is hoisted higher so that the eye of the block is forced outwards by the over-hanging top of the mast; this breaks the lashing and then the spring in the eye holds it out from the mast and the sail is lowered. If a reef is to be taken in, a length of wire is shackled into the head of the sail exactly the depth of the reef.

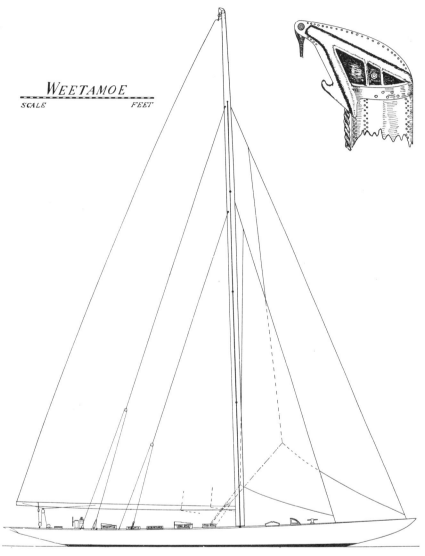

Weetamoe
SCALE   FEET

The sketch on the sail plan illustrates the masthead. It shows the hook which takes the main halyard block, and the angle above, which breaks the lashing holding the eye of the block towards the mast, so enabling the spring that takes it away to come into action when the sail is to be lowered. It will be seen that the main halyard is made fast to the top of the mast, leads through the block on the headboard and then back over a sheave inside the mast-head, and down inside the mast.

Altogether *Weetamoe's* sail plan and her masting and rigging are a great advance and worthy of study.

In *Weetamoe's* fo'c'sle there are fifteen cots, two of which are over the settee just forward of the coal stove. Then there are two double-berthed cabins, which take the cook, steward and the two mates, bringing the crew accommodation up to nineteen. The cook has a roomy galley, 12 ft. by 10 ft., just forward of the mast. In this space is the stove, the crew's sink and pantry, and the owner's sink and pantry. At first sight this does not appear to be a great deal of space; but the number aboard such a vessel as *Weetamoe* is seldom more than thirty all told, and when we remember that on a train the cook has to turn out a dinner of six or seven courses for as many as a hundred people, whose appetites have not been whetted by the keen salt air, gourmands who complain of food, not because the food is bad but because they and their insides are soured, in a galley the width of a carriage, minus the alley-way, bringing his galley down to 12 ft. by 6 ft., which with the train rushing along at 70 or more miles an hour sways and rocks about violently for a train's motion, although not so much as a vessel's at sea, is quicker and more spiteful, we begin to think that a galley like *Weetamoe's* is quite a roomy place.

Weetamoe's ship's company of nineteen men live comfortably and happily in a fo'c'sle 45 ft. long with an average width of 12 ft., from the mast to the bows.

Directly abaft the mast is the main saloon which is 13 ft. 6 in. long by 18 ft. wide with a comfortable lounge each side, two tables, and a companionway which leads straight out on to the deck. Abaft this are four staterooms

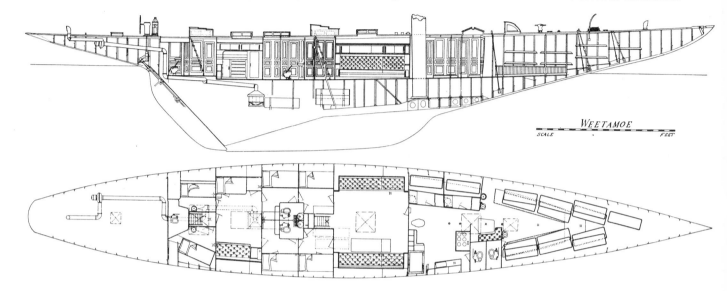

for guests, and in the finest place of the ship is the owner's cabin the full width of *Weetamoe*, 8 ft. fore and aft and 18 ft. athwartships, with a 3 ft. wide sleeping berth to port and a lounge to starboard, leaving a great deal of floor space in spite of the table at the fore end of the cabin. Aft of this is a companionway in the centre, which divides the captain's cabin to starboard from a single stateroom on the port side. In the rest of the ship from these cabins aft the sails are stored in a space 20 ft. long with an average width of 12 ft. and an average depth of 4 ft.

In spite of the ample headroom throughout *Weetamoe* there is still a great deal of room under her floor, which in places amounts again to full headroom, and this causes one to wonder if the displacement of these large racers could be less, and give owners faster vessels.

For if the scantlings were kept the same then all decreased displacement would come off the lead keel, making for an easier vessel in a seaway, and smaller spars and sails with no loss in speed. So with little damage to accommodation these large cutters would cost less and be as fast, for lead keels and sails as well as spars cost less as they grow smaller.

This is not meant to suggest any alteration in the " J " class rule, but is intended to hold off the many misguided yachtsmen who look upon heavier displacements in all vessels as the cure for all ills, for if *Weetamoe's* displacement is compared to *Britannia's* and *Satanita's*, it will be seen that taking an increase of 5 tons of displacement for every foot of water-line length (as the " J " class rule demands around 85 ft.), *Britannia* is 9 tons short of the " J " class displacement, and after forty years of service is still as good a racer as could be devised. *Satanita* is practically 76 tons short of the " J " class displacement for a 93 ft. 6 in. water-lined vessel, yet when racing she used to sail across the Bay of Biscay and down the Spanish and Portuguese coasts to take part in the Mediterranean regattas. On one return passage she came across a noted large cruising vessel of her day hove-to in the bay, and *Satanita*, after asking her if she needed help, carried on under her trysail and arrived in Southampton some days ahead.

Weetamoe is placed at the end of these chapters on the large racers as she is the modern vessel, and in her we see the changes time brings about, changes in ideas and changes in yacht measurement rules. There is no doubt that the present " J " class yacht is as fine a racer as ever seen, and a far better cruiser than that produced under any other rule, as a study of *Weetamoe's* lines, sail plan and accommodation plan will prove.

· 5 ·

12 METRES

THIS is the largest class to the International Yacht Racing Union rule, and there is no doubt the speed, sea-worthiness and cabin accommodation of the 12-metre racers makes them very dear to the seaman's heart. In 1928, when we sailed the 14-footer across Channel to Havre for the regatta there, we came upon the *Vanity* anchored inside the breakwater, ready for the morrow's race, and filtering up through the cabin skylight came the

CLYMENE WINNING FROM THE OCEAN RACERS IN THEIR WEATHER

sweet strains of music from a violin, for her owner, Johnny Payne, was below whiling away an hour with his fiddle. That picture of comfort and contentment always rises before my eyes as I think of the 12-metres, and with it another picture, that of the 12-metre *Clymene* converted to a yawl beating the ocean racers, in their own hard weather and under their own racing rules. The photograph of *Clymene* taken that day by Beken gives a good idea of a 12-metre in action and illustrates the speed and seaworthiness of the class. It must be remembered that in the race that day the finest ocean racers, *Dorade* and *Mistress* of America, and *Neptune* and *Lexia* of this country, were ranged against the *Clymene*, and yet she beat them under their own rule and weather conditions. The picture of her flying along in that race is the finest argument I know for the 12-metre class, especially when beside it rises the picture of restful content *Vanity* made in Havre, with her owner living aboard and enjoying the life.

187

The photograph of *Iris* shows the rather heavy displacement (from a purely racing point of view) called for by the I.Y.R.U. rules, but because of the comfort and room this gives below, it is a virtue in the 12- and 8-metre classes, but as the 6-metres have no cabin accommodation they should not be forced to have such a heavy displacement, for their huge quarter waves cry aloud to the I.Y.R.U., " Why this heavy displacement when we have no cabin accommodation ? "

THE 12-METRE IRIS SHOWS THE QUARTER WAVE CAUSED BY THE I.Y.R.U. DISPLACEMENT RULE

Now although this displacement is a virtue at present, the time will come when it is too heavy for all the metre classes unless the rule makers are careful, as too much of a good thing is bad. For the rules rightly enough force longer boats into heavier displacement, but as the scantlings are not increased all this extra weight goes into lead keels, and the tendency of the class is to get longer, heavier and narrower. Because they are smaller more vessels are built to the 6-metre class and development is faster there, and these little boats act as testing models to the larger classes, which always follow along a year or so later with ideas. The 6-metre racers have become so long and heavy that 80 per cent. of their total weight is in their lead keels, and as with increased length their beam has been lessened, it is easy to realise that they are becoming like half-tide rocks, for their reserve buoyancy is not enough to lift them over head seas. The Norwegians, who have gone farther in this direction than any other country, appealed to the I.Y.R.U. to remove the girth measurement, although girth seems to have little to do with weight, but the girth measurement was removed last winter. All of which seemed to me to be like trying to cure a broken leg by poulticing a little finger.

Length is speed, and it is the striving for length at all costs that has led the racing classes throughout the ages of yacht racing astray. The old plank-on-edge vessels illustrate this; the Norwegians likening their own 6-metres to submarines shows that the International Yacht Racing Union, in spite of its clever formulae, is headed for destruction on the same rock—LENGTH.

And because they are so fond of formulae they cannot see that a simple restriction on length in all classes is their one salvation.

The determination of the length of the luff and leach at the 1932 conference illustrates the futility of too complicated a measurement, for in complicated rules the rule makers lose sight of the goal at which they aim. The circustent spinnakers of the American 6-metre team of 1932 shook the racing world, for in their spinnakers alone they carried double their total allowed area, and a rule had to be made to stop it.

The Americans cabled over a formula which was 90 per cent. of " I " plus " J " squared to be the length of the spinnaker sides. When worked out this proved to be some distance longer than the spinnaker halyard height to the water. Which was rightly thought to be too long. Now, being young and innocent to the ways of the I.Y.R.U. (it was the first conference I had been summoned to as a technical adviser—and also the last) I suggested the sides of the spinnakers should not exceed the length of the forestay on 6-metres, or the luff of the longest headsail on large vessels, and its width in any part should not be more than twice the base of the fore triangle. For such a rule would be suitable for every class from the *Britannia* down to the dinghys, and would also be acceptable to ocean racers and cruiser racers, for just as the I.Y.R.U. racing rules govern the whole world because of their excellent wording and meaning, so should their rules on hulls and rigs. But such a simple suggestion was turned down, and so Nicholson, Fife, Mylne, Ratsey and myself were led to a room with a fine spinnaker by Ratsey laid out on the floor, and we were told to make a rule with the American " I " plus " J " squared in it to control spinnakers. And the rule was made, but was useless for the small classes, and good for a few only. And it is so with the present formula ; this is good but unless a length restriction is put in it the classes to it will get longer, heavier, and narrower until yachts designed to the rule will be like unto the plank-on-edge boats of 1884—wet, miserable and uninspiring.

Now is the time to put the length restriction on while the classes are perfect little ships, with the exception of a few in the 6-metre classes.

And the limit water-line I should propose would be 23 ft. for the 6-metres, 32 ft. for the 8-metres, 45 ft. for the 12-metres and 88 ft. for the " J " class, just to give the I.Y.R.U. a point from which to start thinking.

Unknown to yachtsmen our British designers have saved the classes from worries. For instance years ago they realised that it was bad to set the jib halyards too high up the mast, and so they agreed amongst themselves not to go above 75 per cent. of the mast height with their jib halyards, saving owners in the class many masts, and now the rule has been passed that the jib halyard shall not go above 75 per cent. of the total height. So it is possible that among British designers a similar agreement as to water-line length is saving our classes from the fate of the Norwegian, but as these classes are international our designers handicap themselves by building short boats ; that other nations should build longer ones (as they do) is unfair, for length is speed !

DEVONIA

Length, overall	-	-	-	72 ft. 3 in.	Length, water-line -	- 44 ft. 2 in.
Beam	-	-	-	11 ft. 9 in.	Draught - -	- 8 ft. 8½ in.
Displacement	-	-	23¼ tons	Sail area - -	- 1,825 sq. ft.

Designed by Morgan Giles in 1932, and through the illness of the owner never built, this set of lines is very interesting, for they show a fast and weatherly twelve.

The lines are very pleasing to the eye, for the buttocks are easy and fair.

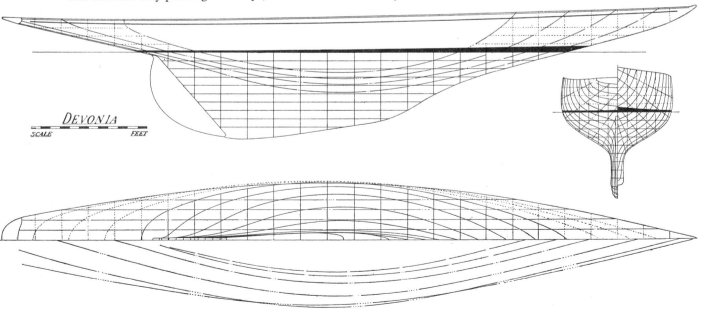

In bygone days these were called the bowlines from midships forward, and buttocks from midships aft, but now through laziness we speak of a bow line as a buttock line. A man looking forward to eating a tasty and tender buttock (rump) steak would be angry if a tough piece of brisket were served up instead, which is exactly what would happen if the looseness that has crept into yacht designing also crept into the butcher's trade.

Devonia's water-lines are easy and the bow endings of the first two above the water-line show a quick round in, which shortens the measured length; the water-line itself as well as the line below is also rounded in quickly to shorten the water-line.

Devonia's water-lines are easy and fair everywhere excepting the fore endings of the load water-line and the lines above and below it. These four lines round in so that she is a foot less in the measured length and the measured water-line, which gives greater sail area and less displacement under the rule.

The sections can be studied without the change from the almost vertical bow section to the horizontal stern section being noticed, for this change from the one to the other is so skilfully carried out that it is practically invisible, the work of a clever designer.

The fin at first seems large, but although few realise it even a 12-metre makes leeway, as will be seen by standing by the mast and looking aft along the centre line at the wake, and so *Devonia's* lead keel and fin is not too large for leeway.

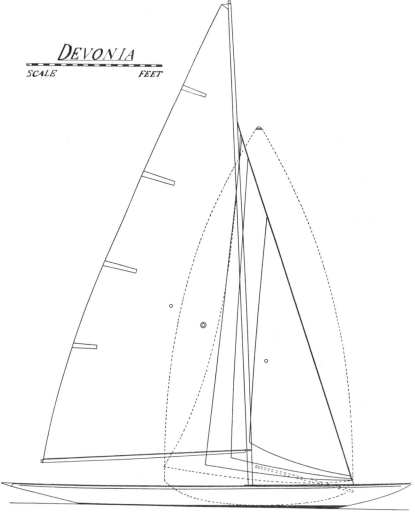

DEVONIA

SCALE   FEET

The sail plan shows the present-day tall and narrow mainsails, as the luff of *Devonia's* mainsail is more than twice the length of her main boom, while the fore triangle has a height equal to almost four times its base.

With the large reaching jib set her actual area is 2,085 sq. ft., although the measured sail is only 1,825 sq. ft. This is due to the fact that the I.Y.R.U. rule measures the spars and not the sails, a very wise and a fair way of measuring. For spars never alter or vary as sails do with the weather and use, and new sails can be used without all the bother of their being measured, for the owner as well as his competitors can see at all times that the sails do not extend beyond the black bands on the spars, which mark the limits of the sail.

The drooping main boom, ugly to eyes unused to it, eases the strain put upon the leach by the main sheet, for if the boom end is high above the deck a far greater strain is needed to haul it amidships, and these racers will stand their main booms practically amidships when going to windward.

The leach of the reaching jib is hollowed; this helps it to clear the crosstrees and at the same time does away with the part of a jib that so frequently spills wind into the mainsail instead of past it.

So altogether *Devonia* is a carefully thought out racer. Her designer, Morgan Giles, who kindly sent me her lines for reproduction, did not send an accommodation plan, and so, to show the accommodation that a 12-metre could have, I have included the accommodation plan of one I designed myself. It will be seen that *Victoria* is a pointed stern racer, because I am a great believer in pointed sterns, for fishes, insects and birds developed for speed through the water or air are pointed at the stern. This canoe stern on the 12-metre would offer less wind resistance when heeled than counter would, and although a boat sailing does not travel fast enough for streamlining to tell, it is needed, for the wind rushes past the boat at sometimes 50 miles an hour, and then the pointed stern prevents the wind eddying round aft.

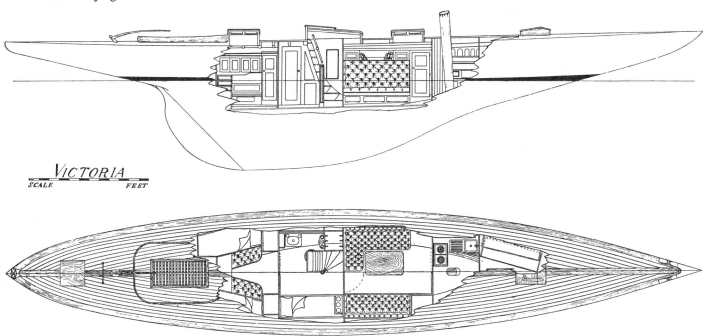

VICTORIA
SCALE   FEET

Victoria is 9 in. longer on the line and 6 in. greater in beam than *Devonia*, but these two differences would hardly alter the accommodation, and the same room would be found aboard either boat. In the fo'c'sle there are four pipe cots, and directly abaft this is the galley and pantry, with a sliding door, leading into the saloon.

Between the saloon and the double cabin aft is the companionway, and under this is the washroom, while opposite is a single-berth cabin. She has no capstan, as the anchor would be hauled up by a tackle along the deck.

So *Victoria* is comfortable and cosy below, and if needed the backs of the settees in the saloon could be swung up and four sleep there, bringing the number that could sleep comfortably aboard up to eleven. Such accommodation in first-class racing vessels makes the displacement called for by the rule worth while.

· 6 ·

8 METRES

HISPANIA VI

Length, overall - - - 46 ft. 0 in.		Length, water-line - - 30 ft. 0 in.
Beam - - - - 7 ft. 9 in.		Draught - - - - 6 ft. 6 in.
Displacement - - - 8 tons		Sail area - - - - 887.6 sq. ft.

Designer, MORGAN GILES   *Owner*, HIS MAJESTY KING ALFONSO

AS a king's wish is a royal command that must be obeyed, we may be sure that of all the designers of Europe King Alfonso chose Morgan Giles to design and build his last 8-metre *Hispania VI*, and so paid England as well as Giles a great compliment. This compliment brings home the fact that once a nation deserts the sea she falls.

HISPANIA VI

At one time Spain was the most powerful nation in the world, but then she was a seafaring nation. This earth is three parts water, and so throughout the ages the power that held the mastery of the seas was master of the world. Directly Nelson had defeated the combined fleets of France and Spain, Napoleon, whose army was waiting in France with but 21 miles of water to cross in order to conquer and overrun Britain, turned tail and made the long march to Austerlitz.

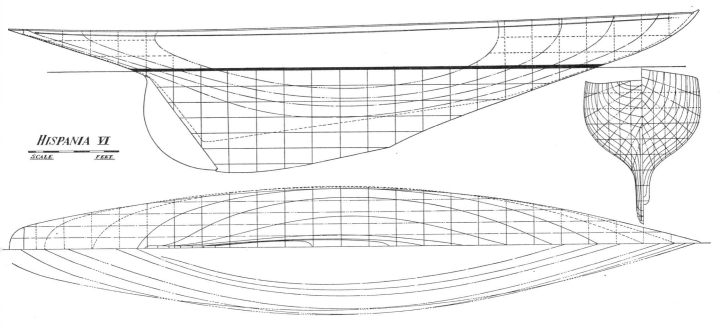

HISPANIA VI
SCALE   FEET.

Napoleon had one of the finest brains for warfare ever possessed by man, and he knew that the successful invasion of Britain was impossible unless he had the mastery of the seas, and his brain power may be gauged by the fact that within a few hours of abandoning the invasion of Britain he had planned the long march to Austerlitz and had perfected the whole details of stopping-places, provisioning and watering so well, that not one of them had to be altered afterwards.

In this last war, because the British Navy held the mastery of the seas, her side was as certain of victory as day follows night.

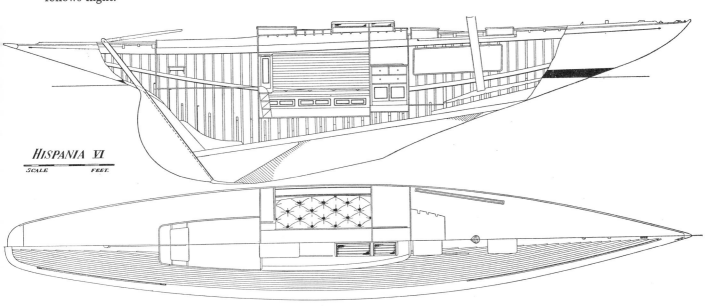

HISPANIA VI
SCALE   FEET.

People foolishly say there will be no more war ; there would not be if after the last war, instead of fiddling about with a League of Nations, all nations had said, " Britain, in spite of all your faults, you are the fairest-minded nation of this earth, keep and improve your Navy, and be the police of the earth ; each country will give you a station, and you must make us all behave, for even now we all come to you in time of trouble."

★   ★   ★   ★   ★   ★   ★   ★   ★   ★   ★   ★

F.S.S.

Hispania's lines show that Morgan Giles did his utmost for King Alfonso, as she is very clean and sweet under water, the sections are firm and yet not too powerful, for it must be remembered that she was designed for Spanish waters, where even if the wind blows the same speed as farther north it has not the same power as it is a warmer wind. For there is no doubt that the colder winds are more dense and powerful, even if they are not faster, a fact soon realised when sailing in summer and winter.

The diagonals are fair and easy, and looking at the lines it is soon realised why she was so successful in the warm winds of sunny Spain.

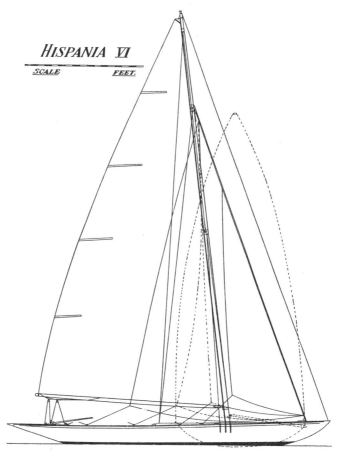

HISPANIA VI

SCALE   FEET.

The 8-metre class is the smallest class to the I.Y.R.U. rules, with cabin accommodation, and the accommodation and construction plan shows that a young owner could live very comfortably aboard throughout the summer months, and sail such a vessel round the coast from regatta to regatta just as the owners in the larger classes do, for coastal cruising in an 8-metre would give owners the two most sought after things in this life, health and happiness, for without doubt sailing at sea brings peace to the mind, and the clean salt-laden air health to the body, which are both needed by all in this mechanical age of irritating noise and poisonous fumes.

The sail plan with its numerous headsails is adaptable for all conditions of wind and weather, for whatever jib the wind calls for is set, then in hard weather there is only the main sail to reef to adjust her sail area to suit the weather conditions.

The 8-metres are very popular, for in the cabin an owner can live, or simply change his wet clothes after a hard race and eat his lunch in comfort according to his ideas of pleasure. Added to this there is the protection the cabin gives in bad weather, for then it seems to make what would otherwise be a boat, a ship.

· 7 ·
6 METRES

THE smallest of the international metre classes is the 6-metre class, which is to the same formulae and has the same heavy displacement for its length of water-line as the larger classes. Because the sixes do not have cabin accommodation this is a mistake, for they would be faster and cheaper if their displacement were lessened. A cabin top would not add much to the expense of a 6-metre, but it would make the heavy displacement excusable besides giving sleeping accommodation aboard, for in this class the owner is generally a young and keen man who would, if he had a cabin, gladly live aboard and sail round the coast to the different regattas as the owners of the " J " class

NADA RE-RIGGED BY UFFA FOX, SHOWING THE MOST ADVANCED MAST IN THE CLASS ; NO TOPMAST RIGGING ; LUFF ROPE AND HALLYARDS RUN INSIDE MAST ; HALLYARD WINCHES ARE INSIDE MAST ; HEADSAIL OF CANVAS HEAVIER THAN MAINSAIL

and 12-metres do, and his lot would be a happy one. Now he generally confines his racing to either the Solent or the Clyde, and the shifting from one place to the other of a 6-metre is practically all carried out by train. Captain Franklin Ratsey, when he owned the *Ayesha*, sailed her to the western regattas with a canvas cockpit cover, and hammocks slung under the deck to sleep in, and was very happy cruising in his six, besides doing well racing her. *Lintie's* run to Burnham and *Nada's* run home to Cowes showed that the boats are weatherly, and only need a cabin top to make them perfect little cruisers for young men.

They will go to windward in heavy weather, for *Nada* in October, 1932, left traders weatherbound in Dover and sailed the whole way to Newhaven to windward in 12 hours, passing three-masted schooners who were anchored under Dungeness, sheltering from the strong westerly wind.

It was too rough to cook, and so *Nada* was hove-to for breakfast and lunch, and the fact that she hove-to comfortably and well shows that the heaving to of a vessel depends not upon a deep forefoot but upon sail balance.

THE BRITISH-AMERICAN CUP

AN EXAMINATION OF THE 1932 RACE FROM COWES

To be asked aboard *Vorsa* as local pilot, for the races off Cowes against the Americans, was very flattering. As our Committee did not (in view of the straightforward tides there) think I would be very valuable for the races off Ryde, I was able to race my canoe at Langston during those three days.

Each night I rang up home in order to hear how the British team had fared, and the news was not good, the American team being first, second, third and fourth in two races, and first, second and third in the other race. So the Americans only needed to win the first race of the Cowes series to take home the trophy.

On Thursday night, after winning the Royal Canoe Club's Challenge Cup, and attending their annual Lobster Supper at Langston, my wife and I set sail in our schooner for Cowes with *Wanderer* in the davits, arriving in the early morning light. Later that morning I met Maurice Clark and Alfred Mylne, owner and designer of *Vorsa*, on the parade, in front of the Royal London, as arranged.

We were soon aboard and sailing to the starting line off the Squadron under mainsail only. *Vorsa* had but two headsails, the working and genoa, being without the intermediate, which I knew, from sailing with them, the American " Sixes " carried and valued highly. The sky was heavy with clouds, each rain squall making up from the south-west affecting the wind in a slightly different manner as it passed. The tide was not yet high, but the narrow eddy between the Squadron and Egypt Point was running fairly strong to the westward. Such a valuable ally could not be ignored, yet to accept the help it offered meant sailing along under the lee of the land in a light fluky wind where a genoa was needed.

JUST BEFORE THE START.   THE LIGHT STREAK SHOWS THE
DIVIDING LINE BETWEEN THE FOUL TIDE AND THE FAIR EDDY

VORSA IN THE LEAD ; NADA, WITH WORKING HEADSAIL,
BETWEEN TWO AMERICANS WITH INTERMEDIATE HEADSAILS

In order to conceal our intentions we jilled along without headsail until the last, when setting our genoa, we made for the line a fraction too soon and were recalled, being forced by competitors close aboard to sail on some distance before turning back.

So we started late, but were soon in first place, for knowing that eddy, and the strange winds encountered in it, we never once fought the foul tide running strongly 50 yards out. When the wind headed us along that shore we let *Vorsa* drive with everything shaking until the next free puff came, while the rest of the fleet bore away as the wind headed them, and were at once in the foul tide.

While we know it is wind that drives a sailing vessel, we must also remember that the tide, like the poor, we have always with us (if not against us), and where the dividing line between a foul tide and a fair eddy is so sharply defined the tides are all important. That foul tide was running at 3 knots and the fair eddy at 1 knot, and as a 6-metre's speed dead to windward is $3\frac{1}{2}$ knots it is only possible for her to make good $\frac{1}{2}$ knot to windward against a foul tide of 3 knots, but by creeping along the shore (as *Vorsa* did) at an average of 4 knots in the fair eddy the speed over the ground becomes 5 knots.

This easily explains how *Vorsa* came from last into first place in the short beat from the Squadron to Egypt Point, where we stood across at once for the easier tide under the north shore. Once to the north of Lepe we were in less tide, and thinking *Vorsa* would do even better with her working instead of her genoa headsail we changed, and this was our undoing, for two American " Sixes " caught and passed us in the beat along the north shore, so we rounded West Lepe third, but by taking a great circle course to the south into stronger tide we picked up one place on the run to West Bramble and held our second place round Old Castle Point buoy, through the line to Egypt Point. Then the intermediate jibs of the Americans told their tale again, and two of them passed us in the hard going to windward to East Lepe, so that we rounded there fourth, but hard upon their heels.

AMERICAN TEAM SET ABOUT VORSA WHILE BOB KAT SETS HER SPINNAKER

THREE AMERICAN "SIXES" ROUND VORSA

We again took our great circle course southward into the last of the main flood, whilst the Americans sailed the straight course to West Bramble, in, if any, a foul tide. We arrived at West Bramble first, but only by inches.

Olin badly wanted to put *Nancy* in between us and the buoy, but Alfred Mylne watched him like a cat with a mouse, and as he darted for our weather Alfred said, " No, no, laddie," as firmly as a policeman on point duty.

Rebuking Olin as he did, Alfred Mylne looked every inch a policeman, even to the brawny " police muscles." [1] And so we rounded first, but as soon as the protection to weather the buoy had given us was left astern, the four American boats were upon us like a pack of hungry wolves, two to weather, one astern, and one to leeward. Our best course to the next mark was a great circle course to leeward, for here the very last of the flood was still with us, while in Cowes Roads it had turned against us.

But a " Six " reaching is faster than one running, and the two reaching to windward would soon take our wind and then run past us unless we defended our weather by luffing towards Cowes and the foul tide.

NANCY HOLDS ON TO HER SPINNAKER TRYING TO BEAT VORSA ROUND THE OLD CASTLE POINT BUOY. BOB KAT IS ROUND AND JILL TO LEEWARD

BOB KAT SAILS THROUGH IN A FAIR TIDE, WHILE VORSA AND THE TWO AMERICANS FIGHT IT OUT IN A FOUL TIDE

Oh for an equal fight ! For some of our team alongside to help, or to go through into the lead to leeward while we took three Americans the longest way home. And so we luffed and luffed into Cowes Roads, while *Bob Kat*, the last American boat round the West Bramble buoy, carried on her own sweet way to leeward, and arrived at Old Castle Point buoy with a minute lead, next came *Jill*, then we in *Vorsa*.

[1] " Police muscles " : The full midship section usually found under a policeman's waistcoat.

Once round the buoy the fair tide through the Roads made the close reach home very short and we finished as we rounded, *Vorsa* coming in behind two and in front of two of the invincible American team.

It was a relief to allow our tense nerves to slacken back to normal again, and give three cheers for such victors.

VORSA FINISHES THIRD, AHEAD OF NANCY AND LUCIE

	H.	M.	S.
Bob Kat (American), Robert B. Meyer -	3	5	51
Jill (American), J. Seward Johnson -	3	6	54
Vorsa (British), Maurice Clark -	3	7	9
Nancy (American), Olin Stephens -	3	7	11
Lucie (American), Briggs S. Cunningham	3	7	24
Nada (British), F. G. Mitchell -	3	7	50
Ancora II (British), Cyril Wright -	3	8	36
Finetta (British), James S. Bacon -	3	15	26

Points : America, 24¼. Britain, 12.

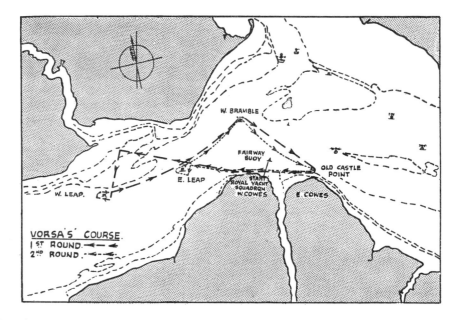

So the American team, by winning four straight races, won outright the British American 6-Metre Cup, and the other three races were not needed. We shall have a chance to avenge our defeat this summer, and in the meantime we can look over things and learn the lessons taught by the American team.

The greatest of all is the team spirit and comradeship. The American team, captained by Bob Meyer, lived under one roof, each night they dined together at one large table, helmsmen and crews talking over the day's events, for they were in Cowes three weeks before their first race, sailing every day round the course.

Nelson, the finest fighter and seaman England has produced, put the team spirit above almost everything, proved by the fact that, whenever possible, he had the captains of his fleet aboard his own vessel during the whole of his pursuit of the French fleet in the Mediterranean, explaining his ideas and hearing theirs. The result was that when they came upon the French fleet (superior in ships, guns and men) in Aboukir Bay they practically annihilated them, only four French ships escaping by cutting their cable and running.

Again, the day before Trafalgar, when Admiral Collingwood and the captains of the various ships were aboard the *Victory* planning the battle, Nelson asked for Collingwood's captain, only to be told that he and Collingwood were not on good terms, so Rotherham was sent for, and as soon as he arrived Nelson took him to Collingwood and said, " Look ! Yonder are the enemy ! " And they shook hands and were friends again.

Next day the *Royal Sovereign* was the foremost ship to engage the enemy, and Collingwood, delighted at being first in the battle, turned to his captain, saying, " Rotherham, what would Nelson give to be here ? "

There was little understanding between the British " Sixes " ; *Vorsa* did not assist any of her team mates excepting that she delayed the first three American " Sixes " a minute and a half on the last run from West Bramble to Old Castle Point, while the only help we received was from *Nada*, who, just after the start, came in on the starboard tack, put an American about, leaving us free to continue close hauled on the port tack.

Not having intermediate headsails, and not understanding fully the uses of the huge parachute spinnakers, we were at a disadvantage where sails were concerned. The parachute spinnaker, made possible by the altering of the rule, so that the sheet could now be taken round the forestay, had 750 ft. of sail in it, almost double the 6-metre's allowed sail area. (*Vorsa's* measured sail area was 460 sq. ft., of which 350 was in the mainsail, so off the wind her actual sail area was 1,100 sq. ft., for the Americans taught us that it actually paid to carry these enormously baggy spinnakers with the wind abeam.)

JONQUIL

Length, overall - - - 35 ft. 0 in.		Length, water-line - - 20 ft. 6 in.
Beam - - - - 5 ft. 8 in.		Draught - - - - 4 ft. 3 in.
Displacement - - - 3 tons		Sail area - - - - 583.5 sq. ft.

Designer, MORGAN GILES   *Owner and helmsman*, CAPTAIN R. T. DIXON

JONQUIL DRIVING INTO A HEAD SEA

Designed and built in 1912 *Jonquil* swept the board of that year and her remarkable record is a credit to her designer and owner for seldom do racers have such a record as hers for a season :

> 44 first prizes,
> 8 second prizes,
> 3 thirds,
> 55 prizes out of 57 starts.

So *Jonquil* can be safely looked upon as the fastest 6-metre of 1912, and a good example of the design of 6-metres of that time. The reason for putting her into the book is to draw attention to the improvement in windward ability of the different classes after 1912 to the present day. Most of this is in the rig and is due to aeronautical research, for the aeroplanes of 1912 were rather more like box-kites than birds, and our Air Ministry spent something like two millions in research to bring aeroplanes to their present state, when they more closely resemble birds. Their research showed the advantage of aspect ratio, which is the proportion of length to breadth, and designers of sailing vessels were quick to make use of this knowledge, and the only thing that prevents sails, in most classes, being taller than they are is the height limit rule makers were wise enough to bring in. In classes where there is no restriction on height the natural limit is somewhere near three times the length of the base, as above this limit it is extremely difficult and almost impossible to make a well-setting mainsail, as the top falls off to leeward through being so narrow.

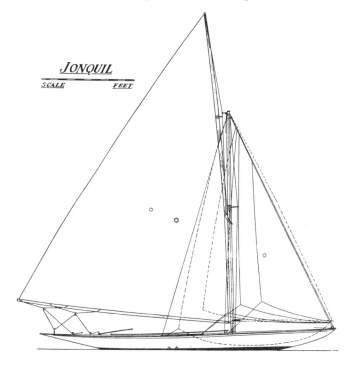

JONQUIL

SCALE   FEET

Jonquil's sail plan has a height of 36 ft. to a base of 37 ft., so its aspect ratio is less than unity, and compared with present sail plans is very inefficient. Yet a few years ago she topped her class, as her record above shows, and no boat could compare with her.

The great advantage of her Gunter lug rig is the fact that as she reefs her mainsail she reefs her topmast, for her yard on end may be considered her topmast.

The advantage of this in really hard weather is great, as it saves the weight and windage aloft that the present-day vessels stagger along with when close reefed, and it is known from aeronautical research that two spars close

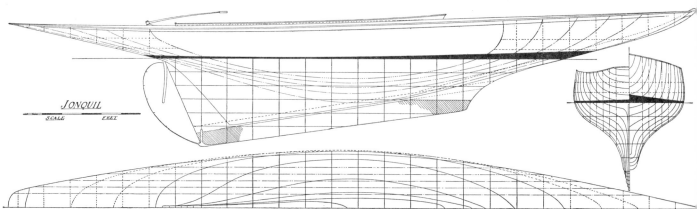

JONQUIL

SCALE   FEET

behind each other offer no more resistance than one, and the yard naturally swings dead to leeward of the mainmast on different tacks.

Jonquil's beam and draught are less than the present-day 6-metre's, and a comparison of her lines with those of *Quixie* by the same designer to the 6-metre class will illustrate the advance in hulls of this class.

QUIXIE

Length, overall	-	-	-	35 ft. 0 in.	Length, water-line	-	-	21 ft. 9 in.
Beam	-	-	-	6 ft. 3 in.	Draught	-	-	5 ft. 0 in.
Displacement	-	-	-	3·15 tons	Sail area	-	-	500 sq. ft.

Designer, MORGAN GILES   *Owner,* BENJAMIN GUINESS

The lines show the type of 6-metre likely to be suitable in the Mediterranean, for *Quixie* has been most successful out there, winning many prizes for her owner, and her short water-line (compared to Solent 6-metres) was chosen for and suited the warmer and lighter winds usually found farther south.

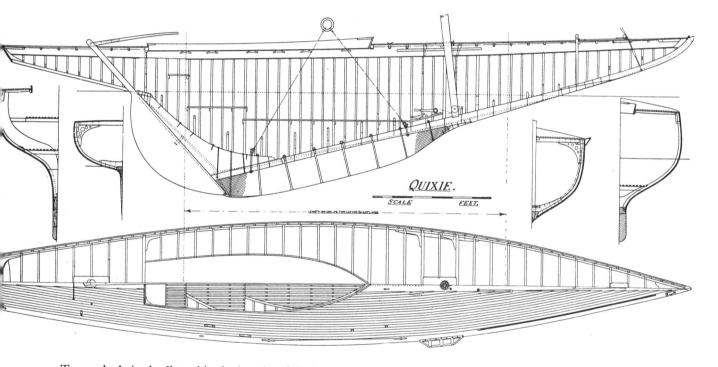

QUIXIE.

SCALE   FEET.

To me the latitude allowed in the lengths of the international classes seems wrong, for it leads to different boats being designed to different weather conditions, so that we in Britain have to design and build shorter and lighter 6-metres to be successful in the Baltic or Mediterranean where the winds are generally lighter, while people from those parts have to build boats especially for the stronger winds that prevail in our country.

For, looking back at the centenary of the Royal Swedish Yacht Club at Stockholm in 1930, with thirty or so 6-metres racing, I have a picture of the hard weather 6-metres slogging away hopelessly in light winds waiting for their weather, and they had two days out of one month's racing in which they could and did win handsomely. The international 14-footers illustrate what I mean, for being all one length and weight and having the same sail area there are no hard weather or light weather boats amongst them, and the same boat can and does win races in hard winds on the sea, and then wins in the calm sheltered waters of the upper Thames. And so it seems that if in the years to come length could be governed in the I.Y.R.U. classes it would be better for all concerned.

Quixie's lines show Morgan Giles' work, and give, as well as an example of his proved ability, the method of measuring the girth and girth difference amidships. The two black marks on either side of the water-line ending show the length taken at 1·5 per cent. of the rating above the water-line, and the girth at these two stations is shown in the sections.   The I.Y.R.U. Rules will be found in the Y.R.A. book printed by Harrison & Sons, of St. Martin's Lane, London, in which book, besides the rating rules, are the rules under which yachts race practically all over the world.

The sail plan shows the tall rig now used as compared with *Jonquil's*.

The construction plan shows the slings for hoisting, and almost every 6-metre is fitted with these for lifting on and off steamers, as 6-metres travel by steamer, train and heavy motor-wagon a great deal.

The dotted line for three-quarters of the water-line marks the length, which has to be constructed with the full-sized scantlings required by Lloyds, but the ends beyond this can be built with frames and timbers a little lighter.   These construction plans give an idea of the work entailed in designing even such a small vessel as a 6-metre, for the weights of every piece of material must be worked out from the lead keel to the jib sheet cleats, otherwise she will not float to her designed water-line.

If too heavy she will be below her marks, and if too light she will float high, and if bow heavy her bow will float heavy and the stern light.

And to pass the rules she must float with her marks just kissing the water.

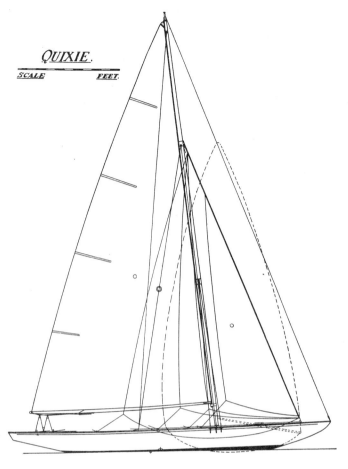

QUIXIE.

SCALE   FEET.

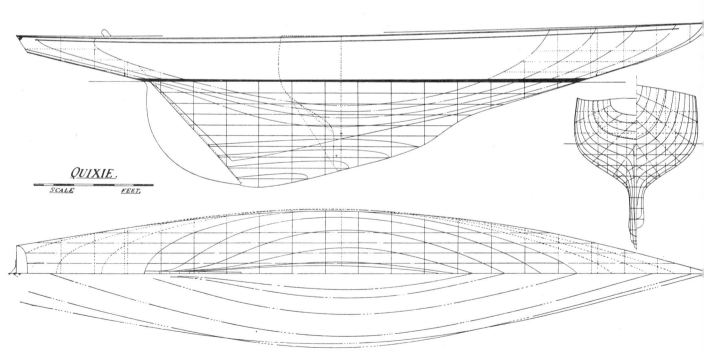

QUIXIE.

SCALE   FEET.

NANCY

Length, overall	-	-	-	36 ft. 9 in.	Length, water-line	-	-	23 ft. 3 in.

Length, overall - - - 36 ft. 9 in.   Length, water-line - - 23 ft. 3 in.
Beam - - - - 6·66 ft.   Draught - - - - 5 ft. 3 in.
Displacement - - - 4 tons   Sail area - - - - 452 sq. ft.

Designer, OLIN STEPHENS   *Owner and Helmsman*, OLIN STEPHENS

As the last 6-metre to be designed and built for the American team of four that defeated the British team on the Solent in 1932, *Nancy* is very interesting, from several points of view. In 1921 several Americans thought it would

THE AMERICAN 6-METRE SHEILA. NOTE ABSENCE
OF OVERHANG AND ASPECT RATIO

THE AMERICAN 6-METRE JILL, SHOWING THE PARACHUTE
SPINNAKER DRAWING WELL WITH THE WIND ABEAM

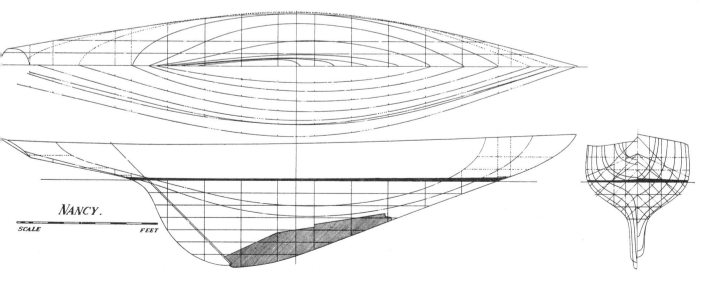

NANCY.
SCALE   FEET

be fine if Britain and America could race against each other under a common rule, and so they built a fleet of four 6-metres to our I.Y.R.U. Rules, which were strange to them, and brought them over to the Solent for the first British-American 6-metre contest. Designing to an entirely new rule they were at a great disadvantage, for our designers with years of experience behind them brought out faster boats, and so Britain won that contest, and generally because

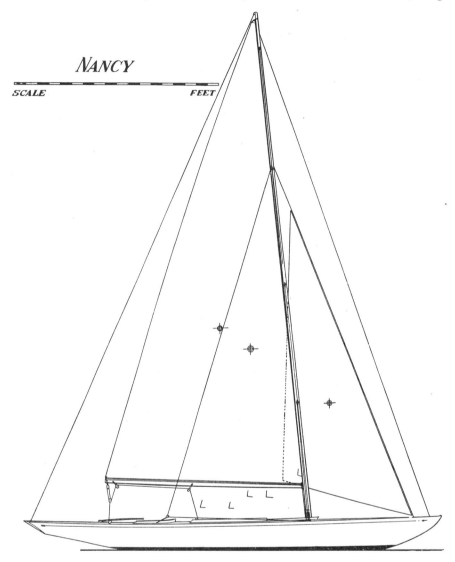

NANCY

SCALE   FEET

we had more experience we won the team races for the 6-metres both here and in America. Till by 1932 the Americans had ten years of experience behind them, and brought over the best four 6-metres for a team we had ever faced, for they had caught us up and passed us at our own game, not so much in hull design as in the rigging and handling of the sails. For though their hulls were without doubt equal to ours they were no better, a comparison between *Nancy* by Olin Stephens and *Vorsa* by Alfred Mylne, the latest and presumably the best American and the fastest of the British team, shows that there is practically no difference in hull design. But a comparison of the two sail plans will show that while *Vorsa* had but two headsails *Nancy* had no less than six, her largest and second smallest being the two corresponding to *Vorsa's*. So she had a headsail to suit every weight of wind, and in the last race for the cup off Cowes *Vorsa* needed a headsail halfway between her two, which was the size used by all the American team, and not having this sail *Vorsa* had to use her large genoa in wind far too strong for it, as she lost so much to windward with the small jib set. Then besides this great selection and understanding of headsails, the American team brought over great parachute spinnakers that they could carry well with the wind even abeam with great advantage—for these sails had 750 sq. ft. in them, so that when set the Americans carried 1,100 sq. ft. of sail, although their measured sail area was only 450 sq. ft.

The success of the American team lay greatly in their selection of headsails and spinnakers, and the wonderful way in which they handled these great sails. Of their four boats one, the *Lucie*, was designed by Clinton Crane, and the other three all came from the board of Olin Stephens, a youngster of twenty-four years of age, who with all the successful racing and cruising vessels he has designed, is well on the way to become the greatest designer the world has ever seen.

Nancy's lines show a 6-metre designed with the strong winds of the Solent in mind, for she is 23 ft. 3 in. water-line, and that means that her displacement is over 4 tons, which brings out a weakness of the scantling rules, for although increased water-line length forces any racer to the I.Y.R.U. rules into a heavier displacement it does not demand increased scantlings. So, as the hull weight remains the same all extra weight is put into the lead keel, putting greater strains on a hull without calling for a stronger hull to withstand them.

Nancy's length caused her displacement to be 4 tons, and 75 per cent. of her total weight (spars included) is in her lead keel. While a shorter " Six " of 20 ft. on the water-line displaces 2·5 tons, and so only 60 per cent. of her total weight is in her lead keel—for by the rules the hulls remain the same.

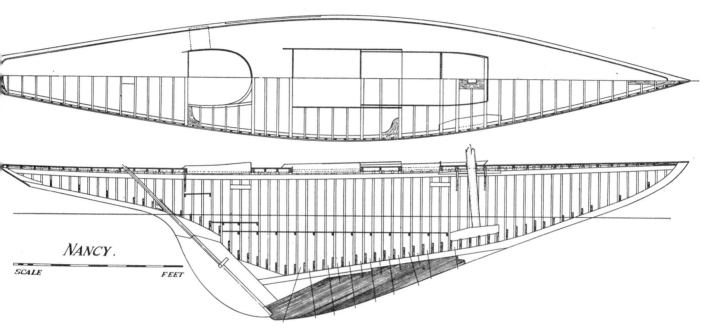

NANCY.

SCALE   FEET

In the construction and arrangement plan of *Nancy* will be seen not two but three cockpits. The hand who cleared the jib if ever it fouled the mast in tacking had the forward cockpit ; the two who worked the jib sheets had the middle cockpit, while the aft cockpit held the helmsman and the technical adviser who while keeping a critical eye on the enemy had also to work the backstays and the main sheet. This dividing up of the crew saves confusion as well as giving each man his exact amount of room in which to work. But more than this, it saves a lot of backchat so often met aboard small racers, for with everyone's nerves strung up to concert pitch the jib sheet men cannot help in their spare moments giving advice to the helmsman, but being separated from the helmsman by a bridge deck without realising it they feel that they are below the salt.

So the lessons to be learnt from *Nancy's* plans are many.

   *   *   *   *   *   *   *   *   *   *   *   *   *

VORSA

Length, overall - - - 36 ft. 6 in.	Length, water-line - - 23 ft. 0 in.
Beam - - - - 6 ft. 10 in.	Draught - - - - 5 ft. 3 in.
Displacement - - - 3·8 tons	Sail area - - - - 463·875 sq. ft.

Designer, ALFRED MYLNE   *Owner*, J. H. MAURICE CLARK

Vorsa was without doubt the best 6-metre of the British team in the 1932 contest, when she was well sailed throughout by Maurice Clark, her owner, who is one of our best helmsmen, for no other boat in our team caused so many anxious glances from the Americans as she did.

VORSA, WITH ALFRED MYLNE AT THE TILLER, UFFA FOX, J. H.
MAURICE CLARK (IN WHITE HAT), AND TWO CREW

In the last race of all she was leading the fleet of eight 6-metres, four British and four American, at the next to the last buoy, and had it not been for the fact that the next four boats close astern of her were all American she would have undoubtedly won the race; as it was she was unable to fight four determined American vessels single handed with a wind over the quarter, which enabled three of them to spread out fan-wise and so starve her of wind, but she held back two, finishing third, ahead of two and behind two of the fastest 6-metres ever sent to Europe by America.

Her length water-line and displacement is hardly different from that of *Nancy*, and her general shape is also little different, the only noticeable thing being the rounding in of her water-line fore and aft to take the utmost out of the rule, for had this line run to the usual sharp point she would have been longer on the line and so forced to be of even heavier displacement than the American *Nancy*. Looking at the profile of both of these long water-lined " Sixes " one is struck by the fact that in order to evade the girth measurement amidships both practically run in a straight line from the fore end of the water-line to the heel of the rudder, and although this puts the weight of the lead keel higher there is so much of this that it does not matter, and besides evading the girth measurement, this cuts down wetted surface, an important point with the long " Sixes ". In looking at wetted surface people seldom realise

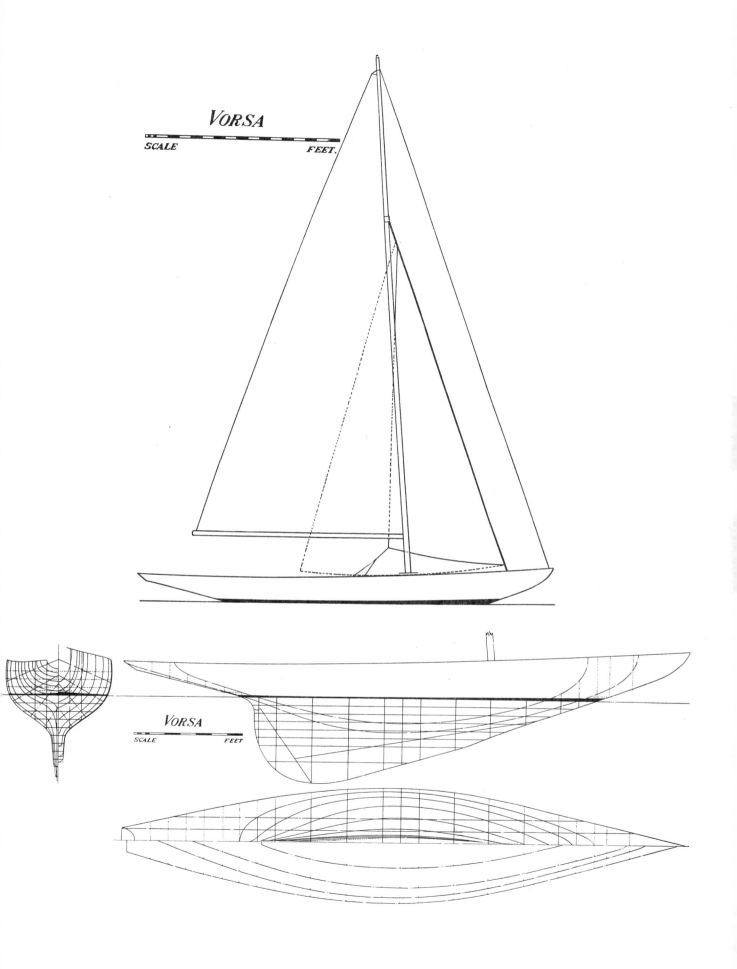

VORSA

SCALE   FEET.

VORSA

SCALE   FEET

that there is just double what there seems, for there are two sides of the boat, and it is the same with a bottom fouled with weed ; if both sides could be laid out and seen at once all owners would take far more care with the under-water surfaces of their vessels, as it is they see one side and then the other, without the total amount really being brought home to them.   It is very like the amount of work and worry a man endures on his passage through life, it is divided up with sleep, and so the total amount is never seen or realised as a whole—and this is just as well.   " Sleep that knits up the ravelled sleave of care."   He wakes up refreshed without thinking of the work that has been done ; there is only the day's work before him to think upon, and so it is with wetted surface and weeds on a yacht's bottom ; there is just the amount in view to impress itself on the brain.

For many years Alfred Mylne has been one of Britain's leading architects, and this design of *Vorsa*, one of his latest, shows that he is still to the forefront as always, for she is a sweet and easy-lined vessel and also very power-ful and weatherly.   She was every bit as fast as any of the American team on all points of sailing, and had she had an intermediate headsail in the last race of the 1932 contest, there is no doubt she would have won handsomely, for even without it she almost won.

LINTIE'S RUN FROM COWES TO BURNHAM, September, 1932

Lintie was designed and built by Fife in 1926 to the International 6-metres Rule ; she was about 22 ft. on the line and, as one would expect, a remarkably sweet little boat.

Buster and I left Kingston on the *Medina* with a fresh south-westerly wind ; hard squalls of wind and rain bustled us out of the river, and at 4.30 p.m. we were tearing through Cowes Roads.   Once clear of the river we took in the spinnaker, and reached along to Ryde under full sail in fast time.

LINTIE (EX REG) WAS DESIGNED AND BUILT BY FIFE IN 1926

There was too much wind for the sea we should find outside the shelter of the Wight, so we reefed off Ryde, and so gave up all thoughts of a record passage to Burnham.   Apart from wind and sea, the mast with full sail showed signs of distress by panting fore and aft below the hounds.   It is far better to make a slow passage than lose a mast.   In ten minutes we were away again, after tucking in two reefs, one on top of the other, so that we could, if we wished, shake out one without touching the other.   We were soon sailing between the Forts, and at 7.05 p.m. we were in a spiteful sea off the Looe.   We had shipped fairly heavy water running from the Forts, and through the Looe a number of steep seas fell aboard, but once through the Looe we felt the shelter of the *Owers*, and drove along in comparatively smooth water, although under a heavy sky full of hard driving clouds, promising a dirty night.

We had chosen the Looe passage in order to cook and eat a comfortable dinner in the lee of the *Owers*, thus saving time by avoiding the necessity of heaving to.   It is a good plan to have a hot substantial meal late in the even-ing, when on the wing, as this stands a man in good stead through the long hours of darkness.

By midnight we were abreast Beachy Head, passing the light at 12.10, having averaged 8 knots from Cowes Roads under a double-reefed mainsail.   Driving along outside the *Royal Sovereign* before a hard wind, rain and heavy seas, we were off Dungeness at 4.45 a.m. and Dover at 8.00 a.m. After Beachy Head the tide had turned against us, and our speed over the ground between there and Dungeness dropped to 6½ knots, and from the Ness to Dover we only averaged 5½ knots.

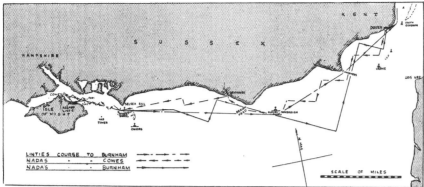

Off Dover the seas were very steep; not only was the wind against the tide, but the trapped water was rebounding and piling itself into steep pyramids with little distance from crest to crest. The valleys of these seas directly beneath our bow was as deep as the distance from our water-line to the cross-trees, as near as we could judge (14 ft.). Although violent in her motion, due to her speed, *Lintie* charged and burst her way through this unnatural popple without getting out of control an instant, although needing very firm handling; then it was I thanked Fife

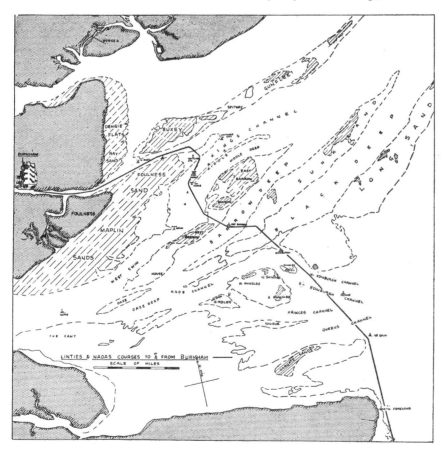

from my heart for designing such a well-balanced vessel—a little thoroughbred. *Lintie*, in spite of the fact that she was double-reefed, had averaged 7 knots from Cowes to the South Foreland, which she rounded at 8.30 a.m.

Laying up inside the Goodwin Sands close to the Kentish shore, we cooked and ate a breakfast fit for a king, while sailing along in smooth water under the lee of the land. On such a day in years gone by the Downs would have been chock-a-block with anchored ships bound down Channel, for once these old square-rigged ships were forced to shorten sail at all they made no progress to windward, the enormous windage of their spars and rigging being too great a handicap. The Downs, with the Goodwins to the eastward and the Kentish shore to the west, was fairly sheltered, and being close to London was a favourite anchorage.

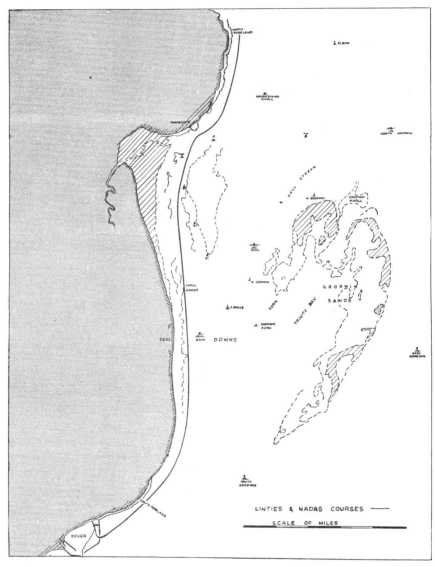

By 11.45 a.m. we were clear of the North Foreland, our speed over the ground having dropped to about 5 knots, owing to the foul tide through the Downs. The Thames estuary looked very stormy with driving squalls and stinging spray whipped off the waves. Into this *Lintie* dashed, and tore across the estuary like a scalded cat, sailing the 20 miles from the North Foreland to the Whitaker Beacon at the mouth of the Crouch in 2½ hours, thus averaging 8 knots with a two-reefed mainsail. This speed (8 knots) may be taken as the maximum speed of a 6-metre through the water, as the tide was almost abeam and so neutral.

Driving into that steep sea we were both at times blinded with the heavy stinging spray, so that we could hardly bear our eyes open ; even when they were, we saw very little. Allowing for the set of the tide we came upon our buoys, lightships and guides without trouble, in spite of the fact that we seldom saw them until they were almost under our bow. This was rather like sailing across in a fog, but a far faster and more exciting sport. *Lintie*, in spite of the fact that she was double reefed, had averaged just 7 knots from Cowes to the Whitaker Beacon, for we had sailed 152 miles in 21¾ hours, as it was now 2.15 p.m.

The ebb tide sluicing out of the river seemed to be running at 2½ to 3 knots, judging from the small amount of headway we made against it beating dead to windward. We struggled on against wind and tide, finally arriving in Burnham in time for the dinner at the Corinthian to the visiting Dutch and German teams.

· 8 ·

22 SQUARE METRES

THE 22 square metre class is about the same length on the line and over all as the 6-metre class but has only half the sail area and half the displacement, the result being easily handled and yet very lively boats. The rule forcing sleeping berths below makes them ideal for young men, for they can live aboard and so save the bother, uncertainty as well as expense of living in a hotel ashore. The same cabin makes a place, in which an elderly owner can keep a dry change of clothes, have lunch and generally be more comfortable than he would be in a 6-metre.

VIGILANT

Length, overall	-	-	- 34 ft. 6 in.	Length, water-line	-	- 25 ft. 6 in.
Beam	-	-	- 6 ft. 4 in.	Draught	- - -	- 4 ft. 3 in.
Displacement	-	-	- 2 tons	Sail area	- -	- 236 sq. ft.

Designer, UFFA FOX

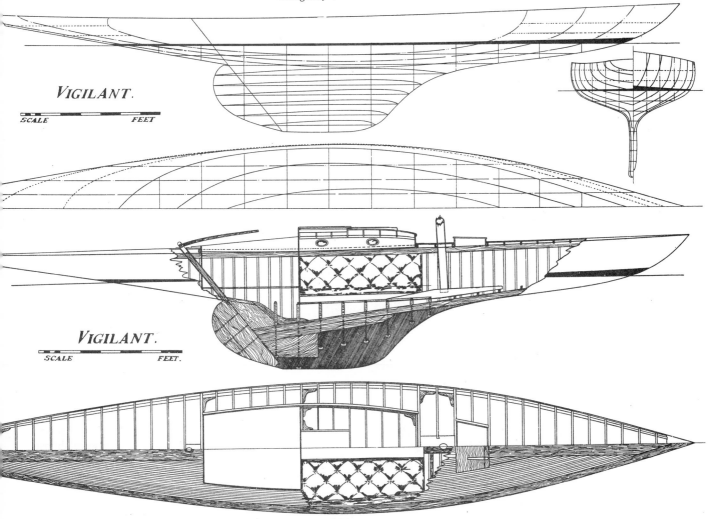

VIGILANT.

SCALE   FEET

VIGILANT.

SCALE   FEET.

Vigilant, as her number shows, is the first of the class in England, and is also the only one yet, though why it is really hard to see.

When the class was first adopted by the I.Y.R.U., writers in our yachting papers said that the twenty-twos would not be man enough for the Solent seas, but *Vigilant's* cruise to Sweden and back, which is described in the cruising half of this book,[1] shows that they were only dribbling down their bibs.

Compared with the 6-metres they are slower in light to moderate winds, but in stronger winds are as fast, while when it is really blowing hard they are faster and more seaworthy than the 6-metres, as their lighter displacement gives them a higher maximum speed, and their cabins keep them dry in a seaway.

Vigilant's submerged counter cut down the wetted surface as it made her keel so short, and though quick and sensitive on the helm she was easily steered and always under perfect control.

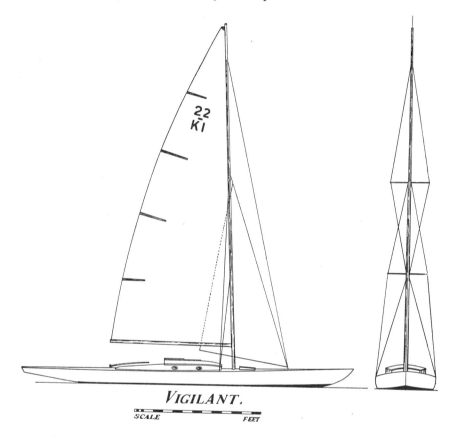

VIGILANT.

SCALE   FEET

Because of her light displacement the hull is very shallow, and skimming along the surface disturbs but little water, and here lies the secret of her high maximum speed, for the hull only draws 15 in. or so of water and in strong winds tends to scoot along the surface.

The accommodation and construction plan shows the cabin arrangement which keeps these boats so dry in a seaway, and protects the helmsman and crew from heavy water. The fore hatch is used for setting the spinnaker, one man going forward to set it, and when it comes down it stows below with its boom.

The sail plan, because of its high aspect ratio (height to base), is the most efficient of all the classes under the international rules, and this accounts for the 22 square metre's speed in moderate weather, for racing round exactly the same course as the 6-metres at Sandham near Stockholm in 1930, the difference between the two classes was just 19 seconds, on a day when no one thought of reefing, and with increasing wind the Skerry cruisers became increasingly faster, for the 6-metres with double their displacement soon reached their maximum speeds.

So the Skerry cruiser class with its liveliness and speed, as well as seaworthiness, is a class worthy of adoption and consideration, especially as its cost is roughly half that of a 6-metre.

[1] See page 105.

· 9 ·
INTERNATIONAL 14-FOOTERS

THE International 14-foot Dinghy Class is, without doubt, the most popular of all classes, for the Y.R.A. dinghy committee founded its rules on solid rock, as they took the rules of the three most popular dinghy classes, the West of England Conference, the Norfolk and the Small Boat Racing Association, and boiled these down into one set of rules, making the National, which afterwards became the International 14-foot Dinghy Class.

Pengelley designed and built the crack dinghies that founded the old West of England Conference Dinghy Class, producing excellent little boats. He might be called the father of the thought, for succeeding designers in after years picked up the threads where he had left off.

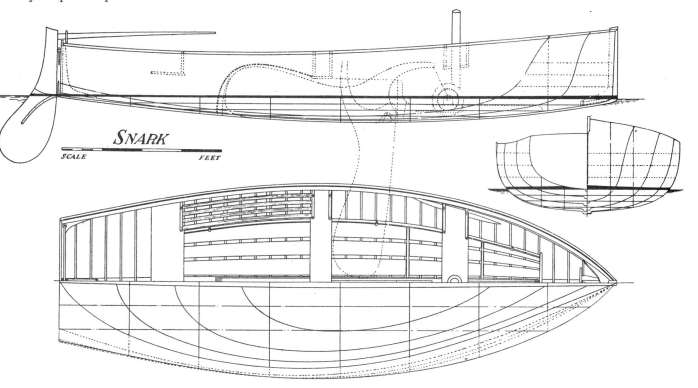

SNARK

SCALE   FEET

Snark, designed and built by Morgan Giles, shows the excellency in design and build reached by the West of England Conference Class in 1911, and the fact that in 1929 this boat, when owned and steered by Mrs. Richardson, was sixth in the Prince of Wales' Cup Race at Plymouth shows how well thought out the National Dinghy Rules were, for they enabled a dinghy eighteen years old to race with every chance of victory. In that race there were thirty-five starters, most of the dinghies being only two or three years of age and many only two or three months.

The lines of *Snark* are those of a boat that will not slow up very much when heeled, for the U-bow section is circular where it is affected by the water, and her sections throughout are generally speaking the bottom halves of circles, and even to-day after an active and successful life of twenty-three years *Snark* is still able to win races, especially on days when the winds are puffy, and it is impossible for a dinghy to be sailed along perfectly upright all the time. Her sail plan is the Gunter lug rig, for the old rules of the class would not allow any spar to exceed the boat's length by more than 18 in., and this rig was the nearest approach to the present Bermudian rig. To-day *Snark* has a rig very like that shown in *Avenger's* sail plan. The construction and arrangement is little altered even to-day, for it is practically identical with to-day's practice. It will be seen that all the weight and gear is in the middle third of the dinghy and the only advancement in all these years is the tendency to concentrate the weights more and more amidships, for although a boat can be trimmed to her designed water-line by the weights spread throughout her length, she is not so fast. In a seaway however small the waves the bow must rise easily and sweetly, and so must the stern, otherwise the two ends tend to dig in, when the bow pushes more water than it should or the stern drags water after it, and it is only by putting the weights amidships that the liveliness in the ends can be obtained.

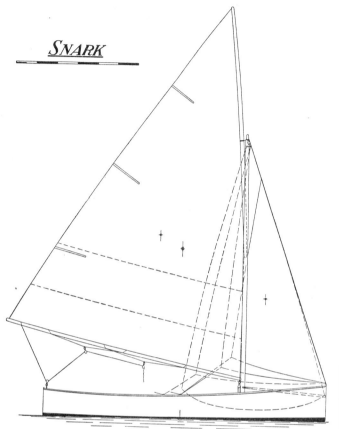

Snark

And *Avenger* shows we have hardly improved upon *Snark's* arrangement of weights, as she left little room for improvement.

When some six years ago I started in to design dinghies the problem was difficult, for Giles as a designer was king of the castle and in a very strong position, having, in twenty years or more, developed and perfected the *Snark* type of lines. If I followed, it was obvious that I would always do so, and so I decided to go off on another tack. One of the maxims of racing is that when last do something different, and this was comforting and helpful.

During my apprenticeship I had worked a great deal on fast motor-boats, hydroplanes and flying machines, and these fast craft went all out for the V section, for while at speed this lifted, a U section tended to bury, but the thing against the V section was that while in power vessels it was ideal, it was not for sailing, as they were often at a large angle of heel.

And *Avenger's* lines show how this V section was carried out, and it was successful, for although when heeled it was slower than the *Snark* type of sections, when upright it was faster with a far higher speed off the wind, due to its lifting tendency, which made it plane easily and so jump from the limited speeds of displacement vessels into the almost unlimited speed of hydroplanes. How successful this V section was can be gauged by *Avenger's* string of prize flags, 52 firsts, 2 seconds and 3 thirds, out of 57 starts. And she was never beaten in strong winds—but she had to be sailed upright at all times excepting in a strong calm when she was listed just enough for the sails to drop naturally into their proper shape, so that the gentle air of a strong calm had not to push the sail at all into its shape, all of its energy being then saved for pushing *Avenger*, and the speeds reached in a strong or a fresh calm were so slow that the shape of the underwater did not matter.

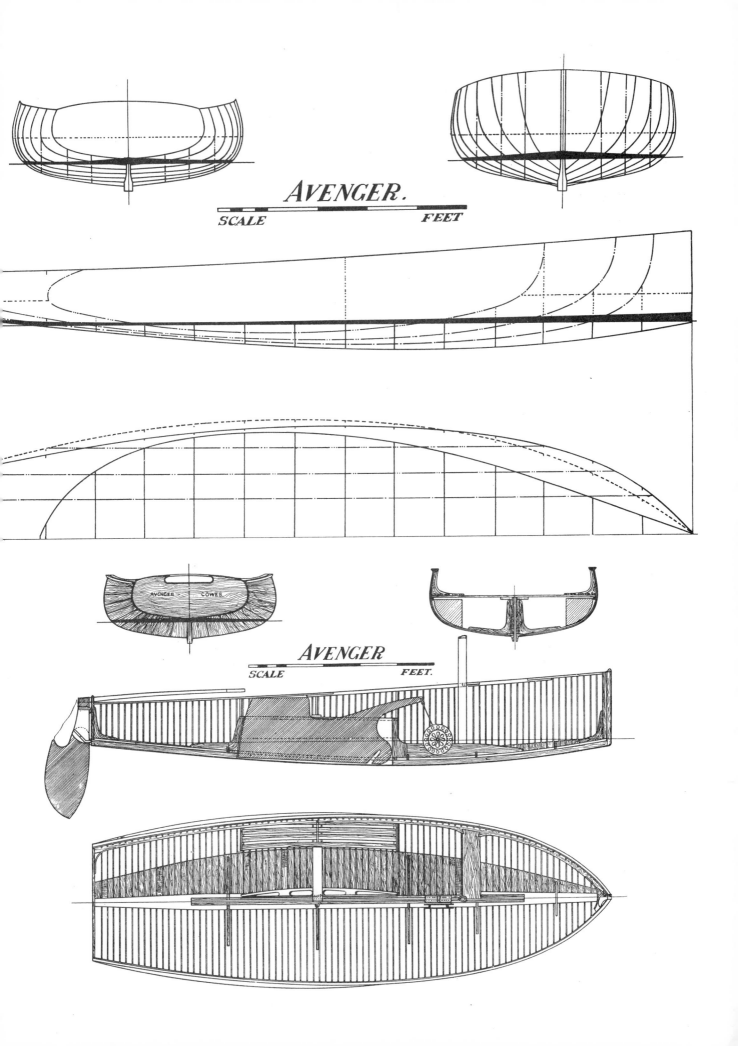

AVENGER.

SCALE   FEET

AVENGER

SCALE   FEET.

Her arrangement shows the weights concentrated as much amidships as possible, the mast is well in from the bow to keep her lively forward, and all the seats are amidships, for Tim (my crew) and I sat as close as possible together either side of the midship thwart, which, besides keeping the ends lively, had the advantage that two men together offer no more windage than one, and when at close quarters and cross tacking to escape from another dinghy I had only to nudge Tim in the ribs and we were about without a murmur, while the other dinghies called, " Lee, oh ! " every time they tacked.

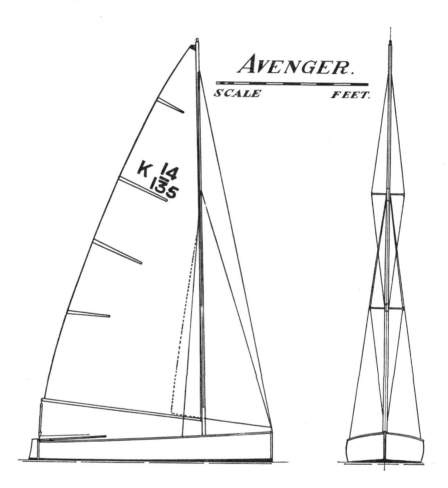

The only times I called " Lee, oh " were when we were actually not tacking, for after cross tacking to escape from another dinghy's dirty wind, say eight times, we almost always escaped easily by my saying " Lee, ho " in an agitated voice, shooting head to wind and then going back to our existing tack, by which time the other man was about and having no way could not tack immediately on us.   And almost always once *Avenger* had her wind clear to windward, she left the fleet.   Her buoyancy tanks are fitted in each bilge amidships, and so keep the water shipped out of the lee bilge, where it takes all the life out of a dinghy, making her sluggish, unstable and slow.

Avenger's lines, sail plan and construction plans shows the present-day dinghies, for her successful season showed the advantage of the V section, and other designers were forced to develop this type of design, and broadly the only difference between the *Avenger* and the *Snark* is in the sections, *Snark* being U sectioned and *Avenger* V, for generally speaking the construction and arrangement are the same.   *Avenger's* rig shows the two cross-tree and double diamond rigging which keeps all cross-trees and rigging close to the mast, and enables the jib to be sheeted in clear outside everything.   In the years to come all larger racing vessels will probably have similar systems of rigging, for the larger classes take years to adopt the more highly developed rigs of the smaller classes.   It must be so, for there is the cost of experiment, a dinghy mast costs no more than the cross-tree of the large cutters, and added to this is the time of making a mast, and the wonder is that the large classes are so well advanced as they are, so the keenest and most popular small class (which at present is the dinghy) will always be the leaders in thought, with the larger classes following in its footsteps according to size.

To illustrate: the 12-metres at one time had two headsails, they now have one; the large classes had three headsails, some now have only two, and future years will see them with but one headsail, in spite of the difficulty in sheeting down such a sail, for winches will overcome this.

In the dinghies we know that to let our boats heel is to slow them, and some years hence all larger classes will discover this simple truth, and they will be sailed as a small boat by the main sheet, which will be arranged and led to a winch so that one man can play it in and out for the puffs of wind just as he would a heavy fighting fish on a rod.

Sailing a dinghy well in strong winds calls for a great deal of anticipation and understanding. The wind is always untrue in strength and direction, varying all the while, be it ever so little in direction it is enough to make a great deal of difference to an observant helmsman, who takes advantage of it, for with a freeing puff he luffs and,

AVENGER, WINNER OF THE PRINCE OF WALES' CUP, 1928

whenever headed, goes about and lays closer on the other tack. The ever varying strength of the wind is looked after by the main sheet, for when racing a vessel is canvassed to suit the lulls in the wind, while cruising she is reefed to suit the squalls, so a racer is always over-canvassed in the squalls, and then her main sheet should be eased until she has no more weight in her sails than she can bear. The photograph of *Avenger* shows her tearing along at her top speed with her mainsail eased away, so that only a few feet at the clew are doing any work. The playing of her mainsheet won her many races, for often she would leave other dinghies standing with her mainsail eased off and flying out to leeward like a flag, while they had theirs full of wind, the difference being that they were heeled over and lifeless while *Avenger* was upright and footing fast. I am a cruising and not a racing man, and excepting for the year in which I raced *Avenger* have averaged under twelve races a season. My reason for pointing this out is to stress the importance of playing the mainsheet in and out in strong winds, which are always squally, for it has enabled a cruiser like myself to win races from purely racing men, and in the keenest class in this or any other country, for with over 300 boats in one class and as many as 50 in a race, competition becomes keen and races hard to win. The helmsmen are scattered all over Britain, and the best from each district travel hundreds of miles every summer to take part in the Prince of Wales' Cup, so the winner has to beat the best helmsmen in the country.

So generally speaking the best and keenest helmsmen in Britain are in the 14-ft. class, which is developed more than any other class, and so all other classes do, or should look to it for ideas. Their rig at present is some years in advance of other classes.

All because a dinghy mast costs no more than a large cutter's cross-tree, and in the event of the mast falling down there is no danger to life and limb on a dinghy as there is with the larger vessel. This is illustrated forcibly by the difference in weights of the mainsails; a dinghy's mainsail weighs 5 lb. and *Britannia's* mainsail weighs three-quarters of a ton.

The difference in the mainsail weights represents the difference in the designer's problems, and because of this great difference the small boat designer is generally in advance of the designer of large vessels, not because his ideas are more advanced, but because he can carry them out so easily and cheaply, and so for some years the racing classes of Britain will follow the ideas of the 14-footers, the leaders in thought.

THE PRINCE OF WALES' CUP
1927 ROYAL YACHT SQUADRON, COWES

The Prince of Wales, by presenting a Cup for the (then) National 14-footers in 1927, gave open boat sailers a trophy, which at once was recognised as the Blue Ribbon of small boat sailing.

The colour blue, denoting the highest attainable, probably came from the highest order of knighthood, the Order of the Garter, which is distinguished by a blue ribbon worn diagonally.

IREX—WINNER   RADIANT—SECOND

The Oxford and Cambridge Universities have chosen blue to denote the highest order in their sports, and it is remarkable, that in spite of the fact that England, since King Alfred's time, owes almost everything to her seamen, neither of these universities awards a blue for sailing and seamanship.

Our old sailing Navy, under Nelson, was undefeatable, otherwise Napoleon would have invaded England, and it might have so happened that both Oxford and Cambridge were sacked. One would think that if only out of gratitude to our Navy the thinkers of the universities would have given blues for sailing and seamanship, considering that they give them to billiards, which is a game and not a sport.

The Royal Yacht Squadron started the first race for the Prince of Wales' Cup from its line at Cowes at 11.45 a.m., Monday, August 1, 1927.

In most battles there is a point, which gained or lost often decides the day, and so with racing, and it is in the defining and winning of this point that victory generally lies. As there was not a tack on the course during this race at Cowes, it was of great importance to lead at the first buoy, as when reaching it is difficult for one boat to pass another.

RESTLESS LEADS AT FIRST MARK

The wind, north by west, meant that the first buoy could be made from the lee end of the line, and as there was a fair eddy here it was the best end to start, providing a boat was on the line and so had a clear wind.

Had the wind been strong, the weather end would have paid in spite of the foul tide there, as the dinghies with a freer wind would have planed thus travelling twice as fast as those on a wind to loo'ard.

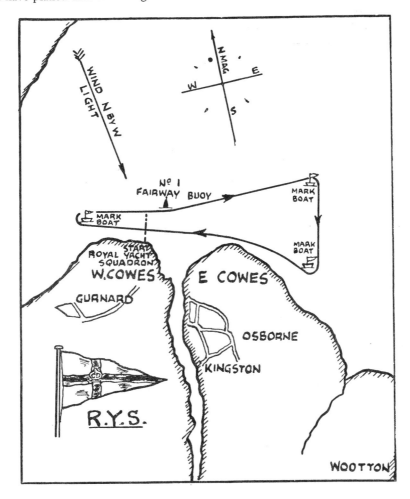

As there were 41 entries in this race, there were no Recall Numbers, but the committee reserved the right to disqualify any dinghy over the line at the start, which rule made the competitors rather shy of the line. This exception to Y.R.A. Rule 28 showed the wisdom of the committee for it had the foresight to realise that it was humanly impossible to hoist twenty or thirty numbers within a reasonable time, even if they could be shown, they would be invisible to the dinghies farthest from the committee as they would be obscured by the sails of the other dinghies. This alteration to Rule 28 has been necessary throughout the contests for the Prince of Wales' Cup, and has worked well, no boat having either been recalled or disqualified for being over the line in the seven contests sailed.

Irex made a fine start, being the weather boat of the batch at the lee end of the line, but James Beale had made even a better one, and led at the first buoy in *Restless* with *Irex* second.

Radiant had started the lee end but half a minute late, and unable to get her wind clear, arrived at the first mark almost last, Morgan Giles, who had started the other end with a clear wind, but a foul tide, arrived just after, and the pair of us started in on our difficult job (which we did not quite accomplish) of sailing past all the dinghies ahead.

The two of us went round the course hand in hand, passing boat after boat, some to leeward and some to windward, finally finishing second and third to *Irex*.

Although we had sailed past so many dinghies we had made no impression at all on *Irex* with Cecil Atkey and Colin Ratsey aboard, for they beat us by almost 6 minutes, proving that they were gaining on us :

BOAT				OWNER					H.	M.	S.
Irex	-	-	-	Cecil Atkey	-	-	-	-	I	48	2
Radiant	-	-	-	Uffa Fox	-	-	-	-	I	53	55
Vamoosa	-	-	-	Morgan Giles	-	-	-	-	I	54	18
Query	-	-	-	C. K. Collyer	-	-	-	-	I	55	21
Foxhunter	-	-	-	A. Cherry Downes	-	-	-	-	I	55	30
Alsani	-	-	-	A. C. Walker	-	-	-	-	I	56	35

In a reaching race such as this the boat leading at the first mark should win, and had *Restless* known the Solent tides she would have taken the cup to the Royal Norfolk and Suffolk Yacht Club, as it was the second boat to round the first mark won it for the Island Sailing Club.

1928 ROYAL NORFOLK AND SUFFOLK YACHT CLUB, LOWESTOFT

The Prince of Wales' Cup Race was on Thursday of Sea Week, and the Trent Cup during Oulton Broad Week, so Tom Thornycroft, A. C. Walker and myself took our three dinghies up for those two weeks' racing.

Tom in *G.E.T.* and I in *Avenger* had challenged as the Island Sailing Club team for the Trent Inland Waters Challenge Cup, which we won in spite of the fact that there were fourteen teams challenging.

PRINCE OF WALES' CUP REPLICA WINNERS, 1928

LADY BEALE PRESENTS PRINCE OF WALES' CUP

Monday, Tuesday and Wednesday of Lowestoft Week we raced round the Prince of Wales' Cup course, so that when Thursday dawned we knew almost as much about the course as those who had raced round it for years.

The first buoy could be laid without a tack, in fact there was not a tack on the course, as the wind was westerly, so it was again most important to be leading at the first mark. To do this a boat must start at the best part of the line, and although the tide had turned against us inshore it was still fair outside and as there was not enough wind to make the dinghies plane, *Avenger* started the outside and lee end of the line with the gun.

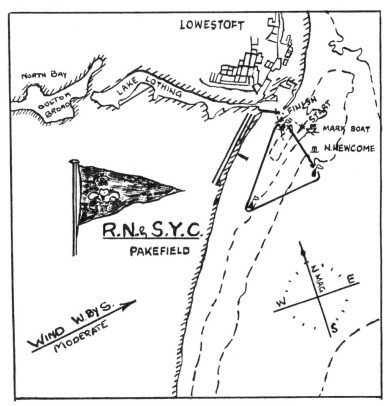

She streaked away and led throughout the race, winning by more than five minutes from Tom Thornycroft in *G.E.T.* :

BOAT				OWNER				TIME		
								H.	M.	S.
Avenger	-	-	-	-	Uffa Fox	-	-	-	-	I	20	35
G.E.T.	-	-	-	-	Tom Thornycroft	-	-	-	I	25	42
Pronto	-	-	-	-	Morgan Giles	-	-	-	I	26	42
Alsani	-	-	-	-	A. C. Walker	-	-	-	I	30	3
Query	-	-	-	-	C. K. Collyer	-	-	-	I	30	50
Worry	-	-	-	-	W. L. Clabburn	-	-	-	I	35	30

As *Alsani* and *Query* were in the first six to finish last year, this was the second time they had won replicas of the cup for their owners. *Alsani* is especially worthy of note, for she was designed by Rayner and built by her owner, both amateurs.

Handling races with forty competitors is difficult, and there is no doubt that the Royal Norfolk and Suffolk did the job well ; there was, however, a puzzling question which I put to the committee.

The course was 12 miles, six times round a 2-miles triangle, the question asked, " When *Avenger* laps competitors is she an overtaking boat ? " The point I wanted clearing was, could *Avenger* in lapping a boat be disqualified by that boat, which was actually 2 miles astern. The answer was good, well worthy of a lawyer, being, " The Sailing Rules will apply." So *Avenger* when lapping boats was very careful to keep clear, as it would have been hard to have been disqualified by the fourteen boats she lapped, and which were actually 2 miles astern when lapped.

It is a point that should be covered, and I suggest this rule, " That the boat being lapped shall not molest the one lapping her, neither shall she disqualify her."

G.E.T. (TOM THORNYCROFT) 2ND, 1928

DARING
WINNER OF THE PRINCE OF WALES' CUP,
1929

1929, ROYAL SOUTH-WESTERN YACHT CLUB, PLYMOUTH

Saturday, August 17, dawned with a fresh south-westerly wind which was cheering to me, as I rather like hard weather races, and it meant that there would be a windward leg at last in the Prince of Wales' Cup Race.

Although Plymouth Sound is probably the finest sailing ground in England, the course as planned had one bad point, for it was a run, and a short one at that, to the first mark. So to me the first buoy was the point of the race, for at it many things could happen with thirty-five boats rounding in a bunch, crosstrees carry away, protests lodged, and accidents generally happen.

The night before the race I decided that *Daring* would either be clear ahead or clear astern at the first buoy, and to be able to stop her when I chose meant a leeward start, which was wrong on this day, for with the wind abaft the beam with such a big fleet it was impossible for the leeward boats to have their wind clear.

Off we went with the gun, and although I endeavoured to be first at the Mallard, Tom Thornycroft in *Pintail* led, and *Daring* would have rounded about seventh had I not borne away and hove-to till the fleet had rounded.

Rounding the buoy we stood about at once on to the port tack, as with every boat ahead it was impossible to be caught by one on the starboard tack ; moreover when we came about again and met the fleet, we should be on starboard tack, which is a powerful weapon, being worth three boats' lengths.

After a short board we tacked and stood towards the breakwater on the starboard tack and soon *Vanda* with James Beale at her helm, had to go under our stern, as he was port tack. As he was second round the Mallard we knew that only one boat could be ahead, Tom Thornycroft's *Pintail*.

Thus encouraged we drove *Daring* even harder and finally arrived at the weather mark an easy first, this enabled us to ease up slightly, for we felt, that having sailed past the entire fleet of thirty-five boats in one beat to windward, the race was ours. *Daring* was in her glory reaching in that weight of wind, and so we went round the course happily, gaining all the while on our opponents. At the end of the third round we had a 4-minute lead from *Pintail* who was still second.

The last round, however, was almost fatal to us ; as we were about to gybe round the Duke Rock Buoy my crew stood up, and being unable to see and afraid of hitting the buoy, I let *Daring* luff. Bringing that weight of wind abeam with no one on the gunwale, caused *Daring* to scoop herself (at that speed) practically full of water. So full she would have sunk with two aboard, but my crew jumped overboard and floating outside baled from there, while I baled from inside, steering all the while.

DARING AND PINTAIL

We drifted to leeward of the Duke Rock without rounding it, and tried to tack in order to weather it, just as soon as the water was low enough to allow my crew back aboard, but *Daring* would not have it. There was no time to waste for Tom in *Pintail* was roaring up all the while, so we had to gybe *Daring* which was like a log in the water. Once at the Duke Rock we gybed her again, still sluggish and dangerously full of water, and once round heaved a sigh of relief, and reached for the Asia buoy and the finishing line, winning by less than 1½ minutes.

Filling-up had cost us 2½ or 3 minutes :

BOAT				OWNER				TIME		
								H.	M.	S.
Daring	-	-	-	Uffa Fox -	-	-	-	1	21	22
Pintail	-	-	-	Tom Thornycroft	-	-	-	1	22	41
Scoulton Pie	-	-	-	Sir Edward Stracey	-	-	-	1	24	8
Avenger	-	-	-	Alan R. Colman	-	-	-	1	34	28
Ermilia	-	-	-	Morgan Giles	-	-	-	1	36	29
Snark	-	-	-	Mrs. H. Richardson	-	-	-	1	37	5

It had been a hard race with all the wind we needed. Half the competitors retired, some damaged at the first mark, some because of so much wind, and some because of fouling at that first mark.

In the first round *Daring* averaged 6 knots, the course being 4 miles to a round, and *Daring* sailing her first round in 40 minutes was being driven as hard as it is possible to drive a dinghy, proved by the fact that she sailed past the whole fleet of thirty-five boats in that beat to windward. As buoys in such a place as Plymouth Sound cannot be out of position, 6 knots may be taken as the utmost a dinghy can be driven round a course with any windward work, for conditions were ideal, hard wind and smooth water.

PINTAIL (TOM THORNYCROFT)
SECOND, PLYMOUTH, 1929

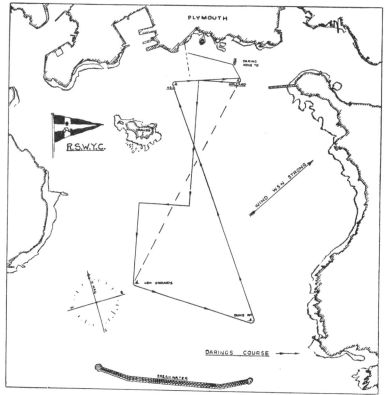

Over the measured mile in the *Medina* I have made 7.9 knots, but that is reaching, and actually a dinghy will, I believe, do 9 knots.

The second and third rounds were not sailed so fast as the first, the second taking $41\frac{1}{2}$ minutes, the third $42\frac{3}{4}$ minutes, and the fourth and last round $45\frac{1}{2}$ minutes, due to the fact that we were not pressed and not being machines we had weakened.

1930, ROYAL NORFOLK AND SUFFOLK YACHT CLUB, LOWESTOFT

There is generally more sea running on the Lowestoft course, due to tides and shallow water, than on any other dinghy course, and so it is very easy to be under-canvassed when racing at Lowestoft, for wind being invisible the state of the sea is generally the best guide to the wind's strength ; but at Lowestoft, and generally in the southern half of the North Sea, it is a bad guide.

GOLDEN EYE (TOM THORNYCROFT)
WINNER, PRINCE OF WALES' CUP
LOWESTOFT, 1930

The 1930 race saw the water off Lowestoft calm and still with but the faintest of airs upon it, so that instead of thinking of reefs every dinghy took a kedge with which to anchor.   Before this race some of the competitors did not know that a vessel on losing her kedge or anchor is disqualified, so after explaining the rule and its reasons, I showed them just how to bend on the kedge warp, so that even if the flukes fouled some object the anchor could be recovered.

The end of the warp is made fast to the crown by a clove hitch and then the warp is led along the shank and stopped down to the ring, with four strands of fine twine, which we tested and found could be broken by one man.

Then if the anchor fluke fouled, a heavy strain would break the stops on the ring, and the pull coming on the crown would clear the fluke, and the anchor could be hauled aboard stern first.

On Thursday and Friday there was not even enough wind to drive such light vessels as dinghies round the course, and after sailing, or rather drifting, for some eight hours on the first day and three hours on the second, such of the competitors as had not retired came to anchor and remained kedged until the race was cancelled.

Saturday came along with a nice breeze, and the full course of six rounds was sailed, and Tom Thornycroft in *Golden Eye* won by eleven minutes.

As Tom had led throughout the two cancelled races as well as this, his victory was well deserved. Mrs. Richardson in *Filibuster* was second, and P. V. Mackinnon, then at Oxford, came third with *Flame*.

Boat	Owner	Time		
		H.	M.	S.
Golden Eye - - -	Tom Thornycroft - - -	1	51	21
Filibuster - - -	Mrs. H. Richardson - - -	2	2	29
Flame - - - -	P. V. Mackinnon - - -	2	4	14
Windjammer - - -	Quiller Gold and G. E. Morris -	2	7	20
Siskin - - - -	H. F. Edwards - - - -	2	7	55
Dazzle - - - -	C. Leslie Lewis - - - -	2	9	50

Windjammer, in the cancelled race of Friday, dropped her kedge before reaching the buoy, and although the tide drove her clear, her anchor fouled the buoy rope, and so she would lay clear until the tide turned. A boat may touch the under-water part of a mark without being disqualified, but if she touches the mark above water she must retire from the race ; so just before the turn of the tide *Windjammer's* crew dived overboard, and swimming under water cleared the anchor from the buoy rope, and with a fleet of thirty dinghies anchored close, and all watching, he was careful not to appear above water till well clear of the buoy.

FLAME (P. V. MACKINNON)
3RD, LOWESTOFT, 1930

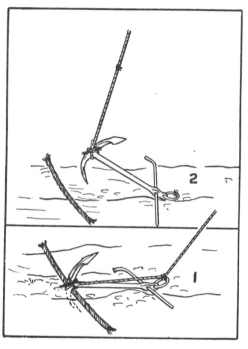

LOWESTOFT, 1930
A GOOD TIP FOR CRUISERS

LOWESTOFT, 1930. TOM THORNYCROFT, WINNER OF PRINCE OF WALES' CUP
WITH HELMSMEN AND CREWS WHO WON REPLICAS

1931, ROYAL THAMES YACHT CLUB, RYDE

The morning of this race came in with a strong north-westerly wind, which against the tide kicked up such a sea for small boats, that the committee postponed the race till the turn of the tide at 2.00 p.m.

During all this time the competitors ran round in small circles, some cutting 3 ft. off their masts to save windage, others taking spinnakers out of their boats and then putting them in again, only to leave them out for the race. It is very trying to competitors' nerves in such weather before the start. However, off they went at 2.00 p.m., on a beat to windward to the outer mark off Wootton, and *R.I.P.*, who had started well out on the line in the last of the

SWIFT (H. F. EDWARDS).
2ND, RYDE, 1931; 2ND, TORQUAY, 1932
(OWNED BY W. H. GODFREY)

NIL DESPERANDUM (T. C. RATSEY)
3RD, RYDE, 1931

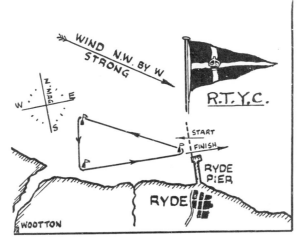

weather-going tide, rounded this first mark with a strong lead, which she seemed to increase on the reach and run back to the buoy off the pier. But after three rounds, this hard driving brought her to grief, for she shipped water faster than her crew could bail, and running along close under the Island shore, where the water was quieter, she dragged her rudder through the sand and tore off her rudder pintle and retired, so ending a young helmsman's chance of winning the Prince of Wales' Cup at his first attempt.

Nil Desperandum led for the next round, then *Swift* came into first place, and leading to the inshore mark off Wootton, seemed a certain winner with only the run home in which to keep her lead.   However, Morgan Giles on this run had passed about four dinghies every round, dropping them again on the beat, but rounding this time second with only one to pass where he had previously passed four, and with the slightly longer run to the line, he had a better chance even than *Swift*.

IT IS ONLY RIGHT THAT THE RACE SHOULD GO TO THE MAN THAT SAILS HARDEST

FILIBUSTER (COL. AND MRS. H. RICHARDSON)
2ND, LOWESTOFT, 1930 ;   4TH, RYDE, 1931

Setting his spinnaker, he started closing the gap between the two, and were he able to keep *Catherine* from capsizing, it was just a question of time before he caught *Swift*, who had left her spinnaker on shore.

Catherine went like greased lightning on that run, and catching *Swift* just before the finish, won by 6 secs., capsizing directly she received her gun. This shows that her helmsman was driving his boat to the utmost, and it is only right that such a race should go to the man racing hardest. It was by far the most exciting Prince of Wales' Cup race, for Stewart Morris in *R.I.P.*, Chris Ratsey in *Nil Desperandum*, H. F. Edwards in *Swift*, all led in turn, but Morgan Giles led at the moment when it counted, and so won the Prince of Wales' Cup in the hardest race for sea, so far, in the contest.

BOAT				OWNER					TIME		
									H.	M.	S.
Catherine	-	-	-	Morgan Giles	-	-	-	-	4	1	4
Swift	-	-	-	H. F. Edwards	-	-	-	-	4	1	10
Nil Desperandum	-	-		T. C. Ratsey	-	-	-	-	4	2	33
Filibuster	-	-	-	Mrs. H. Richardson	-	-	-	4	3	25
Fleetwing	-	-	-	G. K. Collyer	-	-	-	-	4	4	22
Huff	-	-	-	R. D. Heard	-	-	-	-	4	4	40

MORGAN GILES (WHITE SWEATER), WINNER OF PRINCE OF WALES' CUP AT RYDE, SIR JOHN FIELD BEALE (WITH CIGAR), CHAIRMAN DINGHY COMMITTEE, MRS. H. RICHARDSON (BLUE JERSEY), FOURTH, PRINCE OF WALES' CUP, WINNER OF POINTS CUP FOR DINGHY WEEK AT RYDE

The lesson to be learnt from this race is, never race without taking a spinnaker. Its weight is little, and it must help off the wind ; *Catherine*, setting hers every round but one, owed her success to this sail, and her owner's forethought in taking it, as much as to his skill in carrying it when no other boat attempted to set such a sail.

Their Majesties the King and Queen came over from Cowes in their *Admiral's Barge* to watch this race, and it is pleasing to think that they saw the most exciting race for the Cup presented by their son, His Royal Highness the Prince of Wales.

★   ★   ★   ★   ★   ★   ★   ★   ★   ★   ★   ★   ★   ★

1932, ROYAL TORBAY YACHT CLUB, TORQUAY

This race was round a triangular course in Torbay, so practically free from tides.

On Thursday, August 18, the wind was east by north, and light, and the committee, thinking this would swing a point or two southerly through the day, sent the fleet at 11.00 a.m. round the course against the sun.

This gave a dead run to the first mark off Paignton, which meant that there would be no windward work on the first round, for if there is a run on a triangular course there can be no beat, the windward leg being that which is the run the reverse way of the triangle.

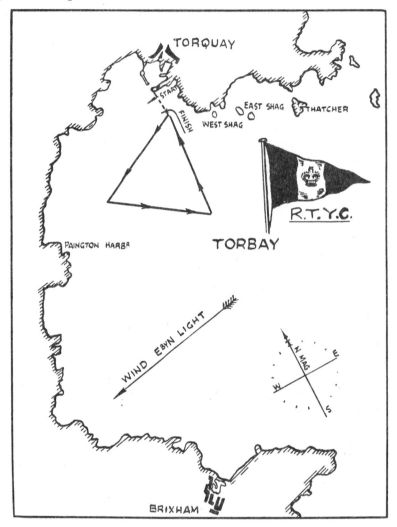

The dinghies made for the Paignton mark with their spinnakers to port, the start being divided into two schools of thought, the one thinking the sea end of the line correct, the other being deceived, by the local draught out of the harbour, into thinking that the inner end, although a little further from the next mark, was right.

At the start those nearest the harbour went fastest, but *Swift*, starting just inside the end of the outer mark, picked up the true breeze earliest and soon opened out from the fleet, and carrying a stronger breeze the whole time arrived at the leeward mark with a long lead.

Swift made the outer mark without a tack, and reaching for the Torquay mark, with the wind abeam, it appeared impossible for the dinghy to catch her.

R.I.P., however, rounding the Paignton Buoy twelfth, started passing boat after boat, and we, watching and timing her and *Swift* over each leg of the course, saw that *R.I.P.* was gaining on *Swift* all the time, seconds only, it is true, but it was steady and untiring, so only a question of time before *R.I.P.* overhauled *Swift*.

My prophecy that *R.I.P.* would pass *Swift* halfway down the fifth run was wrong, for she caught her almost as soon as they started on this run, the reason being that W. H. Godfrey, instead of keeping to seaward in the stronger breeze, that had served him so well in the first round, allowed *Swift* to fall to leeward, and *R.I.P.*, keeping a more weatherly course and carrying a stronger breeze, passed *Swift* and led her through this last round to the finish.

BOAT	OWNER	TIME		
		H.	M.	S.
R.I.P. - - - -	H. A. Morris - - - -	2	53	45
Swift - - - -	W. H. Godfrey - - - -	2	55	17
Golden Eye - - -	Tom Thornycroft - - -	2	55	34
Filibuster - - - -	Mrs. H. Richardson - - -	2	56	2
Fury - - - -	R. Scott Freeman - - -	2	57	25
Sorry - - - -	Morgan Giles - - - -	2	58	25

The start of this course, with no windward work upon it, was very important, even such an experienced and able helmsman as Tom Thornycroft being deceived by the strong local draught out of Torquay Harbour.

The wind, eight days out of ten, would have hauled more southerly, and so made the leg from Paignton to the outer mark into a beat to windward ; as it was, it only hauled a point, which only meant that this buoy could not quite be laid on the port tack.

Above : MAN WEIGHS 154 LB. EVERY DINGHY MUST FLOAT 112 LB. WHEN FULL OF WATER. S. PORTER PASSING A DINGHY AT COWES

Left : R.I.P. (H. A. MORRIS), WINNER, PRINCE OF WALES' CUP, TORQUAY, 1932

Triangular courses are difficult to arrange with windward legs ; the American method of starting the race from a committee boat, which can steam to any corner of the triangle, seems best, for it enables a committee to start the race from the leeward buoy, thus making the first leg a beat to windward.

There was a considerable amount of floating weed in Torbay owing to the exceptional weather conditions prevailing at the time, and some competitors who did not take care to avoid it or to clear their plates and rudders at frequent intervals were unwittingly hampered by it.

It was very pleasant to see another young helmsman come into the prize list, in the person of Bob Scott Freeman, in his first year of serious sailing at sea, for he sailed a splendid race to keep ahead of such experienced helmsmen as Morgan Giles and Collyer.

1933, ROYAL NORFOLK AND SUFFOLK YACHT CLUB, LOWESTOFT

The sands, creeping shorewards, caused the Royal Norfolk and Suffolk Yacht Club to alter its triangular course with three buoys, into a five-buoyed course with two triangles on a long base parallel to the shore.

The start found the faintest of airs stealing across the water from the south-east, and it was almost three minutes before the entire fleet had crossed the starting line against the tide.

Often a large fleet starting to windward across the line, batters a light wind to pieces, so that those coming after lay idle on the water until a new wind fills in once again.

R.I.P., the winner of last year's race, started to windward of the lee bunch; just to leeward was *Desperation*, who led for the first round, showing that this was the best place from which to start.

DESPERATION   R.I.P.

JUST AFTER THE START—SHOWING THE BOATS INSHORE DRAWING AWAY FROM THOSE WHICH HAD STARTED OUT,
NOW BEARING AWAY

DESPERATION LEADING R.I.P., FLIGHT AND LIGHTNING ROUND THE S.E. BUOY

The order at the first mark was : *Desperation*, *Vivid*, *Flight* and *R.I.P.* The first and last of these dinghies pinched for the outer mark with the tide under their lee bows, and *Flight* and *Vivid* fell to leeward. Many bore away for the slack water along the shore tacking out for the weather mark some distance down. Had the wind been the same strength under the land these boats must have led at the outer mark, but gliding has taught me that wind, upon striking an obstacle, rises, so these were sailing in a deadened wind (see sketch).

This sketch also explains the reason for rain in the British Isles from the south-westerly wind. This warm moisture-laden wind off the Atlantic rises, on striking the land, into colder air, condenses and droppeth as the gentle rain from heaven upon the place beneath.

The order at the outer mark was *Desperation*, *R.I.P.*, *Flight* and *Lightning*; the latter had stood down the beach. On the run and reach back to the harbour, *R.I.P.*, in trying to pass *Desperation*, lost a place to *Flight*, the three finishing the first round within six seconds of each other.

In the short beat to the north-east mark both *R.I.P.* and *Lightning* passed *Flight*, and this was their order to the Claremont Pier, and *R.I.P.* rounding dangerously close to the mark was slightly to windward of *Desperation* at the start of the close-hauled leg to the S.E. buoy. Making the utmost of this advantage, *R.I.P.* worked out to windward and ahead of *Desperation*, leading her by 30 seconds at the end of the second round.

These two pulled out from the fleet in the freshening and changing wind, *R.I.P.* finally winning by practically five minutes from *Desperation* and well over 12 minutes from *Sea Serpent*, who was third.

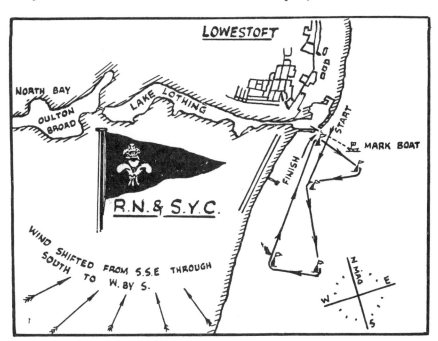

EASTERLY WIND LIFTING OVER THE CLIFF AT LOWESTOFT
BOATS NEAR SHORE BECALMED

BOAT	OWNER	TIME	
		M.	S.
R.I.P. - - -	H. A. Morris - -	0	0
Desperation - -	T. C. Ratsey - -	4	56
Sea Serpent - -	Sir John Field Beale -	12	52
Effort - - -	C. K. Collyer - -	15	0
Joanna - - -	Mrs. C. B. Tracey -	16	10
Tim Too - - -	P. Richardson - -	16	15

In these races for the Prince of Wales' Cup with between thirty and fifty starters, it is difficult to finish within the first twelve, so those who win replicas by being in the first six value them very highly.

R.I.P., by winning the Prince of Wales' Cup twice in her life of three years, proves that the class is becoming more stable, it being increasingly difficult for designers and builders to improve upon their earlier creations. The following story tells how *R.I.P.* came to be built, and to receive her unusual name.

When I met H. A. Morris at the Easter All-in Meet of the Tamesis Club in 1930, he told me of his aches and pains, and agreed to my suggestion that he was only walking about to save funeral expenses.

I said, " Why not have a new dinghy built, she'll finish you off and you can then be buried in her." The idea tickled him so much that he ordered and named *R.I.P.* right away, and throughout her designing and building we wrote letters describing her successful race against *Charon* across the Styx, and his astonishment at being beaten for the first time upon his own waters.

Above : SEA SERPENT (SIR JOHN FIELD BEALE), 3RD, LOWESTOFT, 1933. THE FIRST BONELESS 14-FOOTER ALONGSIDE A TIMBERED DINGHY

Left : DESPERATION (T. C. RATSEY) 2ND, PRINCE OF WALES' CUP, LOWESTOFT, 1933

* * * * * * * * * * * * *

COWES TO HAVRE IN *AVENGER*

Avenger had won twenty races right off the reel in the Solent, the racing had turned to foxhunting, and the sweepstakes from boats, to the number of minutes and seconds by which *Avenger* would win.

It was not yet time to go to Lowestoft and the Broads for the Prince of Wales' and the Trent Cups, so we thought we would have a dart at the French.

We had planned to race *Avenger* at Havre and Deauville to see if she were able to beat the French boats of her class, but as I had to complete the design of a yacht for a South African, it looked as though we would miss Havre.

Then a friend arrived from Havre the Monday of their regatta, and said there would be no dinghy race at Deauville and only four at Havre, that day being the first race, the others the following three days.

So we filled *Avenger* with 3 cwt. of food, water, clothes, compass, lamps, charts and gear, and left Kingston at 4.30 p.m. We were half an hour clearing the river, and once we had left its shelter we picked up a south-west wind, so strong, that the 15 miles from Castle Point to Bembridge Ledge were sailed in 1½ hours, as we arrived there at 6.30 p.m.

This speed I should have thought impossible considering the weight of food, gear and three men that formed *Avenger*'s crew.

We knew we could not stand full sail in the wind and sea clear of the shelter of the Island, so while still in the lee of Bembridge Ledge we reefed the mainsail, so that its head came below the jib halyards, and then let her go across for Havre close hauled on the starboard tack.

Once clear of the Island, we shipped water faster than two could bail it out on this course, so I let her off a point to leeward of Havre, this easing the wind and sea enough to enable one man bailing to keep pace with the water shipped, while the other two sat her up.

About 4 miles outside the Wight we saw a cutter with three reefs in her mainsail running back for the shelter of the Island. She had only just put to sea bound for Havre, where she finally arrived two days after us, her crew explaining that the day upon which they sailed was too rough for her. (Yet she looked wholesome and was a 50-tonner.) By midnight the wind and sea had eased enough to allow us to shake out our reefs and carry full sail, and soon after, the wind easing still more, we gave *Avenger* her large light reaching jib. It was necessary to keep her hard at it even if it did mean shifting sails at night, for with the weight of wind in which we started we hoped to sail the 100 miles from Cowes to Havre at an average of 6 knots, so arriving in time for the second day's race.

Dawn found us gliding along quietly and sweetly over gentle hills and valleys, and although this was very enjoyable after the strong wind and rough sea we had started in, it meant that we could not arrive in Havre in time for that day's race.

At 9.00 a.m. the sun burnt up this light air, and we lay becalmed in the swell left over from the hard breeze until late in the afternoon, when a light air made, and once more we moved o'er the face of the waters.

The high land of Cap de la Heve showed over the skyline at 6.00 p.m., so we washed and shaved, then dressed in our best collars and ties, so that we should look smart when we arrived, and 10.00 p.m. found us dining and wining ashore, in Havre.

AVENGER WON 57 PRIZES IN 57 STARTS
52 FIRSTS, 2 SECONDS, 3 THIRDS

AVENGER CARRIED FULL SAIL WITH ONLY TWO ABOARD
WHEN RACING. THE 8-METRES AND OTHER CRAFT
RACED WITH TWO REEFS IN

The next morning we raced and won, as we did again the day after, for the Havre course is in the shadow of la Heve where there are no tricks in the tide.

Thursday night I attended the dinner of the Société des Regattes du Havre, feeling rather like our Royal National Lifeboat Institution, for like it, I was supported by voluntary contributions, wearing (not having taken a dinner jacket) Commander Eldred's trousers, a French yachtsman's dinner jacket, another's shoes, but my own handkerchief.

The day after our last race was a Friday, and, moreover, the thirteenth, so, of course, we stayed till Saturday afternoon, when we left with the wind dead ahead and the weather report Jolie Brise Nord Ouest. As this meant a beat dead to windward of 100 miles, we stood on each tack for four hours.

(As a boy in the choir, instead of paying attention to sermons, I would wander miles on the wings of thought, and in one of these wanderings suddenly came face to face with the fact, that people fear Fridays because of the first Good Friday, and thirteen because that was the number at the Last Supper.)

The brise was Jolie Saturday, through that night, and Sunday until the afternoon, when it freshened to a hard wind, but still remained north-west and dead ahead. The three of us laid out to windward and letting *Avenger* take all that came fairly smoked along, for as yet there was no sea to stop her. The sea did not make up until four hours later, just before dark, when we had to reef, as she shipped so much heavy water.

During those four hours of hard driving with the three of us laying right out, my brain was at work on the strength of our shrouds, counting 85 per cent. of this, as splicing takes away 15 per cent. of a wire's strength. Against this I put the weight required to depress the lee gunwale as it was, the weight exerted by the dropkeel in its efforts to keep the boat plumb, and the weight of three men intensified through their leverage, for we were completely out of the dinghy, excepting for our legs below the knees.

As the strength of the wire and the strain upon it was equal, it was even betting that the shroud would part and our mast carry away, but as a faint heart never won a fat woman we let *Avenger* stand it, till the sea made up enough to force us into reefing.

Just before dark we lifted the Island on our weather bow, and continuing on our port tack, later saw the *Owers* flashing out dead ahead.

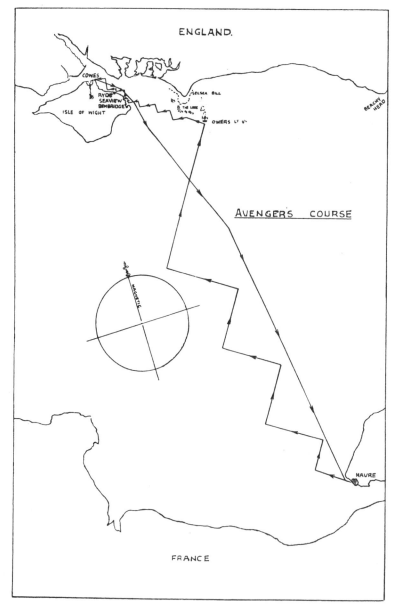

We stood on until close to the lightship and then came about. By this time a very heavy sea was running for such a small boat as *Avenger*, and through my not easing her over a very steep sea, she shipped it solid and was almost swamped. The hurricane lamp was put out of action, the electric lamp was washed off the thwart into the bilge, and everything was soaked, so that it was impossible to strike a match, or make a light of any sort. As we were right in the steamer track with no light, I put *Avenger* about again and hoped to be able to thread her through the passage between the shoals inside the *Owers*, and then work along close up to and in the lee of the land in smooth water, and out of the steamer track.

But after a while I missed the passage, which is difficult to find even in daylight, and is almost unknown, and we found huge breaking seas on either hand and dead ahead, so we put about and threaded our way back into deep water, spending the night evading steamers, as well as fighting to windward in steep breaking seas.

As we tacked close inshore off Bembridge, the light of early dawn gleaming upon the white ruin of St. Helens old church reminded me of the way the stones with which sailors scrubbed their decks received the name of Holy Stones.

St. Helens Roads giving such good shelter from south-westerly winds and being so close to Portsmouth was a favourite anchorage for our old sailing Navy, and as Tombstones were excellent for deck scrubbing, St. Helens old churchyard was plundered, and so the stones became known as Holy Stones.

AVENGER READY FOR PLANKING

AVENGER TIMBERED OUT. STERN VIEW

We beat on past Bembridge to Seaview Pier where we made fast and went ashore for breakfast. Monday is washing day on the Island, and good housewives rise very early to do their washing as well as their day's work, so we went to a house where the smoke was already rising from the chimneys, and asked if we could have breakfast. While this was being cooked, we all three fell asleep on the lawn, which was wet with dew, but as we were wet through, we did not mind this.

" Oh Sleep it is a gentle thing,
Beloved from pole to pole."

Bob and Spike had been bailing all night, and I had been steering for 17 hours, so we were extremely tired, and even *Avenger* had felt the strain, for she had altered shape forward, and ever after was faster in wind and sea.

After breakfast we sailed to Ryde, but our race was not until the afternoon, by which time the wind had died, leaving but the faintest of airs, in which our tired brains refused to sparkle, so we finished third to Tom Thornycroft and A. C. Walker.

Then away for Cowes where the Customs allowed us to keep the three small bottles of scent, as we had opened them, and explained that they were for our own adornment.

Avenger had taken 29 hours to sail to Havre, and 37 hours to beat back. Bob and Spike have bronze medals, whilst I have a silver one and a cup to remind us of *Avenger's* greatness, all of which she won at Havre.

·10·
FROSTBITE DINGHIES

A YACHT'S dinghy is a difficult problem to solve, as it has so many conflicting points.   It must be light, so that it can be hauled out and stowed easily on deck, it must be strong and able to take hard knocks, must row and carry well, and sail too, as sailing makes a tedious journey to the shore a pleasure.   In spite of its lightness it must be so built, that even after weeks on deck, under the strong drying sun of the Trade winds, it is tight when launched. And *Utility* was an effort to combine all these virtues in one dinghy.

UTILITY AND FAY

Length - - - - 11 ft. 6 in.	Beam - - - - 4 ft. 4 in.
Displacement - - - 460 lb.	Sail area - - - - 72 sq. ft.

Owners. GEORGE RATSEY AND DR. COOKE   *Designer,* UFFA FOX

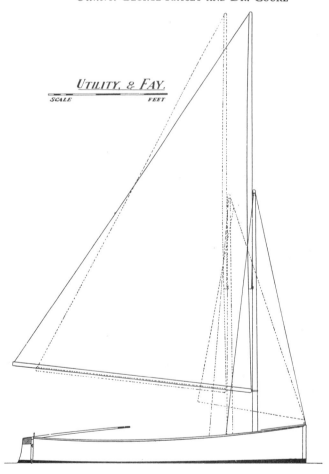

UTILITY, & FAY.
SCALE   FEET

UTILITY HAS TO CARRY FIVE, ROW WELL AND TOW WELL

The American Dinghy Association in 1932 started the Frostbite Dinghy Class with rules, which in time will produce the perfect tender for small yachts, providing its committee is strong minded enough not to alter them and allow Bermudian masts, which would improve the speed of the dinghies at the cost of making the rig an impossible one to carry aboard small boats.

238

The rules are very simple indeed. The length is between 10 ft. 6 in. and 11 ft. 6 in., beam between 58 in. and 52 in. and a minimum depth of 16 in. with a sail area of 72 sq. ft. The weight must not be less than 125 lb. for the stripped hull, or the drop keel to exceed 25 lb. in weight, and all spars must stow inside the dinghy. The rules demand in addition a boat that will row well with five aboard, and also tow well.

The drop keel of *Utility* was just $\frac{1}{2}$ lb. under the maximum weight allowed, and as her hull was only a pound over the minimum weight, she was within $\frac{1}{2}$ lb. of the minimum total weight allowed by the rules ($150\frac{1}{2}$ lb.)

This no doubt was one of the reasons she was so successful, and combined with her powerful lines made her very fast in strong breezes.

For passage making such a dinghy could be easily hauled on deck, and when the yacht lay at anchor it could be lifted on deck so as not to bump the parent ship through the night. Many an enjoyable excursion could be made in the dinghy up strange creeks and rivers, whilst the mother ship remained anchored near the mouth.

To prevent her opening up in the heat of the sun, *Utility* was built of two thicknesses of mahogany planking, the inner running diagonally and the outer fore and aft.

As this dinghy has to tow her parent ship in order to conform to the rule, a cleat was made and fitted under the centre of the midship thwart, on which to belay the tow rope from the yacht, for so many people never realise that the only place from which to tow is the centre of the tow boat. Then she is able to twist and turn about just as she wishes instead of being controlled entirely by the boat she is towing. All our tugs illustrate this, and the sight of several tugs twisting a large liner about just as they wish is an education in towing, and they of course have their towing hook amidships.

We also made a painter for running out a heavy kedge, which is probably the most dangerous task when cruising, for if the kedge is taken in the dinghy, it has to be lifted and flung out, when its weight is liable to capsize a small boat, or worse still, its fluke catch in some part of the occupant's clothing, when he would be taken to the bottom with the kedge and probably drowned. So I have always lashed my anchor over the stern with a painter, the end of which is belayed to a cleat under the thwart and have slipped it at the right moment without any

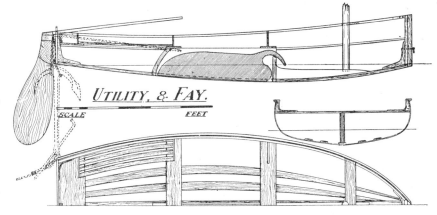

NOTE THE CLEAT UNDER THE MIDDLE THWART FOR TOWING OR MAKING FAST THE SLIP ROPE OF THE KEDGE

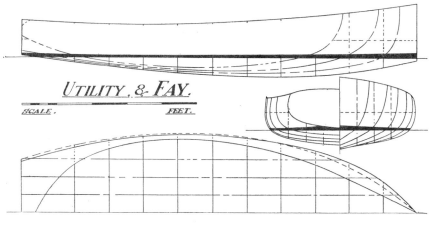

strain or struggling. In this way, the kedge never enters the dinghy at all, only its warp, which is coiled down starting from the anchor end and so runs away clear, and thus, when all out and the painter let go from its cleat, the kedge is launched peacefully and easily without exertion, fuss or danger.

The solid spars, 11 ft. 2 in. just stow inside the dinghy nicely and the halyard leading forward makes the forestay while the main shrouds come 15 in. abaft the mast, making a back stay and shroud in one.

Two dinghies have been built from these plans, one for George Ratsey in America, where she is almost invincible in strong winds, the other by Dr. Cooke, of Ventnor, who built her himself in his stable, and has sailed her around the Isle of Wight where the tides cause steep seas, which are very trying to such small craft. The doctor's rig is shown with dotted lines, as he prefers a jib.

So the plans and photographs of *Utility* are worthy of study, as they are an attempt to produce the ideal yacht's tender, one that will row and tow well, and at the same time sail well, and be easily hauled on deck and stowed.

·II·

WINNING THE CANOE CHAMPION-
SHIP OF AMERICA

ON February 25, 1933, the Royal Canoe Club held its annual dinner and presentation of cups, and as winner of the two most important of these, it was my privilege and pleasure to fill them and pass them round the table.

In olden times, many a man met his end by being stabbed from behind whilst drinking, and often in old pictures a man is shown drinking with his back to the wall. This protected him from behind, and the old tankards had glass bottoms, so that those drinking could see any danger ahead. As the challenge and De Quincey Cups were passed round, three men stood all the while, the man drinking toasted the man on his left, while the man on his right, who drank last, remained standing, so the man drinking had a friend standing either side of him as was the old custom.

Through dinner we toasted canoeists the world over, and afterwards Roger and I departed, he to Oxford and I to the Isle of Wight, hoping that we should both take canoes to America in August, sister ships that would not only conform to the American rules, but also to the English.

Two days later, on the Monday, I sent the following cable to a friend, who is the oldest canoeist in America :

W. P. STEPHENS, 3716 Bay Street, Bayside, New York.

Please send 1933 sailing canoe building rules, latest date for Challenge from England and date of Contest. UFFA.

Letters and cables passed between America and England, mostly cables from England, with the result that we challenged for everything we could, Roger as the Royal Canoe Club, and I the Humber Yawl Club.

Then came the designing of our canoes, Roger helping with letters, full of ideas, from Trinity, and finally the canoes were designed to both sets of rules.

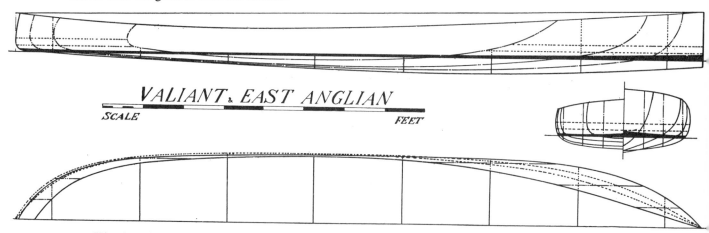

VALIANT & EAST ANGLIAN

SCALE   FEET

The American maximum beam rule forced us to design canoes 3 in. narrower than the English rule, whilst the English rule, demanding a $\frac{1}{4}$ in. planking, forced our hulls 40 lb. over the minimum weight allowed in America.

Time alone would tell if we could afford to give away the 3 in. of beam under the English rule, where no sliding seat was allowed, and carry the extra 40 lb. of hull weight round the American courses, but we thought we might, and it was worth trying.

The rig would have to be different, as entirely different rules prevailed. Under the American rule, we were allowed 111 sq. ft. of sail, actual area, with a height of 16 ft., but no side stays on the mast, while under the English rule we were allowed 96 sq. ft., Y.R.A. measurement, with no restriction as to height or staying of mast.

The Americans had no limit to the depth of centre board, so, while racing there, we thought we would try a very deep one, which was impossible under the English rule, which only allowed a board to extend 1 metre below the canoe.

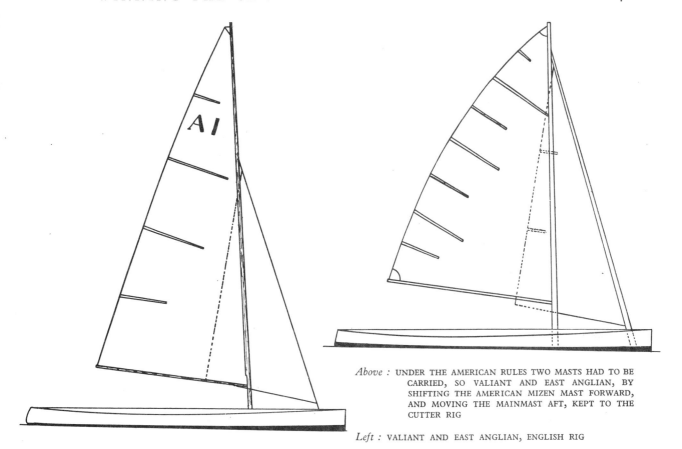

Above : UNDER THE AMERICAN RULES TWO MASTS HAD TO BE CARRIED, SO VALIANT AND EAST ANGLIAN, BY SHIFTING THE AMERICAN MIZEN MAST FORWARD, AND MOVING THE MAINMAST AFT, KEPT TO THE CUTTER RIG

Left : VALIANT AND EAST ANGLIAN, ENGLISH RIG

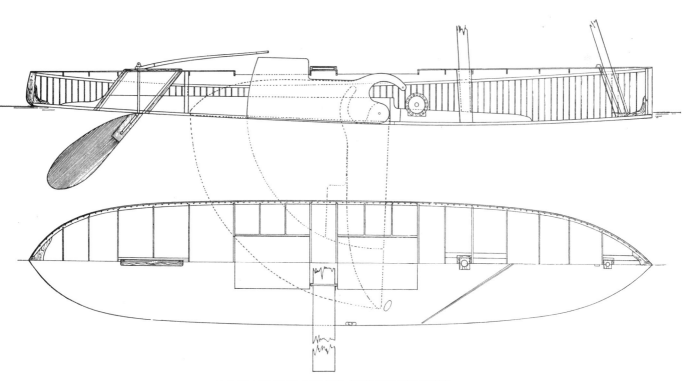

VALIANT AND EAST ANGLIAN, CONSTRUCTION PLANS

The American rules allowed a sliding seat, and the English did not, so by changing rigs and drop keels, and adding a sliding seat, our canoes were changed from the English to the American rules.

The American rule allowing a sliding seat, but no sidestays, made a fair amount of work calculating the leverage and power exerted by a man five foot out on a slide, plus the power of the canoe and balancing this against the strength and elasticity of hollow spruce spars. For, to win races, weight, and so strength, must be cut down to its limit, yet to carry away a spar is fatal.

After the designing, came the building. *Valiant* and *East Anglian* were built upside down, for the bottom of any vessel is the part that decides her speed, and by building upside down this is always in view.

VALIANT'S BOW

EAST ANGLIAN'S STERN

Moulds were made and set up on the stock, the keel, stem and stern post fitted, and the moulds ribbanded out. Next, the $\frac{3}{8}$ in. by $\frac{1}{4}$ in. timbers were steamed and bent 2 in. apart round the ribbands, and the first skin, of $\frac{1}{8}$ in. thick diagonal planking, fitted. Oiled silk, stretched over the diagonals, formed the next skin, on which the $\frac{1}{8}$ in. fore and aft planking was fitted and fastened. After this the keel case, extending almost the full length of the canoe, was fitted, followed by the deck beams and mast steps, and after six coats of varnish inside, the deck, of specially made 3-ply, was fitted, and fastened in one piece.

Spars were made and all was merry and bright, for we were ready for sea. The following verses by my wife will illustrate our pleasant thoughts during the building of *Valiant* and *East Anglian*.

ROGER'S NEW CANOE

There's a shaving in our workshop,
　　It's planed and varnished too,
It trembles in a tiny breeze,
　　It's the keel of R.'s canoe.

And gossamer hangs from the beams,
　　I ask, " What will that do ? "
They tell me 'tis the planking light
　　Of Roger's new canoe.

There's wood so delicate at hand
　　No nails in this, but glue,
And 'tis the deck, so I am told,
　　Of Roger's new canoe.

There is a tube both short and spare,
　　Sans crosstree, stay or shroud.
It is the mast, don't speak so loud,
　　Of Roger's fine canoe.

There is a pocket handkerchief,
　　So small and dainty too,
It is the sail of R.'s delight,
　　The sail of his canoe.

There's a flutter in our workshop,
　　There's happy work to do,
Wish her good luck, a gentle touch,
　　She's launched—the new canoe.

There's no mark upon the water,
　　No ripple, sure 'tis true.
As Roger gaily glideth by,
　　In his wondrous new canoe.

We had had some experience with the English rig, but none with the American, so this was the first to be tried out, and it proved better to windward than expected, and I easily beat an International Star Class Yacht to windward in both light and strong winds, so, as far as windward work went, we were contented with our canoes, for winning, after allowing the Star Class 15 minutes in an hour, showed this to be a good rig.

Then the English rig was fitted in a tabernacle, which allowed the mast to be reefed in strong winds. This too seemed good.

     *   *   *   *   *   *   *   *   *   *   *   *

The Royal Canoe Club's Annual Meet came all too soon, and almost every new yacht or sailing boat finds her first class race too early for her liking. Roger took *Valiant* over to Southsea on board the passenger steamer, where his brother met him with a trailer and motored them both to Langston.

VALIANT AND EAST ANGLIAN, WITH THE ANCIENT MARINERS HUGH CAMKIN, R. C. ANDERSON
AND R. A. SMITH, AT THE ROYAL CANOE CLUB'S ANNUAL MEET

The following Wednesday, I sailed *East Anglian* across, well reefed, with no jib, as it was blowing hard from the south-west.

At the end of the two weeks' meet, I had lost the De Quincey Cup to Eric Freeman in *Genetta*, and the Challenge Cup to Roger De Quincey in *Valiant*, and on July 22 we sailed *Valiant* and *East Anglian* to Cowes in company with *Aquamarine*, having just a week in which to fit out for America, as we were sailing aboard the *Empress of Britain* on July 29.

That week was spent making spars and masts, varnishing our canoes and doing the hundred and one jobs we thought necessary. On Friday 28, we shipped our canoes and gear, including ten spare masts, to Southampton and aboard the *Empress of Britain*, and returned to Cowes for the night. This gave us a double start, which is useful. In this case, it enabled us to leave again, heavily laden with gadgets we had thought of since the previous day.

Roger and I left England full of hope, for we hoped that we should win the American National Championship and also their International Trophy, and return with, as well as these trophies, a rule from America that would be acceptable to England, and so unite canoeists of both countries. If we succeeded in obtaining this, a canoeist would henceforth be able to race in both countries without the handicap of having to design and build to two entirely different sets of rules.

The *Empress of Britain* was most kind to us, and we spent many happy hours in the carpenter's shop, making spare tillers and paddles.

Later, whilst I made a storm jib, Roger made the brake for his centreboard winch ; this brake is Highfield's patent, and due to the smallness of the winch we were unable to buy a brake for it, so, as the only way a man can pass to windward of the patent law is to make the article for himself, Roger was forced to make his brake.

Our voyage across was spent very pleasantly, making gear for our canoes during the day, and dancing at night. Going through the Straits of Belle Isle we saw an iceberg, shaped like an old Spanish galleon with a high stern. This did not seem at all out of place, for although it was summer it was very cold, owing to the Labrador Current, which, bringing this iceberg south, gave us food for thought.

Here we were, in the same latitude as the south of England, where it was very hot, meeting icebergs, and not being surprised, this vast difference being due to the ocean currents, for the warmer water of the Gulf Stream, setting across to the British Isles, makes it possible for tropical trees to grow in the south-west of England, whilst the Arctic Current, coming down the Labrador Coast, is the cause of the coldness of that land.

AS WE STEAMED UP THE ST. LAWRENCE OUR
CANOES WERE HOISTED OUT OF NO. 2 HOLD

DUDLEY MURPHY, CHAIRMAN OF AMERICAN
CANOE ASSOCIATION COMMITTEE

Looking at the high bold land close aboard that morning was painful to our eyes, that for almost a week had been used to looking out into space with an unbroken skyline. Now, looking on this high land so near to us, our eyes found difficulty in focussing it, and yet for almost a week we had been able to go down, after being on deck, and feel no pain in our heads, when we looked at the good food on our table, which was far closer than the land we now saw.

We arrived at Quebec on August 3, five days out from England, which is very fast time indeed. We left Quebec at 6.00 p.m., and as there was no room for our canoes on this train, they were to leave by the next at midnight.

OUR CANOES, GANANOQUE JUNCTION

This gave us six hours in Montreal, in which to find a hotel, turn in, sleep, turn out and meet the canoes. So after a nap at the " Windsor," we met the canoes at 7.00 a.m. and switched them over to the National from the Pacific Railway, arriving at Gananoque junction at noon. We then took a tiny train to the town waterfront, and had our canoes ready for sea by tea time.

Our destination, Sugar Island, was in sight, three miles away, and we were looking forward to our sail there. Just as we were about to put to sea (in the river St. Lawrence) Jack Wright, the Commodore of the American Canoe Association, came along in his launch. He was a friend in need, for we had loaded our canoes right down with suitcases, spare masts and gear, all of which he kindly took aboard his launch, and the three of us made for our tents on Sugar Island, the Commodore steaming in his launch and Roger and I sailing our canoes.

Doing 6 knots, we were soon abreast of the island, with its tents, hills, trees, rocks and sandy bays, and hauling our wind reached past Headquarters Bay, and luffing into New York Bay, were welcomed by Dudley Murphy's wild scream of "Whoopahee," a most unearthly yell, that he had learned from some Indian canoe men who used it as a greeting to other Redskins they met.

Rolf Armstrong had met us in *Mannikin*, and his canoe, with our two, the commodore's launch, and the other canoes all ready there filled the bay completely. We pitched our tent with the help of about ten others, then put up our beds, and piled all our gear into the tent, suit cases, bags of sails, ropes and gear, till it looked just as untidy as our cabin aboard the *Empress of Britain* had done, so we felt at home right away. The poor tent did not even have a chance to look tidy.

The commodore invited us to dinner at his tent across the bay, after which we went for a sail in the light of a full moon.

The island looked very fine by moonlight, while in front of headquarters' tent there was a huge red glow from the camp fire, with figures passing to and fro in front of it, and the sound of their voices as they sang came floating across the water to us. An island has more charm than any other part of this earth, and this island to-night in the moonlight seemed very lovable, and we were both happy and content as we sailed about its bays. It was to be our home for two weeks, we were to know its trails, live with its people, share meals with them in their tents, sit round the camp fire at night with them singing and yarning, and learn to love them all, for their kindness and open-heartedness. They named Roger and I the Babes in the Woods, and it was very nice to be babes to such people.

* * * * * * * * * * * *

The next day (Saturday) Roger and I dressed in our best, white tops, white flannels, neckties and white shoes, for the flags were to be hoisted, and the camp officially opened. After the speeches, and many kind words, we set sail for Gananoque : Rolf Armstrong in *Mannikin*, with Roger all alone in *Valiant*, and Mrs. Rolf with myself in *East Anglian*. There we ate ices, bought several small tools we needed, and sailed back to Sugar Island, Mrs. Rolf coming back with Roger, while I sailed home alone.

Sunday was the day of rest, with tea at Squaw Point, where we saw what comfort there could be in a tent. Mrs. Coggins must have been surprised to see Roger and I drink seven cups of tea each, but we thought we should not often have a chance at tea in America.

That night we went to our first camp fire, and the commodore asked me to sing, so I sang "The Bosun's Story," of how he discovered the north pole by harpooning a whale and being towed there by it, and then being knocked back again by the whale's tail. On Monday we all arrived at headquarters' tent with our sails for measurement, and we found that ours were 11 ft. under their allowed area. They were correct on the foot and luff, but the roach had gone out of the leach, due to the fact that a sail is like a piece of elastic, which, when stretched, becomes narrower, although longer, and therefore measures the same area as when made, but in a different way.

Tuesday was our first race in American waters. This was a tuning up race, with a nice breeze, and we averaged 4½ knots round the course. I hit the first buoy, by catching my drop keel on its wire, and so pulling it towards me. Committees should moor turning marks with chains, but if with rope, they should have a weight 10 ft. or so below the surface to take them down plumb, so that they cannot be caught by the keel of a boat rounding them. In this case, I asked what I should do and was told to carry on, as it was a tuning up race, and we all wanted to see how our canoes sailed, but I should not put any canoe about or take her wind, so keeping clear, I completed the course, and finishing second, reported to the committee, and was disqualified automatically. Rolf Armstrong was first with Gordon Douglas third and Roger fourth. At this speed our canoes and the Americans were equally matched, below it the latter would be faster and above it we should win.

Flags on mark buoys are not very good as guides, for if dead to windward, or dead to leeward, they are invisible, blowing either directly away, or directly toward, the man trying to see them. Besides this, in uncertain winds they flip out, and often just catch a boat rounding close, and so disqualify her. Here, the American Canoe Association had solved the flag problem in a cheap and masterly way. They had tacked shiny tins or buckets upside down on the buoy poles, and they glistened and reflected the sun's rays like mirrors. On dull days, catching what light there was, they showed up brightly as well, and being round showed equally well from all angles.

The camp fire that night was to see the crowning of the king of the island with speeches by him, the Prince of Wales, and Knights of the Bath and Garter. Then these were to be impeached, and a dictator appointed for the duration of the meet. I was chosen King, and crowned, which was all very well until my son, the Prince of Wales (George Denhard, the chairman of the New York Canoe Club) spoke, and he rather let me in for things. However it was not long before the dictator was put in power, and then the fun began. The commodore was made privy councillor, and there was a bees' nest in one of the privies. Mayors were made, cabinets formed and everyone was given a job. After this we had a sing-song, and then to our tents and sleep.

Wednesday was the first race for the Admiralty Trophy. The rules for this race stated that one leg of the triangle was to be sailed, and the next paddled, so by doing this we sailed and paddled over each leg of the triangle in two rounds. It was a paddling start, and a race we had not bargained for, so we knew little about it, and as I had never before paddled a canoe, things looked black. They looked even blacker when my sliding seat fell overboard at the start, and I had to go back and recover it. However, at the end of the second leg, which was a sailing leg, *East Anglian* led the fleet. Then came another paddling leg, and here again I became unbuttoned, for I had stowed my sails, pulled up the drop keel and stowed the sliding seat, and was leading the fleet nicely, with enough lead in hand to hold back the faster paddling canoes of the Americans, when my jib broke adrift, and although it was stopping me as it blew aft, I thought it far better to stow it again, so walked up on the fore deck, and stowed it neatly. Then,

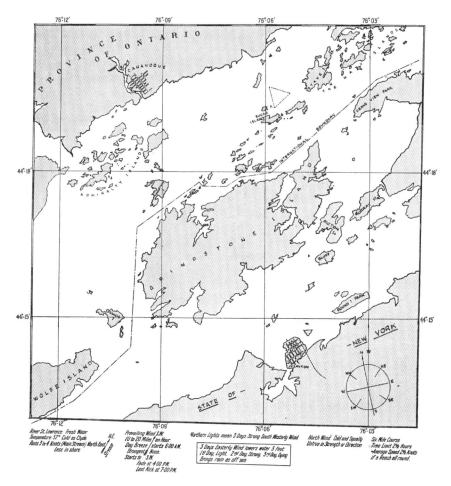

coming aft, I forgot the drop keel was up and *East Anglian* capsized. I tried to right her by standing on the tiny piece of drop keel, that was showing, but could not do it, so swam round and pushed the drop keel out. Even then I could not right her, so rigged the sliding seat, and with this and the drop keel, she was easily righted, and I was all ready to paddle on, when the paddle was seen floating twenty yards away. This meant another swim for the paddle, but at last we were away again. When the next sailing leg came, my sails were like a prune, being a mass of wrinkles, but halfway through this leg, which fortunately was a beat, the wrinkles all came out, and *East Anglian* was first round the weather mark, but not far enough to hold one of the faster paddling American canoes on the next leg. She passed me halfway down this leg, and *East Anglian* could not catch her again on the last reach home, so finished second.

The wetting of the sails, their wrinkling, and then coming as good as gold again after they were dried, showed me the value of using rope for luff and foot, instead of wire, for the rope shrinks and swells with the canvas, whereas the wire remains constant, and so, after a sail has been wet on a wire and shrunk, it is probably stretched unfairly.

That night Roger attended the fancy dress ball in a child's rompers, whilst I was rigged out in a grass skirt from the South Sea Islands, two very nice cool costumes.

On Thursday the Mermaid Trophy was raced for. This trophy was given by Leo Friede for 16 ft. by 30 in. canoes, as he was a great lover of these little canoes, and for years had won the National Championship in one of them, and twice successfully defended the International Trophy in *Mermaid*, his 16 ft. by 30 in. canoe.

Our canoes were 17 ft. by 39 in., so Roger borrowed a 16 ft. by 30 in. and I was loaned the *Damosel*, another 16 ft by 30 in., and we felt very unsafe in these narrow canoes, which, with no one in to balance them, capsized by themselves. However, we managed to sail round the course without capsizing, in spite of the fact that our athwart-ship tiller fouled the sliding seat. Ralph Britton won in *Jonah*, Gordon Douglas was second in *Nymph*, Tyson third in *Oske Wow Wow*, and I was fourth and Roger fifth.

In the afternoon, the second race for the Admiralty Trophy was held. The wind was very light, and away we went sailing slowly round three rounds of the triangle. For what seemed hours I lay 100 yards off the finishing line becalmed, with the rest of the fleet farther astern, when the time limit expired, and the race was called off.

This night the camp fire was under the care of Dr. Wakefield, a past commodore, and he built up the biggest fire of the whole meet. The piano was brought out, and many fine songs were sung. The charm of a camp fire lies in the warmth of its light ; it is soothing and one looks into it, and dreams pleasant dreams, whilst, when a song is sung, the listeners can float away in their little dream-boats with the singer, for a fire, and the twilight of the fire, stirs a man's imagination.

The sunrise and sunset are the two most beautiful parts of the day, and their charm is the charm of the fire. Then, too, outdoor people watch the sun rise and set, for then the Lord tells those that understand the weather for the day or night.

Friday, we sailed the postponed race for the Admiralty Trophy. This time the breeze allowed us to finish within the time, and *East Anglian* won, with Roger second, Chip Tyson third, and Gordon Douglas fourth.

Saturday came with a smart S.W. wind, and the paddling race for the Admiralty Trophy was held. As this was paddling only, Roger and I were advised to take this very easily, as we could not hope to beat the faster American paddling canoes, and the first heat for the National Sailing Trophy was to follow immediately afterwards. But we both agreed, that if we were going to race, we might as well win or burst ! So we took out the drop keel, spars, and as much gear as we could, and came to the starting line to win.

The course was straight along the island to Stave Island, wind on the weather quarter, strong, so as soon as I could I headed *East Anglian* out to sea, where, although it was rougher, the wind was stronger and more of a help, as I stood up to paddle with a fair wind. Away we went, white water flying off our double paddles, and the result was that *East Anglian* finished second unexpectedly, only 30 yards astern of the champion paddler of Canada, and so won the Admiralty combined paddling and sailing trophy by 1 point.

We were towed back to Headquarters Bay, and there quickly rigged our canoes with drop keels, masts, sails and sheets, and were soon ready for the first heat of the sailing trophy. The wind was too strong for most of the American canoes, so *East Anglian* won, with *Valiant* second, Gordon Douglas third in *Nymph*, Rolf Armstrong fourth with *Mannikin*, and *Mab*, who had left her mainsail ashore and set two mizens, fifth. So only five finished out of nine starters.

After the race Roger went to Gananoque to see the paddling races there, while I stayed at Sugar Island to try out our storm jibs, and see if they were good, in case the wind came stronger. They seemed good, so after sailing three times round the island, I set off for Gananoque to watch the last of the paddling races. By this time the wind was easing, and only about half the paddling canoes were swamped in this race. The war canoes, with fifteen men in each, made the finest sight, as they tore through the water. We had tea aboard Frank Palmer's yacht, and returned to Sugar Island for dinner. The island looked very fascinating as *East Anglian* approached it in the twilight ; the hard wind had eased with sundown, and there was time to think of the peace and restfulness of living in tents, on an island with no roads, no motors, nothing except rocks, trees, bushes and wild animals. And it was pleasant to think of, and look upon this island, in the evening light. That evening, after dinner, the executive meeting was held at Headquarters Tent, and the American Canoe Association made Roger and I honorary members for life. This was a great honour, and one we felt deeply. And so to bed, feeling happy and contented.

Sunday was another day of peace. In the morning Roger and I went for a sail off the weather side of the island, as there was a smart breeze. I had my storm jib, and he, with full sail, was faster, as was to be expected, for there was not enough wind to shorten sail on our canoes with sliding seats.

Then, after lunch, we were all peacefully yarning in George Lewis's tent, when in burst Ted Coggins, who had just arrived at camp, wanting to be convinced that our canoes were faster than the Americans in hard weather. He bet the red pants he wore that he could beat Roger and I.

Now two to one is unfair, and as I was dressed for church, Roger took the bet, and the pair went to race, whilst we went on to church in Headquarters Tent.

Rolf Armstrong went out as race officer aboard the committee boat, and started them, while we sang hymns ashore. Suddenly, whilst the lesson was being read, Doc. Wakefield nudged me, and looking out to sea, I saw Ted capsized, and Roger roaring along in fine style. Then Ralph Britton's voice suddenly tailed off faint in the next hymn, and looking up, I saw him twisting his neck round to watch the race, for as he was in the choir he had his back to the sea. So our service and race went on. Roger won the red trousers, and convinced Ted that our canoes were faster in wind, a fact which had been proved beyond all shadow of doubt the day before.

LOOKING OUT TO SEA I SAW TED COGGINS CAPSIZED

That evening Ralph Britton took us to his island home the other side of Gananoque to dinner, and then in the twilight, Ralph, Roger and I explored the group. The magic and fascination of these small islands was strong that night, and it was hard to leave them, and return to our own island and bed.

OUR TENT IN NEW YORK BAY

Amongst the Admiralty group we saw the Natural Open Air Cathedral, surely the finest place in which to worship. People did go there every Sunday evening, sitting in their canoes and boats, whilst the parson conducted the service from the natural pulpit ashore.

The parson who preached at our service at Sugar Island in the afternoon was a brother-in-law of Ralph Britton, and he told us the story of a brother clergyman who was appointed to congress, and when asked if he prayed for congress, he replied that he looked at the congress, and then prayed for the nation.

On Monday came the second heat of the National Trophy over a windward and loo'ard course with a nice breeze from N.W., which shifted during the race, and so spoilt the beat for the last two rounds. At the end of the first round, *East Anglian* led, and held her lead till the fifth round, which was won by *Mannikin*. Then, as the wind had shifted still more to the south, the last beat became a close reach, but *Mannikin* not noticing this, lost her lead by holding on to the starboard tack, when by coming about at the buoy she could have laid the course on the port tack. So *East Anglian* won this race with *Mannikin* second, *Valiant* third and Douglas fourth.

This night was the commodore's ball, and Roger and I wore our dinner jackets in his honour, but they were so hot and uncomfortable that we changed them after about two dances.

Tuesday was the third and final heat for the National Championship in a light wind, when our canoes and the Americans were the same speed. *East Anglian* had only to finish fifth in this heat in order to win the American National Sailing Championship, so I sailed a very careful race, feeling rather like a married man playing cards who will only go nap when he has the ace, king, queen, jack and ten of one suit, and in spite of carefully sailing well clear of every canoe and buoy, *East Anglian* only lost first place by 5 seconds to Gordon Douglas in *Nymph*, with *Mab* third, Roger fourth and *Oske Wow Wow* fifth.

And so *East Anglian* had won two American championships for the Humber Yawl Club of England, the combined paddling and sailing, and the decked sailing, and I felt at peace with all the world.

There was just one other championship, for paddling only, and the fact that the American canoeists one and all asked me to train for this, and try to win it in 1934, illustrates their sportsmanship and love of sport.

On Wednesday, the Paul Butler Trophy was sailed for. It was Paul Butler who adapted to the canoes the Indian trick of sitting out to windward on a plank. These Indians gauged the force of wind by men, a two-man breeze was one where two men sat out at the end of planks, and so on. Paul Butler was a tiny man, and so light that he did not stand any chance in strong winds, so he put the sliding seat on his canoe in the eighties, and won races, until the others fitted them also, and now most canoeists use a sliding seat, although on this side of the Atlantic we have a rule against them.

The sliding seat is of great advantage to canoe sailing, for the power of a sailing canoe is that of the weight of its crew sitting to windward. In England, we are forced to lay out, which is a strain, but, with the sliding seat there is no strain, as the crew simply sit out at the end of the slide. Besides being easier and more comfortable, this is also drier, for the seas, breaking over the canoe as she is driven to windward, do not touch the man on the sliding seat.

Paul Butler's widow gave this trophy, and it is a very pretty cup, rather like a Gaelic quaich with a handle on each side, a Scotsman being so afraid of losing his drink that his cup was made so that he could hold it with both hands.

Roger won this race, and I finished 12 seconds astern of him, with Ralph Britton third, in *Jonah*. In the first beat to windward I made a mistake over one tack; Gordon Douglas in *Nymph* was second and he stood on for about 50 yards, and then came about to port. As he knew the waters and was, moreover, second boat, I put about too; then we came round again, as I had his wind, and away we stood for the islands to windward. By this time, however, Roger, who was a very close third on rounding the buoy, had pulled out ahead, as he had not tacked twice in quick succession as we had, and we were unable to catch *Valiant* during the rest of the race.

Thursday was the last race for us of the meet, and as winner of the National Trophy, *East Anglian* was not allowed to race for the *Mab* Trophy, so I went aboard the committee boat, as one of the officers of the day.

It was a fine race to watch, as it was another day when the wind was light enough for the English and American canoes to be of equal speed.

The first three canoes kept changing places during the beat to windward, first one ahead and then the other as the puffs shifted or the others made false tacks. But in the end Rolf Armstrong won by a minute from Roger, with Ralph Britton third, and Adam Whal fourth.

Then came lunch, and whilst Roger went to Gananoque to do some shopping, I rigged our two canoes, and packed things at the tent, for that afternoon we were to sail our canoes to Clayton, and so enter America for the first time. It was a fine sail there with a strong wind, and on the beat *Valiant* forged ahead of *East Anglian*. Murphy and Ralph Britton escorted us over, and went bondsmen for our canoes, otherwise we should have had to put down money amounting to the third of their value against their being sold to the Americans.

We sailed them into a yacht yard, and stored them in a shed, then went back to Sugar Island for our last night's sleep, after we had been presented with our cups and medals, and the former had been duly filled and passed round. This was a joyful and yet sad evening, for it was our last, and we made the most of it, Roger leaving for Gananoque at 2.00 a.m. to visit his uncle in Vermont.

Heavy rain and wind squalls.

On Friday morning it rained hard, and was not at all pleasant for packing things from our tent, but at last it was all over, and Douglas took Rolf Armstrong, his wife and canoe as well as myself to Gananoque for the ferry to Clayton. At Gananoque I had to change the customs papers of our canoes for others to let them into America. Then we boarded the steam ferry for Clayton, and as she steamed past Sugar Island the friends we had left fired the cannon and dipped the flags, a very sad morning, but all things come to an end, and that camp did, although its memory will live always.

Arriving at Clayton, I paid five dollars for a poor old trailer, last used as a barrow for dung, and into this we fitted a new oak shaft, with steel plates and bolts, to fit the back of Rolf's Packard. He tore off to Watertown for the trailer's licence, after we had weighed it at a baker's. Then he loaded his canoe *Mannikin* on the top of the car, while I loaded *East Anglian* and *Valiant* on the trailer with their ten masts, drop keels, sails, etc. They brought the springs down flat. We stopped for dinner for an hour, and then on with the work till midnight ; then to bed.

Saturday morning we were up at 4.30 a.m., for it would be a long drive to New York and an early start is half the battle. So the car with *Mannikin* on top and four of us inside started off for the trailer at the shipyard, and there bolted it to the buffers at the stern of the car. We were very anxious about the five-dollar trailer, as it had a heavy load aboard, which was still valuable, as the International Canoe Trophy had yet to be won.

ROLF ARMSTRONG'S CAR WITH HIS CANOE MANNIKIN ON TOP, AND OUR CANOES VALIANT AND EAST ANGLIAN
TOWING ASTERN

After 15 miles our fears were justified, for the stem of one of the tyres sheered off, which made the trailer wheel wobble, and almost shook the canoes off. We stopped, unshipped the trailer, and Arthur George and I took off the wheel, whilst Rolf and his wife drove into Watertown for tools, with which to fit another tyre, *Mannikin* looking very cheeky on top of the car all the way.

After the repairs off we went again and arrived at Watertown without further trouble. But the strain began to tell on our nerves, and we were so pleased to be able to relax for a few minutes that breakfast was very noisy, and so full of laughs that people thought we were tight.

I had been riding on the trailer some time to watch and listen to things there, and the noise of a man chopping wood caused my heart to stop for a moment until I realised what it was. After breakfast we left with a quantity of wire and two horseshoes for luck.

About 5 miles from Watertown the bolts holding the buffers to the port quarter of the car carried away, and we had to wire these on. At the same time we wired the starboard side to make sure of these though they had not yet gone, so we continued adding new wires before the others gave way, and consequently they never failed.

And so we came to the Mohawk valley, through which our course lay. This valley was once the home of the Mohawk tribe, and to see its beauty spoilt by roads and railways made me wonder if civilisation is a blessing or a curse. That afternoon I was sure it was a failure, for the redskins, once a vigorous, fierce, and although cruel, an admirable race, were no more. And it seemed wrong, for they were the natives of North America. White men are so sure that their gospel is the only one, and they teach it to strong vigorous races, who drop their own strict moral laws for it, then, following the gospel teachers, come others with fire water, and soon the race fades and dies like a poisoned tree.

With all our boast and pride of civilisation, people still starve in thousands in a land of plenty, millions wither and choke in big cities, living lives humans were never meant to endure, and all because of the introduction of money into the world, the thing that should have made living simple, destroying the simple life.

On and on we went, till late at night we reached New York, and then passed through its streets at 3.00 a.m., seeing crowds of people turning the night into day. We crossed to Long Island by the steam ferry, finally arriving at Rolf's home at 3.30 a.m. after 23 hours of driving all in New York State, and it was not until then that I realised that each state was as large as a country of Europe. Then I gained some idea of the size of North America.

At the end of our journey we were met by dear old W. P., to whom I had sent the first cable some months ago, that started this adventure, and with whom I was to stay for a week or so. We had arrived at the scene of the International Canoe Contest (Bayside) without a scratch on any of the three canoes, weary but triumphant.

On Sunday W. P. and I sailed over to City Island in *Snicker Snee*, a Humber canoe yawl, for W. P. is a member of the Humber Yawl Club. In the afternoon we unloaded the canoes from the trailer, and then visited the New York Canoe Club House, or rather all their furniture on a barge, for the clubhouse had been sold.

LEO FRIEDE, WHO HAD TWICE BEFORE DEFENDED THE NEW YORK CANOE TROPHY SUCCESSFULLY WITH MERMAID

AND WALTER BUSCH, A YOUNG ATHLETE, IN LOON

On Monday we again measured our canoe sails with the same result, that we were 11 sq. ft. under area. So we prepared plans for a larger suit with more round to the leach, which would, when stretched, come out to the designed roach. We decided to give a 6 in. round in the luff of the mainsail, a 21 in. round to the leach, a 4 in. round on the foot, 4 in. round to the luff of the jib, and 1½ in. round to the foot and leach of the jib. This would disappear soon after the sail was used.

Sunday, the new sails were measured, and the mainsail was over area, so we chopped 9 in. off the foot at the clew, lifting the boom that much, and reducing the round of the leach to 1 ft. 6 in. The jib was just right.

All the week we were preparing the canoes for their last effort in America, rubbing down and varnishing, taking off our keel bands, varnishing spars, fitting battens to our mainsails, and all the many little things one can always do to a boat before any race. The Americans, too, were doing the same sort of things.

On Friday the first race of the series was held, to select the two American defenders. There was a smart breeze, which capsized many, carried away the masts of others, and generally shook the fleet up, while *East Anglian* sailed over to City Island without any trouble at all, to see Ratsey about our new sails. On the way back, an 8-metre tried to catch her, but could make no impression at all, for we were on a reach. The next morning with two aboard, *East Anglian*, with *Valiant's* new Ratsey sails, crossed the line a minute or so after the American trial races had started. We easily made the weather mark, while the Americans had to tack for it, so our new sails promised to be good, for besides holding a higher wind, we were footing faster. Down wind we were only as fast as the rest of the fleet, and reaching they were faster. Then we drifted all the afternoon, whilst the competitors, in the third race, were lying becalmed. This race was finally called " off " and the American team selected was Leo Friede, who had twice before defended the New York Canoe Cup successfully, and Walter Busch, a young athlete.

Monday, the mainsail was taken to Ratsey's to be cut, and a new suit ordered for *East Anglian*, the same size. And we still found work to do on our canoes.

We all went into New York to dinner on Tuesday with Leo Friede, the committee and all the canoe racers. The view from the top of his roof was very fine, for the buildings of New York are impressive, like giant's fingers flung up against the sky.

On Wednesday the sails of our two canoes were ready, and they were measured with the American's sails, in Ratsey's sail loft at City Island and found just under area, so we were settled and away we sailed for Bayside across the sound. This was a beat to windward against a light breeze, and as we were trying our new sails, was just right. Earlier in the day we had sailed over from Bayside, Rolf in *Mannikin*, his wife in the *Currey Racer*, which we easily beat to windward, laying a point higher and going as fast, and Roger in *Valiant*, with myself in *East Anglian*. We

AT THE START ROGER LOOKED AFTER LEO FRIEDE WHILE I LOOKED AFTER WALTER BUSCH

had a very short sail in our canoes on Thursday, and devoted the afternoon to fitting battens in the mainsail, whilst the canoes were on shore. We also set the sails in the light wind to see how they stood. We had pockets right across the sail for long battens, but with a batten right across a sail it is possible to be sailing with the mainsail starved of wind, and not know it, till suddenly the battens allow it to flop across, and then one realises that for some time the mainsail has been starved of wind. We finally ended with the second from the top batten right across the sail, but the rest of normal length, making one long batten and six others.

Friday dawned with a light air, just what we did not wish to see, and out we went to the triangle to start. We were surprised at being sent round the course, so that we had no beat to windward. There was a dead run on one leg and this meant that the other two legs were reaches. We should have been sent round the other way, when the run would have been a beat.

At the start, Roger looked after Leo, while I looked after *Loon*, but as they were faster in the light going they slipped out from under our lee by the time we had reached the first buoy. The end of the first lap saw Friede well ahead, Busch second, and Roger and myself almost 2 minutes astern. These times were unaltered for the rest of the race, for the wind lightened slightly, the only difference being that in the third round Busch took the lead from Friede and I went ahead of Roger. Then, on the last leg, I caught the mooring rope of the mark buoy on my drop keel, and this pulled the buoy on to *East Anglian*, so she retired, leaving Roger to finish alone for England.

During the trial races Roger and I had sailed close to the buoys, and found that they were moored with chains, and could be cut very closely, so all was well, but then these trial races had taken place in the shallower waters in the bay, and when the course was laid out for the international contest in the deeper water of the sound, these chains were not long enough, so ropes were used.

After the race we all gathered aboard the committee boat and yarned. The speeds that day worked out at 4½ knots, as 2 hours had been taken to do 9 miles, and as there was no windward work, we had stood no chance at all. But we hoped for more wind on the morrow.

FIRST LAP

								M.	S.
Leo Friede	-	-	-	-	Mermaid	-	-	-	-	27	34
Walter Busch	-	-	-	-	Loon	-	-	-	-	29	0
Roger De Quincey	-	-	-	Valiant	-	-	-	-	29	17
Uffa Fox -	-	-	-	East Anglian	-	-	-	29	24

SECOND LAP

								M.	S.
Leo Friede	-	-	-	-	Mermaid	-	-	-	-	57	35
Walter Busch	-	-	-	-	Loon	-	-	-	-	57	46
Roger De Quincey	-	-	-	Valiant	-	-	-	-	58	58
Uffa Fox -	-	-	-	East Anglian	-	-	-	59	18

THIRD LAP

							H.	M.	S.
Walter Busch	-	-	-	-	Loon	-	-	-	I	27	15
Leo Friede	-	-	-	-	Mermaid	-	-	-	I	28	41
Uffa Fox -	-	-	-	East Anglian	-	-	I	30	15
Roger De Quincey	-	-	-	Valiant	-	-	-	I	30	28

FINISHED ELAPSED TIMES

							H.	M.	S.
Walter Busch	-	-	-	-	Loon	-	-	-	I	59	22
Leo Friede	-	-	-	-	Mermaid	-	-	-	I	59	48
Roger De Quincey	-	-	-	Valiant	-	-	-	2	1	46
Uffa Fox -	-	-	-	East Anglian	(Hit buoy and retired)

That night, after we were in our room, Roger and I had a yarn over things. To win the cup, we had to win the next two races, and if we could only win the next, we should probably win the last whatever happened, for we should be on the upward, while the others would be on the downward path. So we thought, if one went ahead and won while the other stayed back and played about with the American team, and held them back, all would be well. As I was the elder it would be better for me to play Mr. Nuisance if possible, for my football position had been centre half, where I used to fairly successfully prevent the other team from playing football, so I hoped to be able to hold back the two American canoes. By the rules, only the first canoe home counted, so it would not matter where I finished, as long as I attracted the American canoes from Roger, so that he could finish first.

Saturday morning came in with a flat calm; there was not a ripple, and the race was timed for 11.00 a.m., at which time there was still not a breath of wind, so the committee said they would postpone the race, and give us half an hour's notice before the start. So we put our canoes tidy, and did odd jobs to them. Then the four of us, the two Americans and we two English, went off to lunch together. We were still feeding happily when the committee routed us out to race, and Roger and I were delighted to see a smart breeze.

The wind this day was in exactly the opposite direction from the day before, and as we were being sent round the triangle the same way, it meant that we should get a good beat to windward. Everything looked good to us, but to make sure we thought I should still be Mr. Nuisance. Away we went with two reaches, and then a beat to windward, and at the end of the first round *Valiant* was first, *East Anglian* second, with *Mermaid* third and *Loon* fourth.

Now, my job was to delay the first American canoe till the other one came up, and then try to hold the two back or at any rate keep them from causing Roger any fear. So on the second reach *Mermaid* and *East Anglian* luffed, bore away and fought like two wild cats, all of which time *Valiant* pulled out ahead and *Loon* caught up. As we approached the leeward buoy *East Anglian* was in front with *Mermaid* and *Loon* close astern. This would never do, for it would mean that I should round first, then *Mermaid* would split tacks to clear her wind, and I should be forced to tack on her, which would let *Loon* away on the other tack. So *East Anglian* slowed up, and *Mermaid* went round the buoy a length ahead, then round came *East Anglian* shooting up on *Mermaid's* weather quarter, so preventing her from tacking. Later, *Loon* came round far enough astern to have a clear wind. So she stood on the starboard tack as we were, and did not tack until *Mermaid* had been driven well under *Valiant's* lee, where she could bring nothing but delight to Roger's eyes when he saw her. I went off to make sure *Loon* did not pick up any advantageous shift of wind, so the game went on. The newspapers reported that *Mermaid* and *East Anglian* changed places five times on one reach, and this illustrates the combat.

ROGER WINS IN VALIANT

FIRST ROUND

				M.	S.
Roger De Quincey	- - -	*Valiant*	- - -	23	6
Leo Friede	- - -	*Mermaid*	- - -	23	40
Uffa Fox -	- - -	*East Anglian*	- - -	23	40
Walter Busch -	- - -	*Loon*	- - -	24	20

SECOND ROUND

				M.	S.
Roger De Quincey	- - -	*Valiant*	- - -	46	8
Uffa Fox -	- - -	*East Anglian*	- - -	47	27
Leo Friede	- - -	*Mermaid*	- - -	47	40
Walter Busch -	- - -	*Loon*	- - -	49	3

THIRD ROUND

				H.	M.	S.
Roger De Quincey	- - -	*Valiant*	- - -	1	9	9
Uffa Fox -	- - -	*East Anglian*	- - -	1	10	8
Leo Friede	- - -	*Mermaid*	- - -	1	10	22
Walter Busch -	- - -	*Loon*	- - -	1	12	22

FINISH ELAPSED TIMES

						H.	M.	S.
Roger De Quincey	-	-	-	*Valiant*	-	1	32	0¾
Uffa Fox -	-	-	-	*East Anglian*	-	1	33	24
Leo Friede	-	-	-	*Mermaid*	-	1	34	11
Walter Busch -	-	-	-	*Loon*	-	1	35	13

A nine mile course in 1½ hours equals an average of 6 knots, so we were travelling well over 6 knots all the while, as there was a good turn to windward, whereas on the previous day there had been no windward work, so we had only done 4½ knots through the water. As before, we all met aboard the committee boat and yarned. That night Roger and I decided that it was worth while one of us being Mr. Nuisance, and that it was really best for me to play this part, if practicable, but if not, Roger should do it.

The morning of the final race was just what the doctor had ordered for us, as a strong wind was blowing from exactly the same quarter as the day before, and we imagined we should be sent round the triangle the same way, but as we approached the committee boat, running dead before the wind, we were surprised to see the signals hoisted for the course the opposite way round. So we started with a dead run to the lee mark, with no chance of a windward leg, unless the wind shifted. *East Anglian* led over the line and then started her attempt to hinder *Loon* and *Mermaid* hoping to get *Valiant* away, but as *Valiant* rounded the lee mark, her foresail gybed round and fouled her foremast, and so she was practically hove-to. *East Anglian* then fought *Loon* and *Mermaid*, and soon won first place, leaving Roger astern. However, he soon had *Valiant* sailing again, catching *Mermaid* and then *Loon*, but instead of coming on ahead into first place, while I dropped back to the enemy, he stayed with them, and, attacking *Loon*, refused to come on. Roger in *Valiant* was doing such a good job with the foe, that I in *East Anglian* sailed, reaching and running round the course quite happily, until there came a heavy shower of rain at the end of the second round, which knocked the wind down to almost a calm. Then the pace slowed, and Roger had to fight very hard to keep the now faster *Loon* back, but he held her until the wind freshened again at the end of the third lap and all was well once more. On the last lap, after rounding the leeward mark, the wind shifted a little, making the close reach to the weather mark possible with sheets slightly eased. So *East Anglian* romped down this reach, and *Loon*, rounding the leemark behind *Valiant*, tacked at once to starboard. Roger, although he could easily lay the weather mark, swung about with *Loon* and it was not until a motor yacht, under way, put *Loon* about, that Roger came round with him. Then they both reached with sheets well off for the weather mark, round which *East Anglian* had already passed to reach across the line and win, thanks to her team mate's aggressiveness.

So the International Canoe Trophy came to England for a year, with the other canoe cups we had won from the Americans.

FIRST LAP

							M.	S.
Uffa Fox -	-	-	-	*East Anglian*	-	-	23	0
Roger De Quincey	-	-	-	*Valiant*	-	-	23	54
Walter Busch -	-	-	-	*Loon*	-	-	24	7
Leo Friede	-	-	-	*Mermaid*	-	-	25	47

(Broken his mizen sheet.)

SECOND LAP

							M.	S.
Uffa Fox -	-	-	-	*East Anglian*	-	-	54	14
Roger De Quincey	-	-	-	*Valiant*	-	-	54	27
Walter Busch -	-	-	-	*Loon*	-	-	54	32
Leo Friede	-	-	-	*Mermaid*	-	-	54	50

Americans closing up in light wind—Roger fighting hard to hold them.

THIRD LAP

						H.	M.	S.
Uffa Fox -	-	-	-	*East Anglian*	-	1	10	16
Roger De Quincey	-	-	-	*Valiant*	-	1	11	14
Walter Busch -	-	-	-	*Loon*	-	1	11	36
Leo Friede	-	-	-	*Mermaid*	(Gave up, mizen sheet parted			

again.)

FINISH ELAPSED TIMES

								H.	M.	S.
Uffa Fox	-	-	-	-	*East Anglian*	-	-	-	I	27	52
Roger De Quincey	-	-	-	*Valiant*	-	-	-	I	30	I
Walter Busch	-	-	-	-	*Loon*	-	-	-	I	30	18
Leo Friede	-	-	-	-	*Mermaid* (Did not finish, carried away mizen sheet several times and the knots would not render.)					

These were the fastest times of the three races, but as there was no windward work, the speed through the water was far below that of the previous day, 9 miles in 1½ hours equals 6 knots.

So after 48 years, the canoe trophy left America, the first time it had ever been won from them during all those years.

Roger and I were very pleased and proud at having beaten the best canoe sailors of America on their own waters, but this joy was tempered with a strange sadness hard to define. They had welcomed and opened their hearts to us, taken us into their tents and homes, and we had been the best of friends before and throughout the races, and now that the races were over, were better friends if possible than before.

Only in adversity and defeat does real sportsmanship show up, as it is easy to smile after victory, yet when *East Anglian* swept across the line to win the deciding race for the International Trophy, such a shout of joy and noise of tooting went up from the yachts witnessing the race, that I felt a lump rise in my throat. For here were Roger and I, strangers in a strange land receiving cheers that could not have been louder had they been given for Leo Friede and Walter Busch.

And so our canoe races in America ended enjoyably. They had been marked by clean sailing with no protest, or the need for one, throughout, and this added greatly to the pleasure the races had given us.

A few days later the International Canoe Trophy was presented at the New York Athletic Club, by William P. Stephens, and a challenge read out immediately afterwards. Roger and I said we should like to give them a trophy for their canoe racing to show how grateful we were for all their kindness. We suggested a model of *East Anglian* and *Valiant* to be given for a nine mile race on the triangle.

Two days later four cups left America in the *Olympic* with Roger. These cups had never before, in their 48 years' history, been won from America. The International Trophy, the National Sailing Championship, the National Paddling and Sailing Combined Championship, and the Paul Butler Trophy were to sojourn in England for a year.

Roger and I had enjoyed our visit, for we had met in America canoe sailors who had filled us with

> " The stern joy which warriors feel
> In Foemen worthy of their steel."

·12·

RACING MANŒUVRES

"Once more into the breach, dear friends, once more,
Or close the wall up with our English dead.
In peace there's nothing so becomes a man
As modest stillness and humility:
But when the blast of war blows in our ears,
Then imitate the action of the tiger;
Stiffen the sinews, summon up the blood,
Disguise fair nature with hard-favour'd rage;
Then lend the eye a terrible aspect;
Let it pry through the portage of the head
Like the brass cannon; let the brow o'erwhelm it
As fearfully as doth a galled rock
O'erhang and jutty his confounded base,
Swill'd with the wild and wasteful ocean.
Now set the teeth and stretch the nostril wide,
Hold hard the breath and bend up every spirit
To his full height. On, on, you noblest English,
Whose blood is fet from fathers of war-proof!
Fathers that like so many Alexanders,
Have in these parts from morn till even fought
And sheathed their swords for lack of argument:
Dishonour not your mothers; now attest
That those whom you call'd fathers did beget you.
Be copy now to men of grosser blood,
And teach them how to war. And you, good yeoman
Whose limbs were made in England, show us here
The mettle of your pasture; let us swear
That you are worth your breeding; which I doubt not;
For there is none of you so mean and base,
That hath not noble lustre in your eyes.
I see you stand like greyhounds in the slips,
Straining upon the start. The game's afoot.
Follow your spirit, and upon this charge
Cry 'God for Harry, England, and Saint George!'"

IN these days we cannot make such speeches, time does not permit it, yet if such a speech were made to a yacht's crew before a race well enough for it to stir them with a ruthless determination, each individual of the crew would strain every nerve to win, and determined men cannot be held back. When three of us sailed *Avenger*, a 14-footer, across to Havre in a strong south-westerly wind we saw a 50-tonner turn back and run for the shelter of the Wight. Then I wanted to make an inspiring speech to Bob and Spike, but a 14-footer with seas (that could only be kept in check by continuous and hard bailing) breaking aboard was no place for speechmaking, so instead I asked them if they could stand it for 15 hours or so, which angered them, and their reply was that they could stand it a damned sight longer than I could, so *Avenger's* crew of three all had their backs up, and she would have to swamp before we would turn back, and we made Havre.

So everyone should enter a race stiff-legged like a dog about to fight, and then the race is hard and whoever wins has that feeling of joy which comes after winning a hard fought fight.

Racing men often rightly say that the best helmsman leads at the first mark, but the best boat wins the race, meaning that while a skilful helmsman can overcome the slowness of his boat for a short distance, the superior speed of a faster boat in time overcomes his skill.

The various methods of starting correctly I have tried to illustrate in the chapters on the Prince of Wales' Cup Race, in which, because of the size of the fleet, a start is all important. So I will not touch starting in this chapter except to emphasise the fact that it is the most easy and natural thing for a sailing man to luff his boat, for he keeps his wind clear, gets any freshening puff earlier, and this helps the man making a leeward start, for the fleet with its tendency to luff leaves him more wind and room.

VERONICA ON A LIGHT DAY, WITH HER BALLOON
JIB DRAWING HER ALONG

ZORAIDA

Once round the first mark the race generally resolves itself into a series of duels, and a helmsman finds that whilst before reaching the first mark he was fighting the whole fleet at once, he has now to fight them singly. If the boat astern is attacking him he is fighting a rearguard action, and if the boat he is engaged with is ahead, he is the attacker, and as in a bumping race, he finds himself going into first place, boat by boat, or dropping astern boat by boat.

In chess a certain move forces a particular move from the other side, and this is so in practically every game or sport. It occurs in boxing and cricket, whilst in nap or bridge certain moves and cards call forth others and no card player would put out an ace to beat a six if he could win the point with a lower card. And this chapter is an effort to show the correct card to play to win the point. It deals with actual happenings and where I have been fortunate enough to take or receive photographs which illustrate my points, I have named the vessels and the place of the race, in order to make my words clear, and in case any reader is under the impression that I have invented these racing tactics, I should like to say that I think they have been known since the days when sailing ships manœuvred and fought for the mastery of the seas.

THE LEE BOW POSITION

Zoraida's owner, in the absence of Guy Damant, kindly asked me to race with him in the 12-metre from the Squadron, on a day when it blew hard enough for all classes to be double reefed. Our start was to windward and with the south-westerly wind the southern end of the line was the best position from which to start. We tried to get to windward of *Veronica* but Sir William out-manœuvred us, and started to windward, but as we were right on the line we had our wind clear some way to leeward and though we were down, if we could sail half a length ahead and at the same time make good up towards *Veronica* to windward, we should force her into the dirty wind on our weather quarter, when we should immediately go out in front.

So Connel put his utmost into *Zoraida* and she responded nobly to his touch. Slowly we forged ahead and at the same time squeezed up to *Veronica* until finally we had her on our weather quarter in our dirty wind when she fell off a point and was soon under our lee quarter.

Zoraida won that race by her helmsmen sailing with such keenness and feeling for the first 10 minutes after the start.

The pictures, showing *Veronica* out to windward and slowly coming back to us, and finally going across from our weather to our lee quarter, besides illustrating the way a Solent sea flings a 12-metre about, shows the reef earing not pulled sufficiently out on the boom.

Neither was ours, and reefing in the wind that day made it practically impossible for it to be hauled out well. My reason for pointing this out is not so much to criticise as to help owners with their sails, for while often a sail is not set taut enough on the foot it is often set too taut, both stretching parts of the sail unduly and so spoiling its shape and set. So the owner thinks the sail maker has made him a bad sail, while the sail maker thinks, well, if he cannot treat a sail better why bother to make him a good one ? Here we were in two 12-metres with a crowd on board each consisting of helmsmen and crew as fine as any in the country, with sails as good as could be made, and yet they were not set properly. This shows the need for these few words which are an effort to give understanding to all, for understanding in this world is everything. A doctor's job is easy once he understands exactly what is wrong with his patient.

The lee bow position is a powerful weapon of defence, for as the best defence is attack it puts the man with the strongest position on the defence. Starboard tack is worth at least three boats' lengths for it has the right of way over port tack, and a vessel on the port tack would have to be well clear ahead before she dared cross the bows of a starboard tack vessel.

And this is where lee bowing is useful, for a port tack vessel meeting a starboard tack vessel has either to tack or bear away, if she is far enough ahead so that by the time she has tacked and gathered way she will be abreast although to leeward of her enemy, then she should tack and lee bow her opponent, and this forces him to go about, for if he does not do so at once he will lose three lengths very quickly, whereas if he tacks he keeps his wind clear and also when these boats next meet he will have the advantage the starboard tack gives once again.

If a port tack vessel is not far enough ahead to lee bow the starboard tack vessel she should put her helm up and go close under the starboard tack vessel's stern, luffing as soon as she can. The starboard tack vessel will probably try to tack and smother the port tack vessel, but the extra speed given her by bearing away combined with the loss in speed of the starboard tack vessel staying generally enables her to escape, and if the starboard tack vessel holds on, the next time they meet the vessel that was port tack is starboard tack with the advantage that gives.

The pictures illustrate exactly when one boat can lee bow another, for although generally the windward boat has the advantage this is just one point of sailing where she has not.

That this lee bowing was known when sailing ships fought for the mastery of the seas is shown by the painting of the Glorious First of June, 1790, by P. J. de Loutherbourg. This picture took four years to paint, and was then full of mistakes.

The greatest mistake of all was that the artist had painted the *Queen Charlotte a little ahead of the lee beam* of the *Montagne*, where Lord Howe wanted to get, but could not because of the loss of his fore topmast, which was shot away by the *Jacobin*. The officer, whose duty it was to place the *Queen Charlotte* on the lee bow of the *Montagne*, went to see this picture, and at the first glance he pronounced it a libel on the *Queen Charlotte*, inasmuch as had she been in the position represented it would have been her own fault for letting the *Montagne* escape. The flags in the picture show the wind aft, but the diagrams and description in detail of each vessel's manœuvres in the battle show that they were at the time close-hauled on the port tack.

" Frustrated thus in her attempt to reach the lee bow of the *Montagne* the *Queen Charlotte* could only continue to ply her larboard guns at the French three-decker, who, at about 10 h. 10 m., having had her stern frame and starboard quarter dreadfully shattered, and sustained a loss of 100 killed and nearly 200 wounded, set her maintopmast staysail . . . and ranged ahead clear of the *Queen Charlotte's* destructive fire."

So this old trick of lee bowing should be studied carefully by racing men, its greatest use being to my mind when she is meeting a vessel on the starboard tack and has to give way, for unless she can cross the other safely, it is much better to tack under his lee bow, being sure to tack far enough ahead and to leeward so as not to interfere with the other's course, and then when she has regained the speed lost in tacking she can eat up to windward, and giving the enemy the dirty wind off the weather side of her mainsail, knock her back a long way, the distance varying with the size of the vessel. A vessel the size of *Britannia* will knock another of her class back 200 yards, and a

OUR LEE BOW WAVE

SIR WILLIAM OUT-MANŒUVRED US AND STARTED TO WINDWARD

SLOWLY WE FORGED AHEAD, AND AT THE SAME TIME
SQUEEZED UP TO VERONICA

A SOLENT SEA FLINGS A 12-METRE ABOUT

UNTIL FINALLY WE HAD HER ON OUR OWN WEATHER QUARTER

SHE FELL OFF A POINT AND WAS SOON ON OUR LEE QUARTER

PHOTOGRAPHS TAKEN ABOARD *ZORAIDA* SHOWING HOW SHE LEE BOWED *VERONICA*

14-footer will knock another dinghy back 20 yards, and the other classes between will knock their own opponents back varying distances between 200 and 20 yards according to their sizes.

At all times a racer must keep his wind clear of the other vessels, for the wind is his power, and if he sails in wind interfered with by another vessel he either has only half the driving power in his sails that the other vessel has, or else the wind he is using has been deflected by that vessel and so he is unable to sail so close to the wind as the weather vessel. An overtaking, a port tack, or the outside boat at a mark has to give way or room to the other vessels, but if in giving way she can shake their wind she stops them to a certain extent. In running, an overtaking vessel

"THE PAINTING OF THE GLORIOUS FIRST OF JUNE BY P. J. DE LOUTHERBOURG, ALTHOUGH FULL OF MISTAKES, BRINGS OUT THE FACT (SEE PAGE 259) THAT LEE BOWING WAS UNDERSTOOD AND MANŒUVRED FOR AS EARLY AS 1794"

can see when she is disturbing the wind of the boat ahead, for her spinnaker flops about, and the game the overtaking vessel should play, if possible, is to try and make the leading boat luff to windward of the mark, then when the mark is so that both boats are by the lee in running for it, steer for it, for by the Y.R.A. rules the leading boat has to give a free passage to leeward, and the leeward side is counted as the side on which a yacht carries her mainboom, so the overtaking vessel has now a free passage to windward, and can easily pass ahead into first place.

The whole game of yacht racing is very like chess, but far faster and more exciting, for there is no time to think out manœuvres, everything is done almost instinctively, and therein lies its charm—for after the race the helmsmen can sit down and think over it, and can generally pick out several mistakes, resolving never to make the same ones again. And a helmsman who never makes the same mistake twice is soon a first-class racer.

A whole book could be written upon strategy, tactics, tidal work and sailing, but it is hoped that the few illustrations will enable everyone new to racing (and perhaps those old to it) to understand the art of racing a sailing boat. For it is really this, that to attack or defend against another vessel a boat interferes with her wind, and so generally the windward position pays, the exception being the lee bowing manœuvre as taught by our great-grandfathers, forgotten and then rediscovered, as are almost all things. The earliest mention I remember of the rediscovery of this manœuvre is in the description of a race round the Island about 1880.

The easiest way to become a first-class helmsman is to quietly and carefully go over each day's race the evening after, and a man honest and critical with himself will soon be respected as a helmsman, for he sees his own faults and endeavours to correct them.

"O wad some power the giftie gi'e us
To see oursels as others see us!"

EPILOGUE

HEART'S DESIRE

Length, overall - - - 52 ft. 0 in.	Length, water-line - - 36 ft. 0 in.
Beam - - - - 11 ft. 6 in.	Draught - - - - 7 ft. 0 in.
Displacement - - - 14 tons	Sail area - - - - 1,000 sq. ft.

Designed for himself by UFFA FOX

WHEN a small boy in the choir I sang "Oh rest in the Lord, wait patiently for him and he shall give thee thy heart's desire."

So this little cruiser is named *Heart's Desire* and for years I have waited patiently and still have to for her, being only able to own a canoe at present, and this waiting is probably all for the best, as during this time I have designed many cruisers that have appeared perfect, only to find years later they were capable of improvement. This design shows the direction and how far my ideas have developed in the spring of 1934.

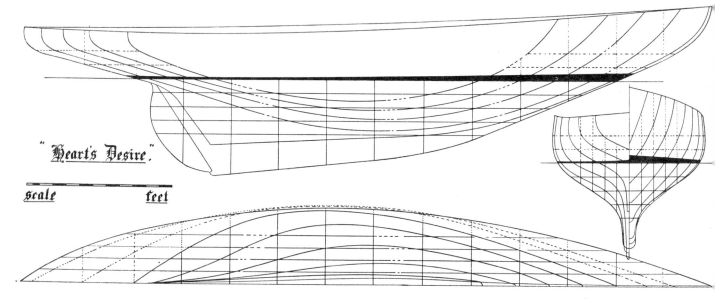

"Heart's Desire".

scale   feet

This 36-ft. water-line cruiser has been chosen as the largest sized boat that could be sailed single handed, for then and only then is an owner free to sail where and when he wishes; and the knowledge that whether from choice or necessity a passage can be made single handed is a jewel beyond compare.

The idea behind the cruiser is a vessel in which my wife and I could cruise in comfort the year round, and yet fast enough to take part in an occasional ocean race, a vessel that in meeting a head wind in the channel could make good on her passage instead of spending weeks weatherbound. For having left trading schooners and ketches and wholesome yachts weatherbound in Dover when in a little 6-metre, which made the passage to Newhaven dead to windward in 12 hours, I realise that the ability to go to windward is very desirable however much cruising men may scorn it, for it was not the weather, although it blew hard, that kept these vessels weatherbound, but the knowledge that with the wind and sea against them they would only fetch back to Dover again after a long tack off and on.

The overhangs do not at first sight give the appearance of a vessel meant for deep water work, but I am convinced that well designed overhangs are of great value to a sailing vessel in a seaway when they increase her length and fore and aft stability by their reserve buoyancy, which can only come into action in rough water, so as *Heart's Desire* is intended for crossing oceans among other things she has overhangs.

Overhangs are bad when the wind suddenly dies away to a calm from gale force, for then there is a heavy sea, and the boat is without life or motion except that given her by the waves, when a counter pounding down on the water seems intent on smashing itself to pieces.   So the canoe stern with its V sections is easier then and more suitable for rough water.

It is a remarkable fact that all things naturally developed without rule or restriction for passage through air and water in this world are pointed at the stern, for example birds, fishes, tadpoles, the Indian canoe, the Viking ships, whale boats, lifeboats (of all nations), racing eights and funneys.

The thing that has put a blunt stern on vessels has been artificial conditions, rating rules, and by this I mean not only the I.Y.R.U. Rating Rules, but also the formula to which cruising as well as fishing boats are built.

One of the greatest factors in this is price, and for a given cost the nearer a boat or a house is to a square box with every dimension equal the more room it will have, and so we have square-sterned boats and now the architect on shore is producing square ugly buildings with economy as his excuse.   In time these square buildings will be considered beautiful.

And so as rating rules which govern length and those which govern cost have produced the square-sterned boat and not the laws of nature, and as the laws of nature will endure to the end, it is far better to design to these than to artificial conditions.

So *Heart's Desire* is designed to a rule which considers nature and her works and the strength of a man's right arm.

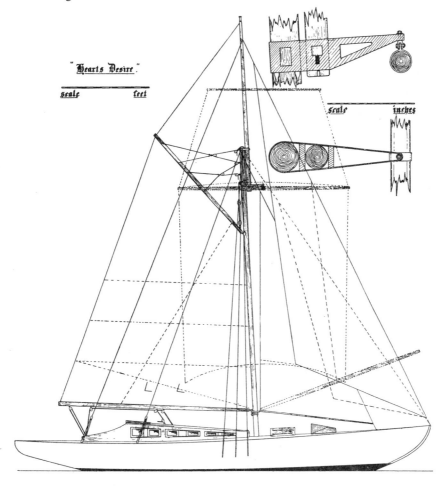

Crossing the Atlantic in *Typhoon* proved that one man could handle a 500 sq. ft. mainsail in all weathers (for we weathered the October and November gales of 1920 in her), and this fact takes away the excuse for making this vessel a yawl, ketch or schooner.   The only excuse for these rigs with their extra spars, blocks and rigging is to split the canvas into smaller and more easily handled sails, so while she would be even more easily handled with a two-masted rig and a smaller mainsail she would be that much slower, that much more expensive to run for extra spars, rigging and blocks, and would require an anchor that much heavier.

The mast is two-fifths the water-line length from its fore end, as forward of this it tends to knock the bow off to leeward as it rises out of the sea, and also by being so far aft it is in a beamier part where its shrouds have more spread, and above all this makes the mainsail smaller.

The mainsail is of tanned flax, in fact all the sails will be tanned, as although tanning like tarring a rope takes away a certain amount of virtue and strength from the fibres, so that when new a tanned sail is weaker than one not tanned, because the tanning keeps out the dampness and rot from a sail, it remains much about that strength ever after, whereas the white sail gradually loses its strength.

Flax is so much softer to handle than cotton, which in wet or frosty weather becomes very much harder. The cloths will run parallel to the leach of the mainsail, for then the sail is stronger, and when we pause to consider the strain put upon the leach of mainsails when all hands are hauling in the mainsheet the reason is apparent, for with the old-fashioned vertical cloths the strain came upon the cloth its strongest way, and not upon the stitches of the seams. A study of the photographs of old vessels will show perfect setting leaches without any sail battens being used, and there is no doubt they are a worry for they break, catch in things, chafe through the sail and generally are best left ashore in a cruising vessel, and the reef points by being in the seams, as they can be of a mainsail with vertical cloths, are far stronger than with a cross-cut sail where they come anywhere, and because of this often tear the sail.

The gaff rig is chosen, not only because it keeps the mainsail down to the 500 sq. ft. area, but also for the fact that when a vessel is cruising off soundings she has to stand up and face whatever weather comes her way, and so she must be able to shorten her spars as well as her sails if necessary.

So as the weather increases from a fresh wind to a heavy gale, the jib and topsail are taken in, the topmast housed, and being only 21 ft. long and hollow, it is no longer or heavier than the spinnaker boom, and so can come right down and be lashed along the deck. Then with only 35 ft. of mainmast showing above the deck the mainsail and staysail are reefed down till finally the 150 sq. ft. trysail is set, and she is ready to face any weather.

For light weather the bowsprit spinnaker can be used as a reaching jib or a spinnaker, while in harder winds the balloon staysail can be used reaching or squared off as a spinnaker, the spare staysail club being the right length for a spinnaker boom for this sail.

For running before the Trades the 500 sq. ft. squaresail and square topsail, with 200 sq. ft. in it can be set making the total up to 700 sq. ft., which will give good speed through the Trades, for they blow far harder than one supposes.

The squaresail yard is fitted with a gooseneck, which extending forward of the forestay, not only takes the squaresail over this, and so frees it from chafe, but also enables it to be braced sharp up before the yard strikes the main shrouds, and so *Heart's Desire* can carry her squaresails with a beam wind. So this gooseneck overcomes the two faults of every squaresail I have seen fitted to small fore and aft vessels. For they all chafe and none can be braced up.

The main shrouds all lead abaft the mast to allow the yard to swing aft, and the tack can be boarded down to the cat davits when on a wind with the square canvas set.

The trysail should be set with the squaresails in the Trades as with no fore and aft sails set a boat rolls first one deck under and then the other. If she used her mainsail and spinnaker the gaff could be taken forward of the shrouds, and so the mainsail would blow forward of these and their constant chafe, which quickly causes seams to part, for the fore and aft rig, while going to windward beyond the dreams of the square rigged ships, that are no more, is badly designed and arranged for long weeks of running with the wind dead astern, for then the chafe with the fore and aft rig is constant, and *Heart's Desire* is an attempt to combine a good rig to windward with a good one to leeward, two opposite things.

With a spinnaker boom, squaresail yard, and topmast all one length and hollow, any one of these spars can replace the other in an emergency, and the staysail boom being the same size as the short spinnaker boom and the square topsail yard, these too can be changed round if necessary, and so with her various combinations of sail ranging from 1,400 sq. ft., with the mainsail, topsail and bowsprit spinnaker set, to 150 sq. ft. with the trysail only set, and her light spars interchangeable and the ease with which the topmast can be lowered and lashed on deck, leaving only 35 ft. of mainmast standing, this rig is well able to take its place with the deep water rigs that have been tried and proved.

Then after having designed and worked out the details of a gaff rig suitable for all weather conditions, from calm to gale, I thought of the Bermudian mainsail and its saving of weight and windage aloft. The thought of the tall naked spar lashing about while hove-to in a gale off soundings had to be weighed and balanced against the gaff, its numerous blocks, and the fact that it ruins the flow of a mainsail in its most important part, three-quarters of its height above the deck, for it hauls it flat, and the peak halyards on one tack flatten the topsail, for if it is the weather side of the halyards the wind presses it flat against them.

The rigging of the Bermudian mast is hardly any more complicated than the mast with the gaff, but the Bermudian saves the weight and windage of the gaff, six peak halyard blocks (two not shown as purchase blocks), four throat halyard blocks, the two purchase blocks not shown, the topsail sheet block at the gaff end, the lead block at the throat, and the two tack tackle blocks. An enormous saving aloft of sixteen blocks, all the halyards, sheets and tacks they involve, and the gaff itself.

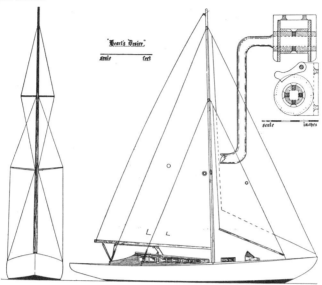

On the Bermudian sail plan will be seen the winch for the staysail, and two similar winches are planned for the jib and main halyards, each winding its entire halyard on the drum, so keeping the decks clear of the fathoms of halyards that have to be coiled down when the sails are set aloft. Looking at the sail plans at present the gaff rig holds my affections, but I am hard at work on the design of a Bermudian mast, where the topmast reefs down inside the mainmast just as a telescope shuts up, and when that has been perfected and tested without doubt the Bermudian mast will be chosen.

For it must be remembered by racers and cruisers that the modern Bermudian masts are in their infancy, designers all over the world are studying their design and construction, and the time will come when the gaff rig will be looked upon as historically interesting only.

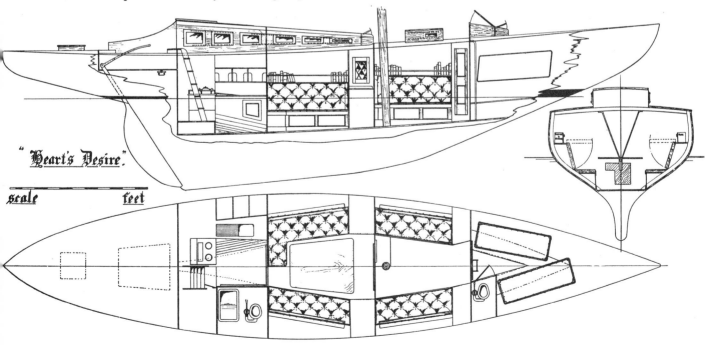

Six foot of headroom under a flush deck enables the beams to run right across the deck, with the advantages of strength and watertightness.

The fo'c'sle has two folding cots, but these would not be used at sea, for in going to windward in hard weather it is impossible to sleep well forward, as the motion and noise is so violent there, due to the bow climbing and crashing its way through the seas.

In the fore cabin and saloon the backs of the bunks swing upward, and forming extra bunks enable eight to sleep in comfort.

Abaft the saloon is the galley, given the most quiet spot on the ship, for in hard weather hot food is important, and can only be cooked, even in the quietest place on a small vessel, with difficulty.

Opposite this is a bathroom, while above it is a berth in the deck house, so that on a dirty night if two are on watch the stand-by man can lay out in the dry and yet be within reach of the helmsman. Opposite this bunk is the chart table, which slides aft, so that sitting on the bridge deck or the top step of the companionway the navigator can study the chart and talk over the position with the helmsman without disturbing anyone below.

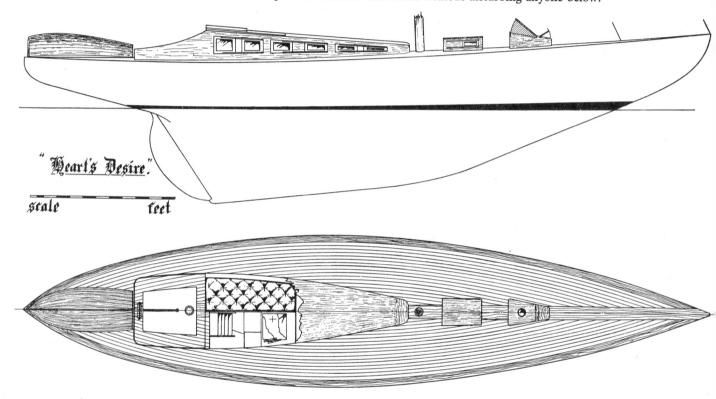

"Heart's Desire".

scale   feet

The helmsman sits in the watertight cockpit well protected by the deck house, forward, and the dinghy upside down on the deck aft clear of the lights to the saloon and the working of the ship, helps to break seas that come in over aft. Cruising vessels usually carry their dinghies over the skylights, which means that they do their sailing with the saloon and cabins in utter darkness, a dismal and unreasonable arrangement.

As openings in the top of a deck or deck house for light and air below are flat, they hold the water, and generally after a few heavy seas leak and drip below; there are no openings above at all. They are all at the sides of the deck house and these windows slide aft to open, so that when hove forward tightly they become watertight as they gain like a tapered pin all the while they are being driven home, and being upright no water clings to them.

Deadlights with small thick glasses cover them when battened down for heavy weather, making them doubly watertight, for nothing is more discouraging than small drips on the face when turned in below.

The forehatch has the side flaps which *Landfall* used, and with such a hatch she sailed across the Atlantic without any water finding its way below, although it was open all the time.

Instead of bulwarks a 3 ft. high fence is fitted, which runs clear round the vessel, which, while preventing the crew from being washed overboard, will not trap any water on the deck; a foot or hand rail with waterways cut in it runs round the deck to which the spars can be lashed. At the bow, stern and in the channels each side is a pulpit, also 3 ft. high, such as is used by the sword fishermen, and these will hold the navigator or leadsman safely, while using the sextant or heaving the lead, as this leaves both hands free, for both jobs require two hands, and without some such an arrangement one hand must be kept to hold on with.

And such at the moment is my *Heart's Desire*, a cruiser in which my wife and I could live and cruise for months, happy in the knowledge that if we wished she would take us to the uttermost parts of the earth.

In *The Beggar's Opera* the Highwayman sang a song in which he likened himself to a bee wandering from flower to flower until he met the most beautiful of all, and there he was content, for Polly was a very charming girl.

But although he said he had reached finality he had not, and perhaps this design will be slightly altered before built, any way the words suit the occasion. For I have sailed in canoes, dinghies, all kinds of racers, from the smallest to the largest, and in every kind of cruiser, pilot and fishing boat, in all weathers fair and foul, and this design is the result of it all, a blend of every one from a square rigged vessel to a canoe.

> " My heart was so free, it roved like a bee,
> Till Polly my Passion requited ;
> I sipped each flower, I changed every hour,
> But here every flower is united."

FINIS

INDEX

LIST OF PHOTOGRAPHS

By BEKEN

By MORRIS ROSENFELD

By EDWIN LEVICK

By WILLIAM WHITE

From paintings by R. F. PATERSON

By IVAN KETTLE

By Miss M. TILL

By the PARKER GALLERIES

The remaining photographs reproduced in this volume were taken by the author.